T

WHERE FOOTBALL IS
KING

WHERE FOOTBALL IS
KING
A HISTORY OF THE SEC

CHRISTOPHER J. WALSH

TAYLOR TRADE PUBLISHING
Lanham • New York • Boulder • Toronto • Oxford

Copyright © 2006 by Christopher J. Walsh
First Taylor Trade Publishing edition 2006

This Taylor Trade Publishing hardback edition of *Where Football Is King* is an original publication. It is published by arrangement with the author.

Published by Taylor Trade Publishing
An imprint of The Rowman & Littlefield Publishing Group, Inc.
4501 Forbes Boulevard, Suite 200, Lanham, Maryland 20706

Distributed by NATIONAL BOOK NETWORK

Library of Congress Cataloging-in-Publication Data

Walsh, Christopher J., 1968–
    Where football is king : a history of the SEC / Christopher J. Walsh.—1st Taylor Trade
Pub. ed.
      p.   cm.
    Includes index.
    ISBN-13: 978-1-58979-355-2 (cloth : alk. paper)
    ISBN-10: 1-58979-355-2 (cloth : alk. paper)
    1. Southeastern Conference—History.   I. Title.
GV958.5.S59W35   2006
796.332′630975—dc22
                                        2006005068

∞ ™ The paper used in this publication meets the minimum requirements of American National Standard for Information Sciences—Permanence of Paper for Printed Library Materials, ANSI/NISO Z39.48-1992.

Manufactured in the United States of America.

To the Greg Pages of the world

Contents

Introduction

To understand football in the Southeastern Conference, you have to know about "The Kingfish."

There was nothing average about Huey Long, Governor of Louisiana from 1928 to 1932 before serving in the United States Senate. A high-school dropout who taught himself and received a law degree after only one year of study, Long envisioned himself as the champion of the "little man" and an enemy of big business. His slogan was "Every Man is King," and he was so confident of becoming president of the United States that he wrote a book entitled *My First Days in the White House*, which included details of his cabinet.

Long was also a huge fan of the Louisiana State University football team.

"As Governor of the State of Louisiana, I protest your calls," he argued during the 1930 game against Arkansas. "I don't mind you penalizing LSU, but penalize us in midfield. Don't do it when we get down to the goal line."

Of course, it wasn't enough for Long to just root for the Tigers. Like nearly every other fan in the SEC, his team had to win, and he had to do his part.

"I don't fool around with losers," Long said. "LSU can't have a losing football team because that will mean that I am associated with a loser."

When ticket sales for the 1934 home opener against Southern Methodist were lagging in part because the Ringling Brothers Circus was also due to perform in Baton Rouge that night, Long politely informed the circus that he would have no choice but to enforce an obscure "animal-dipping" law.

Needless to say, the show did not go on that night. The circus delayed its trip, football ticket sales rose, and LSU managed to tie SMU, 14-14.

Later that same year, Long "secured" six special trains by "reminding" the Illinois Central Railroad that the value of railroad bridges in the state could easily rise from $100,000 to $4 million. He used them to take 5,000 LSU fans from Baton Rouge to Nashville for the LSU game at Vanderbilt. On the day of the trip, he had to work out how dozens of armed Louisiana police could cross the border, with the Tennessee Game and Fish Commission deciding that they could enter the state as "deputy game wardens" to guard whatever "wildlife you may see fit."

Also along for the ride was a 125-piece marching band and 1,500 students wearing new grey uniforms that were rushed from tailors. Newspapers reported that Long loaned any student who was short on funds $7 to make the trip. He was quoted as saying the money came from "contributors."

Although Long deflected speculation that he would announce his bid for the White House during the trip, he did make a pregame speech and boldly predicted an LSU victory. While standing on the sidelines, Long watched the Tigers do just that, 29-0.

Less than a year later, on September 8, 1935, Long was assassinated by the son-in-law of a long-time rival in the capitol building in Baton Rouge. Although his bodyguards killed the assailant, he took a bullet in the stomach and died two days later. Long's last words included: "God, don't let me die, I have so much left to do," and "Who will look after my darling LSU?"

Yes, football is a little different at the 12 schools that make up the SEC. To the fans, and just about everyone else who lives in those nine states, it's so much more than a game, including identity, history, honor, and pride.

"Southerners are proud of their football heritage, their schools, and their teams," said George Mooney, the Voice of the Tennessee Volunteers. "And they share a deep pride that goes with being from the South."

Southern writer and novelist Paul Hemphill once wrote: "Football is less a way out, than a way of life. No other sport has a chance in Alabama."

Actually, that was an understatement.

Since football became the dominant sport on many Southern campuses after World War I, it has meant everything to these people, and been handed down from generation to generation.

They crow at South Carolina, bark at Georgia, and at Florida they Growl—which is the name of the world's largest student-run pep rally, attracting more than 70,000 the night before the homecoming game (performers have included Bill Cosby, Bob Hope, Robin Williams, Jay Leno, Jerry Seinfeld, and Howie Mandel).

Mississippi State fans proudly proclaim, "Friends don't let friends go to Ole Miss." At Alabama, "Secret Witness," a rub against Tennessee, is a popular T-shirt. LSU fans frequently have "Geaux Tigers" displayed on their car bumpers, though one could make a living selling anti-Bama slogans at Auburn.

They even take their mascots very seriously.

When Mississippi State's original bulldog mascot Bully was killed on November 19, 1939, by a campus bus, he was buried under the bench at the 50-yard line of Scott Field. More than 2,500 people paid their respects, and *Life* magazine covered the funeral.

Before LSU home games, Mike the Tiger, who is a real Bengal tiger, rides in a cage on the field and is parked near the visiting locker room. The original Mike, who had the job for 20 years, died during a six-game losing streak in 1956. His death was kept a secret until the string was snapped.

In 1991, Tennessee's coonhound mascot, Smokey VI, was listed on the injury report after suffering heat exhaustion during a game with UCLA. When Georgia's bulldog was to have knee surgery, coach Vince Dooley commented that "Uga's injury has gotten more national attention than my two running backs," referring to Tim Worley and Keith Henderson, who were both coming off serious injuries sustained during the 1986 season.

They scream "War Eagle" at Auburn, "Go Cocks" at South Carolina, and at

Mississippi State the coach once tried to inspire his team before playing the Texas Longhorns by castrating a bull (and you bet it worked).

They play "Dixie" at Ole Miss, cry "Sooey" at the top of their lungs at Arkansas, yell "Go to hell Ole Miss," at LSU, and smoke cigars at Alabama after beating Tennessee.

When Kentucky plays home games at Commonwealth Stadium, which opened in 1973 and has a seating capacity of 67,606, it becomes the third largest city in the state.

At Tennessee, Neyland Stadium (104,079) has been reconfigured so many times to squeeze in more fans that it reminds many of a woman trying to fit into the same girdle after giving birth.

Speaking of women, at SEC schools they're so beautiful that most men risk car accidents whenever they drive through campus. Co-eds often dress up for games, are as vocal as their male counterparts, and insult their counterparts by openly speculating if they have all their teeth.

While fans from the North wonder, "What's the deal with all the majorettes?" their Southern brethren are busy trying to figure out, "How can we beat those Yankee bastards?" The crafty Commodores of Vanderbilt were among the first to figure it out, and everyone else followed.

"I just didn't hear from Georgia people, but from people from all over the South," Dooley said after winning at Michigan in 1965. "To go up there and invade the North and come back a winner was the greatest thing for a lot of people. It was as if we had had a chance to go to Gettysburg again."

The most recent additions to the conference fit in almost immediately.

When word reached Austin that Arkansas was going to join the SEC, the Texas legislature actually passed a bill to try and force the Razorbacks to stay in the Southwest Conference. Instead, the departure proved to be a deathblow to the conference while giving Razorbacks fans another reason to hate Texas.

At South Carolina, which regularly has more than 80,000 on hand at Williams-Brice Stadium to see a team that has never played in a major bowl game, fans stormed the field and tore down the goalposts in 2000 when it snapped a string of 21 consecutive losses by defeating New Mexico State. The Gamecocks came into the game with three winning seasons over the previous 33 years (most of which came prior to joining the SEC).

"Football is the essence of America, but not because of championships or titles," legendary Ole Miss quarterback Archie Manning said. "The drive to compete, the guts to play, the will to come from behind, the grace to walk off the field a loser, that's the essence of football."

Even the media is a little bit different in the SEC. One of the region's signature radio talk shows, hosted by Paul Finebaum in Birmingham, talks college football year-round and makes this quip in the daily introduction: "Where legends are made, and coaches . . . fired."

When Richard Ernsberger was putting together his book *Bragging Rights*, Florida coach Steve Spurrier told him, "You tell Coach [Phillip] Fulmer that the

Swamp is going to be loud this year. As loud as it's ever been." When he did, in a phone interview with the Tennessee coach, the other end of the line got very quiet.

FYI, both Ernsberger and Finebaum are from Tennessee.

"Football is an honest game," Alabama's favorite quarterback Joe Namath said. "It's true to life. It's about sharing. Football is a team game. So is life."

In the SEC, the game is reflected in nearly every facet of society, and it seeps into every crevice of Southern culture.

In the SEC, they are dedicated:

"When I started at LSU in 1983, there were only two sports," said LSU athletic director Skip Bertman, "football and spring football."

They are family oriented:

"When you go to a game in the South, you're likely to see four generations together," Arkansas coach and athletic director Frank Broyles said. "It's part of our heritage, and that heritage is passed along from generation to generation. It means something very important to our people."

They can see things relatively:

"A tie is like kissing your sister," said Alabama coach Paul "Bear" Bryant, who also coached at Kentucky and was an assistant at Vanderbilt.

They ask thought-provoking questions:

"I don't understand why kamikaze pilots wore crash helmets," said Lou Holtz, who coached at Arkansas and South Carolina.

They demand the best:

"It was rot-gut. It wasn't even good stuff," Bertman said after stadium security found 54 fifths of whiskey taped under the student section bleachers before a game at Tiger Stadium. In similar fashion, after Bryant picked up a bottle a Georgia Tech fan had thrown at him, he quipped: "I thought Tech people drank a better brand of whiskey than this." However, Bryant was wearing a helmet at the time for protection, after Georgia Tech's Chick Graning sustained a broken nose, a broken jaw, and lost five teeth on a shot to the face from Darwin Holt during the previous meeting.

They have lofty expectations:

"If I had hired Jesus Christ, then people would just gripe that he had long hair and sandals," LSU athletic director Joe Dean said after hiring Curley Hallman and Gerry DiNardo as football coaches.

They have religion:

"The definition of an atheist in Alabama is a person who doesn't believe in Bear Bryant," Georgia coach Wally Butts said. But there's also a famous joke Auburn fans tell about the time Bryant and Shug Jordan went fishing together, and the Bear openly wondered if he could actually walk on water like all the Bama fans believed. He stepped out of the boat and immediately fell into the water. After swimming back to the boat and reaching up to Jordan, Bryant said, "Shug, promise me you won't tell the Alabama fans I can't walk on water." Jordan replied, "Okay Bear, just as long as you promise not to tell the Auburn fans that I helped you back into the boat."

They have fine dining:

"If you're not a Gator, you're Gator bait," Spurrier said.

They take loyalty seriously, especially after an allegiance changes:

"I know what hell is like," Mississippi State athletic director Dudy Noble said. "I once coached at Ole Miss."

They insult:

"We're looking forward to playing Mississippi State on the road this year," Bertman said. "Word is a tornado blew through Starkville late last season and did $2 million worth of improvements."

They learn:

"Peyton tortured me pretty good," Ole Miss quarterback Eli Manning said about his older brother, who was a pretty good quarterback at Tennessee. "He would pin me down and knock on my cheek with his knuckles and make me name 10 schools in the SEC or in the Big Ten. He wouldn't stop until I did. I probably wouldn't know all my divisions and teams if it wasn't for that."

They play hard:

"It didn't matter if he was big or small, fast or slow, All-American or second team, my job was to beat him and beat him soundly," three-time LSU All-American Tommy Casanova said.

They play *really* hard:

"His ear had a real nasty cut and it was dangling from his head, bleeding badly," Tennessee lineman Bull Bayer said about Alabama's first All-American, Bully Vandegraaff. "He grabbed his own ear and tried to yank it from his head. His teammates stopped him and the managers bandaged him. Man, was that guy a tough one. He wanted to tear off his own ear so he could keep playing."

They go crazy:

"Here, where the hills are high, Tennessee fans are calling on the Volunteers to give the state its first clear claim to national honors," United Press International's Henry McLemore wrote in the midst of the 1939 undefeated season. "Knoxville is the perfect example of civil lunacy. Every suburb is a wing of an asylum." (Incidentally, Tennessee went on to finish the regular season 10-0 without giving up a single point, but endured the first of two shutout losses to Southern Cal in the Rose Bowl, 14-0.)

They pay attention to the competition:

"What did I learn coaching at LSU? Basically, that the conference office in the SEC wants to be able to say they have great football and the conference office in the Big Ten wants to be able to say they graduate their athletes," DiNardo said.

They don't let up:

"You can't be selective about when you compete in this league," LSU coach Nick Saban said. "You can't be selective about when you want to play hard and when you need to play well, because every game you play is a real challenge, and an important one."

They demand:

"To err is human, to forgive divine. But to forgive a football coach is unheard of," Dooley said.

They don't believe in mediocrity:

"The only way I know to keep football fun is to win," Mississippi State coach Darrell Royal said. "There is no laughter in losing."

And they absolutely, positively love their football.

"In the South, college football isn't just a game. It's who we are," said Bill Curry, who left Alabama after someone threw a brick through his window when he won the SEC championship but lost to rival Auburn.

He also once said, "The best way to describe football in the South is hysteria . . . mass hysteria."

Part I

THE SOUTHEASTERN CONFERENCE

· 1 ·

This Is the SEC

Even though the Southeastern Conference didn't become reality until 1933, its roots go back into the late 1800s, when football was barely a blip on the athletic radar screen, especially in the South. With the game just having been introduced on most of the campuses that would eventually form the alliance, most Southern schools were small and baseball was usually the sport of choice.

On December 22, 1894, on the suggestion of Dr. William Dudley, a professor of chemistry at Vanderbilt, faculty representatives from seven schools gathered in Atlanta for an informal meeting to discuss the organizing of an association to establish common rules, settle disputes, and provide general regulation and control of collegiate athletics.

The Southern Intercollegiate Athletic Association (1894–1922) was the first of its kind in the nation, followed by the Intercollegiate Conference of Faculty Representatives, which would evolve into the Big Ten Conference. The schools were Alabama, Alabama Polytechnic Institute (now known as Auburn), Georgia, Georgia School of Technology, North Carolina, University of the South (Sewanee), and Vanderbilt. With an open membership, another 19 schools joined within a year and would be considered charter members. By 1928, the roster included 32 schools, stretching the association from Maryland to Texas.

According to Melvin Henry Gruensfelder, who wrote the thesis "A History of the Origin and Development of the Southeastern Conference" at the University of Illinois in 1964, a primary concern of the organization was "to correct some of the evils of baseball. A key regulation was the requirement for a transfer student to remain in residence for one year before he could participate in an intercollegiate contest. It was enacted in 1894 and known as the migratory law."

Many of the original ground rules still exist in some form today, like participation limited to a time period of five years and eligibility requirements. Additionally, many of the control problems the SIAA faced in its early years the National Collegiate Athletic Association would likewise contend with a half-century later, in that there was a clear division of membership in how best to proceed (especially larger schools vs. smaller schools).

In 1899 the University of the South (from Sewanee, Tennessee)—a future, albeit brief, member of the SEC—pulled off an amazing accomplishment when it won five games in six days on the road against LSU, Ole Miss, Texas, Texas A&M,

and Tulane by a combined score of 91-0. Sewanee had already defeated Georgia, Georgia Tech, and Tennessee, and went on to defeat Auburn, which was the only opponent to score (11-10), and North Carolina before declaring itself the Southern football champion. No one argued the point.

In 1904, the first full-time football coaches, including Mike Donahue at Auburn, John Heisman at Georgia Tech, and Vanderbilt's Dan McGugin, escalated the sport's growing importance in the region, and pretty soon other schools were looking for ways to compensate, especially to keep up with Vanderbilt.

"Charges of ringers and professionalism became so common that a meeting of the association was called in mid-season of 1907 for a hurried hearing regarding the temporary suspension of one school," Gruensfelder wrote. "Bad feeling arising from other charges caused the ending of one intercollegiate rivalry and the de-emphasis of others."

The rivalry, of course, was Alabama-Auburn, now possibly the most intense in the nation.

He continued: "The bad feeling, compounded by efforts to field winning teams, almost destroyed the game in the South. The feeling of distrust was most difficult to overcome and was still evident years later."

At the time, football was essentially a hybrid of rugby and soccer, only incredibly brutal. There was no neutral zone between teams at the line of scrimmage and few limits to what linemen could do to opposing players, or for that matter their own players, as ball carriers could be picked up and thrown over the line. Gang tackling was the norm and, though extremely dangerous, most teams utilized the "Flying Wedge" formation in which teammates would link together—sometimes using a special belt equipped with handles—to form a "V" and charge into the opposition.

In 1905 alone, college football was credited with 18 deaths and 149 serious injuries. With the game at a crossroad and close to being banned, President Theodore Roosevelt, himself a fan of the sport, stepped in and during two White House conferences with collegiate athletic leaders made it clear that football would either be reformed or abolished.

In December of that year, Chancellor Henry M. MacCracken of New York University headed a meeting of 13 schools to initiate changes. It also led to the Intercollegiate Athletic Association of the United States (IAAUS), founded by 62 members. Within four years, it morphed into a much stronger organization with a different name, and thus the National Collegiate Athletic Association (NCAA) was born.

In 1915, in part because the larger and smaller schools were split on freshman eligibility, two new alliances were formed within the SIAA, with members vowing not to play opponents that didn't follow their regulations.

Comprising the Athletic Conference of Southern States were Georgia, North Carolina, South Carolina, Tennessee, and Virginia.

Members of the Southern Athletic Conference were Alabama Institute of Technology, Clemson, Georgia School of Technology, Georgia, Kentucky, Mississippi A&M, and Tennessee.

Perhaps the most famous game of the time period occurred in 1916, when Georgia Tech routed Cumberland College 220-0. With his team up by more than 100 points at halftime, Heisman told his players: "Be careful of that team from Cumberland. There's no telling what they have up their sleeves."

Georgia Tech went 9-0 and won the first of its four national championships in 1917, but declined a trip to the Rose Bowl so that many players could enlist in the military during World War I. With a record of 102-29-7, Heisman had to leave the school in 1919 due to a divorce settlement stipulating that he would not live in the same city as his ex-wife. She chose Atlanta. He was succeeded by William Alexander, who went 134-95-15 and was the first coach to take teams to the Rose, Sugar, Orange, and Cotton bowls.

Note: Georgia Tech won its second national championship in 1928 after defeating California 8-7 in the Rose Bowl. The game is remembered for Cal's Roy Riegels picking up a fumble and running toward his own goal line, only to be tackled by his teammates. When Cal had to punt, Tech blocked it for a safety, earning what would be the game-winning points.

It took five years, but after World War I the issue of freshman eligibility finally split the association, which by 1920 had grown to 30 schools.

Eight joined the Athletic Conference of Southern States to form the Southern Intercollegiate Conference, but still cooperated and competed with association schools after they finally yielded and adopted the freshmen rule.

However, at a meeting at Gainesville, Florida, on December 12–13 of that year, the larger schools formed a completely new league. Making up the Southern Conference were Alabama, Auburn, Clemson, Georgia, Georgia Tech, Kentucky, Maryland, Mississippi State, North Carolina, North Carolina State, Tennessee, Virginia, Virginia Tech, and Washington & Lee. Florida, Louisiana State, Mississippi, South Carolina, Tulane, Vanderbilt, and Virginia Military followed in 1922, while Sewanee and Duke became members in 1923 and 1928, respectively.

This new association, with Georgia's S. V. Sanford serving as president, coincided with the growth of football, placing it among the most popular of spectator sports, thus increasing the role of the NCAA (though few Southern schools belonged at the time).

"It is the purpose and function of this conference to promote intercollegiate athletics in every form, to keep them in proper bounds by making them an incidental and not the principal feature of intercollegiate and university life, and to regulate them by wise and prudent measures in order that they may improve the physical condition, strengthen the moral fiber of students and form a constituent part of that education for which universities and colleges were established and are maintained."

Again there were some problems. For example, the executive committee served merely as a court in matters of enforcement, so there was no investigatory process to discover rule-breakers. Because membership was so large, growing to 23 schools by 1928 despite an original cap of 16, and each deserved an opportunity to be heard on every matter, meetings were excessively long and the travel cumbersome.

One of the favorable issues the new conference faced arose after Alabama became the first Southern school invited to play in the Rose Bowl in 1925. Conference rules did not permit any games to be played after the first Saturday following Thanksgiving. By a unanimous vote the rule was suspended, and four more invitations to conference teams were received before 1932.

But the incredibly large conference had no means for naming an annual football or baseball champion, while championship events were held in basketball, track and field, cross-country, tennis, boxing and wrestling, golf, and swimming. Other issues divided the membership, from academic requirements to recruiting and scholarships, which resulted in sharp differences. The filming of practices and games, even for scouting or instruction purposes, was one of the most hotly debated subjects, and in 1931 it was actually outlawed along with radio broadcasts of football games, while photographers were banned from sidelines.

During a meeting in Knoxville, Tennessee, in December 1932, the decision was made to split the Southern Conference into two geographical entities. The 10 coastal schools east of the Appalachian Mountains kept the Southern Conference name and continued to expand until it again went through a separation in 1953.

Meanwhile, 13 schools, determined to avoid the problems of the previous organizations, formed the Southeastern Conference. Charter institutions were Alabama, Auburn, Florida, Georgia, Georgia Tech, Kentucky, LSU, Mississippi, Mississippi State, Sewanee, Tennessee, Tulane, and Vanderbilt. In a departure from the previous associations, the president of each school became the primary representative to the conference (with the goal of having athletics to better serve the overall educational aims of each institution), and a new constitution and bylaws were quickly adopted. Kentucky's president Frank McVey was elected the first SEC president, followed by Florida's Dr. John Tigert.

"The Southeastern Conference is organized to form a more compact group of institutions with similar education ideals and regulations in order that they by joint action increase their ability to render the services for which they were founded and for which they are maintained, by making athletics a part of the education plan and by making them subservient to the great aims and objects of education and placing them under the same administrative control. The conference proposes to accomplish this end by promoting mutual trust and friendly relations between members; by controlling athletic competition and keeping such competition within the bounds of an educational activity; by promoting clean sportsmanship; and by developing public appreciation of the educational, rather than the commercial, values in intercollegiate sports."

McVey held his first informal meeting with school presidents in Birmingham, Alabama, on February 16, 1933, with the first full meeting called to order in Atlanta on February 27. During the heart of the Great Depression, the league's inaugural championship was a basketball tournament in Atlanta, with Kentucky defeating Mississippi State 46-27 for the title. The LSU men's track team, which was coached by Bernie Moore, won the conference's first national championship, defeating Southern California 58-54 at the national meet in Chicago.

In football, Alabama finished atop the SEC standings (5-0-1, 7-1-1 overall) just ahead of LSU (3-0-2, 7-0-3). With rule changes designed to encourage more passing, the attendance decline of the previous two years reversed, and the sport continued to grow in popularity.

One of the SEC's first controversial decisions was to allow student-athletes to be eligible for normal student aid—for tuition, books, board, and room—resulting in outcry in the media and from other schools, but they were eventually won over. Influenced by the Depression, when many athletes had to leave school in order to support themselves, grant-in-aid for athletics was enacted in 1935.

"This plan has now been in effect a year and I am convinced that it has elevated intercollegiate athletics to a higher plane, and in general has corrected the evils and problems which previously had made falsifiers out of many of the athletes," Tulane's Dr. Wilbur Smith wrote in his report to the NCAA in 1936. In 1938, the Southern Conference adopted its own grant-in-aid policy.

Meanwhile, bowl games other than the Rose Bowl (which wouldn't sign an affiliation agreement with the Pac-10 and Big Ten conferences until 1946) began to emerge. Tulane was allowed to play in the first Sugar Bowl in 1935, followed by LSU the next three years. An affiliation agreement to have an SEC team annually selected was debated and initially turned down.

The Orange Bowl, which played its first game in 1933, invited Ole Miss in 1936, followed by Mississippi State, Auburn, Tennessee, and Georgia Tech in the subsequent years, all of which still had to receive permission from the conference. That same year, all SEC schools had finally joined the NCAA, with Alabama and Kentucky the final two holdouts.

In 1934, the conference negotiated a contract for a game-of-the-week broadcast, with A. J. Norris Hill Company the sponsor, but local broadcasts of games were still prohibited. However, when the financial gain exceeded expectations, the ban was lifted with schools allowed to negotiate their own contracts.

Meanwhile, the SEC recognized recruiting and focused on establishing controls. In 1939, the NCAA adopted its famous Article III regarding recruiting and subsidizing, and mandated that all schools adhere as a condition for membership. It authorized some recognition of the athlete in the granting of aid according to need, but fell short of what the SEC had approved. It marked a new era of regulation and enforcement for the parent organization, with the SEC adjusting its regulations to conform.

In 1939, at the suggestion of Vanderbilt Chancellor O. C. Carmichael, the SEC formed a committee to study the prospect of having a full-time commissioner to enforce conference rules and regulations, investigate alleged violations, and act as a center of communications between athletic departments. Martin Sennett Conner, a prominent attorney in Jackson, Mississippi, and former governor of that state, was appointed on August 20, 1940.

"We assume our duties, when men are shaken with doubt and with fear, and many are wondering if our very civilization is about to crumble," Conner said when he was inaugurated as governor on January 19, 1932, at the age of 41. At the time, Mississippi had a bankrupt treasury and a $13 million deficit. After Conner made it one of the first states to impose a sales tax, Mississippi had accumulated a treasury surplus by the time he left office in 1936.

Conner was given an annual salary of $7,500 with a matching expense allowance. To pay for it, each school was to pay one-half of 1 percent of its gross football receipts (which was quickly increased to 1 percent).

The first change in membership came in 1940, when Sewanee, which had not enjoyed the same kind of growth as the other schools and had yet to win an SEC football game, left the conference.

"A small liberal arts college simply cannot compete in football with large universities," the letter of resignation stated. "Equal competition in other sports is very difficult."

Though the SEC regretted the loss, it did not consider a replacement and aimed to keep its numbers low.

As the country entered World War II, Conner established his office in Jackson and set forth to make sure conference regulations were carried out uniformly. One was that an athlete receiving student aid could work at a job paying no more than $10 per month a term. Normal pay could be received during holiday and vacation periods.

When the SEC's annual meeting in 1941 was held in Lexington, Kentucky, just days after the attack on Pearl Harbor, numerous resolutions were passed, including the following by the presidents and faculty chairmen:

"The Southeastern Conference has assembled at the most critical period in American history. The days of the American Revolution were not so ominous. The conflict which resulted in the War Between the States did not constitute such a critical moment in our history. The First World War in 1917 was far less serious than the present crisis which is upon us. We have met today not merely to consider the minor problems of football, basketball, and other athletic sports but to consider seriously how colleges and universities can meet the issue of national defense and make their contributions in the struggle for our existence."

With many eligibility regulations lifted and eventually suspended (entrance requirements, rule on transfers, participation rules, and the academic progress requirement), competition continued through the early stages of the war, though large crowds were banned on the West Coast, resulting in the Rose Bowl temporarily relocating to Durham, North Carolina (where Oregon State defeated Duke 20-16 before 65,000 fans). In 1943, seven SEC football teams cancelled their seasons. Vanderbilt played an informal schedule, LSU and Georgia played with freshmen and transfers, and Georgia Tech and Tulane competed with Navy players. The following season, 11 schools played schedules of from 7 to 10 games.

Though the conference did not suspend business, the commissioner was reduced to part-time status, with reduced pay. Instead, planning meetings were held to prepare for the postwar years, studying, and in many cases overhauling, everything from recruiting to administration. Among the changes, the $10 per month job was abolished (in favor of a $10 monthly grant), but the idea of creating a balanced, rotating schedule in football was rejected. In 1946, the SEC established its own association of officials.

Regulations regarding returning veterans proved to be tricky and confusing, and due to the various categories the commissioner often had to go on a case-by-case basis. When the conference passed a rule that a veteran could compete only after returning to his preservice college within one year of the date of his discharge, it was met by protest. At Auburn's request a hearing was held, with the most vocal objections being raised over the stipulation that a veteran had to return to his original college (veterans organizations felt that a veteran should be able to choose any school he desired), and the rule was repealed.

With the innovative T-formation, devised by Stanford's Clark Shaughnessy, followed by the split-T and the wing-T, and with player substitutions (to speed up the game and reduce injuries) as well as television, football's growth was unprecedented in the years following World War II. Helping usher in the new era was Smith, who was president of the NCAA, and Conner, a member of its executive committee. However, Smith resigned in 1946 due to personal reasons, and Conner was no longer able to continue on the committee or as SEC commissioner due to health reasons, leaving a temporary void in conference representation on the national level.

Coinciding with their departure, the NCAA began a lengthy period of adjustment and transition. In 1947, the NCAA adopted the self-policing Sanity Code regarding recruiting and subsidizing. It permitted aid for tuition and fees, but not room and board. The SEC and Southwest Conference opposed the new rule, along with a recruiting regulation that prohibited off-campus contact. The Sanity Code was passed at the NCAA convention, but the recruiting regulation did not. While the SEC left the convention unsatisfied, it did get more representation with Vanderbilt Dean C. M. Sarratt and Alabama Dean Albert Moore elected to the council, with Moore becoming the first SEC representative to serve as NCAA president in 1953. Tennessee Dean N. W. Dougherty was elected to the executive committee in 1948, and W. A. Alexander of Georgia Tech added to the inspections and enforcement committee.

In an interview with Gruensfelder, Dougherty humorously said: "The NCAA was the biggest thing to happen to the conference."

Dougherty stepped in as acting commissioner after Conner stepped down, until former LSU coach Moore was named the second full-time commissioner in 1948, the same year Kentucky won the SEC's first national basketball championship.

One of Moore's first steps was to move his offices to Birmingham, a central location within the conference that still serves as SEC headquarters. He also created an information bureau that would disseminate weekly releases, and he authorized annual publication of a records book and season statistics.

In 1949, with the conference taking in 25 percent of its assessment on bowl-game receipts, the SEC essentially became self-sufficient. In 1953 the SEC distributed $120,000 to its members as excess funds, with gate receipts exceeding expenditures long before the first television contract was signed.

At the suggestion of the NCAA, the SEC voted in 1951 to regulate the length of the football season, along with preseason and spring practices (meanwhile, the

Southern Conference banned teams from playing in bowl games and limited rosters to 40 players for conference games. When Clemson and Maryland accepted bowl bids, they were declared ineligible for the conference championship. Two years later, seven of the larger schools broke off to form the Atlantic Coast Conference, or ACC). Otherwise, the biggest areas of concern during that time had to do with gambling and bribery. In addition to the numerous proposals the schools considered, reforms were also passed by federal and state legislatures. The first televised game in the Deep South was also played in 1951, between Alabama and Tennessee.

When the NCAA Council recommended that all schools unable to conform to the Sanity Code be suspended, membership didn't follow suit, signaling a departure in the organization's power structure. Due to concerns that it was creating more inequality in athletics, Kentucky faculty chairman A. D. Kirwan led the debate to repeal the Sanity Code that had been in effect for only three years. As a result, the NCAA was again an advisory board, but the movement toward having national control of recruiting standards and enforcement was on.

"The restrictions in the Sanity Code were such that the majority of institutions felt they couldn't live by it," Bradley University director of athletics Arthur J. Bergstrom said. "In fact, it got to the point where a great many schools, especially in the South and Southeast, said that if the code was adopted, they would withdraw their membership from the NCAA."

In 1952, after reorganization increased the decision-making power to the elected council instead of the appointed executive committee, the NCAA strengthened its investigative arm with stricter penalties. Coinciding with rapid growth of membership, not to mention television, the NCAA consolidated its ability to govern both large and small schools and to handle problems not limited to a single school or region.

While the council approved a 12-point code in August 1951 that picked up where the Sanity Code left off, a nine-member Membership Committee composed of the NCAA president and the eight district vice presidents was charged with considering complaints filed against member schools. A Committee on Infractions was established in 1954 to replace the Membership Committee, and an assistant to NCAA Executive Director Walter Byers was hired to help administer the process. In 1956, that position was assumed by Bergstrom.

The SEC was opposed to the NCAA's return to enforcement, but fully cooperated. One of the first major cases occurred in 1952 when Kentucky, coming off a severe point-shaving scandal, requested an investigation, which found that ineligible basketball players had participated in NCAA events over several years. Both the NCAA and SEC penalized the school, and Kentucky canceled its season.

At the time, former Federal Bureau of Investigation agent W. A. Collier was the SEC's investigator, a position he held for 12 years. Additionally, from 1954 to 1961, the conference was represented on the NCAA Infractions Committee by Sarratt and Kirwan.

In 1953, Moore reported that an average of 40 to 50 percent of freshmen athletes who had participated the year before did not return. In 1954, the average loss was 46 percent, and 30 percent of the students authorized grants didn't show up for their first year. The conference responded by authorizing new standards raising the levels of grants, and the return rates improved immediately.

A year later, the NCAA council appointed a committee to study all aspects of recruiting. One of the changes that came out of it, three years later, was the rule allowing a school to pay for one official visit by a recruit to the campus (putting the responsibility on the schools and curbing potential alumni activities). Though initially opposed by many, the national letter of intent became reality in 1963, and a year later most conferences had established entrance requirements. Neither change was legislated at the NCAA level, but rather they were agreed to by the conferences.

It wasn't until 1956 that the SEC attempted to adopt a round-robin schedule featuring a set number of traditional and rotating games, but the schedule was objected to by nearly every school. Instead, a seven-game schedule was adopted. From 1948 to 1964, the SEC considered inviting Miami and Houston to join the conference, but never did in part because of the disagreements over a rotating football schedule. Meanwhile, the conference's proficiency on the field was reaching new heights. In 1959, for example, four teams finished with rankings in the Top 10: Ole Miss (2), LSU (3), Georgia (5), and Alabama (10).

Two other important developments occurred under Moore's watch. In 1963, women were allowed to participate in conference competition with men in swimming and tennis. On June 1, 1964, at the encouragement of football coach Bobby Dodd, Georgia Tech left the conference.

Dodd, a former Tennessee player who led the Yellow Jackets to the SEC championship in 1951 and 1952 (and his team was named the 1952 national champions by two rating systems and the International News Service, which merged with United Press in 1958), believed that Tech could become a successful independent similar to Notre Dame. He also disagreed with the SEC's decision to limit scholarships before the NCAA mandated restrictions.

"Either love your players or get out of coaching," was the quote associated with Dodd. Perhaps fittingly, Georgia Tech's final conference game was a 14-3 victory against rival Georgia.

The departure left the conference unbalanced, but only for two years. Sweeping cutbacks by Tulane president Rufus Harris beginning in 1951 left the Green Wave unable to effectively compete, with as few as 38 players on the football team one season. On June 1, 1966, Tulane withdrew from the SEC for what many thought was an effort to play a national schedule as well.

"That wasn't it at all," Rix Yard, Tulane's athletic director at the time, told the *Times-Picayune* years later. "The purpose was to lighten the schedule. We had to have some relief on the field. Those were tough days. Remember we had an 0-10 season in 1962. I remember going to Bernie Moore and pleading to allow us to reduce our schedule. He wouldn't allow it."

(*Note:* Things got much worse for Tulane before they got better. In 1983, graduate assistant Bob Davie was caught spying on the practices of Mississippi State, Tulane's first opponent. The following year, assistant coach Wally English wanted his son, Jon, taking snaps instead of Bubby Brister, even though Jon had already played at five schools and been ruled ineligible. English sued the NCAA and the school, and with his son at quarterback, Tulane upset No. 9 Florida State, 34-28. He lost the lawsuit, the game was forfeited, and soon after a point-shaving scandal involving the basketball team was uncovered. After Tulane hired Mack Brown, who would coach Texas to the 2005 national championship, to replace English, a credit-card scandal involving football players was also unearthed. A 14-person committee reviewed the program for months and voted the night before the Southern Miss game in 1985 whether to drop the sport. The vote was a tie. A week later, before the season-ending game with LSU, another vote was taken, and Tulane football survived by one vote.)

Although there was always talk of a "Southern Ivy League" consisting of schools like Duke, Rice, Southern Methodist, Tulane, and Vanderbilt, it never materialized.

When Moore retired as commissioner on April 1, 1966, he was succeeded by Alabama native A. M. "Tonto" Coleman (1966–72), who had—ironically—worked at Georgia Tech for 15 years and was known for his wide grins and keen sense of humor. It was under Coleman that an SEC school admitted its first black athlete, Kentucky football player Nat Northington in 1966, after Syracuse's Ernie Davis became the first black player to win the Heisman Trophy in 1961 and was followed by Southern California's Mike Garrett in 1965 (FYI, O. J. Simpson won in 1968).

In 1971, Dr. Earl Ramer of Tennessee became the second SEC representative to be named NCAA president.

With Coleman's retirement, Dr. H. Boyd McWhorter, the Dean of Arts and Sciences at Georgia and league secretary for approximately five years, became the SEC's fourth commissioner in 1972. Not only did he make the formal agreement for the conference football champion to automatically receive an invitation to play in the Sugar Bowl, but in 1979 he helped to reinstate the SEC Men's Basketball Tournament, which had been discontinued in 1952. Also on McWhorter's watch, the first conference championships were held in women's basketball, tennis, and volleyball, and the SEC signed an agreement with Turner Broadcasting Systems to show a football "Game of the Week" beginning in 1984, which was also when women's sports came under the auspices of the SEC.

To give an idea of the proportional growth the league experienced during his tenure, during McWhorter's first year the SEC distributed $1.57 million to its 10 schools. Fourteen years later, in 1986, the sum was $15 million. Growth continued under the direction of Dr. Harvey Schiller, who became commissioner on September 15, 1986. The Air Force colonel and former faculty chair at the U.S. Air Force Academy left in 1989 and later joined Turner Broadcasting to head all sports programming on TBS and TNT, in addition to serving as president of the NHL Atlanta Thrashers and World Championship Wrestling, director of the U.S. Olympic Committee, and CEO of Yankee-net, a sports media company that owned the New York Yankees, New Jersey Nets, New Jersey Devils, and a cable television division.

Speaking at his alma mater, The Citadel, in 2003, Schiller had the audience pass around five rings. The first, valued at $45,000, was a Stanley Cup ring. He also shared two World Series rings (1999 and 2000), Evander Holyfield's boxing ring, and his commissioner's ring from the SEC.

"The most important thing that you can have is for people to say that they trust you," he told the cadets.

When Roy Kramer, who served on numerous NCAA committees and had been Vanderbilt's athletic director for 12 years, succeeded Schiller on January 10, 1990, he launched both the SEC and college football as a whole into the era of the super-conferences. With the possibility of increasing television revenues, Kramer realized that the SEC could take advantage of a loophole in NCAA rules to create an extra revenue-enhancing championship game, but in order to do so it needed at least 12 teams. He asked, and received, unanimous permission from SEC presidents to begin interviewing potential candidates.

Rumors immediately swirled about potential additions, including Texas, Texas A&M, West Virginia, Florida State, and Miami (which joined the Big East in 1991, but later jumped to the ACC with Boston College and Virginia Tech).

"One of the things we looked at was homogenous institutions," Kramer told ESPN years later. "We wanted schools with a strong fan base that traveled well. TV wasn't a dominating factor. Our people were interested in fan base and a broad-based program. That drove our deliberations a lot more than TV markets."

Somewhat surprisingly, it was Arkansas that first jumped at the opportunity, which also led to the end of the troubled Southwest Conference. In the late 1980s, SWC attendance had plummeted, with the eight Texas schools playing before an average of 65 percent capacity at home—numbers blamed mostly on the lack of winning programs and the success of the Dallas Cowboys and Houston Oilers in the National Football League. Attendance was also declining in men's basketball, in which Arkansas was considered a national power under the direction of controversial coach Nolan Richardson. (He won a national championship in 1994, and among his more famous quotes was his response to being asked why there were so many good players in the SEC: "Where did most of the slave ships stop? In the South.")

With Title IX set to mandate a massive budgetary increase for women's sports, the SWC was hindered by a limited television market consisting of only two states (even if one of them was Texas). Coupled with sagging revenues, the conference also went through a litany of scandals, with seven of its nine schools placed on probation during the 1980s, and many top recruits electing to play elsewhere.

"It was like if you're not cheating, you're not trying to win," former Arkansas football coach Lou Holtz was quoted as saying.

Though the SEC might have had some "sexier" possibilities, an invitation was extended to Arkansas. On August 1, 1990, its board of trustees, acting on recommendations from athletic director Frank Broyles and the school's chancellor, approved the switch.

"I personally was concerned that [Texas] A&M and Texas would leave and not include us," Broyles said.

While the SEC looked for a twelfth school, which would be South Carolina (an independent since 1971), to balance out the schedule, Texas and Texas A&M considered their options. Texas flirted with the Pac-10 and Big Ten, but found both geographically undesirable. Texas A&M did ask about joining the SEC, but the conference would only accept both in a package deal.

Eventually, both schools ended up in the Big Eight, along with Texas Tech and Baylor in a partial merger, but again only after a major move by the SEC. Instead of adhering to a television contract extension with ABC and ESPN that the College Football Association negotiated, the SEC signed a landmark five-year, $85 million deal with CBS, which had just lost the NFL to Fox.

Days later, the Atlantic Coast Conference signed an $80 million deal with ABC and ESPN, and CBS quickly added the Big East for $75 million, including basketball games.

The Big Eight quickly evolved into the Big 12, signed a $100 million deal with ABC and Liberty Sports, and the SWC was no more.

With Arkansas and South Carolina joining league play in 1992, the SEC was split into Eastern and Western divisions, with the top team in each meeting for the conference title. Additional television contracts were signed with Jefferson-Pilot Sports and for ABC to broadcast the SEC Championship Game. Undefeated Alabama beat Florida 28-21 in the first playoff at Legion Field in Birmingham, and two years later the championship was moved to the Georgia Dome in Atlanta.

In 1994, CBS Sports signed a multiyear deal with the SEC to broadcast football, men's basketball, and women's basketball games. The deal was extended though the 2008–09 seasons. Five years later, the SEC extended a deal with ESPN.

But Kramer wasn't done changing the landscape of college football just yet. In addition to turning the conference into a financial behemoth, he persuaded the four major college football bowls to agree to a rotating national championship game. Though the Bowl Championship Series—which places teams in the Sugar, Fiesta, Orange, and Rose bowls—has been immensely controversial, especially regarding the selection process for which two teams play in the title game, it's also been a financial windfall for all involved.

While Kramer's tenure (1990–2002) was tainted by claims of bias against Alabama and numerous incidents that had nearly every SEC program on NCAA probation (some more than once), the league won 85 national championships and pocketed $654 million.

In 1990, the SEC schools divided $16.3 million. In 2002, when Kramer stepped down, the total was up to $95.7 million.

On July 2, 2002, Michael L. Slive became the seventh commissioner of the SEC. A former New Hampshire judge who also worked as an attorney defending universities charged with NCAA rules violations, Slive had served as the first commissioner of Conference USA and helped turn it into a league on par with most others in basketball, and just a step behind in football, before Cincinnati, Marquette, Louisville, and DePaul all left for the Big East.

Among Slive's early accomplishments were the SEC Task Force on Compliance and Enforcement report, which called for having all schools off NCAA probation within five years, and the formation of the Academic Consortium, which linked the academic resources of the 12 schools. In 2005, the league distributed $110.7 million.

"I am keenly aware that to be the Commissioner of the SEC is both a privilege and a challenge," Slive said upon his appointment. "It's a privilege because the SEC is the premier conference in the country, with outstanding academic institutions, unsurpassed winning athletic traditions as well loyal, dedicated and passionate fans, outstanding athletic directors and coaches, and, of course, national championship-caliber student-athletes."

· 2 ·

Rivalries

The essence of the Southeastern Conference is in many ways best exemplified by its rivalries. Basically, each season is the equivalent to a series of border skirmishes, except for the intra-state conflicts that are even more intense. A lot of respect is usually involved, mixed in with some serious animosity.

"Southern football is best," Southern columnist and humorist Lewis Grizzard wrote. "Watching the Michigan–Ohio State game was about as exciting as watching two mules fight over a turnip."

Perhaps the SEC's most amicable rivalry is also its oldest. Although Kentucky and Tennessee had already hosted games (not against each other) prior to 1892, Georgia vs. Auburn stemmed from the friendship of the two people who introduced the game on their respective campuses. Dr. Charles Herty of Georgia and Dr. George Petrie of Auburn had been classmates at Johns Hopkins University, marking the first of many intriguing connections between the two football programs.

Reported the *Atlanta Journal* on February 17, 1892: "Atlanta will be the scene Saturday of the first interstate intercollegiate football game (Atlanta vs. Auburn); both teams have been practicing for weeks."

In front of 2,000 fans at Piedmont Park, the Tigers won the initial meeting 10-0. The two programs have played every year since 1898—except for 1943, when Auburn didn't field a team due to World War II.

Auburn's most famous coach, Shug Jordan, was an assistant at Georgia when he was hired to take over the Tigers, and Georgia legend Vince Dooley graduated from Auburn, which unsuccessfully tried to hire him away. Jordan also used to remember when Herty and Cliff Hare would meet after their games.

"They would come to Dean Hare's house on Gay Street in Auburn after the game in Columbus to divide the money," Jordan recalled. "They would take the gate receipts out of an old cigar box, spread it on the kitchen table, and say, 'a dollar for you and a dollar for us' until the game proceeds were divided equally between the two schools."

In 1942, No. 1 Georgia had the ideal backfield of Heisman Trophy winner Frank Sinkwich and Charley Trippi, but lost to Auburn (27-13) just before its showdown with No. 2 Georgia Tech.

With less than a minute to go in the 1959 game, Georgia quarterback Fran

Tarkenton drew up a play in the dirt, broke the huddle, and threw a 13-yard touchdown pass to Bill Herron for a 14-13 victory to snap a six-game losing streak against the Tigers. It also secured one last SEC championship for coach Wally Butts.

After Georgia upset host Auburn 20-16 in 1986, Bulldogs fans rushed the field and started pulling up pieces of the turf. To stop them, the grounds crew turned the water hoses on, inspiring the title, "The Battle between the Hoses."

The 1996 meeting was the 100th in the series, but the first SEC game ever to go into overtime under new rules. The Bulldogs won 56-49 in the fourth extra session—somewhat fitting, since the all-time series was almost dead even at 47-45-8 in favor of the Tigers.

"It's hard to explain to others, but when Auburn and Georgia play, it's like a game between you and your best friend," Dooley said.

"When Auburn and Georgia play, it's like two brothers going at it in the backyard," Auburn coach Pat Dye said. "I love my brother, but I want to whip him."

However, Georgia fans have a not-so-unique dilemma in the SEC in that they have more than one rival. There's the historical rival in Auburn, the natural in-state rival with Georgia Tech, and then the fun/intense rival, Florida, with "The World's Largest Cocktail Party" played at the neutral site of Jacksonville. The three games are played near the end of the regular season, and essentially decide the Bulldogs' success.

Georgia fullback Theron Sapp's jersey was retired primarily due to his performance against Tech in 1957. The Bulldogs were 2-7 and had lost eight straight to the Yellow Jackets when Sapp scored the game's only touchdown and recovered two fumbles at linebacker (one of which set up his score). Previously, a 12-0 Tech victory in 1929 kept Georgia from playing in the Rose Bowl, and despite the 1942 loss to Auburn, the Bulldogs still crushed Tech 34-0 en route to a Rose Bowl victory against UCLA.

Tech was so thrilled with the 1984 win at Georgia that back in Atlanta, fans broke into Grant Field and tore down the goalposts. The 1900s closed with three of the wildest games in the series by scores of 27-24 (Georgia), 21-19 (Tech), and 51-48 (Tech, led by quarterback Joe Hamilton, who finished second in Heisman voting).

As for the Cocktail Party, kicker Bobby Etter won the 1964 game for Georgia when he picked up a bad snap and ran 22 yards for a touchdown. Florida missed a chance to nail down the 1975 SEC championship when Georgia tight end Richard Appleby stopped on an end-around and threw an 80-yard touchdown pass to Gene Washington for a 10-7 victory. In a similar circumstance the following year, Florida coach Doug Dickey went for a first down on fourth-and-1 at his own 29—and didn't make it. The Bulldogs scored three straight touchdowns en route to a 41-27 victory, thanks to what fans called the "Fourth and Dumb" play.

When Vanderbilt began playing football in 1890, it scheduled its natural rival, the University of Nashville (Peabody), located mere blocks away, and won 40-0. Intensity between the neighboring schools reached its highest point in 1896 when fans from both sides interrupted the game. The incident began after a Vanderbilt player fell on the ball after a failed drop kick, only to take a hard hit. When the instigator was roughly pulled off, a melee ensued.

Reported *The American*: "In a very short time words were supplanted by blows and for a few minutes both sides were engaged in a lively manner. After matters were amicably arranged the play was allowed to go on for a space of time, but a decision of the umpire being unsatisfactory to the University of Nashville, the men walked off the field, and while the two captains were discussing the matter the crowd came together again and necessitated a discontinuance of the game.

"It was decided by the umpire and referee to call the game on account of outside interference. Captains Connell and MacRae both expressed themselves as very sorry that the affair occurred and are of the opinion that it was due to the excited student bodies."

After both sides protested in letters to the newspaper, school administrators met and decided that the game should be forfeited to Vanderbilt.

A near riot between fans after Ole Miss defeated then Mississippi A&M College (7-6) at Scott Field in 1926 led to the creation of the Battle of the Golden Egg. In the 13 previous meetings, all of them A&M victories, Ole Miss had been outscored 327-33, and fans rushed the field to celebrate and went for the goalposts. Regarding the mayhem, the A&M yearbook, the *Reveille*, said: "A few chairs had to be sacrificed over the heads of these to persuade them that it was entirely the wrong attitude."

While the student newspapers continued to lob verbal shots at each other regarding the "Battle of Starkville," an Ole Miss honor society, Sigma Iota, proposed that a trophy be awarded upon the game's conclusion in a ceremony during which both alma maters were sung in hopes of keeping fans calm. "The Golden Egg" was a regulation-size, gold-plated football mounted on a pedestal. The original cost of the trophy was $250.

Ole Miss won the first Golden Egg with a 20-12 victory and has dominated the series since, with a 52-21-5 record through 2005. In 1977, the *Jackson Clarion-Ledger* used the headline: "Egg Bowl up for scramble," leading to the popular slang term for the game, "Egg Bowl."

Among the highlights, Arnold "Showboat" Boykin scored seven touchdowns for Ole Miss in the 1951 game. And in 1962, sophomore quarterback Jimmy Weatherly missed a handoff to David Jennings, only to run 43 yards for a touchdown in the Rebels' 13-6 victory.

Another memorable moment came in 1992, when host Mississippi State ran 11 plays inside the Ole Miss 10-yard line in the final 2:30 of the game, but was unable to score as the Rebels held on for a 17-10 win. It was also the first on-campus meeting since 1972, with the series rotating between campus sites thereafter.

"Rivalry between the University of Mississippi and Mississippi State University is not just an on-field thing," W. G. Barner wrote in the book *Mississippi Mayhem*. "It's an ongoing thing. Like a smoldering feud. But more than a feud, this one never wanes in intensity."

However, some Rebels fans consider LSU their biggest rival due to a string of fierce games ranging from 1947 through 1971, occasionally with the SEC and/or national title aspirations at stake. In 1959, Bill Cannon's amazing 89-yard punt return gave LSU a 7-3 victory and cost Ole Miss a chance to win a consensus national championship, but the Rebels got even in the Sugar Bowl with a 21-0 thrashing.

There was a time in which LSU considered Tulane its biggest rival, and the Tigers' first game ever in 1893 was a 34-0 loss to the in-state neighbor. For years, the teams used to play for "The Rag," which was a flag splitting each team's colors: half purple and gold, half green and white. Though the original rag vanished, a new one was awarded to LSU after its 48-7 victory in 2001, giving the Tigers a 65-22-7 advantage in the series.

In 1939, the Green Wave was unbeaten and poised for a Sugar Bowl bid when end Ralph Wenzel caught a long pass for an apparent touchdown, but then he confessed to the nearest official, "I think I stepped over the line while running for the touchdown. I think the fair thing to do is to tell you." Tulane went on to score anyway and won the game 33-20.

Probably the biggest scare regarding the rivalry had to do with LSU's mascot, Mike the Tiger. Tulane students were actually able to kidnap the original Bengal tiger (Mike I, 1936–56), but in the mid-80s they just cut the locks on the cage and freed Mike IV during the early morning hours a few days before their game. The tiger freely roamed, knocking down some small pine trees before being cornered in Bernie Moore Track Stadium and shot with a tranquilizer gun by police.

FYI, fans used to believe that the Tigers would score a touchdown for every growl Mike made before each game, and thus he was frequently provoked. Objections of cruel punishment stopped the practice.

Arkansas' long-standing rival was Texas, but the Razorbacks have since taken up with LSU. Even though the schools weren't in the same conference until 1992, their first meeting was 90 years previous and both have played spoiler in key situations. In 1996, the Golden Boot Trophy—which stands 4 feet tall, weighs almost 200 pounds, and is valued at $10,0000—was introduced, going to the winner of the annual regular-season finale.

South Carolina vs. Clemson is the fourth-oldest uninterrupted series in college football, but one of the few in which the state school has been the predominant underdog (Clemson leads the series 63-36-4). The ninety-sixth meeting in 2004 might have been the low point of the rivalry, when players fought on the field and cost both squads the bowl trips for which they were eligible. South Carolina coach Lou Holtz said afterward that he was "embarrassed like I've never been before," and he retired at the end of the season.

Actually, that wasn't the first such incident between these teams. In 1902, when the game was played on the Columbia fairgrounds and called Big Thursday (from 1896 to 1959), only one official was available for the game because of a train accident. South Carolina won 12-6, but Clemson's cadets responded by marching on the South Carolina campus with fixed bayonets, causing a riot. Consequently, the series was put on hold until 1909.

The most controversial game was in 2000. With less than a minute remaining,

Thomas Hill fell on Derek Watson's fumble in the end zone to give the Gamecocks an apparent 14-13 victory. However, with 10 seconds remaining, Woody Dantzler completed a 50-yard pass to Rod Gardner, whom South Carolina fans will be forever convinced pushed a defender out of the way but received no penalty. Clemson won the game on a 25-yard field goal.

Another dramatic finish was in 1964. Down 3-0 late in the fourth quarter on the road, South Carolina replaced injured quarterback Dan Reeves—yes, the same Dan Reeves who holds the National Football League record for being in nine Super Bowls as a player or coach—with Jim Rogers. A 45-yard completion to J. R. Wilburn set up Rogers' dramatic 15-yard scramble into the end zone for a 7-3 victory.

Meanwhile, Clemson fans are quick to point out that even though South Carolina's George Rogers won the 1980 Heisman Trophy, he never scored a touchdown against the Tigers (most Gamecock fans consider it a fair trade-off).

The series is also known for its hijinks. For example, counterfeiters printed thousands of bogus tickets in 1946, resulting in the crowd storming the gates and surrounding the field during the game.

One of the more humorous moments was a prank in 1961, when the men of South Carolina's Sigma Nu chapter dressed up as Clemson players and actually took the field at Williams-Brice Stadium (then known as Carolina Stadium) for pregame warm-ups.

"They planned that thing forever," said Tommy Suggs, who was in the stands that day rooting for Clemson. "It was absolutely hilarious."

In borrowed uniforms from nearby Orangeburg High School—which were similar in appearance to Clemson's—the fake players performed calisthenics before breaking down into position groups. Linemen were pretending to pull udders, and the punter kicked the ball backward. When the student impersonating coach Frank Howard, with a stuffed shirt and wide-brimmed hat, walked by the sideline, an elderly female fan yelled out, "Coach Howard, I love you." He replied, "Go to hell."

Eventually, some Clemson students took matters into their own hands, and the resulting pandemonium required the state police to restore order.

"It's the greatest hoax in college football history," said Suggs, who wound up attending South Carolina and pledging Sigma Nu. As a quarterback, he led the Gamecocks to their lone Atlantic Coast Conference championship in 1969, and in 2005 was in his 32nd year as color analyst on South Carolina radio broadcasts.

Occasionally a team or a coach came along that was basically seen by every other team as a rival and worthy of nothing short of an all-out effort.

Steve Spurrier was one such person when he coached at Florida, and he had a habit of irking just about everyone.

For example, after a blowout against Kentucky in 1996, Spurrier commented: "These sort of games don't prove very much. All it proves is we're better than Kentucky."

When a non-sellout crowd attended a victory at Vanderbilt, Spurrier was asked if he was surprised by the sparse turnout. "Surprised?" he answered. "It's Vandy. There must have been something good on TV."

In 1996, Spurrier found out that LSU defensive coordinator Carl Reese, whose squad gave up "only" 28 points to Florida the previous season (during which Reese dubbed Spurrier "Shiny Pants"), had sent the game tape to Nebraska in preparation for the national championship at the Fiesta Bowl. The Cornhuskers won handily, 62-24.

"Hopefully LSU's defensive coordinator won't be giving clinics on stopping the Gators next year," Spurrier said after Florida crushed LSU 56-13.

But Spurrier saved many of his best rips for Georgia, which had kept him as a quarterback from fulfilling the dream of winning Florida's first SEC title in 1966. After scoring 50 points in Athens—which will forever draw the ire of Bulldogs fans—he was asked about going for a last-second passing touchdown. "Because no visiting team has ever scored 50 points in this stadium and we wanted to be the first," Spurrier said.

Georgia fans also received an extra jab when Spurrier was asked about whether he would be able to even the 15-game margin in the Largest Cocktail Party in the World: "I don't know, 15 years is a long time."

A rivalry also grew against Tennessee, with the two teams frequently butting heads atop the Eastern Division standings in the 1990s. From 1992 to 2004, the division was won by either Florida or Tennessee 11 times, and both won a national title. When Florida finished No. 1 in 1996, quarterback Danny Wuerffel won the Heisman Trophy. The following year, Tennessee quarterback Peyton Manning finished second to Michigan cornerback Charles Woodson. When the ballots were cast the Vols had one loss, to—you guessed it—Florida, 33-20. Of Manning's six losses as a starter, four were to Florida.

With the Gators frequently having the upper hand, Spurrier made Tennessee fans grimace with his cracks that you can't spell Citrus without UT because, while the SEC champion went to the Sugar Bowl, the runner-up often played in the Florida Citrus Bowl.

Florida's more modern rival is Florida State, which was a girls' school until after World War II, didn't field a team until 1947, and had its first taste of success under Bill Peterson in the 1960s. Of course, after being hired in 1976, Bobby Bowden turned the Seminoles into a powerhouse. The intra-state showdowns of the 1990s, including the 1996 national championship game in the Sugar Bowl, made them worthy of the spotlight they received.

However, the roots of that rivalry are deep, extending to seasons when Florida did everything it could to avoid playing the upstarts from Tallahassee. Due in part to pressure from the state legislature, the first meeting was in 1958, won by the Gators 21-7. Because Florida State's stadium seated only 25,000, Florida refused to play there, citing the financial hit the schools would take, and thus the first six games were all played in Gainesville. When Florida athletic director and coach Ray Graves said it would take another 10,000 seats for the Gators to play there, Florida State immediately agreed.

"The president wanted to fire me because we had to have 35,000 seats by the next year," Florida State athletic director Vaughn Mancha, a former All-American at Alabama, recalled to the *Fort Lauderdale Sun-Sentinel*.

But the school made it happen in time for the 1964 season. With the Gators leading the series 5-0-1, some wore stickers reading "Never, FSU, Never," on their helmets during practice, and the game-day jerseys had the words "Go for Seven" above the numbers. The host Seminoles won 16-7. Florida came back to win nine straight, a streak that was finally snapped in 1977, 37-9.

One of those victories occurred in 1966, in a game forever remembered for Lane Fenner's diving 59-yard touchdown catch that was ruled incomplete by game official Doug Moseley, who said that the Florida State receiver did not have control of the ball. Florida held on for a 22-19 victory, but both the game film and a *Tampa Tribune* photograph appeared to show that Fenner had indeed made the reception, resulting in a student protest and Peterson claiming the team was robbed. While Gators supporters mockingly posted copies of the picture in their homes, offices, and taverns, Moseley was hounded for years by angry fans who thankfully didn't have access to the Internet back then.

Somewhat similar to the way Spurrier was viewed as the coach everyone wanted to beat, Alabama has frequently been the team to beat due to its success and legacy. It's even more so for the neighboring schools, which directly compete against the Crimson Tide in recruiting.

Tennessee considers Alabama its biggest rival, primarily because the Crimson Tide is the only program to have won more games, SEC titles, and national championships, and by a wide margin. The teams' annual showdown is known as the "Third Saturday in October," though it's now usually held the following weekend. Both sides treat the annual event as a benchmark for the season, with the winner more often than not challenging for the SEC championship, if not more.

"You never know what a football player is made of until he plays Alabama," Tennessee coach General Robert Neyland said. He was also once quoted as saying, "Tennessee sophomores don't deserve citizenship papers until they have survived an Alabama game."

Legendary coach Paul "Bear" Bryant enjoyed victories over Tennessee so much that he began the tradition of handing out cigars in the locker room after victories. Not to be outdone, the Volunteers picked up the habit in the 1990s.

"We all remember the things we do in the Alabama game," Tennessee coach Johnny Majors said.

But Bryant's history with the Volunteers goes back to when he was a senior end at Alabama, before he coached Kentucky (1946–53)—which like Vanderbilt, where he was an assistant, considered Tennessee its biggest football rival. In 1935, Bryant sustained a broken leg against Mississippi State, but he played the following week against Tennessee.

He recounted in his autobiography the pregame speech given by assistant coach Hank Crisp in the locker room: "I'll tell you gentlemen one thing. I don't know about the rest of you, you or you or you. I don't know what you're going to do. But I know one damn thing. Old 34 will be after 'em, he'll be after their asses."

"In those days they changed the players' numbers almost every week . . . to sell those quarter programs," Bryant wrote. "So he's up there talking about old 34, and I look down, and I'm 34! I had no idea of playing."

Bryant helped key a 25-0 victory, but it would be the last time Bryant was on the winning side against Neyland, going 0-7 at Kentucky.

The rivalry grew to a fever pitch approximately 65 years later. Court records indicated that Tennessee coach Phillip Fulmer had been instrumental in helping the NCAA Committee on Infractions build a case against Alabama during a recruiting scandal that nearly resulted in the Crimson Tide being issued the death penalty. Though numerous coaches had pointed the finger at Alabama, Fulmer lobbied the SEC to take action and went out of his way to direct a key witness to investigators, while at the same time seeming to sidestep numerous issues that plagued his own program. Because Tide fans viewed Fulmer as someone who tried to take away their beloved program in order to gain a competitive edge, he became the most hated man in Alabama.

However, the quintessential rivalry of the SEC is undoubtedly Alabama vs. Auburn, a contest nicknamed "The Iron Bowl" when it was held at the "neutral" site of Legion Field in Birmingham (less than an hour away from Tuscaloosa). Everything else in the state stops that day, and those who relocate there are asked to declare an allegiance almost immediately.

"This is the number one football state in America," said Pat Dye, who was an assistant under Bryant at Alabama (1965–73) and Auburn's head coach from 1981 to 1992. "People in Wyoming are talking rodeo in July. The people in Alabama are talking the Alabama-Auburn football game. The people in North Carolina are talking the four corners defense [in basketball]. In Alabama, they're talking about why you didn't run the ball on third down and one instead of throwing it."

The rivalry is so intense that it took a four-decade hiatus due to a dispute between the schools. Friction intensified during the 1906 game, when Alabama coach J. W. H. Pollard unveiled the "Military Shift," a maneuver he learned at Dartmouth but that had never been seen in the South. Pollard held secret practices to work on the formation, which was described as every player except the center lining up on the line of scrimmage and joining hands, but then turning one direction or another to form an unbalanced line.

Alabama won the game 10-0, but Auburn coach Mike Donahue was so upset that he threatened to cancel the series. A year later, with the teams in disagreement over expense money and referees, Pollard came up with another unique scheme, the "Varsity Two-Step," which was a variation of the Military Shift only much more confusing. Alabama used it to score the touchdown it needed for a 6-6 tie in what would be the teams' last meeting until 1948.

The debate on renewing the series went on for years, with Alabama in particular hesitant to play a less-successful program that had never finished better than third in the SEC. Citing problems—including brawls and other incidents—at rivalry games in Georgia, Kansas, Louisiana, Maryland, Minnesota, South Carolina, Tennessee, and Texas, the school's Committee on Physical Education and Athletics report argued: "We hazard nothing in saying that the game would not make a single constructive contribution to education in the state." It concluded, "The fundamental question is: Do the people of Alabama need a tranquil, sane kind of athletics in their two major institutions, or an irrational rabid kind?"

When representatives of the state legislature threatened to hold back funding to both schools if they didn't meet on the football field each and every year, students met in Birmingham and buried a symbolic hatchet in Woodrow Wilson Park. On December 4, 1948, at Legion Field, 46,000 attended the first Iron Bowl since 1907, with another 2,000 at the Birmingham Armory for a pay-per-view broadcast.

Gordon Pettus' touchdown pass to Butch Avinger set the tone. Ed Salem passed for three touchdowns, ran for another, and kicked seven extra points as Alabama destroyed Auburn 55-0. The following year, the Tigers turned the tables, 14-13, to earn the bragging rights.

It's a game that few people from other regions can fully appreciate and is by far the most heated intra-state football rivalry in the country, if not biggest overall.

"I thought I understood something about rivalries," said Billy Curry, who coached Alabama from 1987 to 1989, but never defeated Auburn. "But until I'd experienced Alabama-Auburn, I didn't understand anything at all."

Although fans on both sides obviously have their favorites, five games in particular stand out:

1971: Even though Auburn quarterback Pat Sullivan went on to win the Heisman Trophy, Alabama running back Johnny Musso led a 35-31 victory. Coming in, both teams were undefeated, with the Crimson Tide ranked third and the Tigers fourth.

1972: Undefeated Alabama led 16-0 going into the fourth quarter, and had given up a field goal when Auburn's Bill Newton blocked consecutive Greg Gantt punts with David Langner returning both for touchdowns and a 17-16 victory. More than 30 years later, Tigers fans still relished "Punt, Bama, Punt" like it happened yesterday.

1981: Bryant recorded victory No. 315, making him the winningest coach in major college football history.

1985: Just before running back Bo Jackson won the Heisman Trophy, Auburn was No. 7 with Alabama unranked. The lead changed hands four times in the fourth quarter before Tide kicker Van Tiffin, who missed a 52-yard field goal into the wind earlier, made a game-winner from the same distance against the wind.

1989: No. 2 Alabama (10-0) was thinking national championship when it traveled to Auburn for the first time. But the Tigers had been waiting for nearly 100 years to get the Tide on their turf, and they pulled out an emotional 30-20 victory. "After years of bondage, our people were finally delivered to the Promised Land," Auburn athletic director David Housel said.

But no one understood the rivalry better than Bryant did.

"Sure I'd like to beat Notre Dame, don't get me wrong," he said shortly before retiring in 1982. "But nothing matters more than beating that cow college on the other side of the state."

The feeling's more than mutual.

· 3 ·

The Good . . .

In late July of every year, the Southeastern Conference officially kicks off the upcoming football season with a journalistic smorgasbord called Media Days at the Wynfrey Hotel, just outside of Birmingham, Alabama. Since 1985, reporters have descended on the posh locale and helped turn it into something resembling a toy store the day after Thanksgiving. Prior to that, a dozen or so newspaper reporters used to partake in the SEC Skywriters Tour, in which Elmore "Scoop" Hudgins, who handled media relations for the conference, organized a league-wide traveling contingency that visited every school.

In 2005, more than 700 journalists attended Media Days, and many stuck around for the entire three days of interview sessions. Four schools would participate a day, with the coach and two players making the rounds and being peppered with questions from newspapers, television, radio, Internet, etc.

But before the interview assembly line could begin, the commissioner had to deliver introductory remarks on the state of the conference and how it expected to improve in the coming year. As usual, he—in this case, Mike Slive—often had a lot to talk about.

"Sometimes we lose sight of the broad base programs that this league enjoys and it is one of the reasons why we deal with our financial issues," Slive said during his speech. "It gives us the opportunity to create tremendous opportunity for student athletes in sports. The evidence of our competitive success in all sports is simply in the numbers.

"Last year, SEC teams won seven national championships and had eight runners-up. In half of the 20 sports we sponsored, we had either a national champion or a runner-up. In 16 of the 20 sports we sponsored, SEC teams placed in the top five nationally. Seventy-two of our student athletes won individual national championships and 554 of our kids won first-team All-America honors. And finally, 159 SEC teams participated in NCAA postseason play. That represents almost 75 percent of all the teams in the league.

"Equally for me, if not more importantly, more than 2,000 of our kids who are student athletes, representing close to 40 percent of all athletes, earned SEC academic honor roll status."

The numbers adequately reflect a conference that has made its top priority being the best at everything. Since 1990, the SEC had won 107 team championships, an average of more than six per year.

In football alone, here are the SEC's national champions (selected by The Associated Press poll unless otherwise noted):

Year	Team
1951	Tennessee
1957	Auburn
1958	LSU
1960	Ole Miss (Football Writers Association of America)
1961	Alabama
1964	Alabama
1965	Alabama
1973	Alabama (United Press International)
1978	Alabama
1979	Alabama
1980	Georgia
1992	Alabama
1996	Florida
1998	Tennessee
2003	LSU (*USA Today* coaches' poll)

Note: Arkansas was named the 1964 FWAA National Champion before it joined the SEC.

Factor in the years before the conference was created in 1933, and SEC teams have won nearly two dozen national championships, beginning with Georgia Tech in 1917. Coached by John Heisman, Tech (9-0) outscored opponents 494-17.

The SEC has had at least one team finish in the Top 10 every year since 1944, and the conference record for bowl teams in one season is eight.

Of course, numerous other barometers are used to measure its success.

MONEY

It should surprise no one that the SEC is immensely successful in creating revenue, especially from football, which finances many other sports.

In the summer of 2005, the SEC distributed $110.7 million to the 12 schools as part of the revenue-sharing plan for the previous academic year. From what had become an annual press release announcing that the amount was the most ever, the conference reported:

"Broken down by categories and rounded off, the $110.7 million was derived from $45.4 million from football television, $20.2 million from bowls, $12.4 million from the SEC Football Championship, $11.6 million from basketball television, $3.3 million from the SEC Men's Basketball Tournament and $17.8 million from NCAA Championships. The average amount distributed to each school which participated in all revenue sharing was $9.22 million.

"Not included in the $110.7 million was $7.1 million retained by the institutions participating in bowls and $660,000 divided among all 12 institutions by the NCAA for academic enhancement."

Here's the yearly breakdown since 1980:

1980	$4.1 million	1993	$34.34 million
1981	$5.57 million	1994	$34.36 million
1982	$7.24 million	1995	$40.3 million
1983	$9.53 million	1996	$45.5 million
1984	$18.4 million	1997	$58.9 million
1985	$9.34 million	1998	$61.2 million
1986	$13.1 million	1999	$68.5 million
1987	$13.56 million	2000	$73.2 million
1988	$14.34 million	2001	$78.1 million
1989	$13.85 million	2002	$95.7 million
1990	$16.3 million	2003	$101.9 million
1991	$20.6 million	2004	$108.8 million
1992	$27.7 million	2005	$110.7 million

ATTENDANCE

The SEC has essentially led the country in attendance since 1980, including 5,719,678 in 2004 by averaging an all-time best 74,282 fans per game, and stadiums close to 96 percent capacity (95.87 percent).

In comparison, the Big Ten finished second by totaling 4,591,722 fans and averaging 69,572 per game. The Atlantic Coast Conference drew 3,678,508 fans. On average, the Big 12 averaged 57,312, the Pacific-10 55,684, and the ACC 55,735.

Four of the Top 10 schools in home attendance were from the SEC, with Alabama in the midst of stadium renovations to place it in the Top 5.

School	Average
1. Michigan	111,025
2. Tennessee	106,644
3. Ohio State	104,876
4. Penn State	103,111
5. Georgia	92,746
6. LSU	91,209
7. Florida	88,409
8. Southern Cal	85,229
9. Oklahoma	84,532
10. Texas	83,094
11. Auburn	83,085

12. Florida State   82,841
13. Wisconsin   82,368
14. Alabama   81,870
15. Notre Dame   80,795

AWARDS

Seven SEC players have won the Heisman Trophy, the biggest award at the collegiate level:

1942   Frank Sinkwich, halfback, Georgia
1959   Billy Cannon, halfback, LSU
1966   Steve Spurrier, quarterback, Florida
1971   Pat Sullivan, quarterback, Auburn
1982   Herschel Walker, running back, Georgia
1985   Bo Jackson, running back, Auburn
1996   Danny Wuerffel, quarterback, Florida

Note: Running back George Rogers won in 1980 when South Carolina was an independent.

Among other major awards (see Appendix F), the SEC has won four Maxwell Awards, nine Walter Camp Awards, six Outland Trophies, and two Lombardi Awards. Approximately a dozen national Coach of the Year awards have been earned, led by Paul "Bear" Bryant's three to go with his six national championships. Bryant's 323 victories, most of which were at Alabama and Kentucky, had not been topped when he retired in 1982, with a winning percentage of .780. Only General Robert R. Neyland of Tennessee retired with a better winning percentage among SEC coaches, at .829 (173-31-12).

Other SEC coaches who retired with top winning percentages include Dan McGugin of Vanderbilt (.762), Bobby Dodd of Georgia Tech (.713), John Vaught of Ole Miss (.745), and Vince Dooley of Georgia (.715).

(FYI, Dodd spent his entire head-coaching career at Georgia Tech, where he was 165-64-8 from 1945 to 1966. He won two SEC titles with 13 bowl teams and had two unbeaten seasons.)

MISCELLANEOUS

• On the 2005 opening-day rosters, the SEC had 261 former student-athletes playing in the National Football League—the most of any conference. Florida and Tennessee led with 37 each, trailing only Florida State's 42. Georgia was tied with Ohio State for fourth with 35, and Auburn and LSU were in the Top 10. The Atlantic Coast Conference was second (231), ahead of the Big Ten (223), the Pac-10 (188), and the Big 12 (176).

- In the 2005 NFL Draft, the SEC had 10 players selected in the first round alone.
- The SEC's television package included alliances with CBS, ESPN, Jefferson-Pilot, and Fox Sports Net. The nine states it covered represented roughly 20 percent of television households in the United States and published more than 70 daily newspapers.
- During the 2003–04 academic year, the SEC had 35 student-athletes named CoSIDA Academic All-Americans, tying with the Big 12 for the most of any conference. The SEC had 15 student-athletes make first team, 15 make second team, and 5 make third team of their respective sports.
- The 12 member institutions provide nearly $45 million in scholarships for more than 4,000 student-athletes each year.
- For the 2003–04 academic year, the SEC had 170 teams participate in NCAA postseason competition among the 20 league-sponsored sports, an average of more than eight teams per sport. The SEC also had 498 first-team All-Americans, including 81 individual national champions.

· 4 ·

. . . And the Not So Good

At that same session of Media Days prior to the start of the 2005 football season, it didn't take long for the first coach to be asked about off-field incidents and how they could be avoided. It was probably the most asked-about topic during the three-day gathering.

"If we have issues, I want to come get you because you just jinxed us," University of Florida coach Urban Meyer said. "You're like my wife when someone is throwing a no-hitter. She comes in and says, 'Do you realize there's a no-hitter going?'"

That the National Collegiate Athletic Association has often had a black eye when it came to controversy was nothing new. The NCAA instituted a "Sanity Code" shortly after World War II because of academic, financial, and gambling concerns, especially in football. But the SEC, in particular, has seemingly always been synonymous with trouble.

The conference's biggest scandal was arguably during 1951 in men's basketball, when six members of the Kentucky Wildcats faced charges of accepting bribes to control scores and frustrate oddsmakers' point spreads. Coach Adolph Rupp had claimed his team was untouchable, that "They couldn't reach my boys with a ten-foot pole," but the NCAA suspended the 1952–53 season.

In 2005, football was again on the front burner due to numerous off-field incidents.

"Well, to be honest with you, it's awful," said Meyer, who had yet to coach a game at Florida after being hired away from Utah. "You know, Friday night, as a coach, you go sleep with one eye open."

Leading the offseason rap sheet was Tennessee, with players cited for shoplifting, assault, gun charges, and failed drug tests. Additionally, two university students had been struck by football players in separate incidents (one coldcocked during a pickup basketball game), leaving one with a broken jaw and the other requiring a metal plate in his mouth.

"We're not the only one out there," coach Phillip Fulmer said. "We've had our issues, and we'll get through them. We can't stick our head in the sand and think things haven't gone very well. Fortunately, we haven't had anyone murdered or bank robbed, or anything like that. I don't know how many times I've gotten mad at a pickup basketball game. I haven't taken a swing at someone. Or citations for God's sake? You get embarrassed nationally because you have four [traffic] citations?"

Right behind the Vols were the Gamecocks. Twelve players were arrested in the first half of 2005, including six facing felony charges for taking laptops and player photos from Williams-Brice Stadium after South Carolina's bowl appearance was cancelled due to a brawl against Clemson.

To be more specific, the six were charged when $18,000 worth of computer and video equipment and framed photographs were taken from the stadium in late November. Among the players, offensive lineman Woody Telfort was charged with a felony count of grand larceny. On March 1, leading rusher Demetris Summers was dismissed from the team. A day later, tackle Kevin Mainord was arrested for stealing televisions from dorm rooms. Defensive end Moe Thompson was arrested on similar charges six days later. On April 16, Josh Johnson and Ty Erving were arrested and charged with simple marijuana possession. Soon after, wide receiver David Smith pleaded guilty to third-degree burglary. In May, linebacker Dustin Lindsey was charged with DUI. On June 23, running back Cory Boyd was dismissed from the team. (He was reinstated.)

"I know sometimes in college I probably personally did some things I wasn't very proud of," new South Carolina head coach Steve Spurrier admitted. "But [a player] taking [his own] picture off the wall and bringing it back, I didn't think [that] deserved quite the national punishment that those guys got.

"Then we had some stealing incidents. We are not going to have guys that steal on the team. Sometimes you need some guys to maybe go by the wayside to tell the other guys if you are going to play football at South Carolina and be a student-athlete, [you've] got to do things the right way. Simple as that."

However, the incidents did lead to some brief fireworks between the coaches. In response to an incident involving junior Syvelle Newton, Spurrier told *USA Today*, "It wasn't a full-blown fight. If you want to read about some full-blown fights, read about the Tennessee players, not our guys."

Fulmer responded, "He needs to take care of his own house and leave mine alone. He's got plenty of issues over there, I'm sure, to deal with. Maybe it rained that day, and he didn't get to play golf."

(*FYI:* Although both coaches tried to play down their comments, South Carolina upset Tennessee 16-15 on a last-second field goal that season. Spurrier led the Gamecocks to a 7-4 record, while Tennessee, No. 3 in the preseason polls, lost for the first time to Vanderbilt in 22 years. At 5-6, Tennessee wasn't bowl eligible for the first time since 1988.)

But it's not like bad behavior was unique to those teams.

At Mississippi State, 17 players either transferred, quit, were suspended, or graduated early. Many left because coach Sylvester Croom came in and cracked the whip on those who weren't used to it, and because he held them accountable for their actions.

"There are things that happened when I was playing that went unreported and nobody ever found out about. That's a whole lot worse than what these kids are doing now," said Croom, a former All-American center at Alabama. "It's just different now."

He later added, "A lot of it goes into the kind of players you recruit."

Interestingly enough, Croom was involved in another issue when he was with the Crimson Tide, from 1972 to 1974, as one of the conference's first black players.

The first black player was Nat Northington, who signed on at Kentucky in 1966 along with Greg Page. After preseason practices, Page was second on the depth chart only to defensive end Jeff Van Note, who went on to play 18 years in the National Football League with the Atlanta Falcons. While Page was making a tackle during a pursuit drill, his teammates swarmed on from behind. He was paralyzed, went into a coma, and died after 38 days on a respirator. The heartbroken Northington was injured in his first game against Indiana, didn't play the rest of the season, and chose to quit the team. However, before he left, Northington encouraged the handful of black players in the incoming freshman class to stick it out. Among them was Wilbur Hackett, who as a junior was named a Kentucky co-captain. Croom was honored with a similar distinction at Alabama in 1974.

Racial tension that had been building in the region for decades overflowed into SEC athletics in other ways. In 1955, Georgia governor Marvin Griffith asked Georgia Tech to withdraw from the Sugar Bowl because its opponent, Pitt, was integrated. Louisiana and Mississippi lawmakers subsequently passed legislation prohibiting schools from competing against integrated teams (but it didn't stop Jones College in Mississippi from crossing the border to play Compton College in the Junior Rose Bowl).

In 1963 Rupp, who was far from an advocate of civil rights, sought approval from his SEC counterparts to allow games against integrated teams. Alabama, Auburn, LSU, Mississippi, and Tennessee did not reply to the request. Three years later, Texas Western, with an all-black starting lineup, beat Kentucky in the landmark NCAA title game.

Alabama football became the focal point of the debate in the SEC, with Paul "Bear" Bryant winning his first three national championships with all-white teams. The first came in 1961, with the Crimson Tide subsequently honored in New York at a Hall of Fame dinner, at which President John F. Kennedy was named an honorary letterman.

However, a year later Kennedy was at the Orange Bowl when Alabama defeated Oklahoma 17-0. Although he visited Sooners coach Bud Wilkinson, who was on his physical fitness council, the president did not step inside the Crimson Tide locker room, which many took as a snub due to the hot issue of racial integration.

Months earlier, on October 1, 1962, two people were killed and at least 75 injured in rioting over the admission of the first black student, James Meredith, at Ole Miss. Kennedy addressed the nation, urging nonviolence, but also "federalized" the Mississippi National Guard and brought in U.S. marshals and military police to help keep the peace (FYI, Meredith eventually did graduate).

After winning the national championship in both 1964 and 1965, despite having a loss during both seasons, Alabama was the preseason No. 1 team. The Crimson Tide was undefeated in 1966, but wasn't rewarded with the title. That year, both the Associated Press and United Press International decided to have their final voting before the bowls. Many believed the state's racial issues—including governor George Wallace's "Stand in the Schoolhouse Door," the Rosa Parks bus incident in Montgomery, and the Selma civil rights marches—were factors in the voting, with Notre Dame and Michigan State, both 9-0-1, finishing ahead of 10-0 Alabama at 1 and 2.

Especially since Alabama was a public school—and because it was under the auspices of Wallace, who was against integration—Bryant, who greatly respected authority, was stuck in a difficult situation. While taking criticism, he maintained that the local social and political climate wasn't ready for football integration; but by 1967, he was openly predicting the inevitable. During a deposition for an anti-discrimination lawsuit filed against the school, Bryant testified that he had been actively trying to recruit black players, but had found no takers.

In 1968, Wilbur Jackson became the first black player to accept a scholarship to play football for the Crimson Tide, and he was followed by Bo Matthews. In the 1970 season opener against Southern California, played at Legion Field in Birmingham, Sam Cunningham, who had rushed for 135 yards and scored two touchdowns, led USC to a 42-21 victory. Noted assistant coach Jerry Claiborne: "Sam Cunningham did more to integrate Alabama in 60 minutes than Martin Luther King did in 20 years."

By 1973, one-third of Alabama's starters would be black, and any SEC school that wasn't heavily recruiting black athletes by that point would soon follow suit. Croom eventually became the SEC's first black head football coach when he was hired by Mississippi State in 2004.

Game days on campuses are usually incident-free, though they can present their own unique problems. In 2005, the region was devastated when Hurricane Katrina struck near New Orleans, causing the levy system to fail and the city to flood. After the rest of the South and the country opened their hearts and homes to storm victims from Louisiana, Mississippi, and Alabama, LSU was finally able to play a home game roughly three weeks later. When Tennessee complained about the traditional nighttime kickoff and lack of hotel rooms, the Volunteers received a rude welcome to Baton Rouge, prompting the following letter to athletic director Mike Hamilton:

Dear Mike,

Congratulations on a great effort by the Tennessee football team on Monday night.

While the football game was exciting, I am especially writing to express my sincere apology and regret to you, your president and all Tennessee fans for the incident which took place on our campus as your team buses were approaching Tiger Stadium.

As you know, there is unfortunately an element in every crowd that does not exhibit good sportsmanship, and when crowds grow to the size of those on a football game day, it takes only a very small percentage of offenders to ruin the day for so many.

As I am sure you are proud of Tennessee's following, we are extremely proud of our fans at LSU. Their enthusiasm and loyalty to our program make our many successes possible, and it is the passionate base of fans in the SEC that makes our league truly unique. I think you will find that an overwhelming majority of LSU fans respect and enjoy healthy competition with fans from other schools.

The offenders you encountered on Monday night are not representative of the many great fans we have at LSU. They are the unfortunate few who do not understand that their embarrassing and insulting behavior reflects poorly on LSU's athletics program and does nothing to lend support to our team.

We are working hard to address the problem presented by the small percentage of people who, by their actions, damage the reputation of an entire University. We will continue to work to make LSU football an enjoyable atmosphere for everyone who attends our athletics events, regardless of the school colors they wear.

Sincerely,
Skip Bertman, LSU Athletics Director

While Bertman's letter may have been an honest gesture, it certainly raised more than a few eyebrows around the rest of the conference because it had hardly been a lone incident. In addition to being incredibly loud, LSU fans had the reputation for occasionally being lewd, rude, and quite often crude, and they were proud of it.

It's not too difficult to figure out why.

"The difference between a day game and a night game at LSU? At night you can smell the bourbon on the field," LSU coach Mike Archer (1987–90) said.

Granted, a visiting fan might get the car keyed at just about any football stadium, but at LSU they've always gone after the buses.

"LSU always had a great atmosphere for college football. You had more energy, more electricity at night. It was one way to beat the heat and the humidity, and, let's face it, the fans could drink more. Yeah, they were into it. You knew you were in for a dog-cussin' when you walked into that place," Ole Miss coach Billy Brewer (1983–93) said.

"When we played in Baton Rouge, I'd have the police escort put on his siren, which would like basically be announcing, 'The Rebels are here.' The LSU fans would abuse us, they'd accost us, and a couple of times I thought they might turn the bus over. All it did was get us ready for a football game."

There are numerous other instances of bad behavior made by those associated with SEC football programs, both past and present.

For example, Billy Cannon's 89-yard punt return against Ole Miss probably secured the 1959 Heisman Trophy and turned him into a local legend. In 1983, he was sentenced to five years in prison after pleading guilty to his part of a counterfeiting operation that printed $6 million in bogus $100 bills (he went on to become a dentist).

In 2003, Auburn school officials flew on a trustee's private plane with boosters and athletics director David Housel in an attempt to secretly woo Louisville coach Bob Petrino. The problem was that Auburn already had a coach under contract, Tommy Tuberville, who was preparing for the Iron Bowl, and neither he nor Louisville officials knew anything about it. Not only was it an ethical breach in college athletics, but university president William F. Walker was forced out and Housel stepped down. The trustees were cited in a report by the Southern Association of Colleges and Schools (SACS), which placed Auburn on probation and threatened to pull the school's accreditation as an academic institution in good standing.

That same year, Terry Bowden, who had served as Auburn's head coach from 1993 to 1998, admitted that when first arriving on campus, he discovered there was a system in place whereby football players could get paid.

Additionally, lawsuits are nothing new to the SEC.

In 1963, Bryant was already suing the *Saturday Evening Post* regarding an article by an Atlanta-based sportswriter who called the Crimson Tide a dirty team (from the 1961 Georgia Tech game), when another accused Bryant and Georgia athletics director Wally Butts of fixing their game so they could bet on it. The article also alleged that Bryant had thrown a loss to the Yellow Jackets. Both Bryant and Butts filed suit, and investigating attorneys found that the story had been based on false and fabricated evidence. A court awarded Butts $460,000, and Bryant later settled with Curtis Publishing for $300,000.

But far and away the leading issue with SEC football programs has been the number of times they've been in trouble with the NCAA for rules violations. Since 1953, SEC programs have been sanctioned 47 times for major violations, of which 31 are football related.

While Southern Methodist, which received the death penalty, and Arizona State have the most major infractions in college athletics with eight apiece, here's the breakdown:

> 7—Auburn
> 6—Georgia and Kentucky
> 5—Mississippi State
> 4—Alabama, Florida, and South Carolina
> 3—Arkansas and Ole Miss
> 2—LSU and Tennessee
> 1—Vanderbilt

As of January 1, 2006, Alabama, Arkansas, Auburn, Mississippi State, and South Carolina were all under NCAA probation, with the longest lasting until 2008. That's also the time frame SEC commissioner Mike Slive set as a goal in hopes of getting every program probation-free.

Some called that challenge overly optimistic, but necessary considering not only how long the members had been on a collision course with potential disaster but also how the conference's reputation had become "win at all costs."

According to NCAA records, 28 SEC football titles were won by programs that would be sanctioned within four years. Some were more extreme than others, but here are a few examples:

- Of Kentucky's two SEC football titles, the second came in 1976 when it was cited for "Improper entertainment, financial aid, lodging and transportation; extra benefits; out-of-season practice; complimentary tickets; improper recruiting entertainment, inducements and transportation; excessive number of official visits; outside fund; questionable practice; institutional control; certification of compliance." The program was issued a one-season postseason and television ban. In 1977, the Wildcats finished 10-1 overall, 6-0 in the SEC. Since then, Kentucky's best showing has been third in the Eastern Division (in 1993). Incidentally, in a Pulitzer Prize–winning investigative series, the *Herald-Leader* reported that 26 former Kentucky basketball players said they accepted either cash or gifts from boosters. After investigating for almost three years, the NCAA said in March 1988 that it had been unable to substantiate the infractions reported by the newspaper, but reprimanded the school for not cooperating with the investigation.
- After winning its first SEC championship in 1984, Florida was forced to vacate the title because of recruiting violations under head coach Charlie Pell. The Gators were later hit with NCAA sanctions. It marked the only time in SEC history that a football championship was vacated.
- In 1978, Georgia was cited for improper financial aid and transportation, and extra benefits, and received a public reprimand. In 1982, it again was cited for improper recruiting contacts, inducements, and transportation. Georgia won the SEC championship in 1980, 1981, and 1982, with a national championship.
- Ole Miss was placed on probation in 1959 for "improper recruiting inducements" when it finished 10-1. The Rebels were named national champions in 1960 and won the SEC title in 1960, 1962, and 1963. Ole Miss hasn't won a championship since, but it was cited in 1986 (and again in 1994) when it finished 8-3, sandwiched between campaigns of 4-6 and 3-8.
- When Mississippi State won its only Western Division title in 1998, it came two years after being penalized for impermissible recruiting, extra benefits, unethical conduct, and lack of institutional control.

Auburn is the epitome of the cause-effect relationship (or incredibly bad timing, if you listen to a fan). When the Tigers finished 12-0 in 2004, it marked the third time Auburn went undefeated during the same year the athletic program was placed on probation.

After being placed on three years of probation for improper recruiting inducements in 1957, the Tigers went undefeated and won their lone national championship. The following year, the program was cited again and consequently banned from all NCAA voting and committee privileges, and television, until its probation was completely served.

In 1993, the NCAA found that a player received improper gifts from coaches and boosters. Bowden's first team finished 11-0, 8-0 in the SEC, but was unable to claim the conference title or play in a bowl.

In 2004, the men's basketball team was accused of offering thousands of dollars and cars to two men's basketball prospects, with a summer AAU sponsor/coach acting as a booster or representative of a university.

With basketball violations apparently increasing across the board, it was only part of a long string of NCAA sanctions penalizing nearly every SEC athletic program from 1990 to 2000 (Kentucky was the lone exception, and South Carolina was cited before joining the SEC). Among the more notable cases, as cited by databases on ESPN.com and the NCAA's website:

Florida, 1990: Former coach Galen Hall was accused of giving defensive back Jarvis Williams $360 and providing a ride so he could pay overdue child support. Hall admitted to providing transportation, but denied giving Williams any money. Also, an assistant coach was cited for allegedly providing a loan of at least $70 to a player using money from a booster. Florida was given a one-year bowl ban, to which Hall's replacement Spurrier complained vigorously. "Florida got the biggest discount on major penalties that's ever been given in the NCAA's history," NCAA Committee on Infractions member John Nowak said. With the men's basketball program also penalized, Florida vacated its 1987 and 1988 NCAA basketball championship records and had to return revenue from the 1988 tournament.

Tennessee, 1991: An assistant coach allegedly arranged for an airline ticket so a prospect could attend a special camp. The Volunteers were also cited for improper off-campus contacts, impermissible transportation, and recruitment of prospects before completion of their junior year. Tennessee was limited to 85 scholarships for two years, but avoided all other major penalties.

Auburn, 1993: An assistant coach, staffer, and boosters allegedly all gave money to defensive back Eric Ramsey, who had secretly tape-recorded conversations, including with coach Pat Dye. The school was cited for lack of institutional control, with a two-year bowl ban and one-year television ban. Dye retired early.

Ole Miss, 1994: The recruiting scandal included allegations of a staff member offering cash and a booster offering a car. Boosters were also accused of improper contact, including occasions when recruits were taken to strip clubs in nearby Memphis. Because the violations were similar to those in 1986, Ole Miss was issued a two-year bowl ban, a one-year television ban, and a signing limit of 13 players for two years. Fired coach Billy Brewer sued Ole Miss.

Alabama, 1995: When junior cornerback Antonio Langham signed a cocktail napkin for an agent in the early morning hours after the national championship victory against Miami in the Sugar Bowl on January 1, 1993, it constituted a contract. Running back Gene Jelks had also received $24,400 in loans, based partly on his potential future earnings, and the school was cited for lack of institutional control. Alabama was penalized with a one-year bowl ban, limited to signing 12 players for one year, and had to forfeit all the games Langham played in 1993. However, an NCAA appellate panel later vacated an erroneous finding that Alabama's faculty athletics representative, Tom Jones, had provided false information to the NCAA. It ruled that the Committee on Infractions had judged Jones guilty without ever notifying him or Alabama of the charge. The scholarships were reinstated.

Mississippi State, 1996: A booster allegedly gave improper bonuses, meals, and loans to athletes who worked at his publishing firm. A staff member was also cited for offering money to two prospects if they visited the campus. The school was charged with lack of institutional control for failing to investigate after it had received warnings, and it was limited to signing 12 recruits for one year.

Incidentally, when the NCAA came back and ruled in 2004 that Mississippi State had participated in "improper recruiting contacts and inducements" and "unethical conduct," resulting in four years of probation and a postseason ban that year (even though the Bulldogs clearly weren't going to get enough wins to be eligible), Coach Jackie Sherrill sued the NCAA, NCAA investigators Rich Johanningmeier and Mark Jones, and businesswoman Julie Gibert for contributing to unfair business practices and forcing him out of football.

"Those who point fingers have the most to hide," Sherrill had said two years earlier when responding to charges that he broke NCAA rules.

Georgia, 1997: A booster in Florida allegedly gave recruits cash, meals, and other benefits to sign with the Bulldogs. Georgia was limited to signing 20 recruits one year and banned for two years from recruiting in Palm Beach. Even though the school self-imposed all the penalties, the process didn't go over well with coach Ray Goff, who said, "I can remember people around town making jokes like, 'Hey they're buying players and they still can't win.'"

After the turn of the twenty-first century, two overlapping scandals rocked both the conference and college football as a whole and nearly stripped the SEC of its most prized program.

The first was at Kentucky, with the NCAA's Committee on Infractions determining in 2002 that more than $7,000 was spent by Kentucky, primarily through football operations director Claude Bassett, for impermissible recruiting inducements and monetary gifts to high school coaches and prospects. In addition to Bassett, the committee implicated two other assistant football coaches, a recruiting assistant, three student workers, a football camp director, members of the football equipment staff, eight players, at least six prospective players, two high school coaches, and "numerous" boosters.

The Wildcats received a one-year bowl ban, the first the NCAA had handed down since 1995, and voluntarily agreed to a potential loss of 19 scholarships. Bassett resigned and was effectively banned from college sports for eight years. Cited for unethical conduct, he received a show-cause order, which means any NCAA institution that wanted to hire him during that period would have to demonstrate to the committee why it should not be penalized by doing so.

Head coach Hal Mumme was charged with failing to properly monitor the program, although no restrictions were placed on his being hired for another job in college football. He also resigned. Mumme wound up helping revive the Division I-AA program at Southeastern Louisiana, for an annual salary approximately $700,000 less than what he made at Kentucky.

But that paled in comparison to the recruiting scandal at Alabama, which barely escaped the death penalty, resulting in a federal criminal trial and numerous lawsuits.

At the heart of the scandal were allegations that booster Logan Young, a wealthy businessman in Memphis, had paid approximately $150,000 to a high school football coach to influence star defensive tackle Albert Means to accept a scholarship and play for the Crimson Tide.

With Alabama fully cooperating with investigators—unlike what Auburn would do in its wake, challenging both the charges and the enforcement community as a whole—the NCAA brought the hammer down on the football program by sentencing it to a two-year bowl ban, five years of probation, and the loss of 21 scholarships over a three-year period.

The penalties were considered among the harshest ever handed out by the NCAA, and they came under criticism for their inconsistency (for example, witnesses implicated numerous other schools in offering money for Means, including Arkansas, Georgia, Memphis, Michigan State, Ole Miss, Tennessee, and yes, Kentucky, yet none were punished). It was the first two-year bowl ban since Ole Miss and Washington in 1994, and the loss of scholarships was the most since Miami in 1995.

The NCAA Committee on Infractions justified the penalties by citing Alabama's status as a repeat offender. Under NCAA bylaws, schools guilty of more than one major infraction during a five-year period were automatically subject to more severe penalties. However, in this case, that status was in question.

Prior to the start of the 1995 football season, when the NCAA finally announced its decision regarding Langham, the Committee on Infractions also ruled that Tom Jones had lied to the governing body, resulting in further sanctions. Even though no school had successfully appealed an NCAA penalty, Alabama did; and thanks to further investigation, won, and the ethics charges were dismissed. Seventeen of the scholarships were restored, but Jones went on to sue the NCAA for libel and won, also in unprecedented fashion.

In 1998, Tide assistant basketball coach Tyrone Beaman was fired after allegedly asking boosters for money to secure a player's services. The boosters reported Beaman to the university, which reported the violation to the NCAA. The school received no penalties, but it extended Alabama's repeat-violator period even though the NCAA never reopened the previous football investigation following the appeals.

Instead, the NCAA said that Alabama's cooperation was what saved the football program, with Committee of Infractions chairman Thomas Yeager quoted as saying it was "staring down the barrel of a gun."

As more and more details became public knowledge, the entire process came under scrutiny, even while Young was being prosecuted in federal court for conspiracy, crossing state lines to commit racketeering, bribing a state official, and structuring a financial transaction to evade reporting requirements. In building a case against him, investigators went through Young's garbage and used provisions allowed in the Patriot Act designed to fight terrorism.

Additionally, while a number of coaches had reported concerns about recruiting in the Memphis area, the NCAA used secret witnesses, including Fulmer and Tom Culpepper, a recruiting analyst the Tennessee coach introduced to investigators.

At that time, Tennessee was taking heat for a number of issues, including former quarterback Tee Martin, who led the Volunteers to the 1998 national championship. Former sportswriter Wayne Rowe had told the *Mobile Register* that he wired $4,500 to Martin on behalf of insurance agent Dianne Sanford in February 1999. The NCAA enforcement staff ruled that neither Rowe nor Sanford were considered boosters, so there was no penalty.

At roughly the same time, English professor Linda Bensel-Myers lodged complaints about academic misconduct concerning Tennessee athletes, which she believed had been going on for at least a decade.

Among her statements:

"It's clear that the integrity of the system continues to decline, and that the athletics department is mandating unacceptable tutoring practices that can only be described as institutional plagiarism."

"If teaching athletes the importance of education ruins the football program, then the football program does not belong in the university."

Tennessee suspended four players during the subsequent investigation, but later cleared them, ruling that no NCAA rules were broken because it was an academic issue and not an athletic one. That surprised the University of Minnesota, where the athletic department had been sentenced to four years probation and the men's basketball team lost five scholarships due to academic fraud.

Unfortunately for Bensel-Myers, the university decided that while football did belong at Tennessee, she didn't. The professor moved on to the University of Denver and became director of The Drake Group, which has the mission of "Defending academic integrity in the face of commercialized college sport."

"Because the NCAA has a vested interest in keeping profitable collegiate teams viable, using the NCAA to oversee academics within the athletics department makes as much sense as letting the fox protect the chicken farm," she argued.

Court records indicated that even though the enforcement community was based on the notion of self-policing, SEC commissioner Roy Kramer knew well before Means signed with the Tide that there were alarming issues regarding his recruitment, yet Kramer didn't notify Alabama officials until after Means both accepted a scholarship and played for the football team, thus making Alabama eligible for penalties.

This was the same commissioner who provided guidance in the Lester Earl basketball case, with LSU successfully arguing that postseason bans usually came only with institutional control issues. The appeals committee eliminated Earl's penalty on the eve of the 1999 SEC Tournament.

"I think Roy Kramer is a little worried about his legacy," Bensel-Myers said.

Although he was named in lawsuits, Fulmer refused all efforts to testify under oath about what he knew, said, or did to aid the NCAA's investigation. When told he would be subpoenaed in an Alabama civil case, the coach accepted a $10,000 fine from the SEC rather than risk crossing the state border to attend the 2004 Media Days.

However, according to court documents, Fulmer sent a series of confidential memos to Kramer, often on pages displaying Tennessee logos, telling of rumors he had heard and asking for assistance. They are included below.

Note: The only changes were to correct misspelled names and to block personal information such as phone numbers.

April 13, 1998
Confidential

Logan Young has been "dealing" with Alabama recruiting since the days of Coach Bryant. It's common knowledge around the conference that he is illegally paying either the players, the parents or the coach of selected great athletes— usually defensive linemen that are black and poor. He has typically operated mostly in Mississippi and Northern Alabama, but recently has been involved with kids and a coach from Memphis and Murfreesboro, Tennessee. He is very wealthy and often drinks a lot and brags about his boys he gets to go to Alabama. Recently, at a restaurant, he "sent word" back to "those boys at Tennessee" not to bother trying to recruit David Payne from Memphis Melrose because he already had him wrapped up.

This is not sour grapes . . . this guy is making a mockery of recruiting and now is doing it in our state. He bought Michael Myers (who was coming to Tennessee until Logan bought him a new All-Terrain truck). He bought Dewayne Rudd after Rudd said publicly that he was coming to Tennessee. This year he bought Kindal Moorehead after Moorehead told me "Coach, I want to come to Tennessee, but it's real complicated with my mother. . . . I can't talk about it." Jerome Woods, currently an NFL player from that school, said "Logan came through for the Mooreheads with a new house."

Other players on the Alabama roster I know he has been involved with are Deshea Townsend—Corner, Fernando Bryant—Corner, Kenny Smith—DT, and Chris Howard—DE, Rod Rutledge—TE, Steve Harris—L'ber, Curtis Alexander—TB.

I truly believe he "bought" Eric Locke and Kindal Moorehead this year—Kindal through the mother and Eric through the father who played for Logan at the Memphis Showboats.

Logan seems to always "third party" his deals and makes it hard to prove.

Fernando Bryant recently showed up on our campus driving a new Mercedes. His mother gets up at 4:30 a.m. everyday to water plants at a nursery. You tell me how he did that!

At Michael Myers' home, I almost fell through the porch because the boards were rotten—and he drives a new truck the entire time at Alabama. Myers asked me in my office what "special" things we would do for him if he came to Tennessee. I knew exactly what he was talking about, explained to him that he would lose his eligibility and me my job for something above the scholarship and opportunity to play. He would not say what "special" things at Alabama were.

This is a great disadvantage for us and it's getting ready to happen again with David Payne.

Tuberville called his hand on a kid in Mississippi that started for Ole Miss as a Freshman OL. He and Tuberville are friends through Lacewell, but Tuberville got mad. He won't talk about Logan because he wants the Alabama job. Logan likes Tuberville and will let Tommy "keep a few."

Logan heard I was asking a bunch of questions and said Tennessee had better watch out. . . . Roy Adams recruits for Tennessee! This is not even close! Roy Adams is a queer who associates with anyone who will hang around him from any school anywhere. He has been disassociated from any contact with our program for the whole time I've been the head coach and well before that.

A couple of my coaches said I'd better be careful that Logan was connected to the Mafia. I don't know if he is or not, or how far he would take retaliation, but I can't operate my program with that jerk buying players from under our nose!

The SEC should investigate—start with Tuberville, Sherrill and Bowden. Just ask around Memphis about him and surely there are some tracks. Also, one of our sign-ees, a really bright kid from Mississippi, said "I don't know how they do it, but almost every Alabama player had a new car." He is from an affluent family whose Dad is an attorney and very knowledgeable. There is just too much smoke not to be a hell of a fire somewhere!

April 17, 1998

Contacts & Rumors

1. Roy Adams, Memphis, probably won't say anything because he's involved with kids himself from all over. He's a bad guy! He knows exactly what goes on.
2. Larry Lacewell, Dallas Cowboys, I'm sure won't talk about it. He's a good friend of Logan, but he knows what goes on.
3. Ray Keller, Stevenson, Alabama, insurance—Logan's contact in North Alabama. Logan 3rd in North Alabama. He probably won't say anything either, but he's dirty!
4. Duke Clement—Tennessee guy—knows Logan through business. Would have second-hand information. (O) 870-735-XXXX. (Wealthy businessman whose interior decorator dates Logan. A lot of second-hand information.)
5. Tim Thompson—Melrose High School coach. We believe he got money to get Kendal Morehead to go to Alabama. They at least need to question him and stop it with this year's kid—David Payne—6'6"—240# DE.
6. Chuck Cole—Tennessee guy that follows recruiting closely. Networks with all the Memphis people. Should be able to at least tell them where to look. He is in the middle of the recruiting rumor circle.

7. David Payne is a prospect at Melrose and he should at least be alerted that the NCAA and the SEC is concerned.
8. Stan Collins—former coach at Whitehaven—now an assistant principal. Rumor has it that he went to every Alabama bowl game with his family for free. He coaches Curtis Alexander at Whitehaven and he is their starting TB.
9. When Andre Lott, our signee, made his official visit to Alabama, his coach, Tim Thompson, flew to Alabama that weekend—supposedly to encourage him to go to Alabama. Andre's mother is a strong lady and wanted him at Tennessee. Coach Thompson made him take the trip to Alabama, and was mad at Andre's mother because she went against him.
10. Danny Pearman, former coach at Alabama, that got fired at Alabama, knows what has gone on and although I don't know that he cheated, was the assistant that recruited all those players from Northern Mississippi—Dewayne Rudd, Deshea Townsend, etc.
11. No Alabama coach has been in schools before Kenny Smith, Meridian, Mississippi; Eric Locke, Murfreesboro Riverdale or Kendal Moorehead, Memphis Melrose, committed to them in early January according to their high school coaches. Supposedly the deals were done by Logan through parents in each case—only DuBose and Logan were involved.
12. Danny Ford, former coach at Arkansas, knows what went on. I don't know if he'll talk.

The following are some players that Logan Young has supposedly been involved with.

1. Kindal Moorehead, Melrose High School, Memphis, TN

Kindal is a player who just signed with Alabama this past recruiting season and is still a senior at Melrose HS right now. The rumor is that his mother either just moved into a new house or will be moving into one very soon. It is believed that his coach at Melrose, Tim Thompson, is the one Logan is working through in this situation. It is known that Tim is driving a new Lexus. Kindal's home phone is (901) 452-XXXX. Mom's (Claria) work phone number is (901) 327-XXXX.

2. Michael Myers, Hinds Community College, Raymond, MS
   originally from Vicksburg HS, Vicksburg, MS

Michael originally signed with Ole Miss out of High School and was supposedly given $10,000, but didn't qualify academically and went to Hinds CC. Everyone assumed he was still obligated to go to Ole Miss because of the prior arrangement, but with the coaching change at Ole Miss, he got out of that and was once again available to the highest bidder. He got in trouble and was declared ineligible by the NCAA because of his dealings with an agent prior to his senior year at Alabama. He is currently waiting for the NFL draft. Michael's home number in Vicksburg was 601/638-XXXX. His parents are Herman and Gloria Myers.

3. David Payne, Melrose High School, Memphis, TN

David is currently a Junior at Melrose HS, but the word is that Logan is already involved with him, and I would assume it is through his coach, Tim Thompson, again. There is really nothing known or rumored at this time other than Logan is involved with him. If nothing else, this is one situation that can be watched as it progresses.

4. Dwayne Rudd and Deshea Townsend, South Panola HS, Batesville, MS

Dwayne and Deshea were teammates in high school and both ended up signing with Alabama. Dwayne was the most highly recruited of the two being an All-American in most all recruiting publications, and there were a lot of strong rumors about him during the recruiting process. People had a lot of questions about his character and, as things have turned out, everyone was right to question it. It was widely rumored that an Ole Miss fan in Batesville, . . . Dunlap, had offered Rudd $5,000 up front and then $500 a month while he was in school at Ole Miss, but he still chose Alabama. Rudd is currently playing with the Minnesota Vikings while Townsend just finished up at Alabama. Dwayne's home phone number is (601) 563-XXXX. Dad's (Clarence) work number is (601) 563-XXXX and Mom's (Mary) work number is (601) 563-XXXX.

5. Kenny Smith, Meridian High School, Meridian, MS

Kenny lived alone with a brother in Meridian, his parents were separated and one lived somewhere up north and one was out west. He had some cousins or an uncle that lived in Meridian that supposedly looked after him and his brother, but it was just the two of them in the house. The deal was rumored to have been done through either this cousin or uncle, and was done early in the recruiting process. When it came down to signing day, Kenny had changed his mind and wanted to go to Florida, but he could not get out of the deal and ended up having to go to Alabama. Kenny's home number is (601) 485-XXXX.

6. Jamie Carter, Neshoba Central High School, Philadelphia, MS

I really don't know whether anything happened in this case or not, but it was widely rumored that Logan was involved with him. Both of Jamie's parents teach at Neshoba Central HS, and on the surface do not appear to be the typical family that Logan is able to get to, but the rumors were so persistent that I am including him to check out. Jamie is currently at Alabama and will be a third year player next year. Jamie's home number is (601) 656-XXXX. Mom's (Helen) work number is (601) 656-XXXX.

7. Terrence Metcalf, Clarksdale High School, Clarksdale, MS

Terrence ended up going to Ole Miss and just completed his first season, but it was also widely rumored that Logan was very involved with him. It isn't really known whether Ole Miss out-bidded Logan or if the kid is just really interested in the illegal stuff or what, but the rumors were very strong. Terrence's home number is (601) 624-XXXX.

8. Romero Miller, Shannon High School, Shannon, MS

Romero really wanted to go to Tennessee, but they couldn't take him and his choice got down to between Ole Miss and Alabama. This is when Logan supposedly became involved with him, and a lot of people were surprised when he ended up at Ole Miss instead of Alabama. He just finished his first season at Ole Miss. Romero's home number is (601) 767-XXXX.

9. Fernando Bryant, Riverdale High School, Murfreesboro, TN

Fernando chose Alabama over Tennessee and Logan was rumored to be involved. Fernando has one year of eligibility remaining. He has a new car that everyone that knows him knows that he and his family could not afford to buy it without some help from somewhere or someone. Fernando's mother (Karen) lives in the Atlanta area and her phone number is (912) 377-XXXX.

10. Eric Locke, Riverdale High School, Murfreesboro, TN

Eric chose Alabama over Tennessee this past recruiting season, he is still a senior at Riverdale High School. No one really knows if Logan was involved with Eric or not, but the rumors surfaced in January. Supposedly Logan and Eric's dad, Richard Lott, got to know each other when Richard was playing football at Memphis State University several years ago. Eric's home number is (615) 896-XXXX. Dad's (Richard) work number is (615) 459-XXXX and Mom's (Debbie) work number is (615) 896-XXXX.

May 11, 1998

Official University of Tennessee stationary
Confidential memo to: Coach Roy Kramer
                              Commissioner, SEC

From: Phillip Fulmer

Here are a couple nos. that I had that I thought you might need:

Duke Clement (Wife, Janet knows a lot about what we are talking about since she is a friend to decorator/girlfriend.)
(Home) 901-767-XXXX
(Office) 870-735-XXXX

Chuck Cole—901-755-XXXX (Same no. for home & office)

May 20, 1998

[*Note:* Fax cover sheet had a big Tennessee football helmet at the top and stated it came from the "University of Tennessee Football Office."]
Confidential

For Your Eyes Only!!!

Just to keep you updated on what I hear:

1. Bob McGee in Jackson, Mississippi is one of Logan Young's 3rd party contacts. This is from a former staff member that was fired at Alabama last year. Call me if you want the name.
2. Tuberville called me and said he knows Logan Young "bought" Freddie Milons last year. I believe Logan got to the father, if not both of them.
3. Eric Locke's father took Santonio Beard (prospect at Pearl Cohn High School) to the Alabama spring game at the request of Logan. Coach Rankin at Locke's old high school says that Locke is moving to B'ham and going to work at the Mercedes factory.
4. Janet Clement was talking to her decorator (Logan's girlfriend) and she said Logan had gone to Nashville to talk to a football player . . . (Santonio Beard) about Alabama. In my opinion . . . Janet and Duke know the most about all this and are close enough to help you the most.
5. I can't afford to let another recruiting season go by and they sign two more players (1. David Payne—Melrose, 2. Santonio Beard—Pearl Cohn) from my state. I get the feeling we are falling behind fast on these two kids because of Logan.
6. I know they bought and paid for both Kindal Moorehead and Eric Locke last year. If you find this out and can prove it, they should be declared ineligible to participate in the SEC.
7. Tuberville said he is mad. He might help.
8. Jackie Sherrill pulled me aside at a golf tourney and told me that your FBI guy had been to talk to him. If he knows, lots of people will know!

August 10, 1998
[Official Tennessee football stationary]

Confidential
Dear Coach Kramer:
    As we discussed, this is another person that said he knows a lot about the Kindal Moorehead situation. Use as you see fit!

    Carl Lyles
    XXXX Cochese
    Memphis, TN 38118

Home: 901-794-XXXX
Office: 901-452-XXXX
Cell: 901-832-XXXX

Best wishes.
Sincerely,
Phillip Fulmer

[*Note:* Lyles was a bartender from a country club. Enclosed was a copy of his business card.]

Sept. 16, 1998
[Official Tennessee football stationary]
Memo To: Coach Roy Kramer
From: Phillip Fulmer

For Your Information . . .

The name of the coach in Memphis is Darrell Montgomery. He was at Melrose as an assistant coach and is now the Head Football Coach at Hamilton.

Fulmer made a number of other accusations during interviews with investigators, forwarding information and rumors he had heard from "friends" and boosters. None of those interviews were conducted under oath.

Though the school quickly moved on, as of January 1, 2006, several court cases surrounding Young and the scandal had yet to be resolved. In March 2005, Young was found guilty and sentenced to six months in prison and six months of house arrest, a verdict that no one appeared to be in a rush to carry out. Young, who had a kidney transplant later that year, appealed, but the case was otherwise inexplicably at a standstill.

On the morning of Tuesday, April 11, 2006, housekeeper Amy Hughey found Young, 65, dead on his bedroom floor, with copious amounts of blood throughout the house. Memphis police initially described it as a "mystery murder investigation" after a "brutal death," but two days later ruled Young's death an accident, saying he had fallen backward down his staircase and hit the back of his head on a wrought iron post. Young then walked around the house, visiting the kitchen and laundry room before climbing the same staircase to a bathroom and the bedroom before bleeding to death.

However, police officials inexplicably reversed themselves on one key detail. After initially saying Young had to be identified through fingerprints because his face was unrecognizable, it was later disclosed that Young was identified by his housekeeper. The medical examiner listed the probable cause of death as "blunt force trauma due to fall down stairs," and as of this writing the case remained open awaiting final testing results.

Former Alabama assistant coaches Ronnie Cottrell and Ivy Williams, who were seen as the "fall guys," filed a lawsuit against the NCAA and Culpepper, only to see most of their case dismissed during the high-profile civil trial. When a Tuscaloosa jury found in favor of Cottrell to the amount of $30 million from Culpepper, the judge threw the verdict out and ordered a new trial. That too was appealed. Interestingly enough, the only piece of evidence not made public in the case was an indemnity agreement between Culpepper and the NCAA.

Former Tennessee player Kenny Smith and his family filed a lawsuit against the NCAA and Fulmer. Specifically, Smith and his mother, Vicki Smith Dagnan, claimed they were defamed when Fulmer told investigators about rumors that Smith's mother was having an affair with Alabama assistant Pearman. Both denied the allegation. (To clarify, Smith initially signed with Alabama, but after failing to qualify academically, he later enrolled at Tennessee.)

To counter the Smith case, Fulmer filed a lawsuit along with the American Football Coaches Association, asking a Knoxville, Tennessee, judge to rule that a coach can't be sued for defamation over information given to investigators. In November 2005, Smith's defamation claims were dismissed, but a judge upheld a charge that the NCAA may have invaded his privacy when spokesman Wally Renfro commented on Smith's private academic records while being interviewed on ESPN.

Others named in the NCAA investigation, including Alabama boosters, filed lawsuits as well. Overall, the cases were expected to take years to resolve.

In part to avoid future incidents, the SEC appointed the "Task Force of Compliance and Enforcement," to set forth a series of recommendations and principles tailored to streamline the way conference institutions implicated fellow members of NCAA violations. Under the new "Phillip Fulmer Rule," allegations against another program must first go through a school's athletic director or president, who then reports to the SEC under the promise of anonymity. If the conference office believes the accusation has merit, the accused institution is then required to investigate the information and report to the SEC office within 30 days. The league office would determine whether the investigation was complete and whether the matter should be reported to the NCAA.

While the coaching community had a reputation for being ruthless, especially against rivals, Lou Holtz, who had some incidents of his own to deal with at Arkansas and South Carolina (among others), suggested: "If you burn your neighbor's house down, it doesn't make your house look any better."

Part II

THE EASTERN DIVISION

· 5 ·

Florida

Location: Gainesville, Florida
Founded: 1853
Enrollment: 48,673
Nickname: Gators
Colors: Orange and blue
Mascot: Albert and Alberta Gator
Stadium: Ben Hill Griffin Stadium at Florida Field (88,548)
2005 officials: Dr. Bernard Machen, president; Jill Varnes, faculty representative; Jeremy Foley, athletics director

THE PROGRAM

National Championships (1): 1996
SEC Championships (6): 1991, 1993, 1994, 1995, 1996, 2000
Bowl appearances: 33 (15-18)
First season: 1906
College Football Hall of Fame (6): Charlie Bachman, 1928–32, coach, inducted 1978; Doug Dickey, 1970–78, coach, 2003; Ray Graves, 1960–69, coach, 1990; Steve Spurrier, 1964–66, quarterback, 1986; Dale Van Sickel, 1927–29, end, 1975; Jack Youngblood, defensive end, 1968–70, 1992
Heisman Winners (2): Steve Spurrier, quarterback, 1966; Danny Wuerffel, quarterback, 1996
National Honors: Judd Davis, 1993 Lou Groza Award (best kicker); Danny Wuerffel, 1996 Maxwell Award (outstanding player), 1995 and 1996 Davey O'Brien Award (best quarterback), and 1996 Johnny Unitas Golden Arm Award (best senior quarterback); Lawrence Wright, 1996 Jim Thorpe Award (best defensive back)
First-Team All-Americans: Dale Van Sickel, E, 1928; Forrest "Fergie" Ferguson, E, 1941; Charlie LaPradd, T, 1952; John Barrow, G, 1956; Vel Heckman, T, 1958; Larry DuPree, FB, 1964; Charles Casey, E, 1965; Steve Spurrier, QB,

1965–66; Lynn Mathews, E, 1965; Bruce Bennett, DB, 1965; Larry Gagner, G, 1965; Bill Carr, C, 1966; Guy Dennis, G, 1968; Larry Smith, FB, 1968; Carlos Alvarez, FL, 1969; Steve Tannen, DB, 1969; Jack Youngblood, E, 1970; John Reaves, QB, 1971; Ralph Ortega, LB, 1974; Burton Lawless, G, 1974; Sammy Green, LB, 1975; Wes Chandler, SE, 1976–77; David Little, LB, 1980; Cris Collinsworth, WR, 1980; Wilber Marshall, LB, 1982–83; Lomas Brown, T, 1984; Alonzo Johnson, LB, 1984–85; Jeff Zimmerman, G, 1985–86; Jarvis Williams, DB, 1986–87; Louis Oliver, DB, 1987–88; Clifford Charlton, LB, 1987; Trace Armstrong, DT, 1988; Emmitt Smith, RB, 1989; Huey Richardson, LB, 1990; Will White, DB, 1990; Brad Culpepper, DT, 1991; Judd Davis, K, 1993; Errict Rhett, RB, 1993; Kevin Carter, DL, 1994; Jack Jackson, WR, 1994; Jason Odom, T, 1995; Danny Wuerffel, QB, 1995–96; Ike Hilliard, WR, 1996; Reidel Anthony, WR, 1996; Jacquez Green, WR, 1997; Fred Taylor, RB, 1997; Fred Weary, DB, 1997; Jevon Kearse, LB, 1998; Mike Peterson, LB, 1998; Alex Brown, DE, 1999, 2001; Lito Sheppard, DB, 2000; Mike Pearson, T, 2001; Jabar Gaffney, WR, 2000–01; Rex Grossman, QB, 2001; Keiwan Ratliff, DB, 2003; Shannon Snell, G, 2003; Ben Troupe, TE, 2003; Channing Crowder, LB, 2004

First-Team Academic All-Americans (CoSIDA): Charles Casey, E, 1965; Carlos Alvarez, WR, 1969, 1971; David Posey, KS, 1976; Wes Chandler, RB, 1977; Cris Collinsworth, WR, 1980; Gary Rolle, WR, 1984; Brad Culpepper, DL, 1991; Michael Gilmore, DB, 1993–94; Terry Dean, QB, 1994; Danny Wuerffel, QB, 1995–96

First-round NFL draftees: 35

Retired jerseys: None

All-Century Team (selected by the *Gainesville Sun*): **Offense**—Burton Lawless, G, 1972–74; Donnie Young, G, 1993–96; Lomas Brown, T, 1981–84; Davis Williams, T, 1985–88; Jeff Mitchell, C, 1993–96; Jim Yarbrough, TE, 1966–68; Carlos Alvarez, WR, 1969–71; Wes Chandler, WR, 1974–77; Danny Wuerffel, QB, 1982–85; Neal Anderson, RB, 1982–85; Emmitt Smith, RB, 1987–89; Judd Davis, K, 1992–94; Jacquez Green, KR, 1995–97 **Defense**—Jack Youngblood, DE, 1968–70; Kevin Carter, DE, 1991–94; Brad Culpepper, DT, 1989–91; Ellis Johnson, DT, 1991–94; Scot Brantley, LB, 1976–79; David Little, LB, 1977–80; Wilber Marshall, LB, 1980–83; Steve Tannen, CB, 1967–69; Jarvis Williams, CB, 1984–87; Bruce Bennett, S, 1963–65; Louis Oliver, S, 1985–88; Bobby Joe Green, P, 1958–59

THE COACHES

Jack Forsythe, 1906–08, 14-6-2; G. E. Pyle, 1909–13, 26-7-3; Charles McCoy, 1914–16, 9-10; A. L. Busser, 1917–19, 7-8; William Kline, 1920–22, 19-8-2; Gen. James Van Fleet, 1923–24, 12-3-4; H. L. Sebring, 1925–27, 17-11-2; Charles Bachman, 1928–32, 27-18-3; D. K. (Dutch) Stanley, 1933–35, 14-13-2; Josh Cody, 1936–39, 17-24-2; Tom Lieb, 1940–45, 20-26-1; Raymond

(Bear) Wolf, 1946–49, 13-24-2; Bob Woodruff, 1950–59, 54-41-6; Ray Graves, 1960–69, 70-31-4; Doug Dickey, 1970–78, 58-42-2; Charley Pell, 1979–84, 33-26-2; Galen Hall, 1984–88, 40-18-1; Gary Darnell, 1989, 3-4; Steve Spurrier, 1990–2001, 122-27-1; Ron Zook, 2002–04, 23-14; Charlie Strong, 2004, 0-1; Urban Meyer, 2005, 9-3

National Coach of the Year: None

SEC Coach of the Year, AP: Galen Hall 1984; Steve Spurrier 1990, 1995, 1996
  Coaches: Ray Graves 1960; Steve Spurrier 1991, 1994, 1995, 1996

SEC Championships: Steve Spurrier 6

National Championships: Steve Spurrier 1

RECORDS

Rushing yards, game: 316, Emmitt Smith vs. New Mexico, Oct. 21, 1989 (31 carries)

Rushing yards, season: 1,599, Emmitt Smith, 1989 (284 carries)

Rushing yards, career: 4,163, Errict Rhett, 1989–93 (873 carries)

Passing yards, game: 464, Rex Grossman vs. LSU, Oct. 6, 2001 (22 of 34)

Passing yards, season: 3,896, Rex Grossman, 2001 (259 of 395)

Passing yards, career: 10,875, Danny Wuerffel, 1993–96 (708 of 1,170)

Receiving yards, game: 246, Taylor Jacobs vs. UAB, Aug. 31, 2002 (eight receptions)

Receiving yards, season: 1,357, Travis McGriff, 1998 (70 receptions)

Receiving yards, career: 2,563, Carlos Alvarez, 1969–71 (172 receptions)

Points, game: 24, seven players tied

Points, season: 110, Reidel Anthony, 1996 (18 touchdowns, one 2-point conversion); Tommy Durrance, 1969 (18 touchdowns, one 2-point conversion)

Points, career: 368, Jeff Chandler, 1997–2001 (67 field goals, 16 PATs)

There's a misconception in the college football world. Some people think that other than Steve Spurrier winning the Heisman Trophy and coming back as coach to vault the program into national prominence in the 1990s, the University of Florida football doesn't have any history.

It does . . . just not a lot of it favorably compares.

Otherwise, Florida's biggest contribution to the sport, and all others, was kidney specialist Dr. Robert Cade inventing an electrolyte beverage for the football team at the request of an assistant coach. The university still receives 20 percent of Gatorade's profits, which as of this writing was more than $80 million.

That and the Gator persona. According to local legend, the nickname first appeared on a pennant in 1908, but *Florida Times-Union* columnist Laurence "Kiddo" Woltz was credited with being the first to refer to the team as Gators in print in 1911. Later on, a 12-foot alligator named Albert served as the official mascot until he died in 1970. Today, bronze statues of the cartoonish Albert Gator and Alberta Gator costumed mascots stand across the street from Ben Hill Griffin Stadium.

Florida began play in 1906, a decade later than most SEC teams, under the direction of Jack Forsythe (14-6-2), who enjoyed modest success along with his replacement, G. E. Pyle (26-7-3). Joining the Southern Conference in 1922 pre-dated by one year the arrival of the most notable figure in Florida football history, volunteer coach James Van Fleet, who was also commander of the school's ROTC unit as a major in the Army and had earned two Silver Stars before being wounded in action during World War I. With Van Fleet moonlighting as football coach, the Gators had two winning seasons of 6-1-2 and 6-2-2, with two of the losses ironically coming to Army.

The program acquired its first national attention in 1923 with a 7-7 tie to powerhouse Georgia Tech, which had to rally late in the game for its score, and a stunning upset against Alabama in the season finale at Tuscaloosa. With rain turning the field into a quagmire, the Gators trailed 6-0 at halftime when Van Fleet had his best players change uniforms with the reserves, then kept the starters in the locker room until the last possible moment. Apparently the strategy worked, because all-Southern back Edgar Jones scored 16 points in the second half to lead Florida's comeback victory.

Van Fleet pulled off another tie against Georgia Tech in 1924 and a 7-7 tie against Texas as well. However, his accomplishments on the football field paled in comparison to his military career. He commanded the 8th Infantry Regiment when it spearheaded the landing of the 4th Infantry Division at Utah Beach on D-Day, June 6, 1944. He also led a division that relieved the Allies at the Battle of the Bulge, the last major offensive by the Germans in World War II. General Patton, in briefing a congressional delegation at his headquarters in Bad Tolz, Germany, stated that Van Fleet was the best of all combat generals who served under him.

When the Army announced his death at the age of 100 on September 23, 1992, the order included the following: "On April 11, 1951, he was appointed Commanding General of the Eight Army and United Nations troops in Korea. General Van Fleet drove the Chinese Army north until he was ordered to halt and to go on the defensive in order to achieve an armistice. Van Fleet, shortly after his arrival in Korea, instituted a tremendous program of retraining. In this regard, he established numerous military schools: Infantry schools, Artillery schools, small unit officers schools, staff schools, and even established a war college and most important of all for leadership, a Military Academy—the 'West Point of Korea.' The Koreans erected a life-size bronze statue of Van Fleet in front of the military academy and refer to him as 'The Father of the Korean Army.'"

Following Van Fleet's departure, the Gators enjoyed an eight-win season under H. L. Sebring (1925) and two with Charles Bachman (1928 and 1929). Led by its first All-American, end Dale Van Sickel (who went on to become a Hollywood stuntman), Florida led the nation in scoring in 1928 with 336 points in nine games, thanks to lopsided wins against Mercer (73-0), Sewanee (71-6), and Washington & Lee (60-6). The Gators finished 8-1, losing only the season finale to Tennessee on a wet Knoxville field 13-12.

"The greatest all-around end I've ever seen," Bachman said about Van Sickel.

From 1935 to 1951 Florida had only one season with a winning record, but during that time had one of the program's best players, Forrest Ferguson. From 1939 though 1941, "Fergie" set numerous receiving records, in addition to being a collegiate state boxing champion in 1942 and winning the National AAU javelin championship. He enlisted in the Army that same year and was severely wounded during the Normandy Invasion; his injury eventually took his life 10 years later. Florida honors his memory with the annual Fergie Ferguson Award, given to the senior who displays outstanding leadership, character, and courage.

Coach Bob Woodruff disrupted the losing ways with an 8-3 season in 1952 that resulted in an invitation to play Tulsa, fittingly the first of four early appearances for Florida in the Gator Bowl. Led by All-American tackle Charlie LaPradd and running back Rick Casares, Florida won 14-13. Six years later, Florida, led by quarterback Jimmy Dunn and end Dave Hudson, returned and lost to Ole Miss 7-3.

Running back Don Goodman and quarterback Larry Libertone were featured in a 13-12 win against Baylor at the end of the 1960 season, and Florida pulled off a big upset against No. 9 Penn State (17-7) in 1962—thanks, in part, to some solid defensive play and quarterback Tom Shannon. In 1963, the upset came against No. 3 Alabama 10-6 in Tuscaloosa, where the Tide wouldn't lose again until 1982.

Until 1965, when Florida played Missouri in the Sugar Bowl, where Spurrier (27 of 45 for 352 yards, two touchdowns, and one interception) set six bowl records and was named the game's most outstanding player, its postseason history was limited to the Gator Bowl, with no championships and not a single 10-win season. Oh, and the Gators lost to the Tigers 20-18.

Under the direction of coach Ray Graves—who wrote two books on football and was the originator of the "Monster Defense," an alignment known for incorporating the positions now called free safety and strong safety—the Gators came back to post records of 9-2 and 9-1-1 in 1966 and 1969, respectively, due in part to a pair of impressive bowl wins.

The first was against Georgia Tech in coach Bobby Dodd's final game, 27-12 in the Orange Bowl. The second was 14-13 over Tennessee, in—surprise—the Gator Bowl.

"Graves is one of the greatest defensive coaches of all time, and a fine gentleman," said Dodd, who had Graves as an assistant coach for 13 seasons.

Graves had the Gators close to greatness, but he wasn't the only one. Florida's rise to the top of the conference actually began well before the 1990s, with various teams and individuals standing out along the way.

Among the first of these, of course, was Spurrier, who not only launched himself into Florida lore but also essentially won the Heisman Trophy on October 29, 1966, on a play he *didn't* line up at quarterback.

Undefeated and ranked seventh, Florida was tied against Auburn, facing fourth down in the closing moments. Spurrier had passed for 259 yards (and to give you an idea of how times have changed, he finished with 2,012 passing yards that season) and averaged 47 yards a punt. But instead of letting the kicker attempt the 40-yard game-winning field goal, Spurrier did it himself, clearing the crossbar by about a foot for a 30-27 victory. Graves could only smile about it afterward, and when Auburn coach, Ralph "Shug" Jordan, referred to him as "Steve Superior," it more than seemed to fit.

The following week, Florida was stifled by Vince Dooley's tough defense at Georgia (27-10), but with Larry Smith accumulating 94 rushing yards, the Gators spoiled Dodd's sendoff.

Another standout on hand for Graves' final two years, and former Tennessee coach Doug Dickey's first season with the Gators in 1970, was defensive end Jack Youngblood, an All-American who went on to be twice named the National Football League's Defensive Player of the Year.

"He added weight in an honest way," Graves said. "This was before the days bodybuilding became so widespread."

Youngblood's signature play in college came against Georgia in 1970. Leading 17-10, the Bulldogs had the ball at the 1-yard line when Youngblood stopped a running back short of the goal line, knocked the ball loose, and recovered the fumble. Florida went on to win 24-17.

Not surprisingly, the defense slipped without him in 1971, when quarterback John Reaves became college football's all-time leader in career passing with 7,549 yards (a record that has since been obliterated).

Beginning in 1973, Florida enjoyed an unprecedented streak of four straight bowl appearances, though it lost each game, starting with a 16-7 defeat to future Gators coach Ron Zook and Miami of Ohio in the Tangerine Bowl. That was followed by a 13-10 loss to Nebraska in a controversial Sugar Bowl in which running back Tony Green was ruled out of bounds on an apparent 26-yard touchdown run, a 13-0 shutout by Maryland in the Gator Bowl, and 37-14 pounding against Texas A&M in the Sun Bowl.

Leading that last team, in 1976, was All-American split end Wes Chandler, who gave way to another outstanding receiver, All-American Cris Collinsworth.

In coach Charley Pell's first bowl victory, 35-20 against Maryland in the Tangerine Bowl after the 1980 season, Collinsworth (eight catches for 166 yards) and defensive tackle David Galloway were named the offensive and defensive players of the game. It was the first in another string of four straight bowl games, and of seven overall during the 1980s when the Gators posted 76 victories.

"I want my players to think as positively as the 85-year-old man who married a 25-year-old woman and bought a five-bedroom house next to the elementary school," Pell said.

Under coach Galen Hall, Florida went 9-1-1 in both 1984 and 1985, and with a 14-10 victory at Auburn was ranked No. 1 for the first time in school history—but ineligible for postseason consideration, due to National Collegiate Athletic Association sanctions.

Florida didn't have one of its best teams in 1986, but played one of its most memorable games. The Gators were struggling at 3-4 when No. 5 Auburn came calling in Gainesville and built up a 17-0 lead in the third quarter. After being out for a month with an injury, Florida quarterback Kerwin Bell limped onto the field and with a throw to wide receiver Ricky Nattiel, who had a separated shoulder himself, they mounted a comeback. Down 17-16 with 30 seconds remaining, the Gators went for the 2-point conversion and victory. Bell dropped back to pass, only to limp into the end zone himself when all of his receivers were covered.

One of the key players of the 1980s was two-time All-American linebacker Wilber Marshall, who was named college football's player of the year in 1983 and went on to have an All-Pro career for the Chicago Bears.

The later part of the decade was highlighted by running back Emmitt Smith, who set most of the school's rushing records (58 of them, to be exact) and was named both the national Freshman of the Year in 1987 and SEC Player of the Year in 1989 before leaving after three years. He eventually broke Walter Payton's career rushing record (18,355 compared to 16,726 yards), and was the NFL's all-time leader for rushing touchdowns (164), rushing attempts (4,409), 1,000-yard seasons (11), and postseason rushing touchdowns (19).

"What does it take to be the best?" Smith said. "Everything. And everything is up to you."

Florida's playbook with Smith was said to be Emmitt left, Emmitt right, Emmitt up the middle, and fans would cheer it.

Despite Smith's prowess, the program was soon in disarray again. Years before, legendary Alabama coach Paul "Bear" Bryant once said that the only thing that Florida lacked was simply having the right person in charge at the right time. He was right. That person proved to be Spurrier, who answered the call to return to Gainesville. Actually, it wasn't the first time he'd heard from his alma mater. After retiring as a player, Spurrier was hired as the Gators quarterbacks coach in 1978 but let go after one season when Pell questioned his work ethic. From there, Spurrier served as offensive coordinator and quarterbacks coach at Georgia Tech, only to see Bill Curry fire the entire staff after one season.

At the age of 35, Spurrier finally got a chance to cultivate his system at Duke, where Red Wilson made him the offensive coordinator. His first play called was a double-reverse pass, and no one benefited more than quarterback Ben Bennett, an All-American who set the NCAA record for career passing yards (9,164 yards) and had a school-record 55 touchdowns.

When Spurrier became the "Head Ball Coach," as he would say, Duke had its first seven-win season since 1961 during his second season, and in 1989 the Blue Devils played in a bowl game for the first time in 29 years.

Florida had numerous demons to slay, but Spurrier was brash, arrogant, and unbelievably confident—and that was as a player. He was an unrelenting coach, and the only thing stronger than the Gator faithfuls' love for him was his opponents' animosity toward him; they would wildly celebrate after the few times they beat him (if at all). The offense was nicknamed Fun 'n' Gun, which was true except for anyone trying to stop it—it was wide open, creative, and it changed the landscape of the SEC.

For example, in 2001, when asked if he considered running the ball instead of passing with less than two minutes remaining against Mississippi State, Spurrier said: "Run it out to keep the shutout? No, I didn't think about that. We felt having 35 points at the half, we only needed 17 more to break 50."

The Gators won 52-0.

"Mississippi State was No. 1 in pass defense coming in," he said. "They won't be going out."

"He was a little different," said Tommy Tuberville, who at Ole Miss and Auburn was winless in his first four games against Spurrier until finally winning in 2001 (23-20). "He was outspoken. You can be pretty much outspoken when you're kicking everybody's butt like he was."

"If people like you too much, it's probably because they're beating you," Spurrier said.

Under Spurrier's direction, Florida became only one of six schools in major college football history, and one of two in SEC history, to win 100 games during a decade (100-22-1). The Gators were the first team in the conference to win at least 10 games in six straight seasons and the third school ever to be ranked for 200 consecutive weeks. Amazingly, he didn't win a national coach of the year award, but Spurrier became the first Heisman winner to coach another Heisman winner.

"Danny Wuerffel is a better person than he is a quarterback, and he is a great, great quarterback," Spurrier said.

To put that statement into context, Spurrier has also said many times that Wuerffel, who like his coach was the son of a Presbyterian minister, should be considered the greatest quarterback to ever play the game. When Wuerffel left Florida after the 1996 season, he was the most efficient quarterback in NCAA history, with a career rating of 163.6. He's also the only Heisman winner to win the Draddy Award as college football's top scholar-athlete.

The NCAA tabbed the Gators a college football dynasty. Here's what one looks like:

1990 (9-2): The Spurrier era kicked off with a stunning 50-7 pounding of Oklahoma State and followed with a solid 17-13 victory at Alabama. Even though the Gators were not bowl eligible, nor could they claim the conference title because of NCAA sanctions (among the violations, Hall supposedly helped a player make a child support payment), they lost only to Tennessee and Florida State. In its debut season alone, the offense sent defensive coordinators scrambling, especially to recruit quality defensive backs.

1991 (10-2): For the first time, the Gators defeated Alabama, Auburn, Florida State, Georgia, and Tennessee all in the same season. With the impressive wins against Alabama (35-0) and Tennessee (35-18), Florida went a perfect 7-0 in SEC play to claim its first conference championship and topped it off by avenging the previous loss to Florida State, 39-28. A 38-21 loss at Syracuse was the only blemish heading into the Sugar Bowl for its first-ever meeting against Notre Dame. It was a crazy contest, with 34 points scored in the fourth quarter alone. Shane Matthews threw for 370 yards, and the Gators amassed 511 yards only to see the Irish, coached by Lou Holtz, score three touchdowns in the final 5 minutes to win 39-28.

"I can't wait to get back to the restaurant and see the waiter who said, 'Cheerios and Notre Dame are different: Cheerios belong in a bowl,'" Holtz said.

1992 (9-4): Early season losses at Tennessee and Mississippi State marked the only time Spurrier had a losing record at Florida, only to be nullified by a seven-game winning streak that put the Gators in the first SEC Championship Game a week after losing at Florida State, 45-24. Alabama, which went on to win the national championship, won 28-21 at Legion Field in Birmingham. Led by game MVP Errict Rhett's 182 rushing yards, Florida defeated North Carolina State 27-10 in the Gator Bowl.

1993 (11-2): Despite a narrow 38-35 loss at Auburn, in addition to a 33-21 defeat to Florida State, Florida returned to the SEC Championship Game and won a rematch with Alabama, 28-13. Against undefeated No. 3 West Virginia in the Sugar Bowl, Rhett set the school record for career rushing yards thanks to a 105-yard, three-touchdown performance. Wide receiver Willie Jackson caught nine passes from quarterback Terry Dean for 131 yards and a touchdown, and the defense gave up just 265 yards and one touchdown for a 41-7 final.

1994 (10-2-1): Florida was ranked No. 1 in the preseason polls and lived up to expectations. Spurrier won the rubber match against Alabama in the SEC Championship Game 24-23, but the rivalry with Florida State reached new heights at Doak Campbell Stadium when the Seminoles came back from a 28-3 lead late in the third quarter to pull off an amazing 31-31 tie. Florida State fans still refer to it as the Choke at the Doak, as it was essentially a loss for the Gators. The two teams met again in the Sugar Bowl, combining for 855 yards of offense. Wuerffel completed 28 of 39 passes for 394 yards, but Florida could muster only 5 rushing yards in the 23-17 defeat.

1995 (12-1): Florida got back at Florida State with a 35-24 victory to complete its first perfect regular season, and the Gators destroyed Arkansas 34-3 in the SEC Championship Game. But against Nebraska in the national championship Fiesta Bowl, the Gators couldn't compensate for the physical play of the Cornhuskers, who easily won 62-24. Reidel Anthony's 93-yard kickoff return in the fourth quarter was one of the few highlights. The loss prompted Spurrier to hire Bobby Stoops, who had built the No. 1 defense at Kansas State, as defensive coordinator. (*Note:* Stoops became Oklahoma's head coach in 1999 and a year later won the national championship.)

1996 (12-1): The season was initially highlighted by an early matchup against Tennessee, which was led by quarterback Peyton Manning. Weurrfel won the shootout 35-29, propelling the Gators to both a No. 1 ranking and an eventual 1 vs. 2 meeting against Florida State. After the Seminoles won 24-21, dropping Florida to No. 4 in the polls, Spurrier vehemently complained that FSU had gotten away with a number of late hits on Wuerffel and put together a video to back up his claim. Florida State fans laughed that Spurrier was being a crybaby, but soon the joke would be on them. When Florida routed Alabama 45-30 in the SEC Championship Game—thanks to six touchdown passes by Wuerffel—and Texas defeated No. 2 Nebraska in the Big 12 Championship Game, the Sugar Bowl would be another rematch. Ike Hilliard caught three touchdown passes, Terry Jackson ran in two fourth-quarter touchdowns, and the defense limited Florida State to just 42 rushing yards. With No. 2 Arizona State losing earlier in the day to No. 4 Ohio State, Florida won its first national championship, 52-20.

"Call me arrogant, cocky, crybaby, whiner or whatever names you like," Spurrier said. "At least they're not calling us losers any more."

1997 (10-2): Though Florida scored 247 points in its first five games, a 28-21 loss at LSU dashed any hopes of repeating, and a 37-17 setback to Georgia knocked the Gators out of contention for the SEC championship. Running back Fred Taylor accumulated 234 rushing yards to help lead a 21-6 victory against Penn State in the Citrus Bowl, but it was the defense, led by players like Jevon Kearse, Reggie McGrew, Mike Peterson and Johnny Rutledge, that dominated the headlines. The Nittany Lions had just 139 total yards, the lowest ever under coach Joe Paterno, and were twice stopped on fourth-and-goal from the 1 in the second quarter.

1998 (10-2): Florida stumbled in overtime at Tennessee 20-17, keeping it out of the SEC Championship Game, and again 23-12 at Florida State. Ranked No. 7, the Gators played in their first Orange Bowl since Spurrier concluded his college career in 1967. Quarterbacks Doug Johnson and Jesse Palmer combined for 308 passing yards in the 31-10 victory, giving the Gators their sixth straight 10-win season.

"We didn't play up to our potential last year," Spurrier declared. "We only scored 50 points once and only one team accused us of running up the score."

1999 (9-4): Florida squeaked by Tennessee 23-21, but was upset 40-39 in overtime by Alabama, led by running back Shaun Alexander. The two teams met again in the SEC Championship Game in Atlanta, but this time the outcome was decided relatively early, with the Crimson Tide victorious again, 34-7. Although receiver Travis Taylor had 156 yards on 11 catches in the Citrus Bowl, Michigan State pulled out a 37-34 victory on a last-second field goal.

2000 (10-3): A 27-23 victory at Tennessee had the Gators off to a promising start, until they stumbled 47-35 at Mississippi State. Florida rebounded against LSU (41-9) and Auburn (38-7) before completing the sweep of its own division to return to the SEC Championship Game, where it defeated Auburn again 28-6. Despite 136 rushing yards from running back Earnest Graham, Florida lost to Miami in the Sugar Bowl 37-20, the first meeting between the schools since 1987.

2001 (10-2): Florida was again No. 1 in the preseason polls, with a narrow defeat at Auburn (23-20) interrupting an otherwise dominating season. Florida was still in the running to play for the national championship until December 1, when it lost the rescheduled game (due to the September 11 terrorist attacks) against No. 5 Tennessee 34-32. Just like when he was a player, Spurrier's coaching finale at Florida was at the Orange Bowl. With 659 total yards and 456 passing yards, both bowl records, the Gators dominated Maryland 56-23 for a No. 3 final ranking. On January 4, 2002, Spurrier resigned and went on to become the head coach of the Washington Redskins.

"I simply believe that 12 years as head coach at a major university in the SEC is long enough," Spurrier said in his release.

The immediate post-Spurrier years were a bit of a disappointment to Gators fans, who had come to expect championships. Under Zook, Florida reached the 2002 and 2003 Outback Bowls—only to lose 38-30 to Michigan and 37-14 to Iowa—by posting eight-win seasons. In 2004 Zook was fired after a stunning upset at Mississippi State, and at the end of the season Florida enticed Urban Meyer to leave Utah (in the process, he spurned Notre Dame). The innovator of the spread-option offense had accumulated an impressive 39-8 record in just four seasons as Utah's head coach, and he vowed to return the offensive bite to the Gators.

THREE THINGS THAT STAND OUT ABOUT FLORIDA FOOTBALL

1. *Brothers (and Sisters) in Arms:* The popular mascots, each player touching the massive gator head in the middle of the central rotunda before each game, and the fans spreading their arms out and snapping them shut like a gator's mouth are all Florida trademarks. But the program's finest tradition is when all fans sway arm in arm and sing, "We are the Boys from Old Florida" before the start of the fourth quarter.
2. *The Swamp:* The nickname was given to Ben Hill Griffin Stadium by none other than Steve Spurrier, who said that "only Gators can survive a trip to the swamp." Easily one of the loudest stadiums in the country, with a capacity of 88,548, Florida was 70-5 there under his direction. It's the home to Mr. Two Bits (George Edmondson, who at midfield used to lead the cheer: "Two-bits, four-bits, six-bits, a dollar . . . all for the Gators, get up and holler!") and to the Victory Bell from the battleship USS *Florida*. It's also close enough to bars that fans can enjoy pregame, postgame, and even halftime festivities without missing a play.
3. *The World's Largest Cocktail Party:* Until 1993, the annual showdown with Georgia was a moving annual "party" with stops in Athens, Gainesville, Jacksonville, Macon, Savannah, and Tampa before the schools settled on keeping it at the neutral site of Jacksonville. You can probably figure out the meaning of the name all on your own.

· 6 ·

Georgia

THE SCHOOL

Location: Athens, Georgia
Founded: 1785
Enrollment: 33,405
Nickname: Bulldogs
Colors: Red and black
Mascot: Uga
Stadium: Sanford Stadium (92,746)
2005 officials: Dr. Michael F. Adams, president; Prof. Jere Morehead, faculty representative; Damon Evans, athletic director

THE PROGRAM

National Championships (2): 1942, 1980
The "Other" Three: Voted No. 1 in various polls in 1927, 1946, and 1968
SEC Championships (12): 1942, 1946, 1948, 1959, 1966, 1968, 1976, 1980, 1981, 1982, 2002, 2005
Bowl appearances: 41 (22-16-3)
First season: 1892
College Football Hall of Fame (14): Kevin Butler, 1981–84, kicker, inducted 2001; Wally Butts, 1939–60, coach, 1997; Vince Dooley, 1964–88, coach, 1994; Bill Hartman, 1935–37, fullback, 1984; Terry Hoage, 1980–83, safety, 2000; Bob McWhorter, 1910–13, halfback, 1954; John Rauch, 1945–48, quarterback, 2003; Frank Sinkwich, 1940–42, halfback, 2002; Vernon Smith, 1929–31, end, 1979; Bill Stanfill, 1966–68, defensive tackle, 1998; Fran Tarkenton, 1958–60, quarterback, 1987; Charley Trippi, 1942, 1945–46, halfback, 1959; Herschel Walker, 1980–82, running back, 1999; Pop Warner, 1895–96, coach, 1951
Heisman Winners (2): Frank Sinkwich, halfback, 1942; Herschel Walker, running back, 1982
National Honors: Charley Trippi, 1946 Maxwell Award (outstanding player);

1968 Bill Stanfill, Outland Trophy (outstanding interior lineman); Herschel Walker, 1982 Maxwell Award; Garrison Hearst, 1992, Doak Walker Award (best running back among Division IA juniors or seniors); Champ Bailey, 1998 Mike Fox/Bronko Nagurski Award (top defensive player); David Pollack, 2003–04 Ted Hendricks Award (top defensive end), 2004 Vince Lombardi/Rotary Award (outstanding lineman), Chuck Bednarik Award (top defensive player), and Lott Trophy (athletic performance and character)

First-Team All-Americans: Bob McWhorter, HB, 1913; David Paddock, QB, 1914; Joe Bennett, T, 1922–23; I. M. (Chick) Shiver, E, 1927; Tom A. Nash, E, 1927; Herb Maffett, E, 1930; Ralph (Red) Maddox, G, 1930; Vernon (Catfish) Smith, E, 1931; John Bond, HB, 1935; William Hartman Jr., FB, 1937; Frank Sinkwich, FB, 1941–42; George Poschner, E, 1942; Mike Castronis, T, 1945; Charley Trippi, TB, 1946; Herb St. John, G, 1946; Dan Edwards, E, 1947; John Rauch, QB, 1948; Harry Babcock, E, 1952; Zeke Bratkowski, QB, 1953; Johnny Carson, E, 1953; Pat Dye, G, 1959–60; Fran Tarkenton, QB, 1960; Jim Wilson, T, 1964; Ray Rissmiller, T, 1964; George Patton, T, 1965; Edgar Chandler, G, 1966–67; Lynn Hughes, S, 1966; Bill Stanfill, DT, 1968; Jake Scott, S, 1968; Steve Greer, G, 1969; Tommy Lyons, C, 1969–70; Royce Smith, G, 1971; Craig Hertwig, G, 1974; Randy Johnson, G, 1975; Joel Parrish, G, 1976; Mike (Moonpie) Wilson, T, 1976; Ben Zambiasi, LB, 1976; Allan Leavitt, K, 1976; George Collins, G, 1977; Bill Krug, R, 1977; Rex Robinson, K, 1979–80; Herschel Walker, RB, 1980–82; Scott Woerner, DB, 1980; Terry Hoage, R, 1982–83; Jimmy Payne, T, 1982; Kevin Butler, K, 1983–84; Freddie Gilbert, DT, 1983; Jeff Sanchez, S, 1984; John Little, S, 1985–86; Peter Anderson, C, 1985; Wilbur Stozier, T, 1986; Troy Sadowski, TE, 1988; Tim Worley, RB, 1988; Garrison Hearst, RB, 1992; Bernard Williams, T, 1993; Eric Zeier, QB, 1994; Matt Stinchcomb, T, 1997–98; Champ Bailey, DB, 1998; Richard Seymour, DT, 2000; Boss Bailey, LB, 2002; David Pollack, DE, 2002–04; Jon Stinchcomb, T, 2002; Sean Jones, DB, 2003; Thomas Davis, DB, 2004; Greg Blue, DB, 2005; Max Jean-Gilles, G, 2005

First-Team Academic All-Americans (CoSIDA): Francis Tarkenton, QB, 1960; Bob Etter, K, 1965–66; Lynn Hughes, DB, 1966; Bill Stanfill, DT, 1968; Tom Nash, T, 1971; Mixon Robinson, DE, 1971; Jeff Lewis, LB, 1978; Terry Hoage, DB, 1982–83; Todd Peterson, K, 1992; Matt Stinchcomb, OL, 1997–98; Jon Stinchcomb, OL, 2001–02

First-round NFL draftees: 24

Retired jerseys: 21 Frank Sinkwich; 34 Herschel Walker; 40 Theron Sapp; 62 Charley Trippi

THE COACHES

Dr. Charles Herty, 1892, 1-1; Ernest Brown, 1893, 2-2-1; Robert Winston, 1894, 5-1; Glenn "Pop" Warner 1895–96, 7-4; Charles McCarthy, 1897–98, 6-4; Gordon Saussy, 1899, 2-3-1; E. E. Jones, 1900, 2-4; Billy Reynolds, 1901–02,

5-7-3; M. M. Dickinson, 1903, 1905, 4-9; Charles Barnard, 1904, 1-5; W. S. Whitney, 1906–07, 6-7-2; Branch Bocock, 1908, 5-2-1; J.Coulter/Frank Dobson, 1909, 1-4-2; W. A. Cunningham, 1910–19, 43-18-9; Herman J. Stegeman, 1920–22, 20-6-3; George (Kid) Woodruff, 1923–27, 30-16-1; Harry Mehre, 1928–37, 59-34-6; Joel Hunt, 1938, 5-4-1; Wallace Butts, 1939–60, 140-86-9; Johnny Griffith, 1961–63, 10-16-4; Vince Dooley, 1964–88, 201-77-10; Ray Goff, 1989–95, 46-34-1; Jim Donnan, 1996–2000, 40-19; Mark Richt, 2001–05, 52-13

National Coach of the Year: Vince Dooley 1980

SEC Coach of the Year, AP: Wally Butts 1946; Vince Dooley 1966, 1968, 1976, 1980; Mark Richt 2002 **Coaches:** Wally Butts 1942, 1946, 1959; Vince Dooley 1966, 1968, 1976, 1978, 1980; Jim Donnan 1997; Mark Richt 2002

SEC Championships: Vince Dooley 6, Wally Butts 4, Mark Richt 2

National Championships: Wally Butts 1, Vince Dooley 1

RECORDS

Rushing yards, game: 283, Herschel Walker vs. Vanderbilt, Oct. 18, 1990 (23 carries)

Rushing yards, season: 1,891, Herschel Walker, 1981 (385 carries)

Rushing yards, career: 5,259, Herschel Walker, 1980–82 (994 carries)

Passing yards, game: 544, Eric Zeier vs. Southern Miss, Oct. 9, 1993 (30 of 47)

Passing yards, season: 3,525, Eric Zeier, 1993 (269 of 425)

Passing yards, career: 11,528, David Greene, 2001–04 (849 of 1,440)

Receiving yards, game: 201, Fred Gibson vs. Kentucky, Oct. 20, 2001 (nine receptions)

Receiving yards, season: 1,004, Terrence Edwards, 2002 (59 receptions)

Receiving yards, career: 3,093, Terrence Edwards, 1999–2002 (204 receptions)

Points, game: 30, Robert Edwards vs. South Carolina, Sept. 2, 1995 (five touchdowns)

Points, season: 131 Billy Bennett, 2003 (31 field goals, 38 PATs)

Points, career: 409, Billy Bennett, 2000–03 (87 field goals, 148 PATs)

Although Alabama has the Southeastern Conference market cornered when it comes to winning heritage and an established place in pop culture, the University of Georgia is a worthy compatriot when it comes to elite status, especially when you consider its familiar icons.

We're talking about names like Herschel Walker, Wally Butts, and Pop Warner. It's "between the hedges," "silver britches," and a famous bulldog name Uga. It's ringing the chapel bell until midnight following Georgia wins, the historic arch that freshmen were told to avoid walking under, and people yelling out, "How 'bout them dawgs?" which caught on nationally after a victory against Notre Dame.

Yep, Athens is the kind of place any college football fan would enjoy on a Saturday afternoon.

Its roots go deep—back to 1892, when former Georgia student Dr. Charles Herty returned to teach chemistry and brought with him a new game that he had learned at Johns Hopkins University. With the University's Glee Club contributing $50 to finance the removal of rocks and the filling of holes on the field, goalposts were erected; and on January 30, Georgia hosted and crushed its first opponent, Mercer, 50-0. Despite being just 5-foot-6, 125 pounds, Herty's nephew Frank was the offensive star of the game. Georgia's biggest player was center E. W. Frey at 6 foot 1, 202 pounds.

When Herty convinced his former Johns Hopkins classmate Dr. George Petrie to set up a game with his school, Auburn, the South's oldest football rivalry was born. Auburn won 10-0.

After graduate student Ernest Brown ran the team in 1893 (2-2-1), Robert Winston became Georgia's first paid coach and finished 5-1-0. In 1895, Glen Warner was hired to coach the team for $34 a week, which was raised to $40 for his second season when Georgia finished undefeated (4-0). The Cornell graduate who was also known as "Pop" Warner and "The Great Originator" later went on to coach Jim Thorpe at the Carlisle Indian School, in addition to stints at Pittsburgh and Stanford, and compiled 319 career victories.

"You cannot play two kinds of football at once, dirty and good," Warner said.

According to his bio at the College Football Hall of Fame: "He was the first to coach the dummy-scrimmage; he introduced the practice of numbering plays; he was the first to teach the spiral punt and one of the first to advocate the spiral pass; he was the first to use the football huddle; he invented the double-wing formation, with an unbalanced line for more blocking strength.

"What else did Warner come up with during his illustrious career? How about mousetrap plays, the screen pass, the rolling block, the naked reverse, hidden-ball plays, series plays, the unbalanced line and backfield. All came from Warner's fertile and imaginative mind."

Football came exceedingly close to being banned in 1897 when during a 17-4 loss to Virginia at Atlanta's Brisbane Park, Richard Vonalbade Gammon was severely injured and had to be taken by a horse-drawn ambulance to a nearly hospital. After he died the next day, a bill banning the sport passed the state legislature and was on the governor's desk waiting to be signed into law when a letter from Gammon's mother arrived, asking for the sport's pardon.

"It would be inexpressibly sad to have the cause he held so dear injured by his sacrifice," she wrote. "Grant me the right to request that the boy's death should not be used to defeat the most cherished object of his life."

The governor refused to sign the bill, and Virginia gave the university a special bronze plaque to commemorate Gammon's life. Incidentally, the previous week Georgia defeated Georgia Tech for the first time, 28-0.

Beginning with Charles McCarty in 1897, Georgia would have nine more head coaches before Vanderbilt graduate W. A. Cunningham provided both some continuity and success. Led by legendary quarterback George "Kid" Woodruff, Georgia finished 7-1-1 in 1911, with the only loss 17-0 to the coaches' alma mater. The following year saw a similar result, with the team finishing 6-1-1.

Georgia stumbled against Virginia (13-6) and Auburn (21-7) in 1913, but with the school's first All-American, halfback Bob McWhorter, it posted a 6-2 record. Following the outbreak of World War I (after a 6-3 season in 1916), Cunningham enlisted in the Army and later came back to coach one final season before reentering the military. He eventually reached the rank of general. With seven winning seasons, his career record was 43-18-9.

Assistant Herman Stegeman, a University of Chicago graduate who played under Amos Alonzo Stagg (and coached numerous other teams as well), was promoted and during his inaugural season earned Georgia's first title. The original "Bulldogs" prided themselves on defense, giving up only 17 points and recording seven shutouts to finish 8-0-1 as Southern Conference champions.

Before taking over as athletic director, and eventually dean of male students, Stegeman coached two more seasons, finishing 7-2-1 in 1921 (with the losses to East Coast powers Dartmouth and Harvard) and 5-4-1 the following year. In 1923 Woodruff returned, and because he was also a successful businessman insisted on drawing a yearly salary of just $1. After watching the effectiveness of Notre Dame's "Box 4" shift offense against Georgia Tech, he brought in three Knute Rockne disciples with Frank Thomas, Harry Mehre, and Jim Crowley, all of whom went on to have successful careers as head coaches.

Woodruff's first year resulted in a 7-3 season, and the 1925 campaign was best remembered for team captain Ralph "Smack" Thompson, an end who would get so emotional that he was known to scream out in his sleep. For example, on the eve of a 3-0 loss to Georgia Tech, he was yelling "Kill the SOB," referring to standout Doug Wycoff. When the two finally collided on the field, both were knocked unconscious but somehow remained in the game.

"He was absolutely poison," Morgan Blake of the *Atlanta Journal* wrote about Thompson. "With reckless disregard for life and limb, he plunged into the thick of every play."

Woodruff's last season, 1927, proved to be his best. "The Dream and Wonder Team" gave up only 35 points, averaging just 3.5 per game, and pulled off a 14-10 victory at Yale. Led by All-American ends Tom Nash and I. M. "Chick" Shiver, it finished 9-1 and scored 248 points for a No. 1 ranking before losing 12-0 to Georgia Tech.

(*Note:* The Boand and Poling ranking systems both credited Georgia with the national championship, but five other services had Illinois No. 1, with two others opting for Notre Dame and Yale. The Associated Press didn't select national champions until 1936.)

Mehre took over for Woodruff in 1928 with Catfish Smith and Herb Maffett replacing the ends. Georgia came back to finish 6-4 in 1929 and 7-2-1 in 1930.

That 1929 season included a landmark game for the program, thanks to Dr. Steadman V. Sanford, who founded the Henry W. Grady School of Journalism and was referred to as "the best friend of athletics." The university president and chancellor was instrumental in the building of the stadium that would carry his name. At a cost of $360,000, it had a seating capacity of 30,000, which at the time was considered quite large. The famous hedges surrounding the playing field, planted at the suggestion of business manager Charlie Martin, were initially only one foot high.

For the dedication game on October 12, 1929, the sophomore-laden Bulldogs hosted Yale, which was making its first trip below the Mason-Dixon Line. Many expected a one-sided contest, and it was, only for the home team. With the stadium exceeding capacity, Smith scored all the points for a 15-0 victory. He landed on a blocked punt for one touchdown, caught a pass for another, and when he roughly tackled Albie Booth in the end zone for a safety, Booth yelled, "That kind of stuff doesn't go around here." Smith replied, "Neither do you."

Yale never ventured south again.

During his 10 years (1928–37 before leaving for Ole Miss), Mehre had eight teams finish with winning records, four of which contended for the conference championship. Not among them was the 1936 squad, which pulled off a 7-7 tie against the "Seven Blocks of Granite"—including Vince Lombardi—in New York to knock undefeated Fordham out of the Rose Bowl. With Georgia Tech essentially established as the regular-season finale, Mehre lost only twice to the intrastate rival, and he was the only coach to beat Yale five straight times when it was at its height.

Former Texas A&M standout Joel Hunt was hired away from LSU, but after a 5-4-1 season he left, later coaching at Wyoming before returning to LSU. However, he's fondly remembered by Georgia fans for hiring the "Little Round Man" (Wallace Butts) as an assistant. "Wally" wouldn't leave for 22 years, and Georgia football would never be the same.

By 1941, the program had turned the corner. Despite an early tie to Ole Miss and a 27-14 loss to Alabama, Georgia outscored its last five opponents, including Auburn and Georgia Tech, 129-9 and earned its first bowl bid.

Less than a month after the attack on Pearl Harbor, the Bulldogs lined up against Texas Christian at the Orange Bowl. Despite playing with an oversized chin mask to protect a broken jaw, All-American quarterback Frank Sinkwich passed for 243 yards, ran for 139, and scored four touchdowns. With the defense also making six interceptions, Georgia built up a 40-7 lead in the third quarter before TCU came back for a 40-26 final score.

Butts had one more chance before war dismantled his team, and the Bulldogs began the 1942 season by winning nine straight games. Although Georgia lost 27-13 to Auburn, it redeemed itself by routing unbeaten Georgia Tech 34-0 to earn an invitation to the Rose Bowl. With the South's first Heisman Trophy winner, Sinkwich, limited by two sprained ankles, sophomore Charley Trippi keyed the offense with 115 rushing yards on 27 carries. Tackle Red Boyd blocked a punt though the end zone for a safety, and Clyde Ehrhardt's interception set up Sinkwich's plunge for the game's only touchdown. With the 9-0 victory against UCLA, the Bulldogs weren't just atop the SEC, but national champions as well.

Sinkwich, a single-wing tailback who stood at just 5-foot-10, 185 pounds, but wanted to play fullback, set the SEC record with 2,187 yards of total offense. For his career, "Fireball Frankie" ran for 30 touchdowns, passed for 30 more, and accumulated more than 4,600 yards of total offense. He was best remembered for two images. The first was wearing the mask covering half his face to protect the jaw, broken in a pileup against South Carolina. The other was wearing his Marine Corps uniform to accept the Heisman—Sinkwich entered the service shortly after playing in the Rose Bowl.

Georgia was one of the few programs to keep playing throughout World War II, finishing 6-4 in 1943 and 7-3 in 1944. Midseason back-to-back losses to Alabama (28-14) and LSU (32-0) spoiled what was an otherwise terrific 9-2 season in 1945, ending with victories against Florida, Auburn, and Georgia Tech by a combined score of 102-0. At the Oil Bowl in Houston, Trippi threw one touchdown pass and returned a punt—some consider comparable to Billy Cannon's legendary run for LSU—68 yards to score another for a 20-6 victory against Tulsa.

But Trippi was just getting started. As a senior he helped guide the Bulldogs to a perfect regular season, including wins against Alabama (14-0), Auburn (41-0), and Georgia Tech (35-7). Georgia outscored opponents 372-100, with only one opponent able to score more than 14 points. With Trippi never leaving the field and playing the entire 60 minutes, the Bulldogs topped the season with a 20-10 victory against North Carolina, which was led by Charlie Justice. He threw a 67-yard touchdown pass to Dan Edwards, and Johnny Rauch ran in two scores. Georgia finished 11-0 but was not the consensus national champion; Notre Dame edged Army for that distinction.

Rauch, who was almost pulled from high school athletics after being diagnosed with a heart murmur, finished his career as college football's all-time leading passer with 4,044 yards (Bill Walsh also credited him with inventing the West Coast offense). He would help lead Georgia back to two more bowls and win another SEC championship. At the Gator Bowl following the 1947 season, the All-American quarterback completed 12 of 20 passes for 187 yards and led a 13-point fourth-quarter comeback to tie Maryland 20-20. Joe Geri ran in one touchdown and John Donaldson caught the other, but the Bulldogs ran out of time.

After finishing the 1948 regular season 9-1, with the only loss to nonconference North Carolina (21-14), Georgia was invited to play Texas in the Orange Bowl. Although Rauch completed 11 of 17 passes for 161 yards and one touchdown, and Geri ran in two scores, the Longhorns won 41-28 before a record 60,523 fans.

After the 21-13 home win against Georgia Tech, it would be eight long years before the Bulldogs managed to defeat the Yellow Jackets again—the streak lasted through 1956. Butts had only three winning seasons during that span, including 1950 (6-3-3). The Bulldogs played in the first and only Presidential Cup in College Park, Maryland, but despite Zippy Morocco (who later set the SEC's all-time basketball scoring record) scoring two touchdowns, Georgia lost to Texas A&M, 40-20.

Butts didn't return to a bowl game until 1959, and it would also be his last. Led by the "Peerless Pilot"—quarterback Francis Tarkenton, who went on to have an illustrious career with the Minnesota Vikings, Georgia opened with a 17-3 victory against Alabama and won all three big rivalry games for a 9-1 record.

At the Orange Bowl, Tarkenton led touchdown drives of 71 and 62 yards as the Bulldogs defeated Maryland 14-0 for a No. 5 final ranking.

"Leadership must be demonstrated, not announced," Tarkenton was known for saying. He also was credited with this warning: "Beware of the big plays. The eighty-yard drive is better than the eighty-yard pass."

After Butts resigned in 1960, his former freshman coach, Johnny Griffin, who had played on the 1946 team, returned; but he had little success. Griffin pulled out a 30-21 victory at Auburn in 1962 but went 1-8 against Auburn, Florida, and Georgia Tech, and he resigned following the 1963 season only to be replaced by the most successful coach in Georgia history.

When Vince Dooley was hired at the age of 31, athletic director Joel Evans told him it was with the sole purpose of bringing the Bulldogs back to respectability. Dooley did that and much more. When he left the sideline in 1988 to become the full-time athletic director, his list of accomplishments included one national title, six SEC championships, and 20 bowl games.

During his first season, Dooley had two quarterbacks who were as different as chalk from cheese. While Lynn Hughes' precise approach was similar to a Marine ordered to "present arms," Preston Ridlehuber was all improvisation.

"Preston didn't know what he was doing, we didn't know what he was doing, but the thing is that the opponents didn't know what he was doing," Dooley said. "What we all knew was that he would compete."

The contrast helped Georgia finish 7-3-1 and play Texas Tech in the Sun Bowl. Although the Red Raiders had led the Southwest Conference with almost 300 offensive yards per game, the Bulldogs limited them to just 128. Ridlehuber's 52-yard pass to Fred Barber set up the only touchdown for a 7-0 final.

Maybe the biggest break Georgia ever had in a game occurred on September 18, 1965, when defending national champion Alabama was leading 17-10 in Athens. With 2:08 remaining, a flea-flicker going from Kirby Moore to Pat Hodgson to Bob Taylor—with Alabama arguing that Hodgson's knee was down before he let go of the ball (and supported by the game film)—resulted in a 73-yard touchdown. With the two-point conversion, the Bulldogs pulled off an 18-17 upset.

"You don't win the games in the movies," said Crimson Tide coach Paul "Bear" Bryant, who despite the setback went on to win his second straight national title.

Hughes eventually moved to safety, where his quarterback knowledge proved to be crucial against Florida in 1966. Picking up on a tackle-eligible formation, he intercepted what could have been a 39-yard game-winning touchdown by Heisman Trophy winner Steve Spurrier.

After defeating Auburn (21-13) and Georgia Tech (23-14), Georgia was 9-1 and headed to the Cotton Bowl to play Southern Methodist. But even after a 24-9 victory, in which Kent Lawrence rushed for 149 yards on 16 carries, it couldn't overcome the midseason 7-6 loss at Miami in the polls and finished No. 4.

With rambunctious safety Jake Scott—who went on to be MVP of Super Bowl VII—keying the defense, Georgia (7-3) was invited to play in the 1967 Liberty Bowl. Future Bulldogs coach Jim Donnan led North Carolina State on two touchdown drives, but when Lawrence was stopped inches short of the end zone, the play not only stonewalled a 98-yard drive but also preserved the Wolfpack's 14-7 victory.

The 1968 season began with a 17-17 tie at Tennessee, but no opponent would score more than 20 points against the Georgia defense, which featured All-American tackle Bill Stanfill. After winning all three rivalry games against Florida (51-0), Auburn (17-3), and Georgia Tech (47-8), the Bulldogs were 8-0-2 and ranked fourth. But eight turnovers, including one through the end zone, helped Arkansas pull off a 16-2 upset in the Sugar Bowl. Although Georgia was ranked No. 1 by Litkenhous (a difference-by-score formula developed by Edward E. Litkenhous, a professor of chemical engineering at Vanderbilt, and his brother, Frank), Ohio State was the consensus national champion. The Associated Press listed Georgia eighth.

The Bulldogs advanced to the 1969 Sun Bowl, but a 45-6 rout by Nebraska resulted in a 5-5-1 season. In 1971, when tailback Horace King became the first black player to sign with Georgia—with Chuck Kinnebrew, Clarence Pope, Larry West, and Richard Appleby quickly joining him—a nine-game winning streak had Georgia back atop the standings. Auburn ended the title hopes with a 35-20 victory, yet a 28-24 win against Georgia Tech returned the Bulldogs to the Gator Bowl. Sophomore quarterback Andy Johnson had led the offense, but against North Carolina, with Dooley coaching against his brother Bill, it was Jimmy Poulos (161 rushing yards on 20 carries) and defensive lineman Dennis Watson who made the difference in the 7-3 victory.

From 1973 to 1975, Georgia played in bowl games, but found the SEC championship to be elusive. It won a thrilling Peach Bowl against Maryland, 17-16, to finish 7-4-1 in 1973. The following year it lost 21-10 to Miami (Ohio) in the Tangerine Bowl, and in 1975 only a 28-13 loss at Ole Miss kept Georgia from winning the conference title. At the Cotton Bowl, Glynn Harrison returned the opening kickoff to the Arkansas 4 to set up a field goal, and Gene Washington caught a 21-yard touchdown pass, but from then on the Razorbacks dominated for a 31-10 victory.

Despite another loss to Ole Miss in 1976, Georgia came back to win its first SEC championship in eight years, with Dooley keeping a promise to his players to shave his head, and match hairless defensive coordinator Erik Russell, in a show of solidarity. The Bulldogs shut out four opponents, including Alabama and Auburn, and at 10-1 were paired against No. 1 Pittsburgh in the Sugar Bowl. Heisman Trophy winner Tony Dorsett ran for 202 yards on 32 carries, and Matt Cavanaugh passed for 192 as the Panthers proved worthy of their ranking with a 27-3 victory to secure the national championship.

Georgia lost to all three rivals in 1977 to finish 5-6, but the following year the games were as close as ever. After beating Florida (24-22) and tying Auburn (22-22), the Bulldogs were down 20-0 against Georgia Tech when true freshman quarterback Buck Belue entered the game and led the team back to take a 21-20 lead. Not to be outdone, Drew Hill returned a kickoff 101 yards and Tech converted a two-point conversion, only to see Belue drive the offense 84 yards, with a 43-yard touchdown pass to Amp Arnold followed by a Belue-to-Arnold conversion, to secure a 29-28 victory. Despite outgaining Stanford 525 yards to 317, six lost turnovers resulted in a 25-22 defeat in the Bluebonnet Bowl and a 9-2-1 finish.

In 1980 Auburn tempted Dooley by offering to bring him home to direct his alma mater; but after mulling it over, he said no thanks . . . and would be immensely rewarded.

"The overriding factor was I had too much invested here," Dooley said. "I wouldn't leave. This has been my home for 17 years. I'm a Bulldog and proud to be one."

During the season opener at Tennessee, Georgia had freshman Herschel Walker listed as the third-string tailback. But when the Volunteers built up a 15-0 lead, Walker came off the bench and never went back. He ran over future Dallas Cowboys Pro Bowl defensive back Bill Bates on one touchdown and scored another to lead a 16-15 comeback. Walker went on to have four 200-yard rushing performances that season alone, and with 1,616 yards finished third in the Heisman voting (which has never been won by a freshman).

"I thought he would be great, but I didn't think he'd be that great that soon," Dooley said about Walker.

After defeating South Carolina (13-10), Georgia found itself No. 2, but the season was nearly derailed by Florida. Down by one point with 1:03 remaining, the Bulldogs had the ball on their own 7-yard line when Belue's pass to Lindsay Scott resulted in a 93-yard touchdown, securing both their and the team's place in Georgia history. Making the play possible was a block by right tackle Nat Hudson, who came off his initial assignment at the line of scrimmage to force a Florida defender past the pocket.

The rivalry games swept, undefeated Georgia faced No. 7 Notre Dame, which had an outstanding defense, in the Sugar Bowl. With President Jimmy Carter looking on, the Bulldogs' defense, which featured All-American cornerback Scott Woerner, was equal to the task. Two fumbles, recovered by seniors Bob Kelly and Chris Welton, set up Walker touchdowns, and Terry Hoage blocked a field-goal attempt.

"You've got to do everything well, but you've got to play defense first," Dooley said.

Even though Belue completed only one pass, Walker had 150 rushing yards on 36 carries, and Georgia won the national championship with the 17-10 victory.

"When you talk about playing as a team, that was the team," Walker said. "It was unbelievable. I don't know that any team ever played better together than that one. Coach Dooley and the seniors on that team made us believe in each other. We didn't beat people because we were more talented, we beat people because we played together. We won as a team."

Walker was able to lead the Bulldogs to two more SEC titles. After an early season 13-3 loss to Clemson, Georgia ran the table to set up another Sugar Bowl showdown with Pittsburgh with national championship hopes again at stake. But after five lead changes, quarterback Dan Marino connected with tight end John Brown on a fourth-down 33-yard touchdown pass with 35 seconds remaining to give the Panthers a 24-20 victory. At 10-2, Georgia finished No. 6, with Clemson claiming the national title. Walker, who had two touchdowns in the bowl game, finished second in Heisman voting as a sophomore.

"Herschel had world-class speed and strength. I've seen others who had both of those, but he also had mental toughness and self-discipline," Dooley said. "I've never seen another back combine those qualities like he did."

After opening the 1982 season with a 13-7 victory against Clemson, Georgia was ready for another run at the national championship and after defeating Florida 44-0 was promoted to No. 1. All that stood in the Bulldogs' way was No. 2 Penn State (10-1) at the Sugar Bowl. After spotting the Nittany Lions a 20-3 lead in the second quarter, the Bulldogs came back, only to see Gregg Garrity make a diving catch for a 47-yard touchdown from Todd Blackledge to seal a 27-23 victory and the national title.

After rewriting the Georgia record book, and winning the Heisman Trophy as a junior, Walker left to play for the New Jersey Generals of the United States Football League. He had experienced only three losses in a Bulldogs uniform.

"I shouldn't get the credit for all those records at Georgia," Walker said. "I had an extremely good offensive line for three years. A lot of these runs I had were due to excellent blocking."

Another popular Walker quote was: "I never got tired of running. The ball ain't that heavy."

Without Walker, most expected a severe drop-off, especially since the Bulldogs had question marks at both quarterback and tailback. Instead, Georgia surprised practically everyone by piecing together a 9-1-1 regular season. Paired against undefeated No. 2 Texas in the Cotton Bowl, the Bulldogs played just like their nickname indicated, and when the Longhorns fumbled a punt recovered by Gary Moss in the fourth quarter, Georgia took advantage by scoring a touchdown for a 10-9 victory. It finished the year ranked fourth.

Over the next five years, Dooley's teams were always near the top of the standings, but it seemed they could never get over a crucial hump.

The 1984 season resulted in a 7-4-1 record, but was marred by losses in all three rivalry games. Against Florida State in the Citrus Bowl, All-American kicker Kevin Butler's 70-yard attempt as time expired fell just short, resulting in a 17-17 tie. The 1985 Sun Bowl also resulted in a tie, 13-13 to Arizona, after both teams missed potentially game-winning field goals. Georgia finished 7-3-2.

The Bulldogs lost to Florida, 31-19, in 1986, but came back to beat both Auburn (20-16) and Georgia Tech (31-24) to play Boston College in the Hall of Fame Bowl. After Georgia rebounded from a 13-point halftime deficit, with a 5-yard run by quarterback James Jackson giving the Bulldogs the lead, the Golden Eagles scored on a 5-yard touchdown pass with 32 seconds remaining to pull out a 27-24 victory.

Dooley's final two seasons had identical 9-3 records (with losses to Auburn in both), but with bowl wins. In 1987, freshman kicker John Kasay's 39-yard field goal as time expired gave Georgia a 20-17 victory against Arkansas in the Liberty

Bowl. With Wayne Johnson passing for a career-high 227 yards and three touchdowns, the Bulldogs sent the coach off with a 34-27 victory against Michigan State in the Gator Bowl.

Former Georgia quarterback Ray Goff replaced Dooley for his first head coaching job, and in eight years he led the Bulldogs to four bowls. The first came during his inaugural season, with the Bulldogs paired against Syracuse in the Peach Bowl. In what had become typical Georgia fashion, the game was decided by a field goal. The Bulldogs couldn't reach the end zone after linebacker Mo Lewis' 77-yard interception return in the second quarter; in the fourth quarter, the Orangemen were better able to move the ball, and John Biskup's 26-yard field goal with 25 seconds remaining gave Syracuse a 19-18 victory.

Despite an early loss to Alabama and an upset at Vanderbilt, the 1991 team still won eight games during the regular season, including Auburn (37-27) and Georgia Tech (18-15). Against Arkansas in the Independence Bowl, a 24-15 victory, Eric Zeier threw touchdown passes to Andre Hastings and Arthur Marshall, and linebacker Torrey Evans led the defense.

The 1992 season would be even better. Although Georgia lost an early game to Tennessee (34-31) and was edged by Florida (26-24), at 9-2 it drew Ohio State in the Citrus Bowl. Running back Garrison Hearst accumulated 163 rushing yards on 28 carries and scored two touchdowns, and Zeier passed for 242 yards. Both quarterbacks had costly fumbles, but following Kirk Herbstreit's miscue the Bulldogs drove 80 yards to score the winning touchdown for a 21-14 victory. For the first time in a decade, Georgia finished ranked in the Top 10 at No. 8.

Zeier broke most of Georgia's passing records but wasn't able to get the Bulldogs back to a bowl game during his junior and senior seasons. In 1995, six wins returned Georgia to the Peach Bowl, where Hines Ward completed 31 of 59 passes for 413 yards. However, two first-quarter interceptions and a blocked punt gave Virginia a 14-0 lead, and after Georgia defensive tackle Jason Ferguson recovered a fumble and returned it 10 yards for a touchdown with 1:09 remaining, Demetrius Allen returned the kickoff 83 yards for a touchdown and 34-27 victory.

In 1996 Georgia hired Donnan, fresh off his winning streak of 64 games over six seasons at Marshall. While his teams generally had little trouble scoring, the defense could be a bit vulnerable. For example, during his second season, Donnan's team averaged just under 40 points per game in its first four games but then lost 38-13 at Tennessee. A 45-34 defeat to Auburn would be the Bulldogs' only other setback, resulting in a postseason matchup against Wisconsin in the Outback Bowl. Ditching the traditional silver britches for black pants, quarterback Mike Bobo completed 26 of 28 passes—including 19 consecutive attempts—for 235 yards, and running back Robert Edwards scored three touchdowns in the 33-6 victory.

"Mike was on fire," Donnan said.

In 1998, the Bulldogs couldn't complete the sweep against their rivals, losing 21-19 to Georgia Tech, but with eight wins headed to the Peach Bowl. After freshman Quincy Carter had three passes intercepted, Georgia trailed 21-0 in the second quarter, only to rally back. Carter threw for 222 yards and two touchdowns, including a 14-yard score by Champ Bailey, and senior running back Olandis Gary accumulated 110 rushing yards on 19 carries and two touchdowns for a 35-33 victory against Virginia.

Following another loss to Georgia Tech in 1999 (51-48), the Bulldogs played Purdue in the Outback Bowl and again came back from a big deficit. Down 25-0 in the second quarter, with Drew Brees completing four touchdown passes but the Boilermakers missing three extra-point attempts, Georgia scored 28 unanswered points and won 28-25 in overtime on Hap Hines' 21-yard field goal.

In 2000, Donnan gave the quote that would doom him by saying he had "waited 50 years" to coach a team this talented. When he was swept in the rivalry games and lost to Georgia Tech for the fourth straight year (27-15), the coach was fired, but Georgia let him take the team to the 2000 Jeep O'Ahu Bowl against Virginia. This time, with sophomore receiver Terrence Edwards totaling 97 rushing yards and 39 receiving yards, the Bulldogs jumped out to a 17-0 lead they never relinquished, for a 37-14 victory. Donnan finished 40-19 in five seasons.

Two days later Mark Richt, who had served on the staff at Florida State for 15 years, seven as offensive coordinator, was introduced as Georgia's twenty-fifth head coach. In addition to coaching Heisman Trophy quarterbacks Charlie Ward and Chris Weinke, Richt himself had been an outstanding quarterback prospect at Miami under Howard Schnellenberger.

"I figured I'd start my first year, be an All-American my second year, win the Heisman Trophy my third year, and then go pro after that," Richt said.

Instead, he spent most of his college playing career backing up future NFL Hall of Fame quarterback Jim Kelly, and during one season his teammates also included Vinny Testaverde and Bernie Kosar with quarterbacks coach Earl Morral. But Schnellenberger noted that Richt "was more intellectual than the other quarterbacks."

"Mark could have gone to probably 102 other colleges in the country and gotten more playing time than he did at Miami," he said.

The coach who liked to say "Finish the drill" didn't make the mistake of losing to Georgia Tech during his first season, and with eight wins the Bulldogs played Boston College in the Music City Bowl. Running back Verron Hayes concluded his career with 132 yards on 27 carries, but Boston College's William Green was just a touch better with 149 yards and a fourth-quarter touchdown to seal a 20-16 victory. Though David Greene passed for 288 yards, four turnovers proved too much to overcome.

But the groundwork had been laid, and in 2002 the Bulldogs responded to a preseason No. 8 ranking by defeating their first eight opponents, including Clemson (31-28), Alabama (27-25), and Tennessee (18-13). With only one loss, 20-13 to Florida, Georgia advanced to play in its first SEC Championship Game, where it dominated Arkansas 30-3 to win its first conference title in 20 years.

As part of the Bowl Championship Series, Richt had to face his previous team, Florida State, at the Sugar Bowl. Musa Smith rushed for 145 yards, cornerback Bruce Thornton returned an interception 71 yards for a touchdown, and Billy Bennett kicked four field goals as the Bulldogs won 26-13.

"To beat Florida State is a great feeling, since I have a great respect for the

Florida State program," Richt said. "I'm so proud of these kids. They deserve to go out like this."

But instead of an ending, many thought it was just another beginning for Richt and the Bulldogs, who finished the 2002 season 13-1 and ranked third. Georgia went back to the SEC Championship Game in 2003 and won it in 2005 to reclaim its billing as a perennial Top 10 program.

THREE THINGS THAT STAND OUT ABOUT GEORGIA FOOTBALL

1. *Uga:* Although Georgia's original mascot was a goat, the English bulldog with the spiked collar may be the most recognized mascot in all of college sports. Uga has appeared on the cover of *Sports Illustrated,* had a cameo in the movie *Midnight in the Garden of Good and Evil,* and traveled with Herschel Walker to the Downtown Athletic Club in New York for the Heisman Trophy presentation. The first five Ugas are buried near the south stands of the football stadium, and flowers are placed on their graves before each game. "Uga is the best mascot a team could have," receiver Clarence Kay said. "He'll lay on you. He'll lick on you. Give him a bone and he'll love you for life."
2. *"Between the Hedges":* Many schools have shrubbery surrounding the football field, but legendary sportswriter Grantland Rice is credited with the popular term specific to Georgia. Sanford Stadium originally seated 30,000 when it opened some 75 years ago. The current capacity is 92,746.
3. *"Go you silver britches":* Coach Wally Butts introduced them in 1939. Vince Dooley changed them to white, but when he switched back in 1980 the Bulldogs won the national title.

Kentucky

THE SCHOOL

Location: Lexington, Kentucky
Founded: 1865
Enrollment: 25,397
Nickname: Wildcats
Colors: Blue and white
Mascots: Wildcat and Scratch. Live mascots have included Tom, TNT, Whiskers, Hot Tamale, Colonel, and Blue
Stadium: Commonwealth Stadium (67,606)
2005 officials: Dr. Lee T. Todd Jr., president; Dr. Alan D. DeSantis, faculty representative; Mitch Barnhart, athletics director

THE PROGRAM

National Championships (0): None
SEC Championships (2): 1950; 1976
Bowl appearances (10): 5-5
First season: 1881
College Football Hall of Fame (5): Paul "Bear" Bryant, 1946–53, coach, inducted 1986; Jerry Claiborne, 1982–89, coach, 1999; Bob Gain, 1947–50, tackle/guard, 1980; Lou Michaels, 1955–57, tackle, 1992; Babe Parilli, 1949–51, quarterback, 1992
Heisman Winners: None
National Honors: Bob Gain, 1950 Outland Trophy (outstanding interior lineman); Glenn Pakulak, 2002 Mosi Tatupu Award (outstanding senior special team player)
First-Team All-Americans: Clyde Johnson, T, 1942; Bob Gain, T, 1949–50; Vito (Babe) Parilli, QB, 1950–51; Doug Moseley, C, 1951; Steve Meilinger, E, 1952–53; Ray Correll, G, 1953; Howard Schnellenberger, E, 1953; Lou Michaels, T, 1956–57; Irv Goode, C, 1961; Hershel Turner, T, 1963; Sam Ball, T, 1965; Rodger Bird, HB, 1965; Rick Norton, QB, 1965; Elmore Stephens,

TE, 1974; Rick Nuzum, C, 1974; Warren Bryant, T, 1976; Art Still, DE, 1977; Mike Pfeifer, T, 1989; Tim Couch, QB, 1998; James Whalen, TE, 1999; Derek Abney, RS, 2002; Greg Pakulak, P, 2002

First-Team Academic All-Americans (CoSIDA): Tom Ranieri, LB, 1974; Mark Keene, C, 1978; Jim Kovach, LB, 1978; Ken Pietrowiak, C, 1985; Mike Schnellenberger, LB, 1995; Jeff Zurcher, DB, 1998; Hayden Lane, OL, 2005; Taylor Begley, K, 2005

First-round NFL draftees: 13

Retired jerseys: 2 Tim Couch; 2 Ermal Allen; 8 Clyde Johnson; 10 Vito "Babe" Parilli; 11 Rick Norton; 12 Derrick Ramsey; 13 Bob Davis; 16 George Blanda; 19 Howard Schnellenberger; 20 Charlie McClendon; 21 Calvin Bird; 21 Rodger Bird; 22 Mark Higgs; 24 Dicky Lyons; 27 Wallace "Wah-Wah" Jones; 32 Larry Seiple; 33 George Adams; 40 Sonny Collins; 44 John "Shipwreck" Kelly; 45 Jay Rhodemyre; 48 Washington "Wash" Serini; 50 Jim Kovach; 50 Harry Ulinski; 51 Doug Moseley; 52 Rick Nuzum; 55 Irvin "Irv" Goode; 57 Dermontti Dawson; 59 Joe Federspiel; 65 Ray Correll; 66 Ralph Kercheval; 69 Warren Bryant; 70 Bob Gain; 70 Herschel Turner; 73 Sam Ball; 74 Dave Roller; 79 Lou Michaels; 80 Rick Kestner; 80 Tom Hutchinson; 80 Steve Meilinger; 88 Jeff Van Note; 97 Art Still; Paul "Bear" Bryant; Jerry Claiborne; Blanton Collier; Bernie Shively

Centennial Team (selected by the *Lexington Herald-Leader* **in 1990): Offense**—OL Doug Moseley, 1949–51; OL Ray Correll, 1951–52; OL Irv Goode, 1959–61; OL Sam Ball, 1963–65; OL Warren Bryant, 1973–76; E Steve Meilinger, 1951–53; E Tom Hutchinson, 1960–62; QB Babe Parilli, 1949–51; RB Rodger Bird, 1963–65; RB Sonny Collins, 1972–75; RB John "Shipwreck" Kelly, 1929–31; K Joey Worley, 1984–87 **Defense**—DL Bob Gain, 1947–50; DL Lou Michaels, 1955–57; DL Jeff Van Note, 1966–68; DL Dave Roller, 1968–70; DL Art Still, 1974–77; LB Jay Rhodemyre, 1942, 1946–47; LB Joe Federspiel, 1969–71; DB Jerry Claiborne, 1946, 1948–49; DB Darryl Bishop, 1971–73; DB Mike Siganos, 1974–77; DB Paul Calhoun, 1982–84; KR/PR Dicky Lyons, 1966–68

(*Note:* The *Louisville Courier-Journal* had a similar team, adding G Gene Donaldson, G Dermontti Dawson, RB Rob Davis, RB Mark Higgs, LB Jim Kovach, LB Frank LeMaster, and P Ralph Kercheval.)

THE COACHES

A. M. Miller, 1892, 2-4-1; John A. Thompson, 1892–93, 5-2-1; W. P. Finney, 1894, 5-2; Charles Mason, 1895, 4-5; Dudley Short, 1896, 3-6; Lyman B. Eaton, 1897, 2-4; W. R. Bass, 1898–99, 12-2-2; W. H. Kiler, 1900–01, 6-12-1; E. W. McLeod, 1920, 3-5-1; C. A. Wright, 1903, 7-1-0; F. E. Schact, 1904, 15-4-1; J. White Guyn, 1906–08, 17-7-1; E. R. Sweetland, 1909–10, 1912, 23-5-0; P. P. Douglass, 1911, 7-3; Alpha Brumage, 1913–14, 11-5; J. J. Tigert, 1915–16, 10-2-3; S. A. Boles, 1917, 3-5-1; Andy Gill, 1918–19, 5-5-1; W. J.

Juneau, 1920–22, 13-10-2; J. Winn, 1923, 4-3-2; Fred J. Murphy, 1924–26, 12-14-1; Harry Gamage, 1927–33; 32-25-5; Chet Wynne, 1934–37, 20-19-0; A. D. Kirwan, 1938–44, 24-28-4; Bernie Shively, 1945, 2-8; Paul (Bear) Bryant 1946–53, 60-23-5; Blanton Collier, 1954–61, 41-36-3; Charlie Bradshaw, 1962–68, 25-41-4; John Ray, 1969–72, 10-33; Fran Curci, 1973–81, 47-51-2, Jerry Claiborne, 1982–89, 41-46-3; Bill Curry, 1990–96, 26-52; Hal Mumme, 1997–2000, 20-26; Guy Morriss 2001–02, 9-14; Rich Brooks 2003–05, 9-24
National Coach of the Year: None
SEC Coach of the Year, AP: Paul "Bear" Bryant 1950; Fran Curci 1977; Jerry Claiborne 1983 **Coaches:** Blanton Collier 1954
SEC Championships: Paul "Bear" Bryant 1, Fran Curci 1
National Championships: None

RECORDS

Rushing yards, game: 299, Moe Williams vs. South Carolina, Sept. 23, 1995 (40 attempts)
Rushing yards, season: 1,600, Moe Williams, 1995 (294 attempts)
Rushing yards, career: 3,835, Sonny Collins, 1992–95 (777 attempts)
Passing yards, game: 528, Jared Lorenzen vs. Georgia, Oct. 21, 2000 (39 of 58)
Passing yards, season: 4,275, Tim Couch, 1998 (400 of 553)
Passing yards, career: 10,354, Jared Lorenzen, 2000–03 (862 of 1,514)
Receiving yards, game: 269, Craig Yeast vs. Vanderbilt, Nov. 14, 1998 (16 receptions)
Receiving yards, season: 1,311, Craig Yeast, 1998 (85 receptions)
Receiving yards, career: 2,899, Craig Yeast, 1995–98 (208 receptions)
Points, game: 25, Calvin Bird vs. Hawaii, Sept. 13, 1958 (four touchdowns, 1 PAT)
Points, season: 102, Moe Williams, 1995 (17 touchdowns)
Points, career: 246, Joey Worley, 1984–87 (57 field goals, 75 PATs)

The University of Kentucky has the unusual distinction of being the only Southeastern Conference school in which the football program is clearly overshadowed by another sport.

Actually, make that sports. In October, home games are often played at night so fans can enjoy the "daily double" of horse racing at nearby Kenneland Race Course before heading to Commonwealth Stadium. On the way, they might pass a series of tents full of students camped out to purchase men's basketball tickets.

In fact, in really down years, the football program can almost be challenged in terms of attention by both the cheerleading squad, which won its thirteenth national championship in 2004, and the club hockey team posters. Granted, when you have actress Ashley Judd in a hockey jersey to promote the 1998–99 season, that's pretty stiff competition. (*Note:* There's a popular story on campus that Judd, who is a huge basketball fan, was once offered a North Carolina Tar Heels jacket on a chilly movie set and responded, "I'd just as soon freeze to death.")

Considering that the Wildcats have won more than six games only twice since 1984, and have played in just 10 bowl games, most football fans have long since conceded that even though the football team consistently ranks in the nation's top 25 in attendance, Kentucky is first and foremost a basketball school. They instead focus on things like the outstanding rivalry with Louisville.

Just don't tell that to a coach.

"There's nothing like winning," said Guy Morriss (2001–02) after a victory against Mississippi State in which he broke his hand during a halftime locker room tirade. "If it takes hitting a locker, or several of them, I'm going to do it."

It wasn't always that way. In fact, Kentucky was on the doorstep of being a perennial football power—with arguably the best college football coach ever, who had eight straight winning seasons to go with appearances in the Orange, Sugar, and Cotton Bowls between 1946 and 1953.

But when Paul "Bear" Bryant, who won six national championships and 13 SEC titles at Alabama, realized that contrary to promises, basketball would remain the top priority of the athletic department, he quit despite having a 12-year contract. His 60 wins over eight years remain the school record, with Blanton Collier and Jerry Claiborne tied for second with 41.

"When coach Bryant walked into the locker room I always had the urge to stand up and cheer," quarterback/kicker George Blanda (1945–48) said. "Seeing that face for the first time—granite firm, grim, full of grit—I thought, 'This must be what God looks like.'"

Bryant's 1950 team, which finished 11-1, is considered the best in Kentucky history. In the coach's fifth season, the only loss was 7-0 at Tennessee in the regular season finale, played in cold and snow. With Kentucky 5-1 in SEC play and Tennessee only 4-1 (thanks to an early season 7-0 loss at Mississippi State), the Wildcats were awarded their first SEC championship.

As a reward, No. 7 Kentucky was invited to play powerhouse Oklahoma in the Sugar Bowl. Bud Wilkinson's team had won 31 straight games and had already been awarded the national championship (final polls were conducted before bowl games then).

With the No. 2 defense in the country, Bryant kept the Sooners off balance with different looks including a three-tackle formation. One was Walt Yowarsky, who had played less than five minutes of defense during the regular season. With Oklahoma so concerned about Outland Trophy winner Bob Gain, Yowarsky frequently broke into the backfield and interrupted plays. His fumble recovery at the Oklahoma 22 set up Kentucky's first touchdown, a pass from All-American quarterback Babe Parilli (who finished fourth in Heisman Trophy voting and had 50 touchdown career passes) to Wilbur Jamerson.

Kentucky held on for a shocking 13-7 victory, with Yowarsky named the game's most valuable player. Years later, *USA Today*'s Jeff Sagarin's retrospective computer rankings had the Wildcats finishing No. 1, though with No. 2 Army and No. 3 Texas also losing, a good argument could have been made for No. 4 Tennessee, which defeated the Longhorns 20-14 in the Cotton Bowl, as well as for No. 6 Princeton (9-0).

Bryant never had a losing record with Kentucky, which was something that he wasn't able to achieve at his next stop, Texas A&M. While there, he took his players 250 miles west to a barren army base in Junction and essentially ran a brutal boot camp in 100-degree heat. More than 100 made the initial trip, but after 10 days less than one-third remained—the famed "Junction Boys."

"I don't want ordinary people," Bryant was quoted as saying. "I want people who are willing to sacrifice and do without a lot of those things ordinary students get to do. That's what it takes to win."

After a 7-3 campaign in 1946, Bryant led Kentucky to its first-ever bowl game the following season. Thanks to an early Blanda field goal, the Wildcats never trailed, and two Bill Boller touchdowns—on a 15-yard run and a 49-yard interception return—resulted in a 24-14 victory against Villanova at the first and only Great Lakes Bowl in front of 14,908 fans at Cleveland Municipal Stadium.

Kentucky's first New Year's Day bowl came following the 1949 season, when the Wildcats outscored opponents 304-53, with only a narrow 6-0 loss to Tennessee keeping them from winning the SEC championship. But Kentucky committed three turnovers and let a seven-point halftime lead slip away in the Orange Bowl, with Santa Clara coming back for a 21-13 victory. Adding to the disappointment was that the Wildcats blew a chance to score at the end of the first half after Parilli hit Bill Leskovar for a 45-yard gain to set up first-and-goal at the 3, only to see time run out when two running plays came up short.

After the game, Bryant lamented over not calling for a pass play: "If it failed, the clock was killed and then we could have tried a field goal," he said. Still, Kentucky finished the year ranked eleventh.

In 1949 and 1950, Parilli, running Bryant's T-formation and basically playing hide-and-seek with the ball and confusing defenses, directed teams that combined for 684 points against 115 for the opposition. The Wildcats held 10 of 22 opponents scoreless, and all but three of them to seven points or less.

Coming off the Sugar Bowl win in 1951, Kentucky was invited to play Texas Christian in the following Cotton Bowl after a 7-4 regular season. Parilli threw two touchdowns to Emery Clark, and led by All-American guard Ray Correll, the Wildcats controlled the tempo while the defense stopped Texas Christian drives on the Kentucky 4-, 24-, 5-, and 2-yard lines for a 20-7 victory.

Bryant went 5-4-2 and 7-2-1 during his last two years at Kentucky before leaving, and the Wildcats wouldn't play in another postseason game until 1976. As the story goes, after winning the SEC championship Bryant was honored for his efforts with a cigarette lighter at an awards banquet. When Adolph Rupp did the same in basketball, he was a given a Cadillac.

Another Kentucky claim to fame was the group called "The Immortals," which essentially had the perfect season. Not only did W. R. Bass' team in 1898 finish 7-0, but it outscored its opponents 180-0 while playing a slightly unorthodox schedule by today's standards. The wins came against Kentucky University (18-0), Georgetown (28-0), Company H of the 8th Massachusetts (59-0), Louisville Athletic Club (16-0), Centre (6-0), 160th Indiana (17-0), and Newcastle Athletic Club (36-0).

The 1977 team under Fran Curci was arguably Kentucky's other great team, with the season-ending No. 6 ranking its best ever. The Wildcats defeated Penn State (24-20), LSU (33-13), Georgia (33-0), and Florida (14-7) all on the road, and North Carolina (10-7) and Tennessee (21-17) at home to finish 10-1. However, Kentucky was on probation with the National Collegiate Athletic Association and thus ineligible to play in a bowl game.

Curci's reign from 1973, when the Wildcats moved from Stoll Field/McLean Stadium to Commonwealth Stadium, to 1981 was the longest of any coach, but also one that could only be called tumultuous. Though running back Sonny Collins set the career rushing record with 3,835 yards, Curci only had one winning season out of his first three before the roller coaster took an upswing in 1976. Thanks to a 62-yard touchdown pass from Derrick Ramsey to Greg Woods that held up for a 7-0 victory in the season finale at Tennessee, Kentucky went 4-2 in the SEC to share the championship with Georgia (though the Bulldogs won their regular-season meeting 31-7) and with seven overall victories received an invitation to play 9-2 North Carolina in the Peach Bowl to end a 25-year postseason drought.

The Wildcats outgained the Tar Heels 334 yards to 108, while the defense forced five turnovers. Running behind All-American tackle Warren Bryant, tailback Rod Stewart had 104 rushing yards on 19 carries and scored three touchdowns to be named the game's most valuable player in the 21-0 victory. Linebacker Mike Martin, who helped hold the Tar Heels to just over 100 yards and five first downs, was the defensive player of the game.

After failing to record another .500 season, Curci stepped down following the 1981 season with a 47-51-2 record. Claiborne, who had both played under coach Bryant and been one of his assistant coaches, answered the call of his alma mater and was named the school's 31st head football coach. Though the Bear has obviously received the most notoriety, Claiborne won 179 games during his illustrious career that also had stops at Virginia Tech and Maryland. He earned coach of the year honors in three different conferences, and his 1976 team at Maryland finished 11-1 (with the lone loss coming against Houston in the Cotton Bowl).

Under Claiborne, the Wildcats got off to a rough start. But the 1983 squad was the first in NCAA history to go from winless (0-10-1)—after playing the toughest schedule in the country with games against Oklahoma, Clemson, Auburn, LSU, Georgia, Florida, Tennessee, Virginia Tech, Kansas, and Kansas State—to a bowl game in just one year.

When West Virginia scored 17 points in the second half, the Wildcats came up short in the Hall of Fame Classic, 20-16, to finish 6-5-1; but they went back the following year and beat Wisconsin on a late 52-yard field goal by Joey Worley, 20-19. With less than two minutes remaining, the Badgers drove to the Kentucky 8, but the snap from center was bobbled on what could have been the game-winning field goal. The 9-3 record remains Kentucky's best finish since 1977.

When Claiborne (41-46-3) stepped down in 1989 after 28 years as a college coach, including four winning seasons at Kentucky, the program had many things to boast about. Quarterback Billy Ransdell was the school's all-time leader in passing and total offense. Mark Higgs was second in rushing, and tackle Oliver Barnett set a school record with 26 sacks.

However, what Claiborne might have been proudest of was that during his eight years the Wildcats placed more players (68) on the Academic All-SEC Honor Roll than any other school, including a record 17 in 1989 when Kentucky won the College Football Association's Academic Achievement Award (that is, the academic national championship).

In 1990 Kentucky hired Bill Curry, who had actually left Alabama after winning an SEC title the year before. Following three sub-.500 seasons, he had the Wildcats back in the postseason at the Peach Bowl, but ran into misfortune against Clemson. Off the opening kickoff, Kentucky drove to the 2-yard line when quarterback Pookie Jones threw a pass to receiver Alfonzo Browning, who fumbled while reaching for the goal line. Clemson drove 99 yards to take a 7-0 lead and later stopped Kentucky again on the 1. Thanks to a 5-yard touchdown pass to Mark Chatmon, the Wildcats had a 13-7 lead in the fourth quarter, but Clemson scored again in the final minute to win 14-13.

Kentucky finished 6-6, which would be Curry's best season. The team was a woeful 1-10 in 1994, but the lone win was a big one—20-14 over intra-state rival Louisville in the season opener. It was the first meeting between the football teams in 70 years with a record 59,162 fans at Commonwealth Stadium.

While energetic Hal Mumme had enough personality for an entire team, his four years leading the Wildcats were best remembered for the "Air Raid" offense and quarterback Tim Couch, regarded by some to be the best player ever to suit up for Kentucky. Although the 1997 team finished just 5-6, the offense broke or tied 51 school records and 15 SEC records in passing and total offense.

Kentucky returned to the bowl scene in 1998 when the Wildcats won seven games and Couch led the nation in pass attempts, completions, passing yards, and completion percentage. He was named first-team All-American, SEC Player of the Year, and a finalist for the Heisman Trophy, finishing fourth behind Texas running back Ricky Williams, Kansas State quarterback Michael Bishop, and UCLA quarterback Cade McNown. Additionally, wide receiver Craig Yeast became the leading pass catcher in SEC history.

Kentucky capped its season by playing Penn State in the first Outback Bowl to be sold out, and its first New Year's Day bowl in 47 years. Couch completed 30 of 48 passes for 336 yards and two touchdowns—finishing with at least 300 passing yards and at least one touchdown in every game that season—as the Wildcats outgained the Nittany Lions 441 yards to 420, but lost 26-14.

Before leaving early for the National Football League as the first-overall draft pick of the Cleveland Browns, Couch set seven NCAA records, 14 SEC records, and 26 school records, many of which still stand.

Even without Couch, Kentucky was able to return to the postseason in 1999, when the school also celebrated stadium expansion. Led by All-American tight end James Whalen, the Wildcats pieced together six wins to receive an invitation to play Syracuse in the Music City Bowl. Whalen's 45-yard reception set up the first touchdown, a 3-yard carry by Kendrick Shanklin, but he sustained an injury later in the first quarter and was lost for the game. Quarterback Dusty Bonner completed 30 of 43 passes for 308 yards—and despite the Wildcats blocking two field goals (by Dennis Johnson and Jamal White), with linebacker Ryan Murphy making a career-high 15 tackles (and linebacker Marlin McCree had 10 to go with a sack, two forced fumbles, and one recovered), Syracuse came back to score 13 points in the fourth quarter and win 20-13.

Under Morriss, Kentucky had seven wins in 2002, but was back on NCAA probation due to illicit recruiting. Special teams highlighted the season with Derek Abney returning six kicks for touchdowns to set an NCAA record. He was named an All-American along with punter Glenn Pakulak, who also won the Mosi Tatupu Award as National Special Teams Player of the Year.

It all was a far cry from November 12, 1881, when the first of the future SEC schools introduced football. Kentucky, known then as either A&M College, Kentucky State College, and/or State University of Kentucky, defeated Kentucky University by the unusual score of 7¼-1 (how it scored ¼ of a point is unclear).

The *Lexington Daily Transcript* had the following description: "An estimated 500 ladies and gentlemen watched the game. The head-on collisions between the players were equal to the explosion of Spanish bulls crashing into each other. The sight provided much laughter."

At the end of a three-game season—all against Kentucky University, finishing 2-1—Kentucky didn't play again until April 10, 1891, when it defeated Georgetown College, 8-2. Its second game of the season, against Kentucky University, was called because of an injury to an opposing player, but the school's first known coach, Professor A. M. Miller, is credited with a career record of 2-4-1.

In addition to "The Immortals," the early years sported some other winning teams, including 7-1 under coach C. A. Wright (1903); 9-1 with F. E. Schact (1904); 9-1-1 with J. White Guyn (1907), and 9-1 under E. R. Sweetland (1909). Sweetland compiled a 23-5 record over three seasons prior to the nine-year stint by Harry Gamage (32-25-5), which is still the longest coaching reign in team history.

The nickname came after a 6-2 victory against Illinois in 1909, when during the postgame chapel service the head of the school's military department said the team had "fought like wildcats."

Throughout the program's history, there have been numerous memorable moments and important milestones, including the tragic death of Price Innes McLean, a center who died from injuries sustained in the game against Cincinnati on November 6, 1923. The stadium located next to Memorial Coliseum was dedicated in his honor the following year, with Stoll Field named for prominent alumnus, trustee, and benefactor Judge Richard C. Stoll. The seating of Stoll Field/McLean Stadium was 37,000 during its last year of use in 1972.

In 1900, Kentucky managed to beat Louisville YMCA 12-6 without running a single offensive play. Instead, it punted on first down of every possession and scored two touchdowns on recovered fumbles.

Against Maryville in 1930, running back Shipwreck Kelly rushed for a school record 280 yards in leading a 57-0 rout. The mark stood in the Kentucky record book for 65 years—until Moe Williams' 299 yards on 40 carries against South Carolina in 1995, with an SEC-record 429 all-purpose yards that was the second-highest in NCAA history, to lead a 35-30 victory. Williams finished the season with 1,600 rushing yards, broke three SEC records, and set or tied 15 school records.

Tackle Clyde Johnson was Kentucky's first All-American during a 3-6-1 season in 1942. There was no team in 1943 due to World War II, but A. D. Kirwan stayed on and coached the team again in 1944 to finish a six-season stint 24-28-4.

In 1954, Blanton Collier had the thankless task of following Bear Bryant as coach of the Wildcats, and in his first year finished 7-3 overall, 5-2 in SEC play. However, it would also be his best season at Kentucky. After eight years he had a record of 41-36-3, though is fondly remembered for having a 5-2-1 record against Tennessee.

Some of the players Collier coached include two-time All-American tackle Lou Michaels (who doubled as a punter and kicker), Howard Schnellenberger, Tom Hutchinson, Bobby Cravens, Calvin Bird, and Irv Goode. But absolutely amazing was the coaching staff he assembled in 1959, including Don Shula, Ed Rutledge, Bill Arnsparger, Schnellenberger, Ermal Allen, John North, and Bob Cummings.

Collier was replaced by another Bryant disciple, Charlie Bradshaw, a former Kentucky player who inherited a team with 88 returning players on the roster. More than 50 left the squad during the rigorous offseason conditioning program, leaving "The Thin Thirty" to open the season against Florida State and play the Seminoles to a 0-0 tie. The 1962 Wildcats finished 3-5-2, but one of the victories came against Tennessee, 12-10.

Bradshaw managed a 25-41-4 record in seven seasons. His biggest win came early in the 1964 season, pulling off an upset of No. 1 Ole Miss, 27-21, at Memorial Stadium in Jackson, Mississippi. Rick Kestner caught three touchdown passes and finished with 185 yards on nine receptions as the Wildcats twice came back from second-half deficits.

The following year, 6-2 Kentucky turned down a bid to the Gator Bowl, thinking that an invitation to the Cotton Bowl would be forthcoming. But the Wildcats then lost 38-21 at Houston and 19-3 to Tennessee to dash all postseason hopes. A few days later, in December 1965, Nat Northington of Louisville became the first black player to sign a scholarship offer to play football with an SEC school. In 1967 he was the first black player to appear in an intra-conference game, against Ole Miss.

John Ray replaced Bradshaw in time for the 1969 season, and like his predecessor had his biggest win against Ole Miss. This time the No. 8 Rebels were led by quarterback Archie Manning, but they lost 10-9 at Lexington. Ray lasted only four years, never posting more than three wins in a season, to finish 10-33.

Kentucky set an SEC record in 1970 that might never be broken when it held Kansas State to minus-93 rushing yards, thanks in part to seven sacks. Kansas State managed to throw for 307 yards, but also had three interceptions, and Kentucky won 16-3.

In the middle of a nine-game winning streak during the 1977 season, Prince Charles got his first look at American football when he attended the Kentucky game at Georgia. When he was introduced to Curci and All-American defensive end Art Still, who stood at 6-foot-6, Charles said, "You're a tall one, aren't you?" Still helped lead the visiting Wildcats to a 33-0 victory.

On November 23, 1991, Cawood Ledford, the "Voice of the Wildcats" for 39 years, called his last Kentucky football game vs. Tennessee (a 16-7 loss) and retired following the 1991–92 basketball season (his last Kentucky game was the 1992 loss to Duke in the NCAA Tournament on Christian Laettner's buzzer-beater). Ledford had arrived on campus in 1953, Bryant's last season, and was the only non-player or coach to have a jersey retired at Rupp Arena.

"Cawood was a dear friend for 33 years," said former Kentucky director of athletics Larry Ivy after Ledford's death in 2001. "He was a valuable member of our athletics family and was the link between our football and basketball programs and our fans for 39 years—not just in the state of Kentucky, but nationwide. He was the epitome of recognizable class, a true gentleman."

On the emotional flip side was the 1997 home game against Alabama. The Wildcats returned a blocked field goal for a touchdown forcing the Crimson Tide to kick a late field goal to send the game into overtime. When Couch connected with Yeast for the game-winning touchdown and 40-34 victory, fans stormed the field and tore down the goalposts for the only time in school history. It was Kentucky's first victory against Alabama since 1922.

"If I weren't so old, I'd have torn them down myself," athletic director C. M. Newton was quoted as saying.

THREE THINGS THAT STAND OUT ABOUT KENTUCKY FOOTBALL

1. *The Trophies:* The Beer Barrel, which was painted orange and blue and actually filled with beer, used to go to the winner of Kentucky vs. Tennessee, but the tradition was stopped in 1999 when a Kentucky football player died in an alcohol-related car accident. Similarly, the Bourbon Barrel, between Kentucky and Indiana, was also retired. Kentucky and Louisville still play for the Governor's Cup. Comprised of marble, crystal, gold-plated brass, and solid pewter, it stands 33 inches tall, weighs 110 pounds, and cost $23,000.

2. *1A and 1B:* Coach Paul "Bear" Bryant had a unique way of telling apart twin brothers Harry and Larry Jones, who both lettered from 1950–52. Harry wore 1A and Larry wore 1B. Harry led the Wildcats in all-purpose yardage in 1951 with 964, while Larry led the team in kickoff returns (21.1 yards average) in 1952. Previously, in the 1900s, Kentucky had a pair of cousins who were both named William Rodes. William "Red Doc" Rodes lettered three years (1909, 1911–12) as a 140-pound halfback and defensive end. William "Black Doc" Rodes lettered two years (1915–16) as quarterback and also kicked.

3. *"The" Year:* When Kentucky football has a big season, the men's basketball team

has made a habit of following suit. In 1950, when football finished 10-1 and at the Sugar Bowl snapped Oklahoma's 31-game winning streak, Adolph Rupp led UK to its third national championship. In similar fashion, after the 1977 football team went 10-1, coach Joe B. Hall directed the basketball team to its fifth national title.

· 8 ·

South Carolina

THE SCHOOL

Location: Columbia, South Carolina
Founded: 1801
Enrollment: 23,772
Nickname: Fighting Gamecocks
Colors: Garnet and black
Mascot: Cocky
Stadium: Williams-Brice Stadium (80,250)
2005 officials: Dr. Andrew Sorensen, president; Dr. Russ Pate, faculty representative; Eric Hyman, athletics director

THE PROGRAM

National Championships: None
SEC Championships: None
Bowl appearances: 12 (3-9)
First season: 1892
College Football Hall of Fame (1): George Rogers, 1977–80, halfback, 1997
Heisman Winners (1): George Rogers, running back, 1980
National Honors: None
First-Team All-Americans: Frank Mincevich, G, 1954; Warren Muir, FB, 1969; Dick Harris, DB, 1970; John LeHeup, DT, 1972; Rick Sanford, DB, 1978; George Rogers, RB, 1979–80; Andrew Provence, DT, 1982; Del Wilkes, G, 1984; James Seawright, LB, 1984; Sterling Sharpe, WR, 1986–87; Sheldon Brown, DB, 2000; Kalimba Edwards, LB, 2001; Ko Simpson, DB, 2005
First-Team Academic All-Americans (CoSIDA): Mark Fryer, OL, 1987–88; Joe Reeves, LB, 1991
First-round NFL draftees: 8
Retired jerseys: 2 Sterling Sharpe; 37 Steve Wadiak; 38 George Rogers; 56 Mike Johnson
All-Time Teams (selected in 1992): Offense—G Steve Courson, 1973–76; G

Del Wilkes, 1980–81, 1983–84; T Dave DeCamilla, 1968–70; T Chuck Slaughter, 1978–81; C Bryant Meeks, 1945–46; C Mike McCabe, 1973–75; TE Jay Saldi, 1973–75; TE Willie Scott, 1977–80; WR Fred Zeigler, 1967–69; WR Sterling Sharpe, 1983–87; QB Jeff Grantz, 1973–75; RB Steve Wadiak, 1948–51; RB George Rogers, 1977–80; RB Harold Green, 1986–89; K Collin Mackie, 1987–90; KR Robert Brooks, 1988–91 **Defense**—DL John LeHeup, 1970–72; DL Emmanuel Weaver, 1980–81; DL Andrew Provence, 1980–82; DL Roy Hart, 1983–87; DL Kevin Hendrix, 1985–88; LB Ed Baxley, 1979–80; LB James Seawright, 1981–84; LB Corey Miller, 1989–90; DB Bobby Bryant, 1964–66; DB Dick Harris, 1969–71; DB Rick Sanford, 1975–78; DB Brad Edwards, 1984–87; P Max Runager, 1974, 1976–78 **Pre–World War II**—B Tatum Gressette, 1920–21; B Bru Boineau, 1928–30; B Earl Clay, 1931–33; B Fred Hambright, 1931–33; L Luke Hill, 1911–15; L Joe Wheeler, 1920–23; L Julian Beall, 1927–29; L Lou Sossamon, 1940–42; L Larry Craig, 1935–38; L Alex Urban, 1938–40; L Dominic Fusci, 1942–43; L Skimp Harrison, 1942–44

THE COACHES

W. A. Whaley, 1896, 1-3; W. P. Murphy, 1897, 0-3; W. Wertenbaker, 1898, 1-2; I. O. Hunt, 1899–90, 6-6; B. W. Dickson, 1901, 3-4; C. R. Williams, 1902–03, 14-3; Christie Benet, 1904–05, 1908–09; 14-15-3; Douglas McKay, 1907, 3-0; John H. Neff, 1910–11, 5-8-2; N. B. Edgerton, 1912–15, 19-13-3; Rice Warren, 1916, 3-6; Dixon Foster, 1917, 1919, 4-12-1; Frank Dobson, 1918, 2-1-1; Sol Metzger, 1920–24, 26-18-2; Branch Bocock, 1925–26, 13-7; Harry Lightsey, 1927, 4-5; Billy Lavall, 1928–34, 39-26-6; Don McCallister, 1935–37, 13-20-1; Rex Enright, 1938-42, 1946–55, 64-69-7; J. P. Moran, 1943, 5-2; William Newton, 1944, 3-4-2; Johnnie McMillan, 1945, 2-4-3; Warren Giese, 1956–60, 28-21-1; Marvin Bass, 1961–65, 17-29-4; Paul Dietzel, 1966–74, 42-53-1; Jim Carlen, 1975–81, 45-36-1; Richard Bell, 1982, 4-7; Joe Morrison, 1983–88, 39-28-3; Sparky Woods, 1989–93, 24-28-3; Brad Scott, 1995–98, 23-32-1; Lou Holtz, 1999–2004, 33-37; Steve Spurrier, 2005, 7-5
National Coach of the Year: Joe Morrison 1984; Lou Holtz 2000
SEC Coach of the Year, AP: Lou Holtz 2000. **Coaches:** Lou Holtz 2000
SEC Championships: None
National Championships: None

RECORDS

Rushing yards, game: 278, Brandon Bennett vs. East Tennessee State, Oct. 5, 1991 (31 carries)
Rushing yards, season: 1,894, George Rogers, 1980 (324 carries)
Rushing yards, career: 5,204, George Rogers, 1977–80 (954 carries)

Passing yards, game: 473, Steve Taneyhill vs. Mississippi State, Oct. 14, 1995 (38 of 44)

Passing yards, season: 3,206, Todd Ellis, 1987 (241 of 432)

Passing yards, career: 9,953, Todd Ellis, 1986–89 (747 of 1,350)

Receiving yards, game: 206, Zola Davis vs. Vanderbilt, Oct. 24, 1998 (14 receptions)

Receiving yards, season: 1,143, Sidney Rice, 2005 (70 receptions)

Receiving yards, career: 2,497, Sterling Sharpe, 1983, 1985–87 (169 receptions)

Points, game: 24, Stanley Pritchett vs. Mississippi State, Oct. 14, 1995 (six touchdowns); Mike Dingle vs. Virginia Tech, Sept. 22, 1990 (six touchdowns)

Points, season: 113, Collin Mackie, 1987 (25 field goals, 38 PATs)

Points, career: 330, Collin Mackie, 1987–90 (72 field goals, 114 PATs)

Ask a fan of South Carolina what makes football special there, and he or she will almost certainly say: "Loyalty."

How else can you explain Williams-Brice Stadium consistently attracting more than 80,000 fans, putting it in the top 12 nationally for attendance, to support a program that has won no national championships, one conference title, and just three bowl games since 1892?

Put simply, the Gamecocks are college football's equivalent to the Chicago Cubs, and similarly even have an animal curse supposedly keeping them from greatness. With the Cubs, it's the famous goat, which has nothing on South Carolina's chicken.

According to local legend, Ben "Pitchfork" Tillman, South Carolina's governor from 1890–94 who helped establish Clemson, is responsible for than a hundred years of mediocrity on the gridiron. It originated from a dispute between Tillman and the state legislature, which didn't want to support Clemson. Growing increasingly frustrated because the legislature wouldn't approve a land grant for the state's poorer farmers, Tillman supposedly slammed a pitchfork into the ground of the Columbia campus and declared it "cursed."

(*Note:* Tillman was known as "Pitchfork Ben" because he said in a speech that he wanted to "poke" President Grover Cleveland with a pitchfork to prod him into action regarding economic problems in the South. He was also censured in 1902 while serving in the United States Senate for assaulting fellow Senator John L. McLaurin, also of South Carolina, in the Senate chamber.)

At one point during a recent season, the university hired a witch doctor to attempt to remove the curse prior to a game against Georgia. Naturally, the Gamecocks lost, and the football team continued its search for an identity and prominence.

Though a founding member of the Atlantic Coast Conference in 1953, South Carolina left in 1971 due to disputes over the conference's recruiting regulations and the dominance of the four North Carolina schools—North Carolina, North Carolina State, Duke, and Wake Forest. Until 1983, the school competed as a major independent, when it joined the Metro conference in all sports other than football. When the Southeastern Conference was looking for a twelfth member in

1991, South Carolina finally found itself in the right place at the right time and began conference play the following season.

And just like the baseball team from the Windy City, fans of the Gamecocks still love them nonetheless.

"I had great feelings for South Carolina, I had great hopes for it," said Sparky Woods, who was head coach during the transition to the SEC (1989–93). "They had the means to build that kind of tradition and that was an exciting thing to me. When I went to Appalachian State, they didn't have any at that either. When I left there, we had won something like 19 conference games in a row, three conference championships. That was a fun thing to be a part of something new, first time ever kind of thing. But it had its own set of problems, obviously. It's just understanding the situation. Sometimes it's a hard job having a great tradition where they won all the time, like [Alabama]. But I do think South Carolina has the potential to build that kind of thing.

"Joining the conference was a big deal. We went from playing Duke in our first game to playing Georgia."

The tradition began on December 24, 1892, with a 44-0 loss in Charleston to Furman. The team wouldn't score its first point until nearly two years later, and it wouldn't win a bowl game for 103 years. The first time South Carolina posted a winning record for four straight seasons (1902–05), the trustees abolished the sport on campus. That ban lasted only one year, but it still set the program back. Nearly three decades later, coach Billy Laval (1928–34) set the school standard by posting a winning record in each of his seven seasons, the best of which was a 6-2-2 finish in 1928.

The pride and joy of the program is George Rogers, who won the Heisman Trophy in 1980. The running back was the nation's second-leading rusher in 1979, and backed that up with a landmark 1,894 yards as a senior, in the process gaining 100 yards in 22 consecutive games. Rogers solidified his status as the Heisman's front-runner by gaining more than 140 yards in back-to-back road games at national powers Southern California and Michigan, and he led South Carolina to the Gator Bowl against Pittsburgh. Subsequently, the New Orleans Saints made him the first-overall selection in the 1981 NFL Draft.

"George Rogers was the nicest guy you would ever want to meet," play-by-play announcer Bob Fulton said. "He also happened to be the best player we ever had."

Some consider the Michigan game the greatest victory in school history. South Carolina recovered a fumble in its end zone and then drove to the winning touchdown for the 17-14 final score. Rogers finished with 142 yards on 36 carries.

Another candidate is the 1981 game against No. 3 North Carolina. Quarterback Gordon Beckham completed 16 of 17 passes to lead the 31-13 upset.

A final possibility is the 1952 game at Virginia, sponsored by the Shriners and dubbed the Oyster Bowl. With Notre Dame transfer Dick Balka sparking the comeback with his passing, South Carolina recovered a fumble inside its own 5-yard line, and then another in the end zone to score its third touchdown in less than two minutes during the fourth quarter to win 21-14.

Considering its history, that type of game was the kind South Carolina usually lost.

Before Rogers, the school rushing record was held by Steve "The Cadillac" Wadiak, who had 2,878 yards despite never playing football in high school. Instead, he learned the game in the Navy during World War II. Shortly after graduating in 1951, he was killed in an automobile accident before playing a single game as a professional. South Carolina's most valuable player award is named in his honor.

It's just one of many tales of heartbreak the Gamecocks have endured, both on and off the field.

For example, in 1984 coach Joe Morrison's team got on an unprecedented roll, defeating Georgia, Pittsburgh, Kansas State, and Florida State, and it even won at Notre Dame to be ranked second behind Washington. However, the Gamecocks surprisingly slipped at Navy, a game that was rescheduled on the road so South Carolina could have an extra home date the following season. Doubling the disappointment was that Washington lost on the same day, depriving the Gamecocks of their first No. 1 ranking. South Carolina went on to rally from an 18-point deficit to defeat Clemson 22-21, only to lose 21-14 to Oklahoma State in the Gator Bowl and finish No. 11. The Gamecocks mustered only 71 yards of total offense in the first half and lost three of six fumbles, but Quinton Lewis and Mike Hold threw touchdown passes, to Chris Wade and Ira Hillary, respectively, for a late lead that was answered by an 88-yard touchdown drive by the Cowboys.

Maybe it was "Black Magic"—the nickname associated with defensive coordinator Tom Gadd (1983–86), who always wore the color on the sideline. Gadd was also credited for giving players another nickname, the "Fire Ants," after he described the defense as looking like a "bunch of fire ants getting after the football." Whatever it was, the years 1979 to 1984 saw some of the best teams in school history, with three winning seasons and one .500 season, capped by the only 10-win campaign in 1984, which fans considered "magic."

For the most part, those are the high points for a program that has an all-time record under .500:

- Since the Associated Press began ranking teams in 1936, South Carolina has finished in the top 20 only five times and never in the Top 10.
- The Gamecocks have never played in any of the major bowls: Rose, Sugar, Orange, Fiesta, and Cotton. Seventy-two schools had been to nine or more bowl games, and of them South Carolina's .250 bowl winning percentage through 2005 ranked last. The lone conference title was the ACC in 1969 after finishing 7-4.
- Though Paul Dietzel probably came closest, South Carolina has essentially never had a signature head coach, with the school career record for wins just 64 (Rex Enright—and yes, he had the most losses as well with 69). Starting with W. A. Whaley in 1896 (there's no coach of record beforehand), South Carolina has had 32 different head coaches, only five of whom stayed more

than five seasons. Of the 32 coaches, 21 had losing records. No South Carolina coach has gone on to another Division I-A head coaching job.

- Of the 56 programs that have played more than 1,000 games all-time, only four have scored fewer points. Of the 46 teams that had played at least 1,050 games prior to the 2005 season, only South Carolina and Northwestern failed to reach 500 wins.
- Heading into the 2005 season, The Citadel and Davidson College each had defeated South Carolina more times than the Gamecocks had defeated SEC Eastern Division rivals Florida and Tennessee combined.
- Only three times since 1992 has any non-probation member of the SEC failed to win two or more games in a season: South Carolina twice and Kentucky once.

And still the fans have packed the stadium, demonstrating endless loyalty in the face of adversity.

Williams-Brice was originally constructed as part of the New Deal's Works Progress Administration in 1934, seating 17,600. Since then, it's seen numerous renovations and additions, including the enlarging to more than 54,000 in 1972 that was financed by the estate of Mrs. Martha Williams Brice, whose husband, Thomas, had been a letterman (1922–23). Capacity was increased to 80,250 in 1996, but somehow 85,000 crammed in to see the 2001 Clemson game (a 20-15 victory). The most recent addition to the south end zone was a 30,000-square-foot football complex. The $3 million structure was completed in 2004.

Like any football program, South Carolina has its legends from the field, players who are revered by fans. They include Rogers; two-time All-American Sterling Sharpe, the Gamecocks' all-time leading pass receiver with 169 career catches for 2,497 yards; and Dan Reeves, who holds the record for most Super Bowl appearances as a player or a coach with nine.

"Difficulties in life are intended to make us better, not bitter," Reeves said.

Quarterback Tommy Suggs (1968–70) never lost to Clemson. Halfback Alex Hawkins was the 1958 ACC Player of the Year, which Billy Gambrell won four years later. Fullback Bill Wohrman (1953–54) and tackle Jim Moss (1961–62) were the only players in team history to win multiple Jacobs Blocking Trophies as best blocker in the state. Additionally, the practice fields are named after Enright, not so much because he served in World War II or his coaching record, but due to his beating Clemson in seven of his last 10 seasons.

There's also quarterback Todd Ellis, who in throwing for 9,953 yards set more than 20 school passing records in leading the Gamecocks to the 1987 Gator Bowl and the 1988 Liberty Bowl. Other prominent names include Robert Brooks, Duce Staley, Brandon Bennett, Jeff Grantz, Troy Williamson, Andrew Provence, Sheldon Brown, and John Abraham. Many are in the Carolina Athletic Hall of Fame, along with Earl Bennett, Ed Boineau, Bobby Bryant, Earl Clary, Larry Craig, Leon Cunningham, King Dixon, Earl Dunham, Brad Edwards, Dominic Fusci, Johnny Gramling, Harold Green, Tatum Gressette, Fred Hambright, Dickie Harris, Luther Hill, Kevin Long, Harold Mauney, Bryant Meeks Jr., Frank Mincevich,

Jim Moss, Warren Muir, Ed Pitts, Mackie Prickett, Bill Rogers, Rick Sanford, James Seawright, Larry Smith, Lou Sossamon, Bishop Strickland, Alfred Van Kolnitz, J. R. Wilburn, Roger "Red" Wilson, and Fred Zeigler.

Dondrial Pinkins added his name to Gamecock lore in 2003 when he became the only person in SEC history to throw both a 99-yard touchdown pass and a 98-yard touchdown pass during the same season. The league-tying record was to Williamson against Virginia. The "shorter" pass went to Matthew Thomas against Ole Miss.

In 2004, the most famous player on the team was wide receiver Tim Frisby, a 39-year-old father of six and a 20-year Army veteran who had served with the 82nd Airborne Division. Exempt from National Collegiate Athletic Association age rules because of his military service, Frisby walked on and made the team (prompting coach Lou Holtz to joke that was because of the attendance boost his children could provide). One day during summer practice, someone put a strip of tape above his locker with the word "Pops" on it. The nickname stuck, literally and figuratively. During the 2005 reason, he caught a pass for 9 yards.

Otherwise, most of program's memorable moments have to do with personalities or recent instances that inspired catchphrases.

For example, "Fade to Glory" made backup Erik Kimrey a South Carolina folk hero, even though he was the backup quarterback on the 2000 team. When Phil Petty sustained a sprained ankle in the fourth quarter with the Gamecocks trailing Mississippi State 19-13, Kimrey supposedly told Holtz, "I can throw the fade route." He did—perfectly to receiver Jermale Kelly—for a touchdown, and South Carolina went on to win 23-19.

"Lay Down Dogs" originated in a 1993 game against Georgia. Down 21-17 in the closing moments, South Carolina had fourth down at the Georgia 1, prompting Bulldogs broadcaster Larry Munson to say, "Lay down Dawgs. Lay down Dawgs. Don't get up," in hopes time would expire before South Carolina could pull off another play. Tailback Brandon Bennett took the handoff, with Munson calling: "The great back goes over the top. He scores and breaks our hearts."

Quarterback Steve Taneyhill was one of the most colorful players to suit up for South Carolina, and not just because he compiled 8,380 yards of total offense and led the Gamecocks to their first bowl victory in nine tries—24-21 over West Virginia in the 1994 Carquest Bowl at Joe Robbie Stadium near Miami. Taneyhill wore an earring and had a long ponytail that stuck out of his helmet. He practiced his golf swing during pauses in the game and hit fungoes with an imaginary baseball bat after touchdowns. After a victory at Clemson's Memorial Stadium, Taneyhill autographed the Tiger paw in the middle of the field. When asked by a sportswriter how he would like to remembered by South Carolina fans, he replied: "That crazy Yankee quarterback." Taneyhill hailed from Altoona, Pennsylvania.

(As an interesting side note, Taneyhill's career began as a freshman in 1992 when five straight losses supposedly resulted in what was described a "players' revolt." After inserting Taneyhill, South Carolina won five of its last six games, including 24-13 to Clemson, and coach Woods received a one-year reprieve.)

In the mid-1980s, many South Carolina fans had bumper stickers proclaiming, "If it ain't swaying, we ain't playing." It's a reference to the "harmonic vibrations" that caused the newly constructed upper deck on the east side to sway during exciting moments. Eventually, the phenomenon was blamed on the marching band for playing the song "Louie, Louie," which school officials subsequently banned. When the band director defied the order, he was censured, the band was moved to another section of the stadium, and the student section was relocated. Although some fans claimed to have feared for their lives, the stadium remained packed, and engineering officials repeatedly signed off on the structure's safety.

In part because of the limited in-state recruiting base, with two top programs competing for talent in a small state—not to mention desirable powers in neighboring states—South Carolina has on three occasions hired someone who both won a national title and coached a Heisman Trophy winner at another school.

The first was Dietzel, who had been at LSU. From 1966 to 1974, he provided legitimacy to a program that had endured a 15-game winless streak in 1963–64, even though his first season resulted in a 1-9 finish. By finishing 6-0 in the ACC in 1969, the Gamecocks won their first (and still only) conference title, and with a 7-4 overall record received an invitation to the Peach Bowl (a 14-3 loss to West Virginia). Dietzel had three winning seasons, the last in 1973 at 7-4, but like so many others had an overall record below .500 at 42-53-1.

"It's a short trip from the penthouse to the outhouse," Dietzel said. But his most famous quote may have been, "You can learn more character on the two-yard line than anywhere else in life."

Holtz had similar success after a 0-11 finish during his first season in 1999.

"First we will be best, then we will be first," Holtz said.

He backed it up with records of 8-4 and 9-3, finishing second in the Eastern Division in 2000 and 2001. Both seasons concluded with victories against Ohio State in the Outback Bowl—24-7 and 31-28—with the 17 victories the most ever in a two-year span.

"I can't believe God put us on this earth to be ordinary," Holtz said.

South Carolina finished in the Top 25 under Holtz, who became the only coach in NCAA history to lead six different programs to bowl games, and likewise was the only coach to have four different programs finish ranked in the Top 20. However, critics claimed he also may have set the record for programs involved in NCAA investigations and/or probation during or immediately after his reign, which happened at Arkansas, Minnesota, and Notre Dame. He retired after the 2004 season with a 33-37 record leading the Gamecocks.

"We have the greatest fans in the world," Holtz said. "We raise more money per win than any school in America."

Although Holtz's tenure ended under a cloud of disappointment, with his final game marred by a vicious pregame fight with Clemson that resulted in both teams withdrawing from bowl eligibility, twelve of his players being arrested before the start of following season (and even more dismissed from the team), and the NCAA placing the program on three years of probation, Gamecock fans went into 2005 more optimistic than ever.

On November 23, 2004, South Carolina named Steve Spurrier its new head coach, prompting every other Eastern Division coach to mutter words that can't be reprinted here. Though Spurrier had been unsuccessful in the National Football League with the Washington Redskins, his college resume included a .777 winning percentage, six SEC championships, one ACC title, and a national championship at Florida.

He had the all-time highest winning percentage in SEC play, led the Gators to 12 consecutive Top 15 finishes in the Associated Press poll, and was 11-1 against South Carolina's second-biggest rival, Georgia.

"I've got my enthusiasm, my passion, my fire. . . . I've got that back in me," Spurrier said at his introductory press conference. "I'm excited to be here and ready to go. I pledge to you you're going to get my best shot.

"I know our history is not the greatest in the world as far as winning the conference, but we've got everything here. I'd like to borrow a phrase from the Boston Red Sox, 'Why not us?' Why can't we get to the top of the SEC? Certainly that's going to be my dream."

Spurrier even took a stab at debunking the Chicken Curse during his preseason press conference at Media Days in Birmingham, pointing out that both 1969, when South Carolina won the ACC title, and 2005 were the Year of the Rooster on the Chinese calendar.

"I'm just saying, we've got the rooster on our side. . . . That's all I'm saying, we got it really going for us now," he said, smiling. If anything, he embellished the mascot's name better than any other coach in South Carolina history—Cocky.

Although South Carolina didn't win the SEC East Division in 2005, the "Head Ball Coach" (a famous phrase of Spurrier's) probably did more with less than any other coach in the SEC, while simultaneously setting the groundwork for future success. Gamecock Club donations went up more than $1 million over the previous year's total, each of the first three games were nationally televised, and the Gamecocks went from losing three of their first five games to winning five of the final six. Two of those victories came against ranked teams, No. 23 Tennessee (16-15) and No. 12 Florida (30-22).

After being named the SEC Coach of the Year by the Associated Press, Spurrier was able to take a different approach while composing the following letter:

December 8, 2005
Dear Gamecock Fans:

Thank you for your tremendous support of Carolina Football throughout the 2005 season. Your support helped propel us to a 7-4 record and a second place finish in the SEC Eastern Division.

With your support, we were able to win five straight Southeastern Conference games for the first time in school history, win at Tennessee for the first time ever and defeat Florida for the first time since the 1930s.

Now we have a chance to finish the season on a high note at the Independence Bowl in Shreveport, La. on Friday, December 30, when we take on the Missouri

Tigers out of the Big 12 Conference. Our team is excited about this game and we hope you are too.

Over the years, Carolina has earned the reputation of having some of the best fans in the country and we look for a great turnout of Gamecock fans at the bowl game. We hope you will make plans to join us in Shreveport, color the town Garnet and Black and cheer us on to victory. However, if you are unable to attend the game, you can still help out by purchasing tickets to the game and donating them to the service men and women stationed in the Shreveport area. This is a great way for you to support your university and assist the people who serve our country.

Thanks again and we will see you in Shreveport.

THREE THINGS THAT STAND OUT ABOUT
SOUTH CAROLINA FOOTBALL

1. *The Cockaboose Railroad:* Located approximately 50 yards from the main entrance to 80,250-seat Williams-Brice Stadium, the 22 luxurious rail-bound cabooses may be the ultimate in decadent tailgating. They originally opened in 1990 for $40,000 each, and there's now a waiting list. A rival company recently opened seven cabooses in a parking lot down the street for $200,000 each. They sold in two weeks, and most owners spent more than that on the interior design.
2. *The Odyssey Opening:* The team assembles in the southwest corner tunnel as the theme song from *2001—A Space Odyssey* (also known as Richard Strauss' "Thus Spake Zarathustra") is played. As the music soars over the stands, the Gamecocks take the field.
3. *The Mascot:* After having numerous nicknames during the early years, the football players were described in a 1920 newspaper article as having "fought like gamecocks," and it stuck. The following year, Columbia's morning newspaper, *The State*, shortened it to one word. FYI, a gamecock is a pugnacious rooster, bred for fighting. While cockfighting has been outlawed, for years it was considered acceptable. General Thomas Sumter, a Revolutionary War figure from South Carolina, was also nicknamed "The Gamecock." Of course, the fort named after him saw the first engagement of the Civil War, on April 12, 1861.

· 9 ·

Tennessee

THE SCHOOL

Location: Knoxville, Tennessee
Founded: 1794
Enrollment: 25,515
Nickname: Volunteers
Colors: Orange and white
Mascot: Smokey
Stadium: Neyland Stadium/Shields-Watkins Field (104,079)
2005 officials: Dr. John Peterson, president; Dr. Todd Diacon, faculty representative; Mike Hamilton, athletics director

THE PROGRAM

National Championships (2): 1951, 1998
The "Other" Four: The Official NCAA Football Records Book also recognizes Tennessee as producing national champions in 1938, 1940, 1950, and 1967
SEC Championships (13): 1938, 1939, 1940, 1946, 1951, 1956, 1967, 1969, 1985, 1989, 1990, 1997, 1998
Bowl appearances: 45 (24-21)
First season: 1891
College Football Hall of Fame (22): Doug Atkins, 1950–52, tackle, inducted 1985; George Cafego, 1937–39, halfback, 1969; Steve DeLong, 1962–64, middle guard, 1993; Doug Dickey, 1964–69, coach, 2003; Bobby Dodd, 1928–30, quarterback, 1959; Nathan Dougherty, 1906–09, guard, 1967; Frank Emanuel, 1963–65, linebacker, 2004; Beattie Feathers, 1931–33, halfback, 1955; Herman Hickman, 1929–31, guard, 1959; Bob Johnson, 1965–67, center, 1989; Steve Kiner, 1967–69, linebacker, 1999; Hank Lauricella, 1949–51, halfback, 1981; Johnny Majors, 1954–56, halfback, 1987; Gene McEver, 1928–29, 1931, halfback, 1954; John Michels, 1950–52, guard, 1996; Ed Molinski, 1938–40, guard, 1990; Bob Neyland, 1926–52, coach, 1956; Joe Steffy, 1944, guard, 1956; Bob Suffridge, 1938–40, guard, 1961; Reggie White, 1980–83, defensive tackle, 2002; Bowden Wyatt, 1936–38, end (coach 1955–62), 1972

Heisman Winners: None

National Honors: Bob Suffridge, 1940 Knute Rockne Memorial Trophy (outstanding lineman); Steve DeLong, 1964 Outland Trophy (outstanding interior lineman); Peyton Manning, 1997 Maxwell Award (outstanding player), Davey O'Brien Award (best quarterback), and Johnny Unitas Golden Arm Award (best senior quarterback); John Henderson, 2000 Outland Trophy

First-Team All-Americans: Gene McEver, HB, 1929; Bobby Dodd, QB, 1930; Herman Hickman, G, 1931; Beattie Feathers, HB, 1933; Bowden Wyatt, E, 1938; Bob Suffridge, G, 1938–40; George Cafego, HB, 1938–39; Ed Molinski, G, 1939–40; Abe Shires, T, 1939; Bob Foxx, HB, 1940; Bob Dobelstein, G, 1944; Dick Huffman, T, 1946; Ted Daffer, G, 1950–51; Bud Sherrod, E, 1950; Hank Lauricella, HB, 1951; Bill Pearman, T, 1951; Doug Atkins, T, 1952; John Michels, G, 1952; Darris McCord, T, 1954; Johnny Majors, HB, 1956; Kyle (Buddy) Cruze, E, 1956; Buddy Johnson, G, 1957; Steve DeLong, G, 1963–64; Frank Emanuel, LB, 1965; Paul Naumoff, LB, 1966; Austin Denney, E, 1966; Ron Widby, P, 1966; Bob Johnson, C, 1966–67; Albert Dorsey, DB, 1967; Richmond Flowers, WB, 1967; Charlie Rosenfelder, G, 1968; Steve Kiner, LB, 1968–69; Jim Weatherford, DB, 1968; Chip Kell, G, 1969–70; Jack Reynolds, LB, 1969; Jackie Walker, LB, 1970–71; Bobby Majors, DB, 1971; Jamie Rotella, LB, 1972; Conrad Graham, DB, 1972; Ricky Townsend, K, 1972–73; Eddie Brown, DB, 1973; Larry Seivers, E, 1975–76; Roland James, DB, 1979; Willie Gault, WR, 1982; Reggie White, DT, 1983; Jimmy Colquitt, P, 1983; Bill Mayo, G, 1984; Tim McGee, G, 1984; Chris White, S, 1985; Harry Galbreath, G, 1987; Keith Delong, LB, 1988; Eric Still, G, 1989; Antone Davis, T, 1990; Dale Carter, DB, 1991; Carl Pickens, WR, 1991; John Becksvoort, K, 1993; Leonard Little, LB, 1997; Peyton Manning, QB, 1997; Al Wilson, LB, 1998; Cosey Coleman, OL, 1999; Deon Grant, DB, 1999; Raynoch Thompson, LB, 1999; John Henderson, DT, 2000–01; Travis Stephens, RB, 2001; Dustin Colquitt, P, 2003; Michael Munoz, OL, 2004; Kevin Burnett, LB, 2004; Jesse Mahelona, DT, 2004

First-Team Academic All-Americans (CoSIDA): Charles Rader, T, 1956; Bill Johnson, G, 1957; Mack Gentry, DT, 1965; Bob Johnson, C, 1967; Tim Priest, DB, 1970; Timothy Irwin, T, 1980; Mike Terry, DL, 1982; Peyton Manning, QB, 1997

First-round NFL draftees: 36

Retired jerseys: 16 Peyton Manning; 32 Bill Nowling; 49 Rudy Klarer; 61 Willis Tucker; 62 Clyde Fuson, 91 Doug Atkins, 92 Reggie White

All-Centennial Team (selected by fan vote and a panel of school officials):

Offense—G Harry Galbreath, 1984–87; G Eric Still, 1988–89; T Tim Irwin, 1978–80; T Bruce Wilkerson, 1983–86; C Bob Johnson, 1965–67; WR Stanley Morgan, 1973–76; WR Larry Seivers, 1974–76; WR Willie Gault, 1979–82; QB Condredge Holloway, 1972–74; B Hank Lauricella, 1948–51; B Johnny Majors, 1954–56; RB Curt Watson, 1969–71; RB Reggie Cobb, 1987–88; K Fuad Reveiz, 1981–84 **Defense**—DE Doug Atkins, 1950–52; DE Dale Jones, 1983–86; DT Reggie White, 1980–83; DT Marion Hobby, 1986–89; G Steve

DeLong, 1962–64; LB Steve Kiner, 1967–69; LB Jack Reynolds, 1967–69; LB Keith DeLong, 1985–88; DB Bobby Majors, 1969–71; DB Eddie Brown, 1971–73; DB Roland James, 1976–79; DB Bill Bates, 1979–82; P Craig Colquitt 1975–77

THE COACHES

J. A. Pierce, 1899–1900, 8-4-1; George Kelley, 1901, 3-3-2; H. F. Fisher, 1902–03, 10-7; S. D. Crawford, 1904, 3-5-1; J. D. DePree, 1905–06, 4-11-3; George Levene, 1907–09, 15-10-3; Andrew A. Stone, 1910, 3-5-1; Z. G. Clevenger, 1911–15, 26-15-2; John R. Bender, 1916–20, 18-5-4; M. B. Banks, 1921–25, 27-15-3; Robert R. Neyland, 1926–34, 1936–40, 1946–52, 62-15-5; W. H. (Bill) Britton, 1935, 4-5; John H. Barnhill, 1941–45, 33-6; Harvey L. Robinson, 1953–54, 10-10-1; Bowden Wyatt, 1955–62, 49-29-4; Jim McDonald, 1963, 5-5; Doug Dickey, 1964–69, 46-15-4; Bill Battle, 1970–76, 59-22-4; Johnny Majors, 1977–92, 115-62-8; Phillip Fulmer, 1992–2005, 128-37

National Coach of the Year: Bowden Wyatt 1956; Phillip Fulmer 1998

SEC Coach of the Year, AP: Robert Neyland 1951; Bowden Wyatt 1956; Doug Dickey 1967; Johnny Majors 1985; Phillip Fulmer 1998 **Coaches:** Robert Neyland 1936, 1938, 1950; John Barnhill 1944; Bowden Wyatt 1956; Doug Dickey 1965, 1967; Johnny Majors 1985; Phillip Fulmer 1998

SEC Championships: Robert Neyland 5, Johnny Majors 3, Doug Dickey 2, Phillip Fulmer 2, Bowden Wyatt 1

National Championships: Robert Neyland 1, Phillip Fulmer 1

RECORDS

Rushing yards, game: 294, Chuck Webb vs. Ole Miss, Nov. 18, 1989 (35 carries)

Rushing yards, season: 1,464, Travis Stephens, 2001 (291 carries)

Rushing yards, career: 3,078, Travis Henry, 1997–2000 (556 carries)

Passing yards, game: 523, Peyton Manning vs. Kentucky, Nov. 22, 1997 (25 of 35)

Passing yards, season: 3,819, Peyton Manning, 1997 (287 of 477)

Passing yards, career: 11,201, Peyton Manning, 1994–97 (863 of 1,381)

Receiving yards, game: 256, Kelley Washington vs. LSU, Sept. 29, 2001 (11 receptions)

Receiving yards, season: 1,170, Marcus Nash, 1997 (76 receptions)

Receiving yards, career: 2,814, Joey Kent, 1993–96 (183 receptions)

Points, game: 24, six tied

Points, season: 130, Gene McEver, 1929 (21 touchdowns, four PATs)

Points, career: 371, Jeff Hall, 1995–98 (61 field goals, 188 PATs)

When most people think of the University of Tennessee, what usually comes to mind is the trademark "T," the color orange, and a game-day setting that may be second to none.

But what they should be thinking about is the general.

When he took the job in 1926, Robert Neyland (pronounced NEE-land) was also an ROTC instructor who had graduated from West Point and served in France during World War I. Twice he was called upon to leave the football team, first for a peacetime tour in Panama and then by a tour of duty as a brigadier general in the Pacific theater during World War II. Twice he came back to the Volunteers.

As a coach, Neyland was known for organization, discipline, and teamwork. He had a fondness for tough defensive play in particular, and he helped put Tennessee at the forefront of college football again and again.

"If Neyland could score a touchdown against you, he had you beat," said Herman Hickman, one of Neyland's players who went on to join the original staff of *Sports Illustrated*. "If he could score two, he had you in a rout."

Neyland's success boiled down to seven basic principles, which he called his "Maxims." Part of the Volunteers' pregame ritual is to recite them before taking the field:

1. The team that makes the fewest mistakes will win.
2. Play for and make the breaks and when one comes your way, score.
3. If at first the game—or the breaks—go against you, don't let up . . . put on more steam.
4. Protect our kickers, our QB, our lead, and our ball game.
5. Ball, oskie, cover, block, cut and slice, pursue, and gang tackle . . . for this is the winning edge.
6. Press the kicking game. Here is where the breaks are made.
7. Carry the fight to our opponent and keep it there for 60 minutes.

FYI, *oskie* is the signal used when a Tennessee player intercepts the pass; he hollers, "Oskie score," thus alerting teammates to turn and block because now "we have the ball."

Tennessee football goes back to 1891, months before Neyland was born, when the team lost to Sewanee 24-0 under less than ideal conditions in Chattanooga. Tennessee wouldn't score its first victory until the following year, 25-0 over Maryville, and it took another turn of the calendar to 1893 before the first win at home, 32-0, again over Maryville.

After finishing 2-4 that season, which included losses of 70-0 at Trinity (today known as Duke), 64-0 at Wake Forest, 60-0 at North Carolina, and 56-0 at home to Kentucky A&M, only two players returned to campus in 1894. In October the athletic association decided to drop football, and the practice field was deemed unusable (it was being graded and improved).

Senior W. B. Stokely, who had transferred from Wake Forest, organized a club team to keep interest going until the sport was reinstated in 1896, when Tennessee finished 4-0. After the 1898 season was canceled due to the Spanish-

American War, J. A. Pierce was hired as the first full-time coach. His team finished 5-2 in 1899 and 3-2-1 the following year. Still, the program produced lackluster results, going through seven head coaches between 1899 and 1911.

Former Pennsylvania player George Levene (1907–09) was the first coach to win seven games in a season, doing so twice; but it was Z. G. Clevenger, a former Indiana player who introduced the Vols to a straight T-formation, who led Tennessee both to its first victory against Vanderbilt, 16-14 for homecoming, and first championship in the Southern Intercollegiate Athletic Association. Outscoring opponents 374 to 37, Tennessee finished 9-0 in 1914 (Clevenger returned to Indiana in 1923 and remained there until he retired). Clevenger's replacement, John Bender, nearly matched the mark with an 8-0-1 season in 1916 (featuring six shutouts) and a 7-2 finish in 1920.

M. B. Banks took over in 1921, the same year Tennessee first played in the Southern Conference. During his five-year reign, the team participated in its first game at Shields-Watkins Field (which later became better known as Neyland Stadium) and posted an eight-win season in 1922.

Inspired by the thriving daisies that grew in the area near the stadium known as the hill, Tennessee's official school color became orange in 1891, though the football team didn't wear it until the first game of the 1922 season, when the Volunteers crushed Emory & Henry, 50-0.

But then came the man who changed everything at Tennessee, which had lost 18 of its first 21 games against the cross-state rival. Dean Nathan Dougherty, the faculty chairman of athletics, went from proclaiming: "Even the score with Vanderbilt; do something about our terrible standing in the series," to calling Neyland's hiring "the best move I ever made."

Neyland's first stint with the Vols was from 1926 to 1934, when he held the military rank of captain and the team posted an incredible record of 76-7-5.

The Vols lost to Vanderbilt in his debut season and finished 8-1, but the real turnaround came against Alabama the following year. Sparked by tailback Gene McEver—the "Bristol Blizzard," who was Tennessee's first All-American—returning the opening kickoff 98 yards for a touchdown, the Vols held on for a 15-13 victory in Tuscaloosa. Buddy Hackman did the same thing the following week against Washington & Lee, and Tennessee went on to have an unbeaten season, 8-0-1 (with the tie coming against Vanderbilt), and win the Southern Conference championship.

Tennessee didn't lose again until October 18, 1930, 18-6 at Alabama—a span of 33 games—but failed to secure another title due to a tie in each of the three seasons the streak encompassed. However, the Vols played their first postseason game on December 5, 1931, in the New York Charity Bowl at Yankee Stadium. Beattie "Big Chief" Feathers scored on a 65-yard run, and Deke Brackett had a 75-yard touchdown while Herman Hickman keyed the defense in a 13-0 shutout of New York University.

In the midst of a 28-game unbeaten streak, Neyland secured his second Southern Conference Championship in 1932 after finishing 9-0-1. Naturally, the tie came against Vanderbilt, but Tennessee had also developed a knack for tying Kentucky in three of the previous four seasons.

"I'm still trying to figure out those Wildcat games," McEver said while shaking his head years after finishing his career 27-0-3.

When 1932 team captain Malcolm Aiken was asked what he remembered most about Tennessee football, he replied: "The infectious germ of being a winner."

After being dispatched to Panama, with Bill Britton taking his place for a 4-5 season in 1935, Major Neyland returned and put together the nucleus of a team that would dominate college football from 1938–40, winning three SEC championships and two national titles, though not consensus (Texas Christian had that honor in 1938 and Minnesota in 1940).

The first title came following a perfect 10-0 season in which the Vols outscored opponents 293-16. Ranked No. 2, Tennessee received an invitation to play a much bigger Oklahoma squad in the Orange Bowl. Though the two sides combined for more than 200 yards in penalties, the Vols recorded their eighth shutout of the season. Bob Foxx and Babe Wood ran in touchdowns to highlight the 17-0 victory.

Led by George "Bad News" Cafego, Ed Molinski, and Bob Suffridge, the 1939 team shut out all 10 opponents in the regular season, including Alabama and Vanderbilt, with tailback Johnny Butler making a memorable 56-yard touchdown run that took him from sideline to sideline against the Crimson Tide.

Neyland called it a "modern major miracle," and no team has equaled the feat since. He also called Cafego a "practice bum. On the practice field he couldn't do anything right, but for two hours on a Saturday afternoon he did everything an All-American is supposed to do."

Undefeated in 23 games, unscored against in 15, and with an edge in points of 212-0 that season, Tennessee was off to face Southern California in the Rose Bowl. But without Cafego—who had sustained a knee injury in the 34-0 victory against The Citadel—and Suffridge, the Trojans controlled the game, racking up 229 rushing yards for a 14-0 victory.

Undaunted, Neyland's team had another championship run in it, but when Alabama scored a touchdown in the second quarter of their 1940 meeting, it ended a streak of 71 consecutive quarters in the regular season without yielding a point, dating back to second quarter of the 1938 LSU game. The streak still stands as an NCAA record (FYI, the Vols defeated the Crimson Tide 27-12).

Despite being heavily favored against Boston College in the Sugar Bowl, undefeated No. 4 Tennessee had two first-half drives stopped deep in Golden Eagles territory. When Boston College's "Chuckin'" Charlie O'Rourke raised his arm to pass and then ran—a play coach Frank Leahy said he had seen Tennessee run—he scored from 24 yards out for the game-winning touchdown and 19-13 victory.

At the conclusion of the 1940 season, Neyland was called back into military service. John Barnhill, a former Tennessee player who would later coach at Arkansas, took over. The winning ways continued with an 8-2 finish in 1941, followed by a 9-1-1 season that ended with a 14-7 victory over Tulsa in the Sugar Bowl. Quarterback Glenn Dobbs led the Hurricanes, who were outgained in rushing 208 yards to minus-39.

It was under Barnhill that Tennessee had a chance to redeem itself in the 1945 Rose Bowl after a 7-0-1 season that included its first night game (a 13-0 win at LSU). But just like their meeting five years previous, the Volunteers couldn't score against Southern California and lost 25-0.

When General Neyland returned from the China-Burma-India front in 1946, it seemed at first that the program hadn't skipped a beat. Led by tackle Dick Huffman, Tennessee defeated Alabama 12-0 en route to a 9-1 record to win the SEC championship. But thanks to two blocked punts, an 83-yard drive, and a fourth-down interception, Tennessee lost 8-0 to Rice in the Orange Bowl.

"It will take us five years put Tennessee back on top," Neyland predicted.

When the Volunteers followed with lackluster 5-5 and 4-4-2 seasons, whispers began to be heard in Knoxville that maybe Neyland's best was behind him. His single-wing offense appeared to have been passed by in favor of the popular T-formation, and besides, the coach—who'd been born on February 17, 1892, in Greenville, Texas—was advancing in years.

But with another collection of impressive sophomores, Neyland came back strong in 1949, finishing 7-2-1. The Vols took another step in 1950, clinching a memorable 7-0 victory against Kentucky after 17 inches of snow fell in Knoxville during the 36 hours leading up to kickoff. A 7-0 loss to Mississippi State in Week 2 was the only blemish. Against favored No. 3 Texas in the Cotton Bowl, Hank Lauricella's 75-yard run, in which he changed directions three times, set up a 5-yard touchdown pass from Herky Payne to John Gruble. Two fourth-quarter touchdowns by fullback Andy Kozar completed the 20-14 upset by No. 4 Tennessee.

Although the Volunteers were again voted the national champion by one organization, they didn't win their first consensus title until 1951 (when various services also listed Georgia Tech, Illinois, Maryland, and Michigan State as No. 1).

Tennessee recorded its first victory on television, 27-13 against Alabama, and went on to finish the regular season 10-0. Led by 6-foot-8 defensive lineman Doug Atkins, the defense posted five shutouts and the Vols outscored the opposition 386-166.

Playing behind guard John Michels, Lauricella finished second in voting for the Heisman Trophy.

"The general was always in complete control," Michels said. "He never got excited. He was highly organized and a great disciplinarian."

Already voted the national champion, Tennessee played undefeated Maryland in the Sugar Bowl, where a surprise was awaiting. Facing an eight-man front, the Vols could muster only 81 rushing yards and 75 passing yards. Meanwhile, Maryland scored 21 points in the first 16 minutes and returned an interception 46 yards for a touchdown en route to a 28-13 victory.

While Atkins finished off an impressive 29-4-1 record during his three years, an even bigger era was coming to a close. Just before the 1953 Cotton Bowl, Neyland announced that he was stepping down due to health reasons, though he would stay on as athletic director until his death in 1962. When No. 7 Tennessee could get only six first downs and was held to minus-14 rushing yards in the 16-0 loss to No. 11 Texas, the Vols finished 8-2-1.

Neyland's final stint produced a 54-17-4 record, adding up to a career mark of 173-31-12. In those 216 games, the opponent failed to score in 112 of them.

"The general was not the easiest guy to work with Monday through Friday, but on Saturday he was a fatherly figure," Payne said. "On Saturday, he was a warm man who gave you a lot of confidence."

Harvey Robinson, who had been a tailback for Tennessee, had the unenviable task of replacing Neyland, but after seasons of 6-4-1 and 4-6 was dismissed in favor of Wyatt, the former Tennessee player who had won championships at Arkansas and Wyoming. Neyland called it the "the hardest thing I've ever had to do."

"Once they paint orange on you, it never washes off," said Robinson, who after a stint at Florida returned to Tennessee in 1960 as an assistant coach.

What Wyatt's teams may have lacked in pizzazz, they more than made up for in winning prowess, and in 1956 Tennessee ran the table, finishing the regular season 10-0 to win the SEC championship and earn a No. 2 ranking behind Oklahoma. Highlighting the season was a 6-0 victory against Georgia Tech, which was coached by another Neyland protégé, the dynamic Bobby Dodd, who had been Tennessee's quarterback from 1928 to 1930.

"We may have a horse and buggy offense, but we've got a dashboard and a TV set added," Wyatt said.

Although tailback Johnny Majors was named the SEC Player of the Year for a second time and placed second in Heisman voting (won by Notre Dame's Paul Hornung), Baylor spoiled the season, taking advantage of four interceptions and a Majors fumble on a punt return for a 13-7 victory in the Sugar Bowl.

Tennessee was able to play in one more bowl under Wyatt (1955–62)—the 1957 Gator Bowl. The game was remembered for the collision between the Vols' Bobby Gordon and Heisman Trophy winner John David Crow, and because it was Paul "Bear" Bryant's last game at Texas A&M before taking over rival Alabama. Tennessee won, 3-0.

From 1958 through 1964, the Vols were unable to win more than six games in a season and didn't make a single bowl appearance. When Chattanooga football coach Scrappy Moore defeated Tennessee for the first time in 51 years, 14-6 at Knoxville in 1958, he said, "I'll live today the rest of my life."

On March 28, 1962, Neyland died at the Oscher Clinic in New Orleans. In his memory, the football stadium, with the addition of 5,837 seats on the west side bringing capacity up to 52,227, was named in his honor along with an academic scholarship fund.

Perhaps fittingly, Doug Dickey, a top assistant coach under Frank Broyles at Arkansas, brought the T-formation to Tennessee when he was hired as head coach in 1964. Although the Volunteers lost close games to Alabama and Auburn en route to a 4-5-1 season, the record didn't reflect the team's success. It tied No. 7 LSU at Baton Rouge and two weeks later upset No. 7 Georgia Tech 22-14. Middle guard Steve DeLong won the Outland Trophy, and the coaching staff recruited several players who doubled as track stars, including a wide receiver from Montgomery, Alabama, named Richmond Flowers, the self-described "fastest white boy alive."

(*Note:* Flowers' father was Alabama's attorney general from 1963 to 1967 while segregationist George Wallace was governor. Flowers Sr. condemned and prosecuted members of the Ku Klux Klan, and in doing so incurred upon himself and his family death threats and burning crosses. He was convicted in 1969 of extorting money from savings and loan operators and applicants who sought licenses to sell securities, serving 18 months of an eight-year federal sentence before being paroled. Eventually, President Jimmy Carter pardoned him, but Flowers Sr. insisted he was framed by his political enemies. The younger Flowers set off a firestorm of outrage when he spurned Bryant's overtures for Tennessee, and as a senior in 1968 he scored a touchdown in a 10-9 win over the Crimson Tide. "I really wanted to get out of Alabama and get it behind me," Flowers told ESPN Classic's SportsCentury series in 1997. "I didn't want all that heavy stuff laid on me about politics and segregation and civil rights. I was a kid who wanted to be a kid.")

However, during the following season the unthinkable happened. The night after a hard-fought 7-7 tie at Alabama, line coach Charley Rash put a note in each players' mailbox that read: "Play like that every week and you'll go undefeated." Two days later, Rash, Bill Majors, and Bob Jones were killed in an early morning car accident involving a train. Somehow, the Volunteers kept winning, capping off the regular season with a dramatic 37-34 victory against UCLA when quarterback Dewey Warren rolled around the left end for the winning score. Advancing to the Bluebonnet Bowl, Tennessee took advantage of three fumbles and four interceptions in a downpour to defeat Tulsa, 27-6.

The addition of 5,895 seats, increasing capacity to 58,122, brought in more fans to see the Vols crank out a 7-3 season in 1966, setting up an 18-12 victory against Syracuse—led by Floyd Little and Larry Csonka—in the Gator Bowl. Warren completed 17 of 29 passes for 244 yards and two touchdowns.

Tennessee lost its opener in 1967, 20-16 at UCLA, but tore through the SEC schedule, scoring its first victory against Alabama (24-13) since 1960 and defeating Ole Miss (20-7) for the first time since 1958 to win the conference title.

"They're good all right," said Tulane coach Jim Pittman, whose team lost to the Vols 35-14. "They even look strong in the huddle."

Though one service had the 9-2 Vols winning the national championship, they were the consensus No. 2 team behind Southern California. But against Oklahoma in the Orange Bowl, the Sooners jumped out to a 19-0 lead. Jimmy Glover returned an interception 36 yards for a touchdown, only to see Oklahoma match the points with a 25-yard interception return of its own. After being stopped on fourth-and-1, Tennessee's last chance ended with a missed field goal and the Sooners held on, 26-24. After the game, Oklahoma coach Chuck Fairbanks was quoted as saying, "If the Russians had a football team, maybe I'd rather beat them than Tennessee."

Artificial turf was installed in Neyland Stadium (64,429) for the 1968 season (it switched back in 1994), with the first game on the carpet also featuring Lester McClain, Tennessee's first black player in an SEC game. Tennessee tied Georgia 17-17, and led by quarterback Bobby Wade and linebacker Steve Kiner, went on to finish 8-2-1 due to a 36-13 loss to Texas in the Cotton Bowl. The Longhorns outgained the Vols in rushing yards 279 to 83 and had 513 yards of total offense.

Before leaving to take over his alma mater, Florida, Dickey won a second SEC title at Tennessee with a 9-1 record, and ironically faced his future players in the Gator Bowl. While Tennessee had trouble scoring inside the 10 and had to settle for two short field goals, Florida scored on a blocked punt to win 14-13.

Dickey, who would later return and serve as athletic director for 18 years, didn't leave the Volunteers lacking in talent, and when Bill Battle became the country's youngest coach at age 28, he took Tennessee to five straight bowl games—but somehow never won an SEC title.

Despite a loss to Auburn (36-23) in Week 2, Battle became the first Division I coach to win 11 games in his first year. Capping the season was a 24-point first quarter against Air Force in the Sugar Bowl. Tailback Don McLeary scored two touchdowns, and Gary Theiler caught a 10-yard touchdown pass from game-MVP Bobby Scott. Even more impressive was the defense, which limited Air Force to minus-12 rushing yards to go with four recovered fumbles and four interceptions.

Battle backed it up with back-to-back 10-2 seasons, during which the stadium was expanded to 70,650. In 1971, Tennessee beat Arkansas 14-13 in the Liberty Bowl when, after taking advantage of a late fumble, quarterback Jim Maxwell's pass to tight end Gary Theiler set up Curt Watson's 17-yard touchdown run.

"The Artful Dodger" Condredge Holloway, the first black quarterback in SEC history, bested LSU All-American Bert Jones in the 1972 Bluebonnet Bowl, completing 11 of 19 passes for 94 yards and rushing for 74 yards on 19 carries. With All-American cornerback Conrad Graham breaking up a late fourth-down pass, Tennessee won 24-17.

Though the 1972 senior class graduated with a 31-5 record, and Battle never had a losing season—with a 28-18 loss to Texas Tech in the 1973 Gator Bowl and a 7-3 win over Maryland and All-American tackle Randy White in the 1974 Liberty Bowl—he was fired after the 1976 season (after waking up one morning to find a moving van, dispatched by a fan, parked in front of his house). To replace him, Tennessee looked to one of its own—Majors, who had just won the national championship at Pittsburgh.

"Follow me home to Tennessee" took a couple of years to produce results, but Tennessee won four of its last five games in 1978, and the following season had eventual national champion Alabama down 17-0 in the second quarter before finally succumbing 27-17. However, two weeks later, Majors had his first big coaching win with the Volunteers when Hubert Simpson ran for 117 yards and four touchdowns to trounce Norte Dame at home, 40-18. Despite 270 passing and rushing yards by quarterback Jimmy Streater and All-American defensive back Roland James' eight unassisted tackles, Tennessee's late comeback in the Bluebonnet Bowl came up short, with Purdue winning 27-22.

A capacity crowd of 95,288 saw Tennessee open the 1980 season against

Georgia, which won 16-15 and went on to win the national championship. The following year they witnessed a pair of horrendous losses to start the season (44-0 to No. 10 Georgia and 43-7 to No. 5 Southern California), only to see Majors turn things around, with narrow 10-7 victories against Auburn and Georgia Tech snowballing into an eight-win season. Steve Alatorre completed 24 of 42 passes for 315 yards and one touchdown, and Willie Gault returned a kickoff 87 yards for a touchdown to lead a 28-21 victory against Wisconsin in the last Garden State Bowl.

With the 1982 World's Fair in town, the Volunteers snapped an 11-game losing streak to Alabama in Bryant's last appearance at Neyland Stadium, 35-28. But against quarterback Chuck Long in the Peach Bowl, the Vols' last effort was stopped at the Iowa 7 for a 28-22 final score and 6-5-1 finish.

Johnnie Jones scored the game-winning 66-yard touchdown against Alabama in 1983, a 41-34 decision, and scored one of two fourth-quarter touchdowns, along with Alan Cockrell, to lead a 30-23 victory against No. 17 Maryland in the Citrus Bowl. Linebacker Alvin Toles recovered a fumble and had an interception in that game, with the Terrapins limited to 95 rushing yards. But Tennessee's leader for the 9-3 season was the "Minister of Defense," defensive end Reggie White. Once dubbed a "moving nightmare" by a sportswriter, White holds all the school sack records—four in a game, 15 in a season, and 32 during his career.

"There won't be any way to estimate what Reggie meant to us," Majors said. "It's inestimable. He provided humor, leadership, morale."

Majors didn't win his first championship at Tennessee until 1985, when the Volunteers, unranked in the preseason polls, tied No. 10 UCLA (26-26), shocked No. 1 Auburn (38-20), and won at No. 15 Alabama (16-14) to secure the SEC title. The impressive run, with Daryl Dickey, Doug Dickey's son, replacing injured quarterback Tony Robinson down the stretch, set up a meeting with Miami in the Orange Bowl.

"They're not going to beat us because their fans make a lot of noise," Miami quarterback Vinny Testaverde said.

He was right. Instead, Tennessee (9-1-2) beat No. 2 Miami because its defense recorded six turnovers, seven sacks, and five tackles for a loss en route to a 35-7 trashing. Pollsters ranked UT fourth.

Thanks to a late-season rally, the Volunteers (7-5) were invited to the 1986 Liberty Bowl, where quarterback Jeff Francis' three touchdowns bested Minnesota's Rickey Foggie for a 21-14 victory. The following year, it took a come-from-behind effort against another Big Ten team to top off a 10-2-1 season. Francis threw two touchdown passes, but running back Reggie Cobb's second touchdown of the game, on a 9-yard carry, sealed the 27-22 victory against Indiana at the Peach Bowl. Also on that team was DeLong's son, Keith, a linebacker who became a team captain and All-American in 1988.

Majors won back-to-back SEC titles in 1989 and 1990, and the Vols spent most of both seasons ranked in the Top 10. In '89, only a 47-30 loss at Alabama kept No. 5 Tennessee from running the table. A 78-yard touchdown run by Chuck Webb, who finished with 250 rushing yards on 26 carries, and an 84-yard pass from Andy Kelly to Anthony Morgan highlighted an intense 31-27 victory against Arkansas in the Cotton Bowl, which wasn't decided until Alvin Harper recovered an onside kick in final moments.

Two ties and narrow losses to Alabama (9-6) and Notre Dame (34-29) didn't sidetrack the 1990 team, which pulled out a 23-22 comeback victory against Virginia in the Sugar Bowl. Tony Thompson, who had 154 rushing yards on 25 carries, scored his second touchdown on a 1-yard run, capping a 20-point fourth quarter for the No. 8 Vols. Scoring another key touchdown was wide receiver Carl Pickens, who a year earlier was named defensive MVP of the Cotton Bowl.

The 1991 season saw perhaps Tennessee's greatest comeback. It was down 31-7 at Notre Dame when a blocked kick by Jeremy Lincoln was returned for a touchdown and sparked the Vols, who pulled out a 35-34 victory when the Irish missed a game-winning 27-yard field goal as time expired.

Majors was able to post nine-win seasons in 1991 and 1992, with a 42-17 defeat to Penn State in the Fiesta Bowl and a 38-23 victory over Boston College in the Hall of Fame Bowl (with quarterback Heath Shuler completing 18 of 23 passes for 245 yards and two touchdowns, while running in two as well); but heart surgery led to Majors' turning the team over to offensive line coach Phillip Fulmer, who served as interim head coach for the final four games of 1992.

With Fulmer named head coach before the start of the 1993 season, Shuler led the Vols to a 10-win season. The Tennessee quarterback finished second in voting for the Heisman Trophy behind Florida State's Charlie Ward. He had 205 passing yards to go with Charlie Garner's 91 rushing yards and Cory Fleming's 101 receiving yards but Tennessee lost again to Penn State, 31-13 in the Citrus Bowl.

When starting quarterback Jerry Colquitt suffered an injury in the opening minutes of the 1994 season, Tennessee got off to a 1-3 start. Against Washington State, the Vols turned to freshman Peyton Manning, who went on to pass for more than 11,000 yards and 89 touchdowns while setting 33 school, seven SEC, and two NCAA records. He compiled a 39-5 record as a starter, but could never beat one school: Florida.

Tennessee finished 8-4 in 1994 and with three James Stewart touchdowns beat Virginia Tech 45-23 in the Gator Bowl. The Vols went 11-1 in 1995 and aided by 168 rushing yards from Jay Graham and 109 receiving yards by Joey Kent defeated Ohio State 20-14 in the Citrus Bowl to finish ranked third (No. 2 in the coaches' poll). In 1996, it was a 48-28 victory against Northwestern, again in the Citrus Bowl, with Manning passing for 408 yards. His top two targets were Kent (five catches, 122 yards) and Peerless Price (six catches, 110 yards).

In 1997, Manning finally got a title when Tennessee defeated Auburn 30-29 in the SEC Championship Game. However, the Vols went on to lose 42-17 to national champion Nebraska in the Orange Bowl.

"He's raised everyone's play around him to another level because of his competitive spirit, ability, and leadership," Fulmer said.

Like his father, Archie, at Ole Miss, Manning wasn't able to win a national championship or Heisman Trophy (he finished second in 1997), but in 1,381 attempts he was intercepted only 33 times. Fittingly, a road leading to Neyland Stadium was renamed Peyton Manning Pass.

"I'll be a Volunteer the rest of my life," said Manning, who left school as the SEC's all-time leader in total offense (11,020 yards).

Without Manning, many expected the team to plummet in 1998; but the opposite occurred. During the second week of the season, Florida came calling to Knoxville, where 107,653 fans, the largest crowd ever to see a football game in the South, awaited. For the first time since 1992, Tennessee was able to pull out a win, 20-17 in overtime. Energized, the Vols rolled through the regular season—with Auburn (17-9) and Arkansas (28-24) coming closest to pulling off an upset—and into the SEC Championship Game, where they defeated pesky Mississippi State 24-14.

"I knew we were going to win the Arkansas game," linebacker Raynoch Thompson said. "I was trying to figure out how when their quarterback dropped the ball."

"Sometimes you've just got to win ugly," Fulmer said.

In the first year of the controversial Bowl Championship Series, which aimed to pair No. 1 vs. No. 2 for the national championship, the final obstacle was Florida State at the Fiesta Bowl. With Vice President Al Gore looking on, an "oskie" for a 54-yard touchdown by defensive back Dwayne Goodrich gave the Vols a lead they would never relinquish. Darwin Walker's third-down sack of Florida State quarterback Marcus Outzen early in the fourth quarter (what Seminoles coach Bobby Bowden called "a killer") set up Price's reception of a Tee Martin pass in stride for a 79-yard touchdown. Price finished with 199 receiving yards on four catches in the 23-16 victory.

"It wasn't pretty early this year for Tee," Manning told *Sports Illustrated* after watching Martin complete 11 of 18 passes for 278 yards and two touchdowns. "He kept plugging and plugging. He's gotten confidence.

"We roomed together on the road. A couple of times he got phone calls telling him that friends had been killed. I'm thinking, Jiminy, this is unbelievable, but Tee is such a strong person, mentally and spiritually."

Although Tennessee was seemingly always close, it couldn't repeat the championship form over the years to follow. In 1999, nemesis Steve Spurrier at Florida found a way to beat Tennessee again, 23-21. Despite a solid 38-14 victory against Notre Dame, another stumble against Arkansas resulted in a return to the Fiesta Bowl. Twelve months after celebrating the championship, the Vols were outgained on the ground, 321 yards to 44, as Nebraska won 31-21. Tennessee dropped to No. 9.

Quarterback Casey Clausen earned the nickname "The Comeback Kid," and defensive tackle John Henderson won the Outland Trophy as the nation's best interior lineman in 2000. But despite Travis Henry's 180 rushing yards on 17 carries, a 35-21 loss to Kansas State at the Cotton Bowl resulted in an 8-4 season.

Even with an early 26-24 defeat to Georgia, Vols fans thought they were making another championship run in 2001 when Tennessee closed the regular season with a 34-32 victory over Florida (the game had been rescheduled due to the September 11 terrorist attacks) for a return to the SEC Championship Game as the nation's No. 2 team.

However, when Tennessee faced No. 21 LSU, which the Vols had defeated earlier in the season 26-18, the Tigers proved to be more inspired and pulled out a 31-20 victory. Instead of playing Miami for the national championship in the Rose Bowl, Tennessee had to settle for the Citrus Bowl, where it crushed Michigan 45-17. Clausen completed 26 of 34 passes for 393 yards and three touchdowns, and he nearly had two more with wide receiver Donte Stallworth twice tackled at the 1.

"It's been a while since we've played a team as good as Tennessee," said Michigan running back Chris Perry, echoing a sentiment felt countless times throughout the years.

THREE THINGS THAT STAND OUT ABOUT TENNESSEE FOOTBALL

1. *The Volunteer Navy:* Game days are something to behold in Knoxville. Tennessee has the Vol Walk, where thousands of fans gather to wish the players good luck; the checkerboard end zones; and the team running through the marching band's "T" while entering the field. But the tradition of getting to the game by boat on the Tennessee River, started by broadcaster George Mooney, is unique. The floating tailgate party has been known to include a couple hundred vessels.
2. *"Rocky Top":* Though it's not the official Vols fight song, Tennessee fans can't get enough of hearing it played by the Pride of the Southland Band. But it's the exact opposite for anyone else. Hearing 40 to 50 variations, some longer than others, during a game is common.
3. *Smokey:* Several coonhounds were introduced during halftime of the 1953 Mississippi State game, and fans voted on which would serve as the official mascot of the football team. When the last dog, a blue tick named Blue Smokey, was introduced and cheered, he barked. After more cheering, and more barking, he won the job.

· 10 ·

Vanderbilt

THE SCHOOL

Location: Nashville, Tennessee
Founded: 1873
Enrollment: 6,241
Nickname: Commodores
Colors: Black and gold
Mascot: A costumed Commodore, though there once was George the basset hound, followed by Samantha
Stadium: Dudley Field/Vanderbilt Stadium (39,773)
2005 officials: E. Gordon Gee, chancellor; Nick Zeppos, faculty representative; David Williams II, vice chancellor/student life

THE PROGRAM

National Championships: None
SEC Championships: None
Bowl appearances: 3 (1-1-1)
First season: 1890
College Football Hall of Fame (9): Lynn Bomar, 1921–24, end, inducted 1956; Josh Cody, 1914–16, 1919, tackle, 1970; Bill Edwards 1949–52, coach, 1986; Carl Hinkle, 1935–37, center, 1959; Dan McGugin, 1904–17, coach, 1951; Ray Morrison, 1918, 1935–39, coach, 1954; Red Sanders, 1940–42, coach, 1996; Bill Spears, 1925–27, quarterback, 1962; John Tigert, 1901–03, halfback, 1970
Heisman Winners: None
National Honors: None
First-Team All-Americans: Ray Morrison, QB, 1911; Josh Cody, T, 1915–16, 1919; Lynn Bomar, E, 1923; H. C. (Hek) Wakefield, E, 1924; Bill Spears, QB, 1927; Dick Abernathy, E, 1928; John "Bull" Brown, G, 1929; Pete Gracey, C, 1932; Carl Hinkle, C, 1937; Bob Grude, C, 1941; Bucky Curtis, E, 1950; George Deiderich, G, 1958; Chip Healy, LB, 1968; Bob Asher, T, 1969; Barry Burton, TE, 1974; Jim Arnold, P, 1982; Allama Mathews, TE, 1982; Chuck

Scott, TE, 1983; Leonard Coleman, CB, 1983; Ricky Anderson, P, 1984; Chris Gaines, LB, 1987; Bill Marinangel, P, 1996; Jamie Duncan, LB, 1997; Jamie Winborn, LB, 1999

First-Team Academic All-Americans (CoSIDA): Ben Donnell, C, 1958; Jim Burns, DB, 1968; Doug Martin, E, 1974; Damon Regen, LB, 1975; Greg Martin, K, 1977; Phil Roach, WR, 1983; Hunter Hillenmeyer, LB, 2002

First-round NFL draftees: Seven

Retired jerseys: None

THE COACHES

Elliott H. Jones, 1890–92, 8-5; W. J. Keller, 1893, 6-1; Henry Thornton, 1894, 7-1; C. L. Upton, 1895, 5-3-1; R. G. Acton, 1896–98, 10-7-3; J. L. Crane, 1899–1900, 11-6-1; W. H. Watkins, 1901–02, 14-2-1; J. H. Henry, 1903, 6-1-1; Dan McGugin, 1904–17, 1919–34, 197-55-19; Ray Morrison, 1935–39, 25-20-2; H. R. (Red) Sanders, 1940–42, 1946–48, 36-22-2; E. H. (Herc) Alley, 1943, 5-0; Doby Bartling, 1944–45, 6-6-1; W. M. Edwards, 1949–52, 21-19-2; Arthur L. Guepe, 1953–62, 7-29-4; Jack Green, 1963–66, 7-29-4; Bill Pace, 1967–72, 22-38-3; Steve Sloan, 1973–74, 12-9-1; Fred Pancoast, 1975–78, 13-31; George MacIntyre, 1979–85, 25-52-1; Watson Brown, 1986–90, 10-45; Gerry DiNardo, 1991–94, 19-25; Rod Dowhower, 1995–96, 4-18; Woody Widenhofer, 1997–2001, 15-40; Bobby Johnson 2002–05, 11-35

National Coach of the Year: None

SEC Coach of the Year, AP: Steve Sloan 1974; Gerry DiNardo 1991 **Coaches:** Ray Morrison 1937; Red Sanders 1941; Art Guepe 1955; George MacIntryre 1982

RECORDS

Rushing yards, game: 321, Frank Mordica vs. Air Force, Nov. 18, 1978 (22 carries)

Rushing yards, season: 1,103, Corey Harris, 1991 (229 carries)

Rushing yards, career: 2,632, Frank Mordica, 1976–79 (546 carries)

Passing yards, game: 464, Whit Taylor vs. Tennessee, Nov. 28, 1981 (29 of 53)

Passing yards, season: 3,178, Kurt Page, 1983 (286 of 493)

Passing yards, career: 8,697, Jay Cutler, 2002–05 (710 of 1,242)

Receiving yards, game: 222, Clarence Sevillian vs. Tennessee, Nov. 28, 1992 (six receptions)

Receiving yards, season: 1,213, Boo Mitchell, 1988 (78 receptions)

Receiving yards, career: 2,964, Boo Mitchell, 1985–88 (188 receptions)

Points, game: 30, Frank Mordica vs. Air Force, Nov. 18, 1978 (five touchdowns)

Points, season: 90, Jack Jenkins, 1941 (12 touchdowns, 1 field goal, 15 PATs)

Points, career: 209, John Markham, 1997–2000 (47 field goals, 68 PATs)

As an academic institution, Vanderbilt University is among the nation's leading four-year universities and is particularly known for its engineering, law, business, and education schools (among others) along with the Freedom Forum First Amendment Center. The private research university was founded in 1873 and grew into what some consider the South's equivalent to an Ivy League college.

Oh, it also has a football program, which for the most part has upheld the school's reputation for academics and has an exceedingly high graduation rate. In 2001, the Vanderbilt football program was recognized by the College Football Association for its 100 percent graduation rate, sharing the award with Notre Dame. It was the second time in five years that the Commodores achieved the distinction. Since 1990, the football program has been annually recognized by the Coaches Association for graduating at least 70 percent of its players, which places it at the top of the SEC in that category.

Vanderbilt was also the home to maybe the greatest college football writer ever, Grantland Rice, who coined numerous phrases, including "It's not whether you win or lose, it's how you play the game." Also among his seemingly endless stream of poignant and famous statements about the game are these: "Due to its ingredients . . . courage, mental and physical condition, spirit and its terrific body contact which tends to sort the men from the boys . . . football remains one of the great games of all time.

"The drama of sport is a big part of the drama of life and the scope of that drama is endless."

When it comes to football, though, Vanderbilt frequently draws comparisons to the other private institutions that play in major conferences, like Northwestern in the Big Ten and Stanford in the Pac-10. In other words, success on the gridiron has been both fleeting and, well, rare.

"There is no way you can be Harvard Monday through Friday and try and be Alabama on Saturday," coach Art Guepe said.

Vanderbilt has never won a conference championship or, obviously, a national title. It's played in only three bowl games and has become a perennial cellar-dwelling program in the SEC, bottoming out in the 1960s when the Commodores averaged less than two wins per season (15-60-5) from 1960 to 1967.

Nevertheless, the school has advanced many players to the National Football League, including Bill Wade. The 1951 SEC Player of the Year completed 111 of 223 passes that season, including 13 for touchdowns, and went on to help lead the Chicago Bears to the 1963 NFL Championship.

More recently, in 2001, five former Commodores were on active NFL rosters at the defensive back positions alone: Corey Chavous (Minnesota Vikings), Corey Harris (Detroit Lions), Ainsley Battles (Jacksonville Jaguars), Jimmy Williams (San Francisco 49ers), and Fred Vinson (Carolina Panthers).

Simultaneously, the school boasted an impressive collection of pro linebackers including Shelton Quarles (Tampa Bay Buccaneers), Jamie Winborn (San Francisco 49ers), Hunter Hillenmeyer (Chicago Bears), and Matt Stewart (Atlanta Falcons). That didn't include Jamie Duncan, who at the end of his career in 1997 had

425 career tackles, or Chris Gaines, who was once described by a Tennessee writer as "sort of a Rambo on a leash."

However, there was a time, before bowl games, when the Commodores were a national power who left other teams in their wake, desperately scrambling to catch up. When Tennessee hired legendary coach Robert Neyland, it was with the primary objective of beating Vanderbilt, which dominated their early series and from 1915 to 1935 enjoyed 21 consecutive winning seasons.

The man Neyland was hired to try and best was Dan McGugin, who led the Commodores from 1904 to 1934 (though he spent 1918 fulfilling military duty) and compiled an incredible record of 197-55-19.

His first team, which might have been his best team, went 9-0 and outscored opponents 474-4. The victims included Mississippi State (61-0), Ole Miss (69-0), Central (Ky.) (97-0), Tennessee (22-0), Nashville (81-0), and Sewanee (27-0). McGugin's teams were so dominating that the coach didn't experience his fourth loss until his fifth season, when Vanderbilt scheduled both Michigan and Ohio State.

McGugin also didn't mince words in expressing his coaching philosophy and ideology:

"Don't live on the fading memories of your forefathers. Go out and make your own records, and leave some memories for others to live by."

"Play for your own self-respect and the respect of your teammates."

"How you fight is how you will be remembered."

"Hit 'em hard and carry 'em to the ground. It reduces their enthusiasm."

He also had a knack for pregame speeches. When Vanderbilt played at Yale in 1910, McGugin pointed out to his players that many of their grandfathers who fought in the Civil War were buried in the North and had been killed by some of the grandfathers of their opponents that day. Vanderbilt pulled off a 0-0 tie, which was considered quite an accomplishment; what McGugin didn't tell his team was that his own grandfather had served under Yankee general William Sherman.

That team provided McGugin's other unbeaten season. The 8-0-1 squad was led by lineman W. E. Metzger (nicknamed Frog), as Vanderbilt outscored the opposition 166-8 (Sewanee scored six points and Ole Miss two).

But even before McGugin, there was William L. Dudley, considered the father of Vanderbilt football. The dean of the medical college was instrumental in organizing the Southern Intercollegiate Athletic Association in 1893, just three years after the school was issued a challenge by rival Peabody (now the University of Nashville) to play the inaugural game on Thanksgiving Day. With Elliott Jones serving as both coach and captain, Vanderbilt easily won 40-0.

The original Dudley Field, which is the current site of the law school, was named on October 21, 1892, and its first game a 22-4 victory against Tennessee. The field was replaced in 1922 by another facility with the same name, which served the school until 1981 when, except for a section of metal bleachers seating 12,088, the entire stadium was demolished. Replacement Vanderbilt Stadium (39,773) took nine months to build and cost just $10.1 million.

With McGugin the first coach to stay for more than three years (in his two seasons, W. H. Watkins set an early standard with records of 6-1-1 in 1901 and 8-1 in 1902, thanks in part to halfback John Tigert, who was also the school's first Rhodes Scholar), Vanderbilt suffered more than one loss in a season only twice between 1904 and 1912.

In the 1906 season opener, fullback/defensive back Owsley Manier scored three touchdowns and helped the Commodores accumulate a whopping 630 yards for a 28-0 victory against Kentucky. Manier scored five touchdowns against both Alabama (78-0) and Georgia Tech (37-6) en route to an 8-1 season in which the Commodores outscored the opposition 278-16.

In 1912, Vanderbilt set a school record that will almost certainly never be challenged when it scored 105 points against Bethel. Playing in a downpour, which turned Dudley Field into a quagmire, the Commodores recorded 16 touchdowns to go with nine conversions. Leading the scorers was Wilson Collins with five touchdowns, followed by Enoch Brown with three, and Lewie Hardage and Rabbi Robbins both with two (Robbins was the backup to quarterback Zach Curlin, but his game was better suited to the conditions).

The score could have been worse. Vanderbilt did pull most of its starters, and quarters were only nine minutes long; but because of an agreement by both teams, the final two quarters were reduced to seven minutes each.

Reported *The Tennessean*: "Naturally, it makes the Commodores look pretty good on paper to say that they opened the season by breaking a record with only two week's practice, much of which was done in very hot weather and before a number of the varsity men had arrived. Nevertheless, it was not a great victory. Bethel was lamentably weak on defense; on the offense they did come within hailing distance of a first down. But for all that, some of those Bethel men, notably Captain Cody, played gritty football. Their main trouble was lack of unity in action. They were not well trained along football lines, although physically, they seemed never to be in distress."

Actually, Vanderbilt did reach the century mark twice more. The following week it beat Maryville 100-3, followed by Rose Polytechnic (54-0) and Georgia (40-0). The Commodores finished the season 8-1-1 with a loss to Harvard (9-3) and tied Auburn (7-7), but they outscored opponents 391-18.

In 1915, Vanderbilt destroyed Henderson-Brown 100-0 during an impressive 9-1 season that saw the Commodores shut out eight opponents and close with a 28-3 victory against Sewanee. The "point-a-minute" team scored 514 points in 510 minutes, averaging 51 points per game while giving up only 3.8. The lone loss was to Virginia, 35-10.

Running behind future basketball coach Josh Cody, who would help Vanderbilt score 1,099 points in 35 games during his four-year career at tackle, the team was led by versatile ball-carrier Irby "Rabbit" Curry from 1914 to 1916. His final season, the Commodores went 7-1-1, including an 86-0 pounding of Southwestern (Louisiana).

Upon graduating, Curry volunteered for service during World War I, and after completing Ground School was assigned to Flying School. On August 18, 1918, he was shot down over France near Chateau-Thierry and killed.

McGugin took Curry's death hard, but waited to invoke his memory until a pregame speech in 1921. According to *50 Years of Vanderbilt Football*, by Fred Russell and Maxwell Benson, he said the following before Vanderbilt played heavily favored Texas in Dallas:

"You are about to be put to an ordeal which will show the stuff that's in you. What a glorious chance you have. Every one of you is going to fix his status for all time in the minds and hearts of his teammates today. How you fight is what you will be remembered by. If any shirk, the Lord pity him; he will be degraded in the hearts of the rest as long as they live.

"Man is a curious kind of a critter. You will all doubtless eat and have comforts and butt around for a good many days, but during the next hour you must forget yourselves absolutely. You are to hurl yourselves like demons with the fury of hell on the crowd that has come here to humiliate us. The man worthwhile is the man who can rise away above and beyond himself in the face of a great task.

"I am glad Mr. Curry is here. Some of you knew Rabbit. We felt toward him the tenderness a mother feels towards her own little boy. He had a little slender body; he weighed only 128 pounds, but he had a heart as big as that loving cup over there on the mantel. He was modest; his life was absolutely clean; and what a fighter he was. His life was a great contribution to Vanderbilt—traditionally to our athletic traditions. The influence of his spirit will always abide. He always wanted to play with Vanderbilt against Texas. His body is resting only a few miles south of here; but his spirit is hovering above us now. Some of these days I want to see his likeness looking down on our athletic fields. I am glad his father is here so that he can see, face-to-face, how we regard his son.

"There is one thing that makes me sick at heart. I heard repeatedly before we left Nashville that this Vanderbilt team, this crowd of men into whose faces I now look, might win from Texas if it would only fight. Has anybody the right to imply such an insult? And, if so, when before now could such a thing be said of men from Tennessee? How about Pickett's men who moved out of the wood and exposed their breasts and faces to be shattered and torn as they moved up that slope? And how about *The Tennesseans* of the Thirtieth Division, who broke the Hindenburg line—a task even greater because it was accompanied by so much mud and misery. All but a few here are Tennesseans and the rest have elected to be educated here. You are a part of us and you must uphold the traditions of Vanderbilt and Tennessee.

"Who in the devil started all of this bunk about the Texas team? Who thinks they are unbeatable? They say that they have the greatest team in their history and perhaps this is true. They say Vanderbilt never had a team which could defeat theirs of this year, and that is not true. Texas has no shield like ours. We have some scars on it, but there are a lot of stars there, too. Texas has no such athletic tradition and history.

"They say the climate is against us. That is not true. The change should do us good. This light, pure air will help us."

Vanderbilt went out into the pure air and won 20-0, handing the Longhorns their only defeat of the season. In turn, the Commodores finished 7-0-1 and wouldn't sustain a loss for almost two years.

After the new stadium was built in 1922, the original Dudley Field was rechristened Curry Field. Meanwhile, the inaugural game at new Dudley Field was against none other than Michigan, coached by McGugin's biggest nemesis, Fielding Yost, who just happened to be his brother-in-law (and the two had played together for the Wolverines). Yost's team had given the Commodores their only loss in 1905, 1906, 1907, and 1911.

The game came down to a crucial fourth-and-goal at the 1 when a Vanderbilt player was able to push off the goalpost to stop the Michigan ball carrier to preserve the 0-0 tie. Wrote a reporter from Detroit: "Michigan was lucky to escape with their lives."

Led by the passing tandem of quarterback Jess Neely and receiver Lynn "The Blond Bear" Bomar, the 1922 team finished 8-0-1 and outscored opponents 117-16. But during Bomar's senior season in 1924, he suffered a brain hemorrhage from a blow to the chin. For a while he was paralyzed below the waist, and for days doctors didn't know if he would live. Bomar recuperated, and while he never played again, he returned to the bench for the rest of the season.

When the Commodores traveled to Minnesota, which was coming off a victory against Illinois and Red Grange, they defeated the Gophers 16-0. The November 23, 1924, issue of *The Tennessean* boasted the headline: "Vanderbilt Wins First Time in North."

According to reports, McGugin told his team before the game: "Men, those people in the stands out there haven't heard of Southern football. When they think about the South, they think about the Civil War. They think about pain, suffering and death. Many people have no idea of what Southern manhood is all about. Today, we can show them. When your mothers looked on you sleeping in your cradles twenty years ago, they wondered when the time would come when you could bring honor to the South. That time has arrived."

Vanderbilt returned home the following week and lost to Sewanee 16-0. Ironically, the 5-3-2 season was one of McGugin's worst, but the Commodores came back in 1926 to finish 8-1, with five shutouts. The lone loss was to former Vanderbilt assistant coach Wallace Wade and Alabama, 19-7, with the Crimson Tide going on to successfully defend its national championship at the Rose Bowl.

A 10-game winning streak came to a close in Week 4 of the 1927 season, 13-6 to Texas, but quarterback Bill Spears had touchdown runs of 88 and 77 yards to lead a 32-0 victory against Tulane, helping spark Vanderbilt to an 8-1-2 finish.

Raved Rice about Spears: "He is the fastest of the nation's quarterbacks, and one of the most remarkable offensive backs to be seen in college football in years."

The following year, end Dick Abernathy had two touchdown catches to lead a 20-0 season-opening victory against Chattanooga. Later in the season, he blocked a punt that was recovered in the end zone for a touchdown as Vanderbilt got even with Texas, 13-12. The Commodores finished 8-2, losing 19-7 to Georgia Tech, but also had a rare defeat to Tennessee, 6-0.

Arguably Vanderbilt's last two dominating seasons under McGugin's direction came in 1929 and 1930, when it finished 7-2 and 8-2, respectively. But by the time the SEC came into existence in 1933, many of the other SEC programs had caught and/or surpassed Vanderbilt on the playing field. In 1935, when Ray Morrison replaced McGugin, who retired after 30 seasons due to health reasons (he died in 1936 at the age of 56), the team's second-place finish (7-3 overall, 5-1 SEC) set a mark in the standings that the Commodores have not equaled since.

Led by "Iron Man" Carl Hinkle, who was named the SEC's Most Valuable Player, Vanderbilt posted a 7-2 record in 1937 and barely missed a Rose Bowl invitation and chance to play for the national championship. With the bid on the line against Alabama in the season finale, a field goal propelled the Crimson Tide to a 9-7 victory.

Although Hinkle, a center, missed out on the Rose Bowl, during World War II he served as a pilot and won the Distinguished Flying Cross with two Oak Leaf Clusters, the Air Force Medal of Commendation, France's Croix de Guerre, and a Presidential Citation Unit with Oak Leaf Clusters.

Incidentally, one of the more interesting plays of the 1937 season occurred when tackle Greer Ricketson scored the only touchdown of the game against LSU on the hidden-ball trick, for a 7-0 victory.

Red Sanders returned to his alma mater in 1940 (he eventually left for UCLA), and no coach since has been able to match his eight-win seasons of 1941 and 1948. One of his assistant coaches, in charge of the offensive line, was Paul "Bear" Bryant, who was on the Commodores' sideline for one of their biggest upsets against national powerhouse Alabama, ranked seventh.

Vanderbilt held on for a 7-0 victory in Nashville en route to an 8-2 season, but didn't play in a bowl game. Meanwhile, the Crimson Tide went on to finish 9-2, defeated Texas A&M in the Cotton Bowl, and was named the national champion by Deke Houlgate's mathematical rankings system.

On October 7, 1950, Vanderbilt spoiled Alabama's season again, this time 27-22 against the No. 12 Crimson Tide in Mobile. For most of that season, Bucky Curtis led the nation in receiving. His 791 receiving yards, on 27 catches, set an SEC record; the Commodores finished 7-4.

"Winning isn't everything. It's the only thing," Sanders once said (and obviously rubbed off on Bryant). He was once also quoted as saying that "The worst mistake a coach can make is to get caught without material."

When Bill Edwards became head coach in 1949, Vanderbilt was essentially a .500 program. Though the Commodores were competitive and reached No. 13 two weeks after defeating Alabama in 1950, only to lose 31-27 to Florida, they were becoming accustomed to the underdog label.

For example, during the 1951 season Vanderbilt played No. 3 Georgia Tech to a tough 8-7 loss and closed the season with a 35-27 defeat to No. 1 Tennessee, resulting in a 6-5 season.

"I felt like a Yankee and a stranger when I first came here, but I guess I've been reconstructed," said New Jersey native Bob Werckle, a standout tackle (1947, 1949–51). "Vanderbilt is the greatest thing that ever happened to me."

Guepe took the helm in 1953 to start a 10-year reign that saw some significant firsts for the Commodores. Vanderbilt played its first night football game at Dudley Field on September 25, 1954, against Baylor University. Evangelist Billy Graham, who held his crusade at the stadium earlier that year, donated the permanent lights, but Baylor rushed for 312 yards compared to Vanderbilt's 129 to win 25-19.

Though it got off to an uninspiring 1-2 start in 1955 with the victory against Alabama (21-6), Vanderbilt had a three-game winning streak when it pulled off a 34-0 upset against No. 17 Kentucky to suddenly put the Commodores in the running for a potential bowl invitation. Despite a 20-14 season-ending loss to Tennessee, the team's 8-3 record brought the highly coveted bid and a matchup against No. 8 Auburn in the Gator Bowl.

But, as if fate was playing a cruel joke against the Commodores, their quarterback, Don Orr, dislocated his right elbow against the Volunteers. No one knew how he would hold up against the Tigers, considered the SEC's best defensive team that season.

"Orr hadn't hit a lick in practice," Guepe said after the game. "We didn't know for sure his elbow had recovered from the injury in the final season game against Tennessee. I was going to start Tommy Harkins at quarterback if we kicked off, and said so to the team. Something like a tear came up in Orr's eye so I said to him, 'Are you ready?' He said he was, so I said, 'Get in there.'"

In front of 36,000 fans, Orr set up Vanderbilt's first touchdown, a 7-yard touchdown pass to Joe Stephenson, by recovering one of five Auburn fumbles. He added two short touchdown runs for the 25-14 upset.

For the most part, the last 50-plus years have not seen much glory bestowed on the Commodores, whose fans have had to hold out hope for major upsets and enjoyed very few.

But there have been some splashes of success:

November 22, 1969, was a record-setting day for the Commodores, who defeated Davidson 63-8. The 798 total yards remains a school record, but at the time it was both an NCAA and SEC record (Alabama eventually broke it in 1973 against Virginia Tech). Other single-game school records established that day were most pass completions (27), most yards passing (368), most rush-pass plays (99), most first downs rushing (27), most first downs (40, which remains an SEC record), and fewest rushes allowed (16).

In 1974, under the direction of coach Steve Sloan, Vanderbilt pulled off a 24-10 victory against No. 8 Florida for a 3-1 start to the season, and after finishing 7-3-1 (with the tie against Tennessee, 21-21) received an invitation to play Texas Tech in the Peach Bowl. With Mark Adams making both of his field goals and the defense blocking a field-goal attempt after the offense fumbled early in the fourth quarter, the teams played to a 6-6 tie. The Commodores came back the following season—Fred Pancoast's first as coach—to win its last four games, including 17-14 against Tennessee, for a 7-4 record.

On September 10, 1977, Vanderbilt nearly pulled off the biggest upset in the program's history when it opened at No. 1 Oklahoma. When an official, supposedly incorrectly, ruled that the Commodores did not recover a fumble in the end zone, the Sooners were able to eke out a 25-23 victory. Vanderbilt won its next game 3-0 against Wake Forest but then lost seven straight en route to a 2-9 season.

On November 18, 1978, Frank Mordica had 321 rushing yards against Air Force to set both a school and an SEC record. Vanderbilt won 41-27 but finished the season 2-9.

After a 1-2 start in 1982, the Commodores turned things around under coach George MacIntyre, winning seven of the next eight games, including those against No. 14 Florida (31-29) and Tennessee. Against the Volunteers, Whit Taylor completed 24 of 41 passes for 391 yards and led the deciding 84-yard drive in the fourth quarter for a 28-21 victory.

Returning to the postseason, the Commodores were paired against Air Force in the Hall of Fame Bowl, a game that would break 33 bowl records and tie eight. Taylor passed for 452 yards (second in school history to his 464 yards against Tennessee in 1981), and running back Norman Jordan caught 20 passes for 173 yards and scored three touchdowns, but with 331 rushing yards, the Falcons came back from an 11-point deficit to win the shootout 36-28.

Vanderbilt hasn't played in a bowl game since. Gerry DiNardo's teams came close in the early 1990s but never got more than five wins. The Commodores upset No. 17 Georgia 27-25 in 1991 (one week after losing to No. 24 Auburn 24-22) and No. 25 Ole Miss 31-9 in 1992.

Vanderbilt opened the 1996 season by playing No. 6 Notre Dame but lost a tight game 14-7. After his offense fumbled seven times, Irish coach Lou Holtz suggested to his ball carriers that "You take the ball, you put it in the proper position, and then you squeeze the ball until you hear the ball go, 'psshhhhh.'"

"Trying isn't good enough," Commodores coach Rod Dowhower said. "We've got to close."

Instead, when the Commodores finished 2-9, the only thing closed was Dowhower's two-year reign as Vanderbilt's coach.

Although Vanderbilt finished 5-6 in 1999, the season did provide two of the more memorable games in modern history.

On September 11, the Commodores were trailing Northern Illinois 28-3 in the second half when they rallied for a fierce comeback. Quarterback Greg Zolman led three touchdown drives, including one capped by a 61-yard touchdown pass to M. J. Garrett on a slant route. After closing to within 31-26, Jimmy Williams returned a punt 65 yards for the game-winning touchdown and 34-31 victory.

Just a week later, Zolman's touchdown pass to Todd Yoder with 49 seconds remaining tied the game against Ole Miss. After holding the Rebels to a field goal in the first extra stanza, tight end Elliott Carson caught a touchdown pass for the 37-34 victory.

In 2002 Bobby Johnson, who had led Furman to the NCAA I-AA national championship game, took over as Vanderbilt's head coach and immediately promised that the Commodores' days of swearing off the postseason were behind them. That's because he imposed a no-cursing policy on the team.

But Johnson also brought optimism, which paid off in 2005 when Vanderbilt did the next best thing to making a bowl game—it knocked Tennessee out of bowl contention to end its 16-year postseason streak. Earl Bennett's 5-yard touchdown pass from Jay Cutler with 1:11 remaining provided the 28-24 score and started the Commodores celebrating. Vanderbilt (5-6) hadn't won at Neyland Stadium since 1975, and its overall losing streak to UT dating to 1982 was the second-longest between major teams in Division I-A football (trailing only Notre Dame's 42-game string against Navy).

"This is the greatest feeling I've felt in my career," said senior linebacker Moses Osemwegie, who made 16 tackles in the season finale. Cutler, who set 20 school passing records during his career, completed 27 of 39 passes for 315 yards and three touchdowns, while Bennett had 14 catches for 167 yards.

"To turn the corner, you've got to believe, and I'm not saying we've turned the corner, but our guys are starting to believe," Johnson said.

THREE THINGS THAT STAND OUT ABOUT VANDERBILT FOOTBALL

1. *The Commodores:* William Beard, a former quarterback for Vanderbilt, is credited with first using the name in an 1897 story for the *Nashville Banner.* Commodore Cornelius Vanderbilt founded the university with a $1 million gift.

2. *No Director of Athletics:* In 2003 Vanderbilt dissolved its athletic department and opted for a restructuring plan, in part to save money. Instead, football and athletics (14 varsity sports, 37 club sports, and intramural activities) were placed under the auspices of the Office of Student Athletics, Recreation and Wellness, entirely under the Division of Student Life and University Affairs. "In order for us to be successful in the SEC, in order for us to be successful as a Division I-A school we've got to do it differently," Chancellor E. Gordon Gee said. "We've got to do it in a way that provides the opportunity for all of our students to be part of the athletic program."

3. *Star Walk:* The walkway from the McGugin Center to Vanderbilt Stadium, where the players and coaches are cheered by fans before each game, has a black star with a No. 1 in it to honor running back Kwane Doster, the 2002 SEC Freshman of the Year. The running back was murdered while sitting in the back seat of a car in the Ybor City district of Tampa on December 26, 2004. The 2005 season was dedicated in his honor.

Part III

THE WESTERN DIVISION

· 11 ·

Alabama

THE SCHOOL

Location: Tuscaloosa, Alabama
Founded: 1831
Enrollment: 20,969 (with plans to increase to approximately 28,000)
Nickname: Crimson Tide
Colors: Crimson and white
Mascot: Big Al (the elephant)
Stadium: Bryant-Denny Stadium (83,818, but being renovated to bring capacity above 92,000)
2005 officials: Dr. Robert E. Witt, president; Dr. Joe Hornsby, faculty representative; Mal Moore, athletics director

THE PROGRAM

National Championships (12): 1925, 1926, 1930, 1934, 1941, 1961, 1964, 1965, 1973, 1978, 1979, 1992 [*Note:* Not all were consensus.]
The "Other" Five: The Official NCAA Football Records Book also recognizes Alabama as producing national champions in 1945, 1962, 1966, 1975, and 1977
SEC Championships (21): 1933, 1934, 1937, 1945, 1953, 1961, 1964, 1965, 1966, 1971, 1972, 1973, 1974, 1975, 1977, 1978, 1979, 1981, 1989, 1992, 1999
Bowl appearances: 53 (30-20-3)
First season: 1892
College Football Hall of Fame (19): Johnny Mack Brown, 1923–25, halfback, inducted 1957; Paul Bryant, 1933–35, right end, 1986; Johnny Cain, 1930–32, fullback, 1973; Harry Gilmer, 1944–47, quarterback/defensive back, 1993; John Hannah, 1970–72, guard, 1999; Frank Howard, 1928–30, guard, 1989; Dixie Howell, 1932–34, halfback, 1970; Pooley Hubert, 1922–25, quarterback, 1964; Don Hutson, 1932–34, end, 1951; Lee Roy Jordan, 1960–62, linebacker, 1983; Vaughn Mancha, 1944–47, center, 1990; Johnny Musso, 1969–71, halfback, 2000; Billy Neighbors, 1959–61, tackle, 2003; Ozzie Newsome, 1974–77, split end, 1994; Fred Sington, 1928–30, tackle, 1955; Riley Smith, 1934–35, quarter-

back, 1985; Frank Thomas, 1931–46, coach, 1951; Wallace Wade, 1923–30, coach, 1955; Don Whitmire, 1941–42, tackle, 1956

Heisman Trophies: None

National Honors: Cornelius Bennett, 1986 Vince Lombardi/Rotary Award (outstanding lineman); Derrick Thomas, 1988 Dick Butkus Award (outstanding linebacker); Antonio Langham, 1993 Thorpe Award (outstanding defensive back); Jay Barker, 1994 Johnny Unitas Golden Arm Award (best senior quarterback); Chris Samuels, 1999 Outland Trophy (best interior lineman)

First-Team All-Americans: W. T. "Bully" VandeGraaff, T, 1915; A. T. S. "Pooley" Hubert, QB, 1925; Hoyt "Wu" Winslett, DE, 1926; Fred Pickhard, T, 1926; Tony Holm, FB, 1929; Fred Sington, OT, 1929–30; John Henry Suther, HB, 1930; Johnny Cain, FB/P, 1931–32; Tom Hupke, G, 1933; Don Hutson, SE, 1934; Bill Lee, DT, 1934; Millard "Dixie" Howell, QB, 1934; Riley Smith, QB, 1935; Arthur "Tarzan" White, G, 1936; James "Bubber" Nesbit, FB, 1936; James Ryba, DT, 1937; Leroy Monsky, G, 1937; Joe Kilgrow, HB, 1937; Carey Cox, C, 1939; Holt Rast, DE, 1941; Don Whitmire, OT, 1942; Joe Domnanovich, C, 1942; Vaughn Mancha, C, 1945; Harry Gilmer, HB, 1945; Ed Salem, HB, 1950; Bobby Marlow, HB, 1952; George Mason, T, 1954; Billy Neighbors, T, 1961; Lee Roy Jordan, LB, 1962; Dan Kearley, DT, 1964; Wayne Freeman, G, 1964; Joe Namath, QB, 1964; David Ray, K, 1964; Paul Crane, C, 1965; Steve Sloan, QB, 1965; Cecil Dowdy, T, 1966; Ray Perkins, SE, 1966; Bobby Johns, DB, 1966–67; Richard Cole, DT, 1996; Dennis Homan, SE, 1967; Bobby Johns, DB, 1967; Kenny Stabler, QB, 1967; Mike Hall, LB, 1968; Sam Gallerstedt, NG, 1968; Alvin Samples, G, 1969; Johnny Musso, HB, 1970–71; John Hannah, G, 1971–72; Jim Krapf, C, 1972; John Mitchell, DE, 1972; Buddy Brown, T, 1973; Woodrow Lowe, LB, 1973–75; Wayne Wheeler, SE, 1973; Leroy Cook, DE, 1974–75; Mike Washington, CB, 1974; Sylvester Croom, C, 1974; Ozzie Newsome, SE, 1977; Marty Lyons, DT, 1978; Barry Krauss, LB, 1978; Jim Bunch, T, 1979; Don McNeal, CB, 1979; Dwight Stephenson, C, 1979; E. J. Junior, DE, 1980; Thomas Boyd, LB, 1980–81; Tommy Wilcox, S, 1981–82; Mike Pitts, DE, 1982; Jeremiah Castille, CB, 1982; Cornelius Bennett, LB, 1984–86; Jon Hand, DT, 1985; Bobby Humphrey, TB, 1986–87; Van Tiffin, K, 1986; Kermit Kendrick, DB, 1988; Derrick Thomas, LB, 1988; Larry Rose, G, 1988; John Mangum, CB, 1989; Keith McCants, LB, 1989; Philip Doyle, K, 1990; Robert Stewart, NT, 1991; John Copeland, DE, 1992; Eric Curry, DE, 1992; Antonio Langham, CB, 1992–93; David Palmer, WR, 1993; Michael Proctor, K, 1993–94; Jay Barker, QB, 1994; Kevin Jackson, S, 1996; Dwayne Rudd, LB, 1996; Michael Myers, DE, 1996; Chris Samuels, T, 1999; Shaun Alexander, TB, 1999; DeMeco Ryans, LB, 2005

First-Team Academic All-Americans (CoSIDA): Tommy Brooker, E, 1961; Pat Trammell, B, 1961; Gaylon McCollough, C, 1964; Steve Sloan, QB, 1965; Dennis Homan, HB, 1965; Steve Davis, K, 1967; Bob Childs, LB, 1967; Johnny Musso, HB, 1970–71; Randy Hall, DT, 1973–74; Danny Ridgeway, KS, 1975; Major Ogilvie, RB, 1979

First-round NFL draftees: 36
Retired jerseys: None
Alabama's All-Century Team (selected by fans): Offense—E Don Hutson, 1932–34; E Ozzie Newsome, 1974–77; L Fred Sington, 1928–30; L Vaughn Mancha, 1944–47; C Dwight Stephenson, 1977–79; L Billy Neighbors, 1959–61; L John Hannah, 1970–72; QB Joe Namath, 1962–64; QB Ken Stabler, 1965–67; RB Bobby Marlow, 1950–52; RB Johnny Musso, 1969–71; RB Bobby Humphrey, 1985–88; K Van Tiffin, 1983–86 **Defense**—L Bob Baumhower, 1973, 1976; L Marty Lyons, 1975–78; L Jon Hand, 1982–85; LB Lee Roy Jordan, 1960–62; LB Barry Krauss, 1976–78; OLB Cornelius Bennett, 1983–86; OLB Derrick Thomas, 1985–88; DB Harry Gilmer, 1944–47; DB Don McNeal, 1977–79; DB Jeremiah Castille, 1979–82; DB Tommy Wilcox, 1979–82; P Johnny Cain, 1930–32; Coach: Paul W. "Bear" Bryant

THE COACHES

E. B. Beaumont, 1892, 2-2; Eli Abbott, 1893–95, 1902, 7-12; Otto Wagonhurst, 1896, 2-1; Allen McCants, 1897, 1-0; W. A. Martin, 1899, 3-1; M. Griffin, 1900, 2-3; G. H. Harvey, 1901, 2-1-2; W. B. Blount, 1903–04, 10-7; Jack Leavenworth, 1905, 6-4; J. W. H. Pollard, 1906–09, 20-4-5; Guy Lowman, 1910, 4-4-0; D. V. Graves, 1911–14, 21-12-3; Thomas Kelly, 1915–17, 17-7-1; Xen C. Scott, 1919–22, 29-9-3; Wallace Wade, 1923–30, 61-13-3; Frank Thomas, 1931–46, 115-24-7; Harold (Red) Drew, 1947–54, 54-29-7; J. B. Whitworth, 1955–57, 4-24-2; Paul (Bear) Bryant, 1958–82, 232-46-9; Ray Perkins, 1983–86, 32-15-1; Bill Curry, 1987–89, 26-10-0; Gene Stallings, 1990–96, 62-25-0-x; Mike DuBose, 1997–2000, 24-23-0; Dennis Franchione, 2001–02, 17-8; Mike Shula, 2003–05, 20-17 (x—forfeits imposed by NCAA)
National Coach of the Year: Paul (Bear) Bryant 1961, 1971, 1973; Gene Stallings 1992
SEC Coach of the Year, AP: Paul (Bear) Bryant 1958, 1959, 1961, 1964, 1965, 1971, 1973, 1978, 1979, 1981, 1989; Bill Curry 1989; Gene Stallings 1992, 1994; Mike DuBose 1999 **Coaches:** Frank Thomas 1945; Harold Drew 1952; Paul (Bear) Bryant 1961, 1964, 1971, 1973, 1974, 1977, 1979, 1981; Bill Curry 1989; Gene Stallings 1992; Mike DuBose 1999
SEC Championships: Paul (Bear) Bryant 13, Frank Thomas 4, Red Drew 1, Bill Curry 1, Gene Stallings 1, Mike DuBose 1
National Championships: Paul (Bear) Bryant 6, Wallace Wade 3, Frank Thomas 2, Gene Stallings 1

RECORDS

Rushing yards, game: 291, Shaun Alexander vs. LSU, Nov. 9, 1996 (20 attempts)
Rushing yards, season: 1,471, Bobby Humphrey, 1986 (236 attempts)

Rushing yards, career: 3,565, Shaun Alexander, 1996–99 (727 attempts)
Passing yards, game: 484, Scott Hunter vs. Auburn, Nov. 29, 1969 (30 of 55)
Passing yards, season: 2,499, Brodie Croyle, 2005 (202 of 339)
Passing yards, career: 6,282, Brodie Croyle, 2002–05 (487 of 929)
Receiving yards, game: 217, David Palmer vs. Vanderbilt, Sept. 11, 1993 (8 receptions)
Receiving yards, season: 1,000, David Palmer, 1993 (61 receptions)
Receiving yards, career: 2,070, Ozzie Newsome, 1974–77 (102 receptions)
Points, game: 30, Santonio Beard vs. Ole Miss, Oct. 19, 2002 (5 touchdowns); Shaun Alexander vs. BYU, Sept. 5, 1998 (5 touchdowns)
Points, season: 144, Shaun Alexander, 1999 (24 touchdowns)
Points, career: 345, Philip Doyle, 1987–90 (one touchdown, 78 field goals, 105 PATs)

In many ways, the SEC owes a lot of its success to the University of Alabama football program, and not because it's won the most national championships (12), SEC titles (21), or made the most bowl appearances (53).

Rather, it's because Alabama had a series of landmark victories that first helped to put Southern football on the map, taking the initial steps for the region to eventually challenge, if not surpass, the rest of the country.

The first victory came 30 years after William G. Little brought football to the school in 1892. The team was directed by surly coach Xen Scott, a former horse-racing writer from Cleveland who won his first five games in 1919 by a combined score of 225-0, and the following year led Alabama to its first 10-win season. With two losses and a tie already to show for the 1922 season, the Crimson Tide rolled into Philadelphia to play Penn on November 4 as a heavy underdog.

But it didn't play like one. With approximately 25,000 on hand, a field goal by Bull Wesley and the recovery of teammate Pooley Hubert's fumble in the end zone by center Shorty Propst resulted in a 9-7 upset. According to numerous accounts, Scott and his players paraded through the streets of the city and when they eventually got home were greeted by thousands of fans at the Tuscaloosa Train Depot.

The event would also serve as Scott's signature win. Unbeknownst to the players, he had already turned in his letter of resignation and would soon die of throat cancer. With a final 59-0 victory against Mississippi State, Scott's career ended with a 29-9-3 record.

The second landmark victory was more by design. When Dr. George Hutcheson Denny was hired as president of the university in 1912, he was ahead of his time in that he saw football as a tool for building enrollment and gaining notoriety. To give an example of how correct he was, when Denny arrived, the campus had just 652 students and nine principal buildings. When he retired in 1936 there were more than 5,000 students and the campus had 23 major buildings, which still form its central core.

Hoping to build a potential football dynasty, Denny replaced Scott with Vanderbilt assistant coach Wallace Wade, a former Calvary captain in World War I who had lost his right hand in an agriculture accident. His first season produced a 7-2-1 record with Alabama getting pounded at Syracuse, 23-0, in a game Wade claimed taught him more about football than any other.

Alabama (8-1) won its first championship in 1924 by defeating Georgia 33-0 to claim the Southern Conference title. Alabama outscored its opponents 290-24 and recorded seven shutouts, but that was nothing to what the team would accomplish in 1925.

Through its first eight games, the Tide gave up just one touchdown, with Johnny Mack Brown and Pooley Hubert the best backfield combination in college football. A gut-wrenching 7-0 victory against Georgia Tech set up a rematch with Georgia for the Southern Conference title, and, similar to the year before, it was all Alabama, 27-0.

Only the season wasn't over yet. On hand for the victory were representatives of the Rose Bowl Committee, who essentially decided which teams would play for the national championship. When Colgate, Dartmouth, and Yale all turned down invitations due to pressure from the American Association of University Professors, which had issued an unfavorable report on the sport, the first offer to a Southern school was extended. Alabama would play the heavily favored Washington Huskies, and many considered the pairing a colossal mistake.

Led by fullback George "Wildcat" Wilson, Washington jumped out to a 12-0 lead, prompting Wade to walk into the locker room, growl "They told me boys from the South would fight," and walk out. After Wilson unnecessarily twisted Brown's leg while finishing a tackle, the Tide responded by knocking Wilson out of the game for the third quarter. Hubert punched in one touchdown, and Brown scored on both a 59-yard reception from Grant Gillis and a 30-yard catch from Hubert. Washington closed the gap and threatened another touchdown in the waning moments when Brown made an open-field tackle of Wilson to end the threat. Alabama won 20-19 to change the game and the region forever.

"If Alabama had lost badly in 1926, by 40 points or more, would football then have become the sort of important, defining experience that it became over the next five decades? My answer is no, it would not have," Southern historian Wayne Flint concluded. "Because the South would have just been proved yet again to be inferior in some other dimension in life, and what would have happened, I think, is the South would have found some other way to excel. It would have invested this kind of emotional energy and physical commitment to anything else."

Alabama continued its winning ways in 1926 and with a 33-6 Thanksgiving victory against Georgia won a third-straight Southern Conference championship. The only close game was a 2-0 victory against Sewanee, decided by a blocked punt that went out of the end zone. Led by All-Americans Fred Pickhard and Hoyt "Wu" Winslett, along with All-Southern Conference backs Herschel Caldwell and Emile Barnes and center Gordon "Sherlock" Holmes, the Tide outscored its opponents 242-20.

It was back to Pasadena, though this time Alabama didn't have to wait for an invitation to play Stanford, which was coached by the legendary Pop Warner. Because voting was often conducted at the conclusion of the regular season, both teams along with Lafayette and Navy had already been declared national champions by at least one outlet. Alabama was outplayed, but Stanford could never put the game away, resulting in a 7-7 tie.

Wade turned in his resignation at the end of the 1929 season but agreed to stay on for the final year of his contract before heading to Duke. An 18-6 win against Tennessee and a 12-7 victory vs. Vanderbilt had the Tide 5-0, and it had already yielded the only points Alabama would give up all season.

A season-ending 13-0 victory against Georgia meant both a perfect season and Southern Conference championship, resulting in another invitation to the Rose Bowl to play Washington State. Even though the national championship was at stake, Wade started his second unit. Washington State held its own against the backups, but not against the starters, and Alabama easily won 24-0. After what Clyde Bolton of the *Birmingham News* called the "greatest swan song in the history of football," Wade concluded his Alabama career with a 61-13-3 record and third national championship.

For a replacement Wade suggested Georgia assistant Frank Thomas, who had been the roommate of George Gipp at Notre Dame, and Denny concurred. Among his first moves was to adopt Knute Rockne's "Box Formation" offense, which relied on speed and deception but also helped open up the passing game.

Led by back Johnny "Hurry" Cain, Alabama destroyed most of its opponents in 1931, including Clemson (74-7), Ole Miss (55-6), and Mississippi State (53-0), but lost to Tennessee (25-0). The 9-1 record remains the best debut season for a coach in school history, and the 36-point average was an Alabama record.

Even after its first conference game was a scoreless tie with Ole Miss, Alabama won the first SEC championship in 1933, thanks to a key 12-6 victory at Tennessee. The only loss was a 2-0 controversial game against Fordham in front of 60,000 fans at the Polo Grounds in New York. Guard Tom Huke was named All-American, but the Crimson Tide also had an amazing collection of younger players, including fullback Joe Demyanovich, halfback Dixie Howell, end Don Hutson, tackle Bill Lee, quarterback Riley Smith, and a rugged end named Paul W. "Bear" Bryant.

They came back in 1934 to form one of the greatest teams in college football history. After beating Howard 24-0, Alabama practically breezed through its SEC schedule, with the only close game against Tennessee, 13-6. Although many sportswriters thought Minnesota was a more deserving choice, Alabama returned to the Rose Bowl to again face Stanford. The game was a sellout with 84,484, and as usual the Tide was considered the underdog. Duly inspired, and aided by scouting reports from former standout Brown, Alabama dominated 29-13. Howell scored two touchdowns, one on a 67-yard run, and passed 59 yards to Hutson for another. He threw for 160 yards, ran for 111, and averaged 43.8 yards a punt to be named game MVP.

Will Rogers, who referred to the Tide as "Tusc-a-losers" before its first Rose Bowl appearance, noted that "Stanford made a mistake in scoring first. It just made those Alabama boys mad."

Alabama had won its fourth national championship, averaging 31.4 points per game while yielding just 4.5. Howell was named SEC Player of the Year, and Hutson went on to revolutionize the National Football League with the Green Bay Packers.

Alabama finished atop the SEC again in 1935, but the 6-2-1 record was a bit disappointing. Instead the season was best remembered for Bryant's gutsy play against Tennessee, in which he caught a touchdown pass and lateraled to All-American Smith for another score despite playing with a broken fibula sustained against Mississippi State.

"It was just one little bone," Bryant said.

In 1936, Bryant joined Thomas' staff as an assistant coach; and in the first season-ending Associated Press poll, Alabama (8-0-1) was fourth. Inspired by a bowl snubbing, Alabama came back in 1937 to record a perfect regular season, thanks to three narrow victories: 14-7 at Tennessee, 9-6 at Tulane, and 9-7 at Vanderbilt. Otherwise, the Tide dominated, outscoring opponents 225-33 in clinching the SEC championship to secure another invitation to the Rose Bowl. But during a practice on the way to California, a lineman pulled the wrong way and collided with Leroy Monsky, the All-American guard, who needed 25 stitches to close the cut above his left eye. Monsky played, but the team never recovered, losing to California 13-0. It was the only loss Alabama ever recorded in the Rose Bowl. Again, the Tide was ranked fourth.

Unsettling finishes to the two previous seasons didn't sit well with Thomas, who decided Alabama needed to go back to the West Coast and get a victory. So, for the 1938 season opener, he scheduled a trip to Los Angeles to play Southern California. Alabama came home 19-7 winners, but it proved to be the season's biggest highlight; USC went on to play in the Rose Bowl and upset Duke, which was coached by Wade and hadn't been scored on all season, 7-3.

Alabama scored another tangible victory for the region in 1939 when it defeated (7-6) national power Fordham, which was led by its incredibly tough "Seven Blocks of Granite" line that included Vince Lombardi. Years later, after winning the 1966 Super Bowl with the Packers, Lombardi was asked what it felt like to be the greatest football team in the world. "I don't know," he said, "We haven't played Alabama yet."

With back Jimmy Nelson and end Holt Rast, who would be a unanimous All-American selection in 1941, Alabama overcame an early 14-0 loss to Mississippi State to receive an invitation to play Texas A&M in the Cotton Bowl. In scouting the Aggies, assistant coach Harold "Red" Drew said they had "the greatest passing team I have ever seen," but the game was played in poor weather. In its first post-season appearance other than the Rose Bowl, Alabama created 12 turnovers, including seven interceptions, in a 29-21 victory that was nowhere near as close as the score indicated. Although most of the polls had Minnesota No. 1 at season's end, Alabama and Texas, neither of which won its conference title, were able to claim a share of the national championship—Alabama thanks to the Houlgate System (1927–58), a mathematical rating system syndicated in newspapers, and Texas due to two other services (Berryman and Willamson).

With the outbreak of World War II, Alabama scheduled teams comprised of former college all-stars stationed at military bases, including the Georgia Naval Pre-Flight Skycrackers, who were coached by Tide assistant Hank Crisp. Led by All-American linemen Joe Domnanovich and Don Whitmire—who at season's end entered the Naval Academy and eventually rose to the rank of admiral—the Tide made its first appearance in the Orange Bowl and defeated Boston College, 37-21.

After a one-year break, Thomas had enough players—20, down from the then normal 50—in 1944 to put together a team made up of 17-year-olds who were too young to be drafted, students medically disqualified from military service, and returning veterans. It was his favorite of all the teams he coached.

Leading the Tide was a small all-around player from Woodlawn High School in Birmingham named Harry Gilmer, known for his trademark leaping passes—which he used partly because he otherwise couldn't see over his own linemen. With a 5-1-2 record, the "War Baby Tiders" secured the school's first invitation to the Sugar Bowl in New Orleans, where Gilmer put on a dazzling performance in front of 72,000 fans. Though a much older Duke pulled out a 29-26 victory in the final moments, Gilmer was named the game's MVP. Legendary sportswriter Grantland Rice wrote that he was "the greatest college passer I've ever seen."

With a full roster again in 1945, Alabama outscored opponents 430-80 to win the SEC championship. The perfect season resulted in the sixth invitation to the Rose Bowl. Once again the Tide, with many of the grown-up War Babies, was considered an underdog to Southern California, which had won eight straight games in Pasadena dating back to 1923. At halftime, USC had minus-24 yards of offense on 21 plays while Alabama led 20-0. The Trojans didn't get a first down until the third quarter, when they trailed 27-0, but Thomas held back in the second half for a 34-14 victory. It prompted USC coach Jeff Cravath to say, "There goes a great man. I'll never forget what he did today. If he wanted, he could have named the score."

Amazingly, even with the perfect 10-0 record, it didn't add up to a national title (except from the National Championship Foundation). Instead, Army was the consensus choice.

Due to failing health, Thomas resigned following the 1946 season and eventually died in 1954. With a career record of 115-24-7, he was elected to the College Football Hall of Fame in the same class with Hutson. Alabama didn't return to the postseason until the 1952 season when, led by a young quarterback named Bart Starr, it destroyed Syracuse 61-6 in the Orange Bowl and set 15 bowl records in the process.

The 1953 season, which featured the first televised home game, saw Alabama claim its first SEC championship in eight years when a late fourth-quarter field goal gave it a 10-7 victory against Auburn. However, the campaign ended in an unusual way at the Cotton Bowl.

With Alabama down 7-6, Rice halfback Dickie Moegle broke through the line at the Owls' 5, and by the time he was racing past the Tide sideline, a touchdown appeared imminent—until Alabama fullback Tommy Lewis stepped onto the field and drilled the startled Moegle. As if coming out of a daze, Lewis returned to the bench and covered his head with a towel as fans booed. Rice was awarded a touchdown, and at halftime Lewis went to Rice's locker room to apologize. Lewis' fabled explanation was simply, "I'm just too full of Bama."

Moegle finished with 265 rushing yards on just 11 carries, and Rice won 28-6.

After the program endured a 4-28-4 stretch that corresponded with rival Auburn's national championship in 1957, Alabama turned to Bryant, who after serving as a naval officer in World War II had coached at Maryland, Kentucky, and had Texas A&M on the brink of winning a national championship. He met with Alabama officials in secret and agreed to a 10-year contract with an annual salary of $17,000 and a house.

"I left Texas A&M because my school called me," Bryant said. "Mama called, and when Mama calls, then you just have to come running."

Like his approach at Texas A&M with the famous "Junction Boys," Bryant's first training camp was brutal, causing many veterans to quit. But the change was immediate and noticeable during the first game of the 1958 season. LSU, which was led by Heisman Trophy winner Billy Cannon and would go on to win the national championship, was down 3-0 at halftime and struggled to a 13-3 victory.

After a bit of a slow start with a 17-3 loss at Georgia, things came together midway through the 1959 season. While riding a four-game winning streak, Alabama handed Auburn a 10-0 loss to end a five-year drought against the Tigers. Its first bowl invitation in six years paired the Tide against Penn State in the inaugural Liberty Bowl. The game was played in frigid conditions in Philadelphia, and a fake field goal made the difference as Penn State won 7-0, but it was the beginning of 25 straight postseason appearances.

Led by quarterback Pat Trammell, linebacker/center Lee Roy Jordan, and lineman Billy Neighbors, Alabama simply destroyed the competition in 1961, beginning with a 32-6 victory at Georgia. Opponents scored 25 points all season, with North Carolina State, led by quarterback Roman Gabriel, managing the most—7—compared to 297 for the Tide.

After Tennessee tallied a field goal in a 34-3 loss, the Tide finished the regular season with shutouts against Houston, Mississippi State, Richmond, Georgia Tech, and Auburn. The No. 1 ranking following Georgia Tech held true through a 10-3 victory against Arkansas in the Sugar Bowl for the national championship.

"They play like it is a sin to give up a point," Bryant commented.

Although Alabama didn't repeat in 1962, it helped lead the SEC to one of its strongest years ever, with the conference sweeping the four major bowls. Looking for payback for linebacker Darwin Holt's vicious hit, which broke quarterback Emile Granning's jaw the previous year, Georgia Tech pulled out a hard-hitting 7-6 victory when Alabama came inches short of completing a 2-point conversion.

Keyed by Jordan, a unanimous All-American who finished fourth in Heisman Trophy balloting, Alabama came back to crush Auburn 38-0 and Oklahoma 17-0 in the Orange Bowl. Also leading the team was one of Bryant's notorious renegade quarterbacks, Joe Namath.

"If you aren't going all the way, why go at all?" Namath said.

(*Note:* Like Namath, Kenny Stabler would also be suspended by Bryant and was once quoted for saying, "There's nothing wrong with reading the game plan by the light of the jukebox.")

No. 5 Alabama finished 10-1. Fifteen seniors concluded their careers 29-2-2 over their last three seasons. Without them, 1963 was supposed to be a rebuilding year, but only a 10-6 loss to Florida and a 10-8 defeat by Auburn kept Alabama from running the table. Against SEC champion Ole Miss in the Sugar Bowl, the defense made six fumble recoveries and three interceptions, contributing to a 12-7 win.

A knee injury sustained against North Carolina State limited Namath in 1964, but against Auburn he came off the bench to throw a touchdown pass to end Ray Perkins and help lead a 21-14 victory. At 10-0, No. 1 Alabama played Texas in the first night Orange Bowl, a game remembered for its controversial officiating as much as anything else.

Again, Namath came off the bench and completed 18 of 37 passes for 255 yards and two touchdowns. In the closing seconds, Alabama had the ball inches away from the goal line and was down 21-17. The call was a quarterback sneak behind center Gaylon McCollough, who with the snap plowed into the end zone. One official signaled touchdown, but another overruled. Namath said: "I'll go to my grave knowing I scored."

Even with the loss to Texas, Alabama was considered the national champion, but in 1965 the Associated Press delayed the final poll until after the bowl games instead of the conclusion of the regular season. Strangely enough, the situation again worked in Alabama's favor, but only after a controversial start in which Georgia scored a game-winning touchdown, on a play in which the receiver should have been ruled down, for an 18-17 victory.

After beating LSU 31-7 and Auburn 30-3, Alabama was ranked fourth. Bryant turned down an opportunity to play in the Cotton Bowl to meet No. 3 Nebraska in the Orange Bowl and keep its dim national championship hopes alive. Thanks to No. 1 Michigan State losing to UCLA in the Rose Bowl and No. 2 Arkansas getting pounded by LSU in the Sugar Bowl, the Crimson Tide had a chance to defend its title.

Despite being outsized, Alabama outgained Nebraska 518 to 377 yards. Bryant utilized both the tackle-eligible play and more than one on-side kick in completing a masterful 39-28 victory for another national championship.

Alabama looked to make it three straight and rolled nearly every team it faced, allowing just 37 points all season with five shutouts. The team went to the Sugar Bowl for a rematch with Nebraska; on the first snap, Stabler threw a 45-yard pass to Perkins to set up the Tide's first touchdown, and the 34-7 rout was on.

However, the 11-0 finish didn't lead to the coveted three-peat. Going into the bowls, Alabama was ranked third behind Michigan State and Notre Dame, which played to a 10-10 tie with the Fighting Irish running out the clock. Tide fans consider it the "thirteenth" national championship, or the one that got away.

Maintaining that level of excellence was nearly impossible, and in 1967 Tennessee snapped Alabama's 25-game unbeaten streak, 24-13. Stabler's 47-yard "run in the mud" against Auburn resulted in a 7-3 victory, 8-1-1 record, and Cotton Bowl bid to face Texas A&M, coached by Bryant's former assistant Gene Stallings. Five turnovers did the Tide in, including two interceptions by Tuscaloosa-area native Curley Hallman for the Aggies. When the 20-16 game ended, Bryant fittingly gave Stallings a bear hug at midfield.

While defense carried the 8-3 team in 1968, the season was overshadowed when Trammell lost his life to cancer. Bryant said once of his former quarterback, "He can't run, he can't pass, and he can't kick. All he can do is beat you," but upon hearing the news called it "the saddest day of my life."

Alabama came back in 1969 to set offensive records, but as in the following year, the Tide barely won enough to play in a bowl. In one of the rare true shoot-outs in the program's history, Scott Hunter completed 22 of 29 passes for 300 yards against Ole Miss quarterback Archie Manning, who was 33 of 52 for 436 yards and also ran for 104 more. Even though Bryant told his assistants that they were fired numerous times while storming up and down the sideline, Alabama won 33-32 on George Ranager's game-winning touchdown reception.

Unsatisfied, and not having won the SEC championship since 1966, Bryant slipped off during the summer of 1971 to visit Darrell Royal at Texas and study the wishbone offense. Alabama players and coaches were sworn to absolute secrecy about the new scheme, going so far as to run the old offense whenever reporters were at practice. When the Tide rolled into Los Angeles to play No. 5 USC, the heavily favored Trojans were completely surprised and lost 17-10.

For the first time, both No. 3 Alabama and No. 5 Auburn entered the Iron Bowl undefeated, and the Tigers were led by quarterback Pat Sullivan, who would go on to win the Heisman Trophy. But Alabama had Johnny Musso, a unanimous All-American with whom Sullivan would share SEC Player of the Year honors. On national television, Alabama manhandled Auburn, 31-7. The only letdown of the season was a 38-6 loss to No. 1 Nebraska in the national championship Sugar Bowl.

When Alabama opened the 1973 season with a 66-0 victory against a California team that featured quarterback Steve Bartkowski and running back Chuck Muncie, it was obvious that Bryant was ready to make a run for his fourth national championship. Aided by halfback Randy Billingsley's blocks, Alabama had four players each reach 100 rushing yards during a 77-6 victory against Virginia Tech. On Thanksgiving, the Tide handled another unbeaten rival, No. 7 LSU, 21-7, before pounding Auburn 35-0. Alabama would score a school-record 477 points and averaged 480.7 yards per game.

The season culminated at the Sugar Bowl with Alabama's first meeting against Notre Dame in one of the most-hyped games in college football history. Bryant vs. Ara Parseghian lived up to the hoopla, but when Alabama couldn't put the game away in the third quarter, the Irish pulled out a 24-23 victory. Because UPI held its final rankings before the loss, the final time any poll has done so, Alabama was credited with the split, and unsettling, national championship.

"I don't really consider it a loss," Bryant said. "We just ran out of time."

Despite injuries, the 1974 season was almost an exact repeat, including a rematch with Notre Dame in the Orange Bowl. In Parseghian's last game, the outcome was the same, 13-11.

The 1975 season appeared to be as promising as the four before it, in which Alabama was an incredible 43-5, but after a surprising 20-7 opening loss to Missouri there was hardly any title talk in Tuscaloosa. From there, the Tide went on a tirade, allowing just 52 total points with no regular-season opponent finishing a game within 10 points. With the SEC reaching an agreement for its champion to play annually in the Sugar Bowl, Alabama—which, stunningly, was winless in eight straight postseason games—was matched up against Penn State and coach Joe Paterno.

Sophomore Ozzie Newsome's 55-yard slant set up the only touchdown of the game, an 11-yard sweep by halfback Mike Stock, and Alabama won 13-6. With an 11-1 record, Alabama finished third in the polls while Oklahoma (11-1) was credited with defending its national title.

A 1977 early-season 31-24 loss at Nebraska was cause for concern after the defense gave up the most points since playing the Cornhuskers in the 1972 Sugar Bowl. But less than a month later, Alabama pulled off a 21-20 upset at No. 1 Southern California and eventually drew No. 9 Ohio State for the Sugar Bowl, featuring the game's two winningest active coaches, Bryant and Woody Hayes. When the Crimson Tide won a 35-6 rout, Bryant was quoted as saying: "Woody is a great coach . . . and I ain't bad." However, title hopes were again dashed by Notre Dame (11-1), which upset No. 1 Texas in the Cotton Bowl and leapfrogged the Tide from No. 5.

The No. 2 finish motivated the 1978 squad, which would face a murderer's row of Nebraska, Missouri, Southern California, Washington, Florida, Tennessee, LSU, and Auburn, followed by the presumably difficult bowl opponent.

The Tide stumbled only once—against No. 7 Southern California, 24-14—and after defeating Auburn, 34-16, No. 2 Alabama was headed back to the Sugar Bowl to play No. 1 Penn State. The game came down to a goal-line stand, with Penn State facing third down at the 1. Defensive back Don McNeal made the first stop roughly a foot away from the end zone, and when Nittany Lions quarterback Chuck Fusina checked to see how far the ball was from the goal line, defensive lineman Marty Lyons warned him: "You'd better pass."

Instead, Paterno called Mike Guman's name for a run up the middle, where he was met by linebacker Barry Krauss. The impact popped the rivets off Krauss' helmet, but Guman was dropped short of the end zone.

"Here's a moment you dream about happening, and here it was staring at us in the face," linebacker Rich Wingo said. "Gut-check time. Coach always preached it, jaw to jaw, check to check. They weren't going anywhere."

Alabama (11-1) thought the national championship was sewn up, but UPI voters had other ideas. They promoted USC (12-1), which defeated No. 5 Michigan in the Rose Bowl (17-10), from No. 3 to No. 1, resulting in a split title.

There was only one thing to do—go undefeated in 1979 to cap the most dominating decade in college football. With numerous starters returning, the Tide was the preseason No. 1 selection, and it lived up to expectations by outscoring the first five opponents 219-9. Alabama survived scares against No. 18 Tennessee, LSU, and No. 14 Auburn (at that game, Bryant proclaimed that he would have to go back to his home state of Arkansas and plow if the Tide lost, prompting Auburn fans to yell "Plow, Bear, Plow!").

Once again the national championship would be settled at the Sugar Bowl, this time against Arkansas. After turning an early fumble into a field goal, the Razorbacks didn't know what hit them until it was 17-3 in the third quarter. Game MVP Major Ogilvie scored two touchdowns and had a 50-yard punt return to lead a 24-9 victory. At 12-0, Alabama, which had outscored its opponents 383-67 with five shutouts, was the unanimous No. 1.

For the 1970s, Alabama compiled an incredible 103-16-1 record with eight SEC titles and three national championships.

The 1980s wouldn't be as kind. When Ole Miss scored 35 points in the second game of the decade (a 59-35 victory), it seemed like only a matter of time before the winning streak would end. And at 28, it did—a 6-3 loss at Mississippi State on November 1. Two weeks later, Notre Dame won 7-0 in Birmingham, opening the door for Georgia to snare the SEC and national titles.

In 1981, Bryant found himself chasing a different kind of history. At season's start, he was just eight victories away from Amos Alonzo Stagg's record of 314 wins over a 57-year career. Despite Bryant's failing health, the record was a matter of when, not if. When the defense again made a goal-stand against No. 5 Penn State to spark a 31-16 victory, Bryant tipped his hat to the players.

Fittingly, Bryant would go for the record against Auburn, and it may have been the toughest ticket to get in state history. When Alabama won 28-17, two presidents—Ronald Reagan, who had been a sports reporter at the 1935 Rose Bowl, and Jimmy Carter—called to offer congratulations.

Bryant announced his retirement on December 15, 1982, making a Liberty Bowl matchup against Illinois his final sendoff. Led by cornerback Jeremiah Castille's three interceptions and a forced fumble, the Tide won 21-15 and then carried the Bear off on their shoulders one last time. Just 28 days later, the coach's heart gave out on January 26, 1983. He was 69. After the funeral in Tuscaloosa, with eight players serving as pallbearers, hundreds of thousands watched the procession to a cemetery in Birmingham.

Statistically, Bryant's legacy was a 323-85-17 record, 29 bowl appearances, 15 conference championships, and six national championships. In the 1960s and 1970s, no school won more games than Alabama did (193-32-5).

Perkins, who resigned his position as head coach of the NFL's New York Giants, had the impossible task of trying to follow Bryant. Alabama went 8-4 the first season, including a 28-7 upset of No. 5 Southern Methodist in the Sun Bowl. Although the bowl streak ended at 25 in 1984, the Tide defeated Auburn 17-15 thanks to a botched toss sweep at the Alabama 1 with safety Rory Turner making the tackle just short of the end zone.

In 1985, quarterback Mike Shula led a season-opening 20-16 upset of Georgia, which was topped only by the season-ending Iron Bowl. With Auburn leading 23-22 and less than a minute to play, Shula moved the Tide just enough to set up

"The Kick," Van Tiffin's dramatic 52-yard field goal with 6 seconds remaining. For an encore, Alabama went to the Aloha Bowl and beat Southern California, 24-3.

Linebacker Cornelius Bennett came back in 1986 to make "The Sack" when he crushed Notre Dame quarterback Steve Beuerlein. After Alabama's first-ever win against the Irish, 28-10, Beuerlein said, "He knocked me woozy. I have never been hit like that before and hopefully I'll never be hit like that again." Bennett was named an All-American for the third time, SEC Athlete of the Year, and Alabama's first winner of the Lombardi Trophy, signifying him as the nation's best lineman.

At the end of the season, Perkins (32-15-1) left for the Tampa Bay Buccaneers, and Bill Curry of Georgia Tech was hired. In addition to following Bryant, he had the double whammy of being an outsider and the first head coach without an Alabama tie since Thomas in 1937. That he also couldn't beat Auburn proved too much to overcome.

The Tide managed to win the SEC championship in 1989, but when it lost the first meeting on the Auburn campus 30-20, Curry had had enough. After Alabama fell 33-25 to Miami in the Sugar Bowl, clinching the national championship for the Hurricanes, he resigned and accepted the head coaching job at Kentucky.

Alabama didn't dare bring in another outsider and instead hired Stallings, who had also been one of Bryant's "Junction Boys" at Texas A&M.

"What's wrong with people expecting excellence?" Stallings said.

After a slow start in 1990, Stallings returned Alabama to power football. At No. 3 Tennessee, defensive back Stacy Harrison blocked a field goal to set up a last-second 47-yard attempt by All-American kicker Philip Doyle for a 9-6 victory. The Tide went on to win four of its next five games, including a 16-7 victory in the Iron Bowl. Despite a 34-7 loss to No. 18 Louisville in the Fiesta Bowl, where the Cardinals scored four touchdowns in the first quarter, hope had returned to Tuscaloosa.

Alabama fell short of the SEC championship in 1991, but when quarterback Danny Woodson was suspended for violating team rules, freshman Jay Barker stepped in and led a 20-17 victory at LSU, followed by a nail-biting 13-6 win in the Iron Bowl. At 10-1, Alabama drew defending national champion Colorado in the Blockbuster Bowl, where future Heisman contender David Palmer helped inspire a 30-25 victory.

Victories piled up during the centennial season of Tide football, though many of them were not pretty. When No. 1 Washington lost to No. 12 Arizona (16-3), unbeaten Alabama's destiny was in its own hands. Against Auburn, cornerback Antonio Langham stepped in front of a pass and returned it 61 yards for a touchdown. With the defense yielding just 20 rushing yards and getting five sacks, Alabama won going away 17-0. For the season, Alabama outscored opponents 366-122.

In the first SEC Championship Game, Langham again returned an interception for a touchdown to help lead a 28-21 victory. That left a showdown with No. 1 Miami, which had Heisman Trophy quarterback Gino Torretta and was riding a 28-game winning streak, in the Sugar Bowl. One pregame comment that especially attracted attention was made by Hurricanes wide receiver Lamar Thomas: "Alabama's cornerbacks don't impress me one bit. They're overrated. Real men don't play zone defense and we'll show them a thing or two come January 1st."

Alabama made Miami eat those words.

The game was highlighted by possibly the greatest play that didn't count. In the third quarter, Torretta hit Thomas in a full sprint for what seemingly would be a long touchdown—only cornerback George Teague chased him down before reaching the end zone, ripped the ball away in mid-stride, and started running the other way. Even though nullified by a penalty, it's called the "Play of the Century" at Alabama, which won 34-13.

But even with its twelfth national championship, not all was well with the Tide. After a night of celebrating, Langham signed a cocktail napkin for a sports agent, which the agent claimed constituted a contract, and a family member accepted a loan. Langham went to Stallings, who tried to have the deal nullified, but when the agent produced the signature near the end of the 1993 season, Alabama wound up forfeiting all of its regular-season games after reaching the SEC Championship (and losing to Florida 28-13), making a victory in the Gator Bowl its only win. Langham still won the Jim Thorpe Trophy, given to the best defensive back in the nation, and if not for the forfeits Barker would have finished 45-4-1, setting a school record for victories over a four-year period. He won the 1994 Johnny Unitas Award as the nation's best quarterback.

Near the end of the 1996 season, Stallings notified school officials of his intent to retire, and went public after Alabama pulled out a dramatic 24-23 victory against Auburn to reach the SEC Championship Game. Florida, which went on to win the national championship, won a 45-30 shootout in Atlanta, but the Tide sent Stallings off with a 17-14 win in the Outback Bowl against Michigan, which went on to win the national championship in 1997.

"It was real emotional," Stallings said after the coaching staff presented him with the game ball. "I can't think of a more fitting game."

The years following Stallings were nothing short of chaos for Tide fans. His successor, Mike DuBose, went 4-7 in 1997, marking the first time since 1955 that Alabama failed to win a game in Tuscaloosa, and DuBose barely kept his job by beating both LSU and Auburn in 1998. Prior to the start of the 1999 season, the coach admitted to having an affair with his secretary and paid $360,000 to settle the corresponding sexual harassment lawsuit. An overtime victory at Florida saved his job, and led by running back Shaun Alexander the Tide reached the SEC Championship Game, where it pounded Florida 34-7.

But when Alabama finished 3-8 in 2000, DuBose was finally let go. Dennis Franchione left Texas Christian, without warning, to be his replacement. But before he could hold a practice, an NCAA investigation turned into a full-blown recruiting scandal that would land the Tide on probation. Franchione scraped together a 7-5 season in 2001, followed by a 10-3 record in 2002, but after the final game at Hawaii disappeared from Tuscaloosa only to show up in College Station as the new coach of Texas A&M.

Initially, athletic director Mal Moore turned to Washington State coach Mike

Price; but after an illicit night in Pensacola, Florida, Price was promptly fired before coaching a game. Determined to hire someone with Alabama ties, Moore tapped Shula, who at age 37 became the second-youngest head coach in Division I football.

"I had some unfinished business," said Shula, who never won an SEC title as a player.

He came close in 2005 when, despite still feeling the effects of scholarship reductions, Alabama won its first nine games to peak at No. 3 and then shut down the nation's top-rated offense, Texas Tech, 13-10 at the Cotton Bowl.

After a 31-3 trashing of No. 5 Florida, quarterback Brodie Croyle was pictured on the cover of *Sports Illustrated*, which proclaimed, "Bama is Back."

THREE THINGS THAT STAND OUT ABOUT ALABAMA FOOTBALL

1. *The name and the hat:* The Crimson Tide nickname goes back more than 100 years, beginning with "The Thin Red Line," borrowed from Rudyard Kipling's poem "Tommy" about a British soldier. In 1907, sportswriter Hugh Robert of the *Birmingham Age-Herald* called the team the "Crimson Tide," in part from all the red mud it kicked up during games in Birmingham. Additionally, the houndstooth design, one of the most recognizable icons in college football, is one of the most cherished. Bryant nearly always wore his trademark hat, except when the Tide played in a domed stadium, like at the Sugar Bowl. "My mother always taught me not to wear a hat indoors," Bryant said.

2. *The Bryant Museum:* It's a real museum that features everything from newspaper clippings from Alabama's first game in 1892 to championship trophies and grandiose paintings of famous Tide moments. A must-visit for college football fans, it's located on Bryant Drive, next to the Bryant Conference Center, down the street from Bryant-Denny Stadium and not too far from Bryant High School. "I can't imagine being in the Hall of Fame with Coach Bryant," Ozzie Newsome said. "There ought to be two Hall of Fames, one of Coach Bryant and one for everyone else."

3. *The fans:* Not only are Alabama fans the most demanding in college football, with sometimes unrealistic expectations, but they also take every aspect of game days very seriously. Some arrive days early in motor homes and consider barbeque a form of art. Additionally, sorority and fraternity members dress up for games (the women in particular are experts at sneaking in alcohol). Many Alabama women have been known to seriously fret if they don't have dates for games lined up well beforehand.

Arkansas

THE SCHOOL

Location: Fayetteville, Arkansas
Founded: 1871
Enrollment: 17,269
Nickname: Razorbacks
Colors: Cardinal and white
Mascot: Tusk (a Russian boar)
Stadium: Donald W. Reynolds Razorback Stadium (72,000)
2005 officials: Dr. John A. White, chancellor; Howard Brill, faculty representative; Frank Broyles, athletics director

THE PROGRAM

National Championship (1): 1964
SEC Championships: None
Bowl appearances: 34 (11-20-3)
First season: 1894
College Football Hall of Fame (11): Lance Alworth, 1959–61, halfback, inducted 1984; Hugo Bezdek, 1908–12, coach, 1954; Frank Broyles, 1958–76, coach, 1983; Chuck Dicus, 1968–70, wide receiver, 1999; Wayne Harris, 1958–60, center, 2004; Lloyd Phillips, 1964–66, defensive tackle, 1992; Francis Schmidt, 1922–28, coach, 1971; Wear Schoonover, 1927–29, end, 1967; Clyde Scott, 1946–48, halfback, 1971; Billy Ray Smith, 1979–82, defensive end, 2000; Bowden Wyatt, 1953–54, coach, 1997
Heisman Winners: None
National Honors: Bill "Bud" Brooks, 1954 Outland Trophy (outstanding interior lineman); Lloyd Phillips, 1966 Outland Trophy
First-Team All-Americans: Wear Schoonover, E, 1929; Jim Benton, E, 1937; Clyde Scott, TB, 1948; Bud Brooks, G, 1954; Jim Mooty, HB, 1959; Wayne Harris, LB, 1960; Lance Alworth, HB, 1961; Billy Moore, QB, 1962; Ronnie Caveness, C, 1963–64; Bobby Crockett, E, 1965; Glen Ray Hines, T, 1965;

Lloyd Phillips, DT, 1965–66; Martine Bercher, S, 1966; Jim Barnes, G, 1968; Rodney Brand, C, 1969; Chuck Dicus, E, 1969–70; Cliff Powell, LB, 1969; Dick Bumpas, DT, 1970; Bruce James, DE, 1970; Bill McClard, K, 1970–71; Steve Little, K, 1976–77; Leotis Harris, G, 1977; Dan Hampton, DT, 1978; Jimmy Walker, DT, 1978; Greg Kolenda, T, 1979; Bruce Lahay, K, 1981; Billy Ray Smith Jr., DE, 1981–82; Steve Korte, G, 1982; Ron Faurot, DE, 1983; Greg Horne, DE, 1986; Tony Cherico, G, 1987; Wayne Martin, DT, 1988; Kendall Trainor, K, 1988; Jim Mabry, T, 1989; Brandon Burlsworth, G, 1998; Kenoy Kennedy, S, 1999; Anthony Lucas, WR, 1999; Jermaine Petty, LB, 2001; Ken Hamlin, S, 2002; Shawn Andrews, T, 2002–03; Felix Jones, KR, 2005

First-Team Academic All-Americans (CoSIDA): Gerald Nesbitt, FB, 1957; Lance Alworth, B, 1961; Ken Hatfield, B, 1964; Randy Stewart, C, 1965; Jim Lindsey, HB, 1965; Jack Brasuell, DB, 1965; Bob White, K, 1968; Bill Burnett, HB, 1969; Terry Stewart, DB, 1969; Brad Shoup, DB, 1978

First-round NFL draftees: 20

Retired jerseys: 12 Clyde Scott; 12 Steve Little; 77 Brandon Burlsworth

All-Centennial Team (selected by a committee of former players, sportswriters, sports information directors and fans): Offense—OL Bud Brooks, 1952–54; OL Glen Ray Hines, 1963–65; OL R. C. Thielemann, 1973–76; OL Leotis Harris, 1974–77; OL Steve Korte, 1981–82; OL Freddie Childress, 1985–88; WR Wear Schoonover, 1927–29; WR Bobby Crockett, 1963–65; WR Chuck Dicus, 1968–70; WR Jim Benton, 1970–72; QB Lamar McHan, 1951–53; QB Bill Montgomery, 1968–70; QB Joe Ferguson, 1970–72; QB Quinn Grover, 1987–90; RB Leon Campbell, 1946–49; RB Clyde Scott, 1946–48; RB Jim Mooty, 1957–59; RB Lance Alworth, 1959–61; RB Barry Foster, 1987–89; K/P Pat Summerall, 1949–51; K/P Steve Little, 1974–77; P Steve Cox, 1979–80 **Defense**—DL Dave Hanner, 1949–51; DL Fred Williams, 1949–51; DL Billy Ray Smith Sr., 1954–56; DL Lloyd Phillips, 1964–66; DL Dan Hampton, 1975–78; DL Billy Ray Smith Jr., 1979–82; DL Wayne Martin, 1985–88; LB Wayne Harris, 1958–60; LB Ronnie Caveness, 1962–64; LB Cliff Powell, 1967–69; LB Dennis Winston, 1973–76; DB Alton Baldwin, 1943–46; DB Billy Moore, 1960–62; DB Ken Hatfield, 1962–64; DB Martine Bercher, 1964–66; DB Steve Atwater, 1985–88

THE COACHES

John C. Futrall, 1894–96, 5-2; B. N. Wilson, 1897–98, 4-1-1; Colbert Searles, 1899–1900, 5-5-2; Charles Thomas, 1901–02, 9-8; D. A. McDaniel, 1903, 3-4; A. D. Brown, 1904–05, 6-9; F. C. Longman, 1906–07, 5-8-3; Hugo Bezdek, 1908–12, 29-13-1; E. T. Pickering, 1913–14, 11-7; T. T. McConnell, 1915–16, 8-6-1; Norman Paine, 1917–18, 8-3-1; J. B. Craig, 1919, 3-4; G. W. McLaren, 1920–21, 8-5-3; Francis Schmidt, 1922–28, 42-20-3; Fred Thomsen, 1929–41, 56-6-1; George Cole, 1942, 3-7; John Tomlin, 1943, 2-7; Glen Rose,

1944–45, 8-12-1; John Barnhill, 1946–49, 22-17-3; Otis Douglas, 1950–52, 9-21-0; Bowden Wyatt, 1953–54, 11-10; Jack Mitchell, 1955–57, 17-12-1; Frank Broyles, 1958–76, 144-58-5; Lou Holtz, 1977–83, 60-21-2; Ken Hatfield, 1984–89, 55-17-1; Jack Crowe, 1990–91, 9-15; Joe Kines, 1992, 3-6-1; Danny Ford, 1993–97, 26-30-1; Houston Nutt, 1998–2005, 57-40
National Coach of the Year: None
SEC Coach of the Year, AP: Houston Nutt 2001 **Coaches:** Houston Nutt 2001
SEC Championships: None
National Championships: Frank Broyles 1

RECORDS

Rushing yards, game: 271, Dickey Morton vs. Baylor, Oct. 13, 1973 (28 attempts)
Rushing yards, season: 1,387, Madre Hill, 1995 (307 attempts)
Rushing yards, career: 3,570, Ben Cowins, 1975–78 (635 attempts)
Passing yards, game: 387, Clint Stoerner vs. LSU, Nov. 28, 1997 (18 of 38)
Passing yards, season: 2,629, Clint Stoerner, 1998 (167 of 312)
Passing yards, career: 7,422, Clint Stoerner, 1996–99 (528 of 1,023)
Receiving yards, game: 204, Mike Reppond vs. Rice, Nov. 6, 1971 (12 receptions)
Receiving yards, season: 1,004, Anthony Lucas, 1998 (43 receptions)
Receiving yards, career: 2,879, Anthony Lucas, 1995–99 (137 receptions)
Points, game: 36, Madre Hill vs. South Carolina, Sept. 9, 1995 (six touchdowns)
Points, season: 120, Bill Burnett, 1969 (20 touchdowns)
Points, career: 294, Bill Burnett, 1968–70 (49 touchdowns)

What can you say about a college football program whose fans include former presidents of the United States, whose history and heritage are celebrated as proudly as nearly any other, and whose war cry is a boisterous pig call?

Though a relative newcomer to the Southeastern Conference, the University of Arkansas has a national championship to its credit, along with numerous conference championships that were based on the sole principle of, "Yes, we dare to mess with Texas." It boasts a legendary coach, has the distinction of having played two seven-overtime games and winning both (58-56 at Ole Miss in 2001 and 71-63 at Kentucky in 2003), and answers to one of the most unique nicknames you'll ever come across.

A little unusual? Yes, but don't tell that to a Razorbacks fan, especially when they're wearing a hat with a big pig on it and screaming "Go hogs!" at the top of their lungs. They simply don't care how they may look or what you may think of them. Either join in or prepare to be plowed down. That's the way it's been for roughly 100 years.

"The passion they have for the game," replied coach Joe Kines (1992) when he was asked what's the first thing that comes to mind about Arkansas football. "Those are good people there, good folks."

It was 1909, and the Arkansas Cardinals were 6-0 and on their way to a perfect season, scoring 186 points while allowing only 18. After the train from Memphis—where they had just defeated LSU 16-0 for the second of four shutouts—pulled in, coach Hugo Bezdek decided to address some of the students who had gathered to celebrate the victory.

"[They play] like a wild band of razorback hogs," he said, and no one referred to the football team as the Cardinals ever again. The Razorbacks—which had become the official nickname by the start of the following season—were born, providing one of the most unique heritages in all of college sports.

Actually, the program's roots go back to 1884, when students first petitioned the board of trustees to set apart 2½ acres for baseball and football. The land was granted, but with no expenditures. It wasn't until 1893 that an athletic association was formed to "foster and encourage the growing interest which the student body is manifesting in the development of the physical man," making it possible for the first team to form the following year under the direction of John C. Futrall. Arkansas played two high schools and was then promptly crushed at Texas 54-0.

It wasn't until 1908, when Bezdek became the first football coach to be paid at the university, that any effort was put into the program. However, the gains were both immediate and dramatic. Thanks to the strong play of quarterback Steve Creekmore, Arkansas backed up the 7-0 campaign of 1909 with a 7-1 record that included a 51-0 season-ending thrashing at LSU, and Arkansas outscored its opponents 221-19.

Bezdek, who managed baseball's Pittsburgh Pirates from 1917 to 1919 as a summer job between football coaching assignments in the fall, went 29-13-1 in five years, but he set the standard for all Arkansas coaches to follow. It wasn't until Francis Schmidt arrived from Tulsa in 1922 that anyone could compare, with the Razorbacks compiling a 42-20-3 record during his seven-year reign. His best season of 1927 saw an 8-1 record, led by Wear Schoonover, George Cole, and Glen Rose. During Schmidt's final season before heading to Texas Christian, Garland "Bevo" Beavers was named the most valuable player in the Southwest Conference, with the Razorbacks finishing 7-2.

(*Note:* Schmidt, who had a career record of 158-57-11, is best remembered for his pregame speech at Ohio State before the 1934 game against Michigan, when he said, "Those fellows are human; they put their pants on one leg at a time." Ohio State won 34-0 and founded the Pants Club. Any Ohio State player who takes part in a victory over Michigan is an automatic member.)

Little did anyone know, this was all only setting the scene for Fred Thomsen, one of the early innovators of the passing game, which was nowhere near as popular as it is today. Under Thomsen's direction, Schoonover threw the Razorbacks to a 7-2 record to become Arkansas' first All-American.

An ineligible player, who didn't tell coaches he had previously lined up for Nebraska, kept Arkansas from winning its first SWC title in 1933; but the passing combination of Jack Robbins to Jim Benton was ahead of its time. Robbins threw for 2,582 yards and 19 touchdowns, while Benton had 83 catches for 1,303 yards and 13 touchdowns.

Before forfeiting the title, however, Arkansas played Centenary to a 7-7 tie in the last Dixie Classic, which would evolve into the Cotton Bowl, when a 14-yard game-winning field goal went wide.

The conference title finally came in 1936, topped by a 6-0 victory against Texas in Little Rock.

Until Donald W. Reynolds Razorback Stadium debuted on September 24, 1938, celebrated by a 27-7 victory against Oklahoma A&M (with a 9-6 loss to Baylor on the day it was dedicated), the team played in a 300-seat facility known as "The Hill." Constructed as a Works Progress Administration project, the stadium's initial capacity was 13,500. Numerous renovations later, the latest being an elaborate $110 million project before the 2001 season, the capacity has been raised to 72,000 and the stadium includes what many believe is the best video board in college football, measuring 30 by 107 feet.

As Arkansas' recruiting improved, adding the likes of Olympian and All-American Clyde "Smackover" Scott to coach John Barnhill's squad, the Razorbacks got their first real taste of postseason action at the end of the 1946 season, with an invitation to the Cotton Bowl, where the teams played in 20-degree weather. Even though quarterback Y. A. Tittle led the Tigers, the Razorbacks stopped them within the 10-yard line five times in the first half alone and at the 1-yard line twice in the second half.

Scott, who won the silver medal in the 110-meter hurdles at the 1948 Olympic Games in London, had the play of the game when he tackled receiver Jeff Odom at the 1, and the subsequent field-goal attempt failed due to a bad snap. Arkansas, which had just one first down in the entire game, held on for a scoreless tie, and All-American end Alton Baldwin was named the bowl's outstanding lineman.

A year later, Arkansas defeated William & Mary 21-19 in the inaugural Dixie Bowl in Birmingham, Alabama. A 59-yard touchdown pass by Kenny Holland to Ross Pritchard and a 70-yard interception return for a touchdown by Melvin McGaha gave it a 14-13 lead, and a 97-yard drive, capped by Leon Cambell's 7-yard scoring run, completed the comeback.

Despite having future NFL players like Lewis Carpenter, Dave "Hawg" Hanner, Lamar McHan, Floyd Sagely, Pat Summerall, and Fred Williams, the Razorbacks struggled in the early 1950s. Their first victory against Texas, which was ranked fourth at the time, in Fayetteville, 16-14 in 1951, served as one of the few highlights. Nevertheless, a turning point was at hand.

The 1954 team, known as the 25 Little Pigs, was remembered for a dramatic upset against No. 5 Ole Miss, in a game that saw the lone score on the Powder River Play. With approximately six minutes remaining, quarterback Buddy Benson took the snap and began running a sweep—only to throw the ball downfield to Preston Carpenter, who had slipped behind the defensive backs. The pass was in the air for 33 yards, and Carpenter matched the distance for a 66-yard touchdown.

Coach Bowden Wyatt brought the play with him from Wyoming, where the Powder River is a mile wide and a deceptive six inches deep. But despite an impressive 8-3 season and another Cotton Bowl appearance, the Razorbacks couldn't stop George Humphreys, who had 285 rushing yards and two touchdowns, in a 14-6 loss to Georgia Tech. After just two seasons, Wyatt stepped down to take over his alma mater, Tennessee, concluding a five-year stretch in which Arkansas went 22-38 (Otis Douglas was 9-21 from 1950 to 1952).

Among those who applied for the job was an assistant coach from Baylor named Frank Broyles, but Arkansas chose to promote one of its own—Jack Mitchell. Although Mitchell had three winning seasons, he left for Kansas with a record of 17-12-1, and Arkansas was again left looking for a coach in 1958. It hired Broyles just one year after he had taken over at Missouri.

For six games, all losses and outscored 113-39, fans wondered if another coaching search would soon be at hand. Then, on November 1, Arkansas shocked Texas A&M 21-8 and backed it up by winning its final three games against Hardin-Simmons (60-15), Southern Methodist (13-6), and Texas Tech (14-8). More wins would follow, in addition to bowls and unfamiliar accolades.

In 19 seasons at Arkansas, Broyles won 144 games and six Southwest Conference championships. He led the Razorbacks to 10 bowl games (nine on New Year's Day) and its lone national title. Before he arrived, the Razorbacks had only four All-Americans, but they developed 18 under his tenure, including 88 all-conference players. He retired as coach following the 1976 season to concentrate on being the school's athletic director, a post he continues to hold as of this writing, but his name will forever be synonymous with Arkansas football.

"My wife and family are all very pleased," Broyles said upon his retirement from the sidelines. "They all forgot I had a good disposition."

Broyles' first SWC title came in 1959 and was topped off by a 14-7 victory against his alma mater, Georgia Tech (and college coach Bobby Dodd), in the Gator Bowl. Halfback Jim Mooty was named an All-American, an honor that would befall teammate Wayne Harris (nicknamed "Thumper" for his hard hits) a year later. The season also saw the emergence of one of the most exciting players ever to play football. In 1961, Lance Alworth led the team in rushing, receiving, punt returns, and kick returns as Arkansas went 8-3 for its third consecutive Southwest Conference title and played in the Sugar Bowl. (Alworth later played 11 years for the San Diego Chargers and Dallas Cowboys, picked up the nickname "Bambi" because teammates said he had big brown eyes and could run like a deer, and was the first player from the American Football League inducted into the Pro Football Hall of Fame.)

"Any athlete wants pride to compete against the best," said Alworth, who was president of his senior class, lettered in track and baseball as well, ran the 100-yard dash in 9.6 seconds, and was known for his base-stealing prowess. Upon graduation, he was offered baseball contracts by the Pittsburgh Pirates and New York Yankees but opted for pro football.

The Razorbacks lost 10-3 to Alabama, but led by quarterback/defensive back Billy Moore, they returned the following year and finished an impressive 9-2 despite a 17-3 loss to undefeated No. 3 Ole Miss, which was led by quarterback Glynn Griffing, in the Sugar Bowl.

"You don't think about the close games you win," Broyles said. "It's the close ones you lose that you think about."

Arkansas fans were growing more accustomed to winning, but even they were somewhat surprised by the 1964 team, which struggled to victories against Oklahoma State (14-10) and Tulsa (31-22) to open the season. It led to a showdown with defending national champion Texas, which had not lost a regular-season game in four years, on October 19. The low-scoring game was decided by possibly the most exciting play in Razorbacks history—Ken Hatfield's 81-yard punt return for a touchdown thanks to some terrific blocks, including one by Jim Lindsey—en route to a 14-13 victory.

Arkansas didn't allow another point in the regular season on its way to the Cotton Bowl, where Bobby Burnett's fourth-quarter 3-yard touchdown plunge capped an 80-yard drive to finish a 10-7 comeback victory against Nebraska. All-American center Ronnie Caveness was named the game's outstanding lineman, and Fred Marshall—who completed 11 of 19 passes for 131 yards—was named outstanding back.

Among the more interesting aspects of the national championship was how that specific title was awarded. At the time, a national champion was named by 15 different organizations, and the two most notable—the Associated Press and United Press International—tabulated the votes before the bowl games. In 1964, Alabama finished No. 1; however, the Crimson Tide lost 21-17 to Texas in the Orange Bowl. Two organizations that waited until after the bowls to vote—the Football Writers Association of America and the Helms Athletic Foundation—named Arkansas the national champion. Both AP and UPI changed their procedures the following year (which, strangely, worked to Alabama's benefit again).

The 1964 team, which was the first to don the Razorbacks logo on the helmets, posted an amazing five shutouts. Also interesting is that four men associated with the team—including, of course, Broyles—would coach national championship teams: Jimmy Johnson (Miami), Johnny Majors (Pittsburgh), and Barry Switzer (Oklahoma). Johnson and Switzer are the only coaches in history to win a college national championship and a Super Bowl, both with the Dallas Cowboys, owned by their former Arkansas teammate Jerry Jones. (*Note:* Jones and Johnson were both guards; Majors and Switzer were assistant coaches.)

The 1965 team picked up right where the previous team left off and once again had a memorable showdown with Texas that went the Razorbacks' way. After trailing 20-0, the Longhorns came back to take the lead, only to see Arkansas score a late touchdown for a 27-24 victory.

In similar fashion, the Razorbacks finished the regular season a perfect 10-0 and went into the Cotton Bowl ranked second. Again the No. 1 team, Michigan State lost 14-12 to UCLA in the Rose Bowl, but this time so did Arkansas. Quarterback Jon Brittenum led an 87-yard drive, capped by a 19-yard touchdown pass to All-American end Bobby Crockett, for an early 7-0 lead. Not only did LSU answer, but Brittenum sustained a separated shoulder. Two plays later, LSU recovered a fumble and quickly scored again for a 14-7 lead that would hold up despite Crockett setting a bowl record with 10 catches for 129 yards. The disappointing loss ended a 22-game winning streak for the Razorbacks.

As sophomores, quarterback Bill Montgomery and wide receiver Chuck Dicus had Arkansas back in the national spotlight in 1968, with a 39-29 loss to No. 17 Texas the only blemish in the regular season. The Razorbacks were supposed to be underdogs to 8-0-2 SEC champion Georgia—ranked fourth—in the Sugar Bowl, but the Bulldogs made nine turnovers while game MVP Dicus had 12 receptions for 169 yards and scored the only touchdown in the 16-2 victory. Arkansas finished the year No. 6.

"I've found that God is usually on the side that has the best defensive tackles," Broyles said.

The defense continued its dominating ways as Arkansas won its first nine games of 1969 by a combined score of 317-51. When Ohio State, which *Sports Illustrated* was touting as possibly the best team of all time, lost to Michigan, all eyes were on the December 6 meeting between No. 1 Texas and No. 2 Arkansas. The contest was tabbed as both the "Big Shootout" and the "Game of the Century," and with President Richard Nixon in the stands it lived up to expectations— but not the way Razorbacks fans hoped. Although Arkansas had a 14-0 lead going into the fourth quarter, James Street broke a 42-yard touchdown and later put the game away on fourth-and-3 on a rare long pass, resulting in a 44-yard completion, to set up the winning score.

"They're a great team. They know how to win and they know how to lose," Nixon said outside the Arkansas locker room after the Razorbacks' last effort was intercepted at the 8-yard line for a 15-14 final score.

Even Longhorns coach Darrell Royal admitted that his team had been out-played minus the two long-distance plays. Texas went on to win the national championship, while 9-2 Arkansas finished ranked seventh after losing to Ole Miss 27-22 in the Sugar Bowl. The heartache was topped off by Rebels quarterback Archie Manning, though his numbers (21 of 35 passes for 273 yards and one touchdown) weren't as good as Montgomery's 17 of 34 for 338 yards and two touchdowns.

(*Note:* Actually, the real heartache would soon be with the Longhorns. Three days after the game, Texas safety Freddie Steinmark was diagnosed with bone cancer, which resulted in his leg being amputated. He was on the sideline for the Cotton Bowl victory against Notre Dame, jokingly sporting a shaved head, a gold earring, and acting like a pirate. He died on June 6, 1971, at the age of 22.)

Arkansas went 9-2 in 1970, only to head into the offseason on a down note thanks to a 42-7 loss to Texas. The Razorbacks rode the arm of quarterback Joe Ferguson to an 8-3-1 finish the next year, following its first appearance in the Liberty Bowl. Though Ferguson passed for 200 yards to be named the game's outstanding player, and Louis Campbell was named the outstanding defensive player due to two interceptions, Arkansas lost 14-13 to Tennessee.

With an impressive 31-6 victory against No. 2 Texas A&M, highlighted by Teddy Barnes' touchdown catch from quarterback Scott Bull, the 1975 Razorbacks earned a spot in the Cotton Bowl, where linebacker Hal McAfee had 12 tackles and two fumble recoveries, and Ike Forte ran for 119 yards to lead a 31-10 victory against Georgia. At 10-2, Arkansas finished No. 7.

The man who had the unenviable task of trying to follow Broyles was none other than Lou Holtz, who once said: "Life is ten percent what happens to you and ninety percent how you react to it." The coach turned his first squad into a 10-1 team, with the lone loss 13-9 to Texas. Led by quarterback Ron Calcagni with Ben Cowins rushing for more than 1,000 yards, Arkansas averaged 33 points per game, and the defense, led by tackles Dan Hampton and Jimmy Walker, yielded just 8.6.

"I don't think we can win every game," Holtz said. "Just the next one."

Despite the impressive record, Arkansas was a heavy underdog to Oklahoma in the Orange Bowl. The Sooners, led by running back Billy Sims, were poised to be national champions thanks to No. 1 Texas losing to Notre Dame earlier that day at the Cotton Bowl. On top of that, Holtz had suspended his two top running backs and his best receiver for disciplinary reasons.

The game wasn't close. Thanks to a pair of early turnovers that were converted into touchdowns and a special play Holtz devised, the False-Key Tackle Run, Roland Sales had 205 rushing yards and 52 receiving as Arkansas crushed Oklahoma 31-6 to finish the season No. 3.

Pollsters had either Arkansas No. 1 or 2 behind Alabama heading into the 1978 season, but midseason losses at Texas (28-21) and Houston (20-9) cost a chance at the conference title. Despite Walker's 10-tackle performance, a late touchdown gave UCLA a 10-10 tie in the Fiesta Bowl, resulting in a 9-2-1 record.

With the addition of newcomers like running back Gary Anderson and defensive end Billy Ray Smith Jr., the Razorbacks won 10 games the following year—including at home against Texas (17-14)—to be co-champions of the SWC. Led by quarterback Kevin Scanlon, the conference's offensive player of the year, No. 6 Arkansas got its shot at Alabama in the Sugar Bowl, but in this case perhaps could have been more careful about what it wished for. After recovering a fumble on the opening kickoff and scoring a field goal, the Razorbacks were overwhelmed 24-9 as the Crimson Tide won yet another national championship. Scanlon completed 24 of 39 passes for 245 yards.

Led by Anderson's 156 yards on 11 carries and two touchdowns, and by Smith (who followed in his father's footsteps and set a school record with 63 career tackles for a loss to go with 229 total tackles), Arkansas managed to defeat Tulane 34-15 in the 1980 Hall of Fame Bowl to finish 7-5.

While still reeling from a 28-24 upset loss at Texas Christian, the Razorbacks scored another big victory when they hosted No. 1 Texas in 1981. Smith recovered a fumble on the first play, and from there things only got worse for the visiting team. After the 42-11 victory, fans stormed the field and tore down the goalposts for the first time since the 1951 meeting between the rivals. Arkansas went on to finish 8-4 with a late comeback coming up short in the Gator Bowl, where the only thing more potent than the fog was North Carolina's running game, which amassed 283 yards in the 31-27 victory.

The 1982 team had high expectations and climbed to No. 5 with a 7-0 start, but a loss at Baylor, followed by a controversial pass-interference call that led to a 17-17 tie against Southern Methodist, cost any chance of a conference title. Arkansas responded with a 33-7 loss at Texas, but Anderson had a career-high 161 rushing yards on 26 carries and scored two touchdowns as the senior-laden Razorbacks twice overcame a 10-point deficit to beat Florida 28-24 in the Bluebonnet Bowl—

Holtz's last postseason game leading Arkansas, because he left after the 6-5 1983 season.

"At Arkansas, they made a stamp to commemorate you; then, after last year, they had to stop making it because people were spitting on the wrong side," Holtz said.

Strangely enough, even though the Cotton Bowl is a prominent part of Arkansas' history, Holtz's teams never played in the New Year's classic.

Under the direction of former defensive back Hatfield, Arkansas was known for running the triple option in the 1980s when it played in six straight bowl games and the coach compiled a 55-17-1 record. (*Note:* When asked if he would still like Hatfield if the team went .500, Broyles said, "Sure. I'd miss him too.") Even though opponents knew it was coming, they still struggled to stop the variation of the wishbone, which took advantage of the quarterback's speed. Arkansas led the SWC in rushing three times and posted three 10-win seasons despite going 1-5 in the bowls.

Hatfield's first team managed to win four games in the fourth quarter and squeezed into the 1984 Liberty Bowl, where Auburn had a season-low 168 rushing yards and 252 yards of total offense. But the Razorbacks' last-minute rally came short against the preseason No. 1–ranked team that featured running back Bo Jackson. Auburn won 21-15.

Arkansas would win at least nine games in each of the next five seasons, starting with an impressive 10-2 campaign in 1985 that was topped with an 18-17 comeback victory over Arizona State in the Holiday Bowl, thanks to freshman Kendall Trainor's 37-yard field goal with just 21 seconds remaining. No opponent scored a rushing touchdown over the last nine games.

The 21-14 victory at Texas in 1986 was Arkansas' first win at Austin in 20 years, and a 14-10 victory against Texas A&M in Little Rock led to another Orange Bowl invitation to play Oklahoma. But this time, there would be no dramatic comeback. After the Sooners failed to get a first down in the first quarter, Spencer Tillman scored the first of two touchdowns on a 77-yard run and the rout was on. Although quarterback Greg Thomas had only one pass intercepted during the regular season, Oklahoma picked off five in the 42-8 victory.

The conclusion of the 1987 season was equally disappointing, especially after Arkansas was the preseason favorite to win the SWC. As usual their nemesis, Texas, got in the way and pulled out a 16-14 victory on the last play of the game; Arkansas followed that with a 14-0 loss to Texas A&M. Nine wins resulted in a trip to the Liberty Bowl, but again, untimely interceptions were too much to overcome along with future National Football League kicker John Kasay making a 39-yard field goal to give Georgia a 20-17 win.

A retooled backfield featuring quarterback Quinn Grovey along with James Rouse and Barry Foster had the Razorbacks off and running in 1988, and at the end of the conference schedule No. 8 Arkansas was atop the SWC at 10-0. But even with LaSalle Harper, Wayne Martin, and Steve Atwater leading the defense, Arkansas couldn't put away the No. 3 Hurricanes, who won 18-16 in Miami.

Quarterback Troy Aikman spoiled the first trip to the Cotton Bowl in 13 years, while the UCLA defense allowed just 42 yards for a 17-13 Bruins victory.

Hatfield had a final trip to the Cotton Bowl in his last year of coaching the Razorbacks, thanks to a wild 45-39 victory against Houston, which was led by Heisman Trophy winner Andre Ware, and a 23-22 win at Texas A&M. Arkansas had a record-setting performance, with 568 yards of total offense and 31 first downs, but a pair of turnovers within the 10-yard line paired with a 205-yard rushing performance by Chuck Webb paced Tennessee, which held on for a 31-27 victory.

Ironically, three years later, Arkansas' first SEC victory after joining the conference would be against the Volunteers, who were unbeaten and ranked fourth, 25-24. Later in the 1992 season, under the direction of interim head coach Kines, Arkansas defeated LSU for the first time since 1929, 30-6, but finished 3-6-1.

It wasn't until 1995 that the Razorbacks would make their first big splash in the SEC, when coach Danny Ford—who said, "It doesn't take a scientific rocket to find out what kind of offense we're going to run this year"—finished 6-2 in the conference. Madre Hill scored a school-record six touchdowns against South Carolina (51-21), J. J. Meadors caught a fourth-down pass from Barry Lunney Jr. with 6 seconds remaining to win at Alabama (20-19), and Arkansas held on for a 30-28 victory against Auburn to advance to its first SEC Championship Game. But a 34-3 loss to Florida was followed by a 20-10 defeat against North Carolina in the Carquest Bowl, primarily due to an 87-yard touchdown pass by Mike Thomas to L. C. Stevens.

Arkansas wouldn't return to the SEC Championship Game until 2002, but with the hiring of coach Houston Nutt in 1998 began a streak of six consecutive years with bowl appearances. He also was the first Arkansas coach to win his first eight games, despite being picked to finish last in the Western Division. With quarterback Clint Stoerner and receiver Anthony Lucas rewriting the Arkansas record book, the Razorbacks pulled out close wins against both Kentucky and Auburn, with a 42-6 decision Alabama's worst loss in 40 years.

The first SEC team to stop Nutt was—perhaps fittingly—Tennessee, which was ranked No. 1 and went on to win the national championship. Arkansas saw its 21-3 lead evaporate, and a fumble after Stoerner tripped and fell with less than two minutes to play set up the Volunteers' game-winning touchdown and 28-24 final. A week later the Razorbacks lost again on a last-second field goal against Mississippi State, resulting in a trip to the Florida Citrus Bowl, where Arkansas lost 45-31 to defending national champion Michigan.

Even though no longer in the defunct SWC, Nutt led Arkansas back to the Cotton Bowl at the end of the 1999 and 2001 seasons.

Coming off a loss at Ole Miss (38-16), the Razorbacks defeated three Top 20 teams over its last four games, including a dramatic late comeback against No. 3 Tennessee in which Stoerner had touchdown passes of 53 yards to Boo Williams and 23 yards to Lucas—known as the Double Post Redemption Pass—for a 28-24 victory. Again, the goalposts took the brunt of the celebration, which continued the following week with a 14-9 victory against No. 12 Mississippi State before going state-wide and year-round.

Against Texas in the first game of the new millennium, eight sacks—including two by D. J. Cooper—and a goal-line stand by Arkansas limited Texas to minus-27 rushing yards. However, the low-scoring contest was still close heading into the fourth quarter, when Arkansas scored 17 points to blow the game open. Freshman Cedric Cobbs scored the second of his two touchdowns to be named the most outstanding player, and the 27-6 result snapped the Razorbacks' seven-game losing streak in bowl games.

Thanks to upset wins against No. 13 Mississippi State (17-10 in overtime) and No. 24 LSU (14-3), Arkansas managed to get enough wins for an invitation to the 2000 Las Vegas Bowl (a 31-14 loss to Nevada–Las Vegas). The Razorbacks got off to an uninspiring start in 2001 when they lost the reopening game at the expanded Donald W. Reynolds Razorback Stadium 13-3 to Tennessee and followed that with defeats at Alabama (31-10) and Georgia (34-23). But a six-game winning streak returned the Razorbacks to Dallas to face yet another defending national champion, Oklahoma. Only one touchdown was scored—by the Sooners, who, led by strong safety Roy Williams, recorded almost as many sacks (nine) as points in the 10-3 contest.

Another late-season winning streak in 2002, including three consecutive shutouts against Troy State, South Carolina, and Louisiana–Lafayette, set up a showdown with LSU with a spot in the SEC Championship Game on the line. LSU had a 17-7 lead heading into the fourth quarter when senior tailback Fred Talley scored a 56-yard touchdown to close the gap. The Tigers countered with a field goal, giving the Razorbacks the ball at their own 19 with 40 seconds remaining.

A 50-yard pass from quarterback Matt Jones to Richard Smith resulted in a first down at the LSU 31. Even though Jones had completed only three passes in the game, he threw the ball into the back right corner of the end zone where sophomore DeCori Birmingham leaped between two defenders to make the grab.

Hardly anyone in Arkansas remembers it lost to No. 4 Georgia 30-3 in the SEC Championship Game, and then 29-14 to Minnesota in the Music City Bowl. Also forgotten by most was that in the wild celebration following Birmingham's touchdown the Razorbacks were penalized 15 yards for unsportsmanlike conduct. The penalty was marked off prior to the extra point, which Arkansas had to make to break the 20-20 tie. But David Carlton drilled it to cap off the "Miracle on Markham" (War Memorial Stadium in Little Rock, where the Razorbacks usually play a couple times a year, sits along Markham Street), which was in many ways typical for Arkansas football.

It was spectacular, impressive, and a little unusual, all in one.

THREE THINGS THAT STAND OUT ABOUT ARKANSAS FOOTBALL

1. *Tusk:* Real razorbacks, which can be found only in remote parts of Australia, have little resemblance to the hogs that frequent most farms today; but Tusk,

the mascot, is still pretty intimidating even if it is in a cage. Fortunately for Arkansas fans, the Russian boar isn't susceptible to the team's code of conduct, because its predecessors have been known to escape and create mischief, including killing a coyote, a 450-pound domestic pig, and numerous rattlesnakes. As far as anyone knows, no one has been brave or stupid enough to try stealing the mascot.

2. *"Hog Call":* Novices are strongly encouraged to practice the call before attempting it at a game or even just in public. "Woooooo, Pig! Sooie! . . . Woooooo, Pig! Sooie! . . . Woooooo, Pig! Sooie! Razorbacks!" Done correctly, the call starts with both hands in the air, fingers waving during the "Woooooo" part. Arms pump down on the word "Pig," and then back into the air for "Sooie." Serious fans have been known to spontaneously yell it at bars, airports, and even an occasional wedding.

3. *The Golden Boot:* Until 1992, Arkansas' biggest rival was Texas, which it often played with conference, if not national, titles at stake. But when they joined the SEC, the Razorbacks turned their attention to LSU. The 2005 game was the 48th meeting, dating back to 1901, with the series played in six different cities and four different states. The Golden Boot trophy, molded from 24-karat gold in the shape of the two states, debuted in 1996 and goes to the winner of the season-ending game. It stands 4 feet tall, weighs approximately 200 pounds, and is valued at $10,000.

· 13 ·

Auburn

Location: Auburn, Alabama
Founded: 1856
Enrollment: 22,928
Nickname: Tigers
Colors: Burnt orange and navy blue
Battle cry/Mascot: War Eagle (The eagle is named Tiger; the cartoonish costumed tiger mascot is named Aubie.)
Stadium: Jordan-Hare Stadium (87,451)
2005 officials: Dr. Ed Richardson, president; Marcia Boosinger, faculty representative; Jay Jacobs, athletics director

THE PROGRAM

National Championships (1): 1957
SEC Championships (6): 1957, 1983, 1987, 1988, 1989, 2004
Bowl appearances: 32 (17-13-2)
First season: 1892
College Football Hall of Fame (10): Terry Beasley, 1969–71, wide receiver, inducted 2002; Michael Donahue, 1904–06, 1908–22, coach, 1951; Tucker Frederickson, 1962–64, halfback, 1994; Walter Gilbert, 1934–36, center, 1956; John Heisman, 1895–99, coach, 1954; Jimmy Hitchcock, 1930–32, halfback, 1954; Bo Jackson, 1982–85, halfback, 1998; Ralph (Shug) Jordan, 1951–75, coach, 1982; Tracy Rocker, 1985–88, defensive tackle, 2004; Pat Sullivan, 1969–71, quarterback, 1991; Pat Dye, 1981–92, coach, 2005
Heisman Winners (2): Pat Sullivan, quarterback, 1971; Bo Jackson, running back, 1985
National Honors: Zeke Smith, 1958 Outland Trophy (outstanding interior lineman); Tracy Rocker, 1988 Outland Trophy and Vince Lombardi/Rotary Award (outstanding lineman); Carlos Rogers, 2004 Jim Thorpe Award (best defensive back)

Six SEC football coaches participate in a televised roundtable discussion. From left, Paul Davis of Mississippi State, Charlie McClendon of LSU, and Paul "Bear" Bryant of Alabama. From right, Doug Dickey of Tennessee, Vince Dooley of Georgia, and Ray Graves of Florida. Courtesy of the Paul W. Bryant Museum, the University of Alabama.

Michael Slive became the SEC's seventh commissioner in 2002. Courtesy of the SEC.

Alabama wide receiver Tyrone Prothro makes "The Catch" for a touchdown against Southern Miss during the 2005 season. Photo by Michael Palmer. Courtesy of the *Tuscaloosa News*.

Alabama running back Shaun Alexander scores a 7-yard touchdown against Florida in the 1999 SEC Championship Game. Alabama won 34-7. Courtesy of the Paul W. Bryant Museum, the University of Alabama.

Maybe the most famous player at Alabama was quarterback Joe Namath, here throwing a pass against North Carolina State in 1964. Courtesy of the Paul W. Bryant Museum, the University of Alabama.

Alabama's Player of the Decade for the 1970s, Ozzie Newsome, holds the school record for career receiving yards. Courtesy of the Paul W. Bryant Museum, the University of Alabama.

Alabama coach Gene Stallings is presented with the trophy by commissioner Roy Kramer after winning the first SEC Championship Game. Courtesy of the Paul W. Bryant Museum, the University of Alabama.

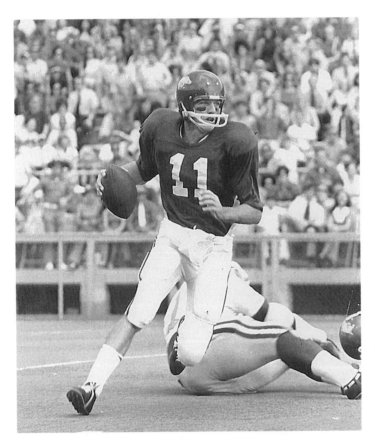

Quarterback Joe Ferguson led Arkansas in passing in 1971–72. Courtesy of the SEC.

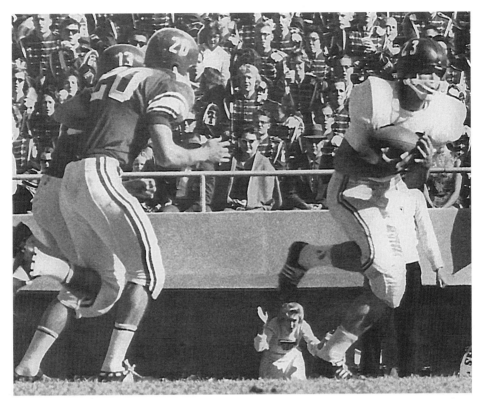

In 1961, Lance Alworth led Arkansas in rushing, receiving, punt returns, and kickoff returns. Courtesy of the SEC.

Ralph "Shug" Jordan was the head coach at Auburn for 25 years and won its only national championship in 1957. Courtesy of the SEC.

Coach Pat Dye compiled a 99-39-4 record at Auburn and led the Tigers to nine bowl appearances. Courtesy of the SEC.

Auburn celebrates after defeating Tennessee in the 2004 SEC Championship Game. Courtesy of the SEC.

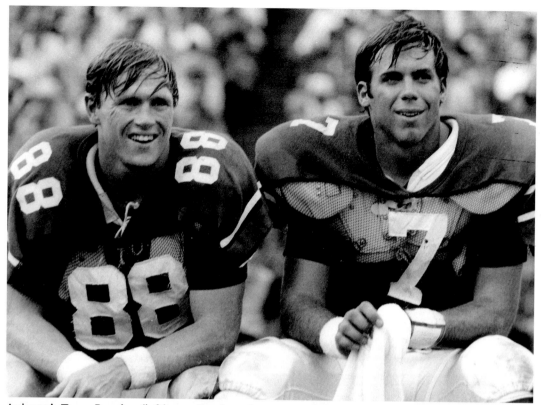

Auburn's Terry Beasley (left) was the favorite target of quarterback Pat Sullivan (right) when he won the Heisman Trophy in 1971. Beasley is one of only two Tigers to reach 1,000 receiving yards in a season. Courtesy of the Paul W. Bryant Museum, the University of Alabama.

Bo Jackson finished the 1985 season with a school-record 1,786 yards and 17 touchdowns en route to the Heisman Trophy. Courtesy of the Paul W. Bryant Museum, the University of Alabama.

Running back Emmitt Smith, who went on to set the career rushing record in the NFL, still holds school records for single-game and season rushing, both set in 1989. Courtesy of the SEC.

Florida players celebrate winning the 1996 national championship after defeating rival Florida State 52-20 in the Sugar Bowl. Courtesy of University of Florida Sports Information.

Forrest "Fergie" Ferguson set numerous receiving records at Florida from 1939–41. He enlisted in the Army in 1942 and was severely wounded in the Normandy Invasion; his injuries eventually took his life 10 years later. Courtesy of University of Florida Sports Information.

Florida had not won an SEC title until Steve Spurrier, who won the Heisman Trophy as a quarterback, returned to his alma mater as a coach. Courtesy of the SEC.

Quarterback Danny Wuerffel won the Heisman Trophy in 1996. Courtesy of University of Florida Sports Information.

Florida All-American defensive end Jack Youngblood went on to be twice named the National Football League's defensive player of the year. Courtesy of University of Florida Sports Information.

Though there's also a live version named Uga, the Georgia Bulldog is one of the most recognizable mascots in college athletics. Courtesy of the SEC.

Coach Vince Dooley is carried off the field after the victory against Georgia Tech, which put the Bulldogs in position to win the 1980 national championship. Courtesy of the SEC.

Georgia's Tony Taylor (43), Tim Jennings (23), and Paul Oliver are all in on the tackle of LSU tight end David Jones during the 2005 SEC Championship Game. The Bulldogs won 34-14. Photo by Mansel Guerry. Courtesy of the SEC.

Running back Herschell Walker helped lead Georgia to a national championship and later won the Heisman Trophy as a junior. Photo by Richard Fowlkes. Courtesy of the University of Georgia.

Kentucky coach Paul "Bear" Bryant (right) poses with Oklahoma's Bud Wilkinson in the days leading up to the 1951 Sugar Bowl. The Wildcats won 13-7. Courtesy of the Paul W. Bryant Museum, the University of Alabama.

Kentucky tackle Bob Gain was awarded the 1950 Outland Trophy as the nation's outstanding interior lineman. Courtesy of the Paul W. Bryant Museum, the University of Alabama.

When full, Commonwealth Stadium is the equivalent to the third-largest city in the state of Kentucky. Courtesy of the SEC.

LSU celebrates winning the 2003 SEC championship en route to the national championship. Courtesy of the SEC.

Billy Cannon's 89-yard punt return against Ole Miss is considered one of the greatest plays in college football history. Courtesy of Louisiana State University.

LSU coach Nick Saban holds up the national championship trophy after defeating Oklahoma 21-14 in the Sugar Bowl. Photo by Steve Franz. Courtesy of Louisiana State University.

Barney Poole was an All-American end for Ole Miss in 1947–48. Courtesy of the SEC.

Even though he never won a championship, many Ole Miss fans consider quarterback Archie Manning the greatest player in Rebels history. Courtesy of the SEC.

Billy Brewer was a quarterback at Ole Miss before taking over as head coach in 1983. Courtesy of the SEC.

Quarterback Eli Manning broke many of his father's passing records at Ole Miss before becoming the No. 1 overall pick in the 2004 NFL Draft. Courtesy of the SEC.

Three of coach John Vaught's teams at Ole Miss (1959, 1960, and 1962) were named national champions by various services. Courtesy of the SEC.

Emory Bellard was the first coach in Mississippi State history to lead the Bulldogs to back-to-back bowl appearances in 1980–81. Courtesy of the SEC.

Former Alabama All-American center Sylvester Croom
was hired as Mississippi State's head coach in 2004.
Courtesy of the SEC.

Paul Davis guided Mississippi State to
its first postseason appearance, a 16-
12 victory against North Carolina
State in the Liberty Bowl. Courtesy of
the SEC.

South Carolina running back George Rogers, here with comedian Bob Hope, led the nation with 1,781 rushing yards in 1980 and won the Hesiman Trophy. Courtesy of the SEC.

Tennessee coach Phillip Fulmer won a national championship in 1998. Courtesy of the SEC.

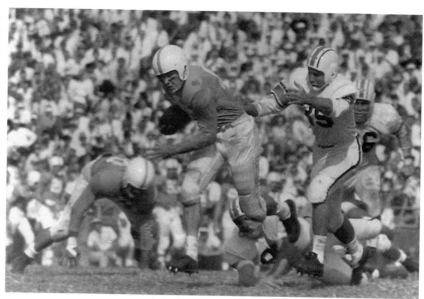

Johnny Majors helped lead Tennessee to a 10-0 regular season as a tailback in 1956 before leading the Volunteers as head coach from 1977–92. Courtesy of the SEC.

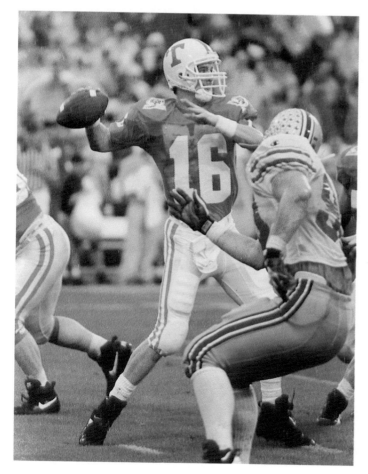

Quarterback Peyton Manning became the third Tennessee player to finish second for the Heisman Trophy in 1997. Courtesy of the SEC.

Tennessee defensive tackle Reggie White was an All-American in 1983 before becoming the NFL's all-time sack leader. Courtesy of the SEC.

General Robert Reese Neyland's 1939 team was the last to shut out each of its regular season opponents, and his Volunteers won the 1951 national championship. Courtesy of University of Tennessee Sports Information.

Quarterback Jay Cutler rewrote many Vanderbilt passing records in 2005. Courtesy of the SEC.

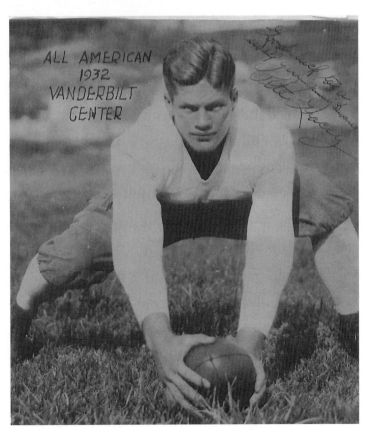

ALL AMERICAN 1932 VANDERBILT CENTER

Pete Gracey was an All-American center for Vanderbilt in 1932. Courtesy of the SEC.

Coach Dan McGugin's first season at Vanderbilt, 1904, resulted in a 9-0 record with the Commodores outscoring opponents 474-4. Over three decades, his teams went 197-5-19. Courtesy of the SEC.

Vanderbilt coach Red Sanders (far left) is pictured with his assistant coaches in 1941, including Paul "Bear" Bryant (second from left). Courtesy of the Paul W. Bryant Museum, the University of Alabama.

First-Team All-Americans: Jimmy Hitchcock, HB, 1932; Walter Gilbert, C, 1937; Ray (Monk) Gafford, HB, 1942; Caleb (Tex) Warrington, C, 1944; Travis Tidwell, QB, 1949; Jim Pyburn, E, 1954; Frank D'Agostino, T, 1955; Joe Childress, FB, 1955; Fob James, HB, 1955; Jimmy Phillips, E, 1957; Zeke Smith, G, 1958–59; Jackie Burkett, C, 1958; Ken Rice, T, 1959–60; Ed Dyas, FB, 1960; Jimmy Sidle, QB, 1963; Tucker Frederickson, FB, 1964; Jack Thornton, T, 1965; Bill Cody, LB, 1965; Freddie Hyatt, E, 1967; Dave Campbell, T, 1968; Buddy McClinton, S, 1969; Larry Willingham, DB, 1970; Terry Beasley, E/FL, 1970–71; Pat Sullivan, QB, 1970–71; Ken Bernich, LB, 1974; Mike Fuller, S, 1974; Neil O'Donoghue, K, 1976; Keith Uecker, T, 1981; Bob Harris, DB, 1982; Donnie Humphrey, DL, 1983; Bo Jackson, RB, 1983, 1985; Gregg Carr, LB, 1984; Lewis Colbert, P, 1985; Ben Tamburello, C, 1985–86; Brent Fullwood, TB, 1986; Aundray Bruce, LB, 1987; Tracy Rocker, DT, 1987–88; Stacy Searels, T, 1987; Kurt Crain, LB, 1987; Walter Reeves, TE, 1988; Benji Roland, NG, 1988; Ed King, G, 1989–90; Craig Ogletree, LB, 1989; David Rocker, DL, 1990; Terry Daniel, P, 1993; Wayne Grandy, T, 1993; Brian Robinson, DB, 1994; Frank Sanders, WR, 1994; Chris Shelling, DB, 1994; Victor Riley, T, 1997; Takeo Spikes, LB, 1997; Damon Duval, K, 2001; Karlos Dansby, LB, 2003; Carlos Rogers, DB, 2004; Carnell Williams, RB, 2004; Marcus McNeill, T, 2004; Junior Rosegreen, DB, 2004; Marcus McNeill, T, 2005

First-Team Academic All-Americans (CoSIDA): Jimmy Phillips, E, 1957; Jackie Burkett, C, 1959; Ed Dyas, B, 1960; Bill Cody, LB, 1965; Buddy McClinton, DB, 1968; Bobby Davis, LB, 1974; Chuck Fletcher, DT, 1975; Chris Vacarella, RB, 1976; Gregg Carr, LB, 1984; Matt Hawkins, K, 1994

First-round NFL draftees: 24

Retired jerseys: 34 Bo Jackson; 7 Pat Sullivan; 88 Terry Beasley

All-Centennial Team (selected by fans): Offense—Walter Gilbert, OL, 1934–36; Ken Rice, OL, 1958–60; Steve Wallace, OL, 1982–85; Ben Tamburello, OL, 1983–86; Ed King, OL, 1988–90; Terry Beasley, WR, 1969–71; Lawyer Tillman, WR, 1985–88; Pat Sullivan, QB, 1969–71; Joe Cribbs, RB, 1976–79; James Brooks, RB, 1977–80; Bo Jackson, RB, 1982–85; Al Del Greco, K, 1980–83 **Defense**—Roger Duane "Zeke" Smith, DL, 1957–59; Donnie Humphrey, DL, 1979–83; Tracy Rocker, DL, 1985–88; Jimmy "Red" Phillips, DE, 1955–57; Aundray Bruce, DE, 1984–87; Jackie Burkett, LB, 1957–59; Mike Kolen, LB, 1967–69; Gregg Carr, LB, 1981–84; Tucker Frederickson, DB, 1962–64; Mike Fuller, DB, 1972–74; Kevin Porter, DB, 1984–87; Lewis Colbert, P, 1982–85; Coach Ralph "Shug" Jordan, 1951–75

THE COACHES

Dr. George Petrie, 1892, 2-2; G. H. Harvey/D. M. Balliet, 1893, 3-0-2; F. M. Hall, 1894, 1-3; John Heisman, 1895–99, 12-4-2; Billy Watkins, 1900–01, 6-3-1; Robert Kent, 1902, 2-2-1; Mike Harvey, 1902, 0-2; Billy Bates, 1903, 4-3; Mike Donahue, 1904–06, 1908–22, 99-35-5; W. S. Kienholz, 1907, 6-2-1;

Boozer Pitts, 1923–24, 1927, 7-11-6; Dave Morey, 1925–27, 10-10-1; George Bohler, 1928–29, 3-11; John Floyd, 1929, 0-4; Chet Wynne, 1930–33, 22-15-2; Jack Meagher, 1934–42, 48-37-10; Carl Voyles, 1944–47, 15-22; Earl Brown, 1948–50, 3-22-4; Ralph (Shug) Jordan, 1951–75, 176-83-6; Doug Barfield, 1976–80, 29-25-1; Pat Dye, 1981–92, 99-39-4; Terry Bowden, 1993–98, 47-17-1; Bill Oliver, 1998, 2-3; Tommy Tuberville, 1999–2005, 60-27

National Coach of the Year: Terry Bowden 1993, Tommy Tuberville 2004

SEC Coach of the Year, AP: Ralph Jordan 1953, 1957, 1972; Pat Dye 1987, 1988; Terry Bowden 1993; Tommy Tuberville 2004 **Coaches:** Jack Meagher 1935; Ralph Jordan 1953, 1963, 1972; Pat Dye 1983, 1987, 1988; Terry Bowden 1993; Tommy Tuberville 2004

SEC Championships: Pat Dye 4, Ralph (Shug) Jordan 1, Tommy Tuberville 1

National Championships: Ralph (Shug) Jordan 1

RECORDS

Rushing yards, game: 307, Curtis Kuykendall vs. Miami, Nov. 24, 1944 (33 carries)

Rushing yards, season: 1,786, Bo Jackson, 1985 (278 carries)

Rushing yards, career: 4,303, Bo Jackson, 1982–85 (650 carries)

Passing yards, game: 416 Ben Leard vs. Georgia, Nov. 13, 1994 (24 of 32)

Passing yards, season: 3,277, Dameyune Craig, 1997 (216 of 403)

Passing yards, career: 8,016, Stan White, 1990–93 (659 of 1,231)

Receiving yards, game: 263, Alexander Wright vs. Pacific, Sept. 9, 1989 (five receptions)

Receiving yards, season: 1,068, Ronney Daniels, 1999 (56 receptions)

Receiving yards, career: 2,507, Terry Beasley, 1969–71 (141 receptions)

Points, game: 36, Carnell Williams vs. Mississippi State, Oct. 18, 2003 (six touchdowns)

Points, season: 102, Bo Jackson, 1985; Stephen Davis 1995; Carnell Williams 2003 (17 touchdowns)

Points, career: 276, Carnell Williams, 2001–04 (46 touchdowns)

It's impossible to explore Auburn University's football program without first explaining its relationship with the Alabama Crimson Tide.

They're like two siblings in high school, with one who gets straight A's and is either the homecoming queen or star athlete (and dates the other), and seemingly has everything go his or her way. The other gets A-minuses and, though exceptional in his or her own right, just doesn't seem to have the same long-term success.

For better or worse, the second sibling is Auburn, which you could also say is college football's equivalent to Jan Brady from *The Brady Bunch*.

In any other conference or just about any other state, Auburn would be considered a college football giant that stood alone. Tabbed "Running Back U," it's produced the likes of Bo Jackson, Rudi Johnson, Carnell Williams, James Brooks,

Stephen Davis, Joe Cribbs, James Bostic, Brent Fullwood, and Ronnie Brown, among others. But when your intrastate rival is the Crimson Tide, well, the shadow cast by Tuscaloosa is long and wide.

Auburn has won a national championship, though the 1957 team was not bowl eligible due to recruiting violations. Since then the Tigers have had two Heisman Trophy winners, neither of whom won against Alabama during his senior year, and 15 finishes in the Top 10 to go with 32 bowl games. The 2004 team went undefeated, yet still didn't play for the national championship.

Similar to "Marsha, Marsha, Marsha," an Auburn fan couldn't be blamed for screaming "Bama, Bama, Bama"—though coach Shug Jordan tried to teach them otherwise, and in 1989 the Tigers took a major step away from that shadow. Instead, their attitude is more one of respect us or not, just don't be surprised when we put on a beatin' on the football field.

In the process, you might hear the fans quote the following:

I believe that this is a practical world and that I can count only on what I earn. Therefore, I believe in work, hard work.

I believe in education, which gives me the knowledge to work wisely and trains my mind and my hands to work skillfully.

I believe in honesty and truthfulness, without which I cannot win the respect and confidence of my fellow men.

I believe in a sound mind, in a sound body and a spirit that is not afraid, and in clean sports to develop these qualities.

I believe in obedience to law because it protects the rights of all.

I believe in the human touch, which cultivates sympathy with my fellow men and mutual helpfulness and brings happiness for all.

I believe in my Country, because it is a land of freedom and because it is my own home, and that I can best serve that country by "doing justly, loving mercy, and walking humbly with my God."

And because Auburn men and women believe in these things, I believe in Auburn and love it.

The Auburn creed was written by George Petrie, a faculty member in the Agricultural and Mechanical College who was credited with forming the first football team and arranging its first game—a 10-0 victory for Alabama Polytechnic Institute over Georgia on February 20, 1892, at Piedmont Park in Atlanta. Team captain Frank Lupton scored the first touchdown and kicked the first conversion.

It was the first college football game in Deep South history, and it helped give Auburn its first football legend, Cliff Hare. He went on to serve as chair of the Auburn Athletic Facility, the dean of the School of Chemistry, and president of the Southern Conference. He would eventually be honored by having his name on the football stadium.

"Athletes make men strong, study makes men wise, and character makes men great," Hare said.

For the first showdown against Alabama, Auburn hired former Penn State player D. M. Balliet just for that one game. He made it count, with a 33-22 victory, at Lakeview Park in Birmingham on February 22, 1893. G. H. Harvey took over the team for the "fall season," when Auburn defeated Alabama again, 40-16. Just like that, Auburn already had its two biggest rivalries established—Alabama and Georgia—in less than a year. In 1894 Auburn defeated Georgia Tech 94-0, but scored only 12 points in its remaining three games to finish 1-3.

The first person to serve as the "head" football coach was a good one—John Heisman, the namesake of college football's highest honor, who led Auburn from 1895 to 1899 and posted a 12-4-2 record before leaving for Clemson and later Georgia Tech (FYI, he later lost 10 of 15 games against Auburn). He won his first game against Alabama, 48-0. Ironically, despite the Heisman Trophy being perennially awarded to the best player in college football, as a coach one of Heisman's personal rules was, "When in doubt, punt." He was also known for saying, "Gentlemen, it is better to have died as a small boy than to fumble this football," and "When you find your opponent's weak spot, hammer it," thus setting a mighty precedent for every SEC coach to follow.

Billy Watkins apparently did in 1900; he posted Auburn's first undefeated and untied season with a 4-0 record with wins against Nashville (28-0), Tennessee (23-0), Alabama (53-5), and Georgia (44-0).

But the first coach to really change the landscape of Auburn football was "Iron" Mike Donahue, who won 99 games during two stints (1904–06 and 1908–22). At times Donahue also served as the team's trainer and athletic director, in addition to coaching baseball, basketball, and track. W. S. Kienholz went 6-2-1 during Donahue's one-year absence in 1907.

Coming off a 4-3 season, the 1904 team finished a perfect 5-0, outscoring opponents 73-11. When Donohue regained the team in 1908—the same year the Alabama rivalry was suspended for 40 years—it went 6-1, with the lone defeat to LSU, 10-2.

The 1913 season brought Auburn its first championship when at 8-0 it finished atop the Southern Intercollegiate Athletic Association standings. The team outscored opponents 223-13, with the closest game a 7-0 win against LSU in Mobile.

Even though the 1914 squad didn't allow a single point, Auburn didn't match the perfect record, finishing 8-0-1 due to a scoreless tie with Georgia. It outscored the other eight teams 193-0 to repeat as SIAA champions.

Donahue's teams posted six-win seasons in 1915, 1916, and 1917 and came back to win one more conference title in 1919. With an 8-1 record, due to a 7-6 loss at Vanderbilt, Auburn shut out five opponents and squeaked out 7-0 victories against Georgia, Clemson, and Mississippi State.

The coach was flexible in his approach. The 1920 team averaged 42.5 points per game despite being shut out twice, scoring 88 points against Samford, 77 vs. Washington & Lee, 56 on Vanderbilt, and 49 opposite Birmingham Southern. In his last season before leaving for LSU, Donahue's team won its first two games by a combined score of 133-0 en route to an 8-2 finish, with the losses coming at Army (19-6) and at Georgia Tech (14-6). However, Auburn again had five shutouts and defeated Georgia 7-3.

Former player Boozer Pitts, who was also a mathematics professor, took over the team and after getting just seven wins over two years was replaced by Dave Morey. But after back-to-back five-win seasons, "King Dave," as the students called him, resigned three games into the 1927 season, leaving Pitts to scrape through a 0-7-2 campaign.

Auburn stumbled through the following two seasons before it hired Chet Wynne, a former All-American fullback at Notre Dame, who was a member of the Nebraska State Legislature when he accepted the job. Among those on his staff was assistant coach Ralph "Shug" Jordan.

Wynne went 3-7 the first year, 5-3-1 the second, and in 1932 Auburn (9-0-1) was the Southern Conference champion, with only a season-ending 20-20 tie against South Carolina in Birmingham preventing a perfect season. Led by Jimmy Hitchcock, "The Phantom of Union Springs" who was the team's first All-American, Auburn outscored its other opponents 255-34.

"Hitchcock was the finest all-around back ever to play against any of my teams," said Wallace Wade, who coached at both Duke and Alabama.

Auburn finished its first SEC season 2-2 (5-5 overall), and Jack Meagher, another former Notre Dame product, replaced Wynne in 1934. Led by Auburn's only three-time All-American, center/linebacker Walter Gilbert, the Tigers went 8-2 in 1935, including a 6-0 loss at LSU.

"LSU put two men on Gilbert for 60 minutes and he took a terrific pounding, but he never stopped charging through to nail the ball-carrier," sportswriter Bill Blake wrote. "Our personal statistics had Gilbert with half the tackles as well as intercepting two enemy passes. There is none who can equal the Auburn center."

During the 1936 season the Tigers earned both their first national ranking (No. 16 after defeating Georgia 20-13) and first bowl invitation, even though the game wasn't in the United States. Billed as the feature event of Cuba's annual National Sports Festival, Auburn played Villanova in the Bacardi Bowl (also dubbed the Rhumba Bowl and the Cigar Bowl) in Havana. The event was almost canceled because dictator Fulgencio Batista's picture wasn't included in the game program; but after a quick trip to the printer, the New Year's Day contest resulted in a 7-7 tie thanks to a 40-yard run by Billy Hitchcock.

A year later, and after SEC officials lifted a ban that didn't allow teams to play in any postseason games other than the Rose and Sugar Bowls, Auburn stayed a little closer to home when it took on Michigan State at the Orange Bowl in Miami. The Spartans were limited to just two first downs and outgained 312 offensive yards to 57. George Kenmore's 60-yard punt return set up the only touchdown, a 2-yard run around the left end by Ralph O'Gwynne. The Tigers finished 6-2-3.

Off the field, one of Meagher's goals was to actually get one—that is, a new stadium, in hopes of minimizing travel as much as possible. For years, Auburn couldn't get opponents to visit, due to the small size of both the town and the facilities. Instead, the Tigers had home games in Mobile, Montgomery, and Birmingham, even though the latter was closer to rival Alabama. Against Georgia, games were also played in Columbus, Athens, Atlanta, Macon, and Savannah from 1892 through 1959.

During his nine seasons at Auburn, Meagher enjoyed only nine games at home. The Tigers' road schedule included stops in Detroit, San Francisco, Philadelphia, Houston, New York, Boston, and Washington, D.C.

The stadium seating 7,500 fans was finally dedicated on November 30, 1939, with a 7-7 tie against Florida. Ten years later another 14,000 seats were added to the renamed Cliff Hare Stadium, although only 12 games had been played there during those years.

That isn't a problem any more. Jordan-Hare Stadium (rededicated in 1973 and the first stadium to be named for an active head coach) added upper decks in 1980 and 1987, increasing the capacity to 87,000 and making it one of the country's ten biggest on-campus stadiums.

With Monk Gafford, the SEC Player of the Year, Meagher's last season in 1942 didn't result in a bowl appearance, but the Tigers (6-4-1) did finish ranked sixteenth after their stunning upset of No. 1 Georgia. Going into the game, the Bulldogs were a heavy favorite; but Jordan noticed that halfback Charley Trippi was tipping off the plays by the way he lined up. With Gafford gaining 119 yards on 21 carries, Auburn won 27-13 to hand Georgia its only loss of the season.

Auburn football struggled after World War II until 1951, when Gerald Washington "Jeff" Beard was named athletic director, one of only five in Auburn's history who didn't coach football. During the following 21 years, he would hire Auburn's signature coach, see the football stadium increase its seating capacity by 40,000, and build a basketball arena (named in his honor) as well as a track and field complex.

One of Beard's first moves was also obviously among his best. When called at Georgia, where he had been an assistant to Wally Butts for five years, Jordan had to be persuaded to apply. In response, he mailed a piece of paper bearing one sentence that read: "I hereby apply for the head football coaching position at Auburn. Signed, Ralph Jordan."

Jordan had been a three-sport standout athlete at Auburn after enrolling in 1928. He was a center on the football team, a forward in basketball, and a pitcher/first baseman in baseball. He led the Southern Conference in scoring in basketball as a sophomore, and he pitched Auburn to a 5-3 victory over Florida to win the conference baseball title his senior year. He went on to join the Army Corps of Engineers and became a major in World War II, taking part in the invasions of Northern Africa, Sicily, Normandy, and Okinawa.

Similar to the experiences of his successful predecessors, things started to click for Jordan during his third season when, despite a 10-7 loss to Alabama, the Tigers (7-2-1) were invited to play Texas Tech in the Gator Bowl. Although Auburn was making its first postseason appearance in 15 years, and boasted a backfield with a future Governor of Alabama (Fob James) and Georgia coach (Vince Dooley), the Red Raiders demonstrated why they had the country's No. 1 scoring offense with a 35-13 victory. Auburn finished No. 17.

"All I ask is that you give everything you've got on every play," Jordan said. "That's not asking very much."

Jordan's first victory against Alabama, after three failed attempts, came in

1954, when the Tigers blew out the Crimson Tide 28-0 to cap a six-game winning streak. At 7-3, it was back to the Gator Bowl, and when Baylor fumbled the opening kickoff, Auburn never looked back. "Joltin' Joe" Childress rushed for 134 yards on 20 carries and scored two touchdowns to lead a 33-13 victory and No. 13 finish.

A 27-13 loss at Tulane was a bump in the road for the 1955 team, which managed to defeat Georgia Tech for the first time in 15 seasons, 14-12. But it responded with narrow wins against Mississippi State (27-26) and Georgia (16-13) before blowing out Clemson (21-0) and Alabama (26-0). Again, it was back to the Gator Bowl, for an unusual intra-conference matchup with Vanderbilt, which was making its first bowl appearance. Five fumbles, including three by Howell Tubbs, were recovered by the Commodores, who won going away 25-13.

A 7-3 season in 1956, featuring a 34-7 victory against Alabama, didn't result in a bowl appearance, but did help set up Auburn for its greatest season ever. With Jimmy "Red" Phillips averaging 23.8 yards per reception, the Tigers ran the table. Despite not being bowl eligible due to improper recruiting inducements, the SEC champions were still voted No. 1 by the Associated Press (No. 2 by United Press International to 9-1 Ohio State).

After opening the season with a 7-0 victory against Tennessee, Auburn jumped up to No. 7, but didn't claim the top ranking until its season-ending 40-0 domination of Alabama. It outscored opponents 207-28, of which only seven points were tallied by an SEC opponent, and—thanks to two goal-line stands against Georgia—shut out its two biggest rivals.

"We went undefeated last year," Jordan said. "It's going to be awful difficult to improve on our record."

Auburn came extremely close. After getting off to a 3-0 start, with shutouts against Tennessee and at Kentucky, the Tigers could manage only a 7-7 tie at Georgia Tech to end a string of 17 straight wins. But with a 6-5 victory at Florida, and a 14-8 victory against Alabama, the unbeaten streak reached 24. At 9-0-1, Auburn was ranked fourth (with LSU winning both the SEC and national championship), and Zeke Smith was awarded the Outland Trophy as the nation's top lineman. When presented with the award, Smith accidentally referred to it as the Heisman Trophy—twice—during his acceptance speech.

"Auburn took me when no one else wanted me," Smith said after turning down an offer to sign with a Canadian League team. "I'm where I am today because of coach Ralph Jordan and Auburn, and I believe I owe Auburn more than I could ever give."

Despite a preseason ranking at No. 3, the winning streak was finally snapped during the 1959 season opener at Tennessee (3-0), and when Auburn lost to Alabama 10-0, it finished 7-3. The scenario repeated itself in 1960, only 10-3 against Tennessee and 3-0 to Alabama, for an 8-2 record and No. 13 ranking.

Meanwhile, upstate, Paul "Bear" Bryant was proving to be an almost unbeatable foe, with Alabama winning the national championship in 1961, 1964, and 1965. The Iron Bowl rivalry grew to new heights of intensity, but wins against the Tide were becoming scarce. During that first title run, Alabama crushed Auburn 34-0.

"I don't know if that's a great team, but they most certainly were great against us," Jordan said. "I don't guess anybody has ever hit us that hard."

Auburn didn't return to the postseason until 1963, when the No. 5 Tigers finished the regular season 9-1, with a 13-10 loss to Mississippi State, by edging Alabama 10-8. With a stingy defense and an option offense featuring All-American quarterback Jimmy Sidle and halfback Tucker Frederickson, Auburn was paired against Nebraska in the Orange Bowl, only to come out flat. Thanks to a quarterback sneak by Dennis Claridge that turned into a 68-yard touchdown on the second snap of the game, the Cornhuskers went on to a 13-7 victory.

"Tucker Frederickson was the most complete football player I've seen in the 40 years I've been connected with the game," Jordan said.

Auburn suffered another bowl defeat in 1965, 13-7 to Ole Miss, which the Rebels practically played at home at the Liberty Bowl in nearby Memphis. Fullback Tom Bryan had 111 rushing yards on 19 carries, but the Tigers finished the year 5-5-1 (4-1-1 against the SEC).

While Alabama continued to roll, Auburn finished just 4-6 in 1966, Jordan's first losing season since 1952, and suffered a 34-0 loss in the Iron Bowl.

No one was eclipsed more by Bryant's success than Jordan, who over 25 years won more than 175 games. But he's remembered by most for his character and how he handled himself, than for his victories.

"Always remember that Goliath was a 40-point favorite over little David," Jordan said.

However, the intense rivalry helped lead to a resurgence on the Plains. In 1968 Auburn won seven games, including a 34-10 victory against Arizona in the Sun Bowl. That game was highlighted by Connie Frederick having a punt blocked, only to see him recover the ball and punt it again, and Buddy McClinton's three interceptions, one of which was returned for a touchdown.

In 1969 the offense was turned over to quarterback Pat Sullivan, who transformed Auburn football forever and won the program's first Heisman Trophy. In 1970 Sullivan led the nation with 2,856 yards, set an NCAA record for most yards per play with 8.57, and tied another with 71 career touchdowns.

"He does more things to beat you than any other quarterback I've seen," Bryant said.

What Sullivan did best, though, was throw to Terry Beasley, whom Dooley described as the "boy wonder" after accumulating 130 yards and two touchdowns during the 1971 meeting. The Sullivan-to-Beasley combination was Auburn's most prolific ever, prompted "Super Sully and Terry Terrific" bumper stickers, and accounted for more than 2,500 yards and nearly 30 touchdowns from 1969 to 1971.

It began with a 57-0 victory against Wake Forest. After defeating Georgia 16-3, Auburn found the 1969 season riding on its annual showdown with Alabama, which it had failed to defeat for five straight years.

"Men, there is a time for everything," Jordan said in his pregame speech. "A time to live and a time to die; a time to love and a time to hate; a time for peace and a time for war; and gentleman, there's a time to beat Alabama. That time is now."

It was, with the final score 49-26. Although the Tigers lost 36-7 to Houston in the Astro-Bluebonnet Bowl (with the Cougars accumulating 376 rushing yards and 516 total yards), Auburn still finished 8-3 and ranked twentieth.

Though they didn't win an SEC championship, Sullivan and Beasley would spend their next two years playing for a national contender. Amazingly, the Tigers were unranked in the 1970 preseason poll, but a 36-23 victory against No. 17 Tennessee catapulted them to No. 12. Losses to No. 14 LSU (17-9) and unranked Georgia (31-17) cost any title aspirations, but Auburn came back to defeat Alabama, 33-28.

It set up a rematch with Ole Miss in the Gator Bowl, dubbed the "Battle of Quarterbacks," with the Rebels led by Archie Manning. He passed for 180 yards and ran for 95 more, but Sullivan threw for 351 yards, including 143 to Beasley, for a 35-28 victory. At 9-2, Auburn was voted No. 10.

"What I remember most is that time after time we had them but he always found a way to make the play," Dooley said about Sullivan.

Sullivan's Heisman season got off to a glorious start in 1971 and No. 5 Auburn was still undefeated heading into the Iron Bowl, with Alabama ranked third. But with the defense looking more susceptible as the season went on, the Tide pounded out a 31-7 victory to win the SEC title and go on to play for the national championship (it lost to Nebraska in the Orange Bowl). Auburn finally received its first invitation to play in the Sugar Bowl, where three turnovers helped Oklahoma take a 31-point halftime lead en route to a 40-22 victory. Again 9-2, the Tigers finished No. 12.

"He was way ahead of his time," Sullivan said about Beasley, who finished eighth in Heisman voting. "He was as fast as anyone playing the game. But the thing that really set him apart was that he was awfully, awfully, strong."

Without Sullivan and Beasley, most people expected a dramatic dip in the program, and again Auburn wasn't ranked in the preseason polls. By winning close games, the Tigers were 4-0 before sustaining a 35-7 setback at LSU, but they responded with another four-game streak. It set up No. 9 Auburn vs. No. 2 Alabama, which was aiming for another national title, in the game Auburn fans relished perhaps most of all.

Alabama had a 16-3 lead when Bill Newton burst into the backfield and blocked a punt, which bounced into the hands of David Langner, who returned it for a 25-yard touchdown. Following the Tide's subsequent possession, Newton and Langner did exactly the same thing—except for only 20 yards on the return—to the dismay of those watching, and the horror of Alabama fans everywhere, for a 17-16 victory. Bumper stickers can still be seen throughout the state, reading, "Punt, Bama, Punt."

Auburn was rewarded with a trip to the Gator Bowl to play Colorado, with the Buffalos heavily favored and Tigers starting quarterback Randy Walls out with a knee injury. But Jordan's favorite team, "The Amazin's," dominated for a 24-3 victory, 10-1 record, and No. 5 finish.

A 34-17 loss to Missouri in the 1973 Sun Bowl resulted in a 6-6 season, but Jordan had one more run left in him. With linebacker Ken Bernich and defensive back Mike Fuller leading the defense, Auburn shut out three of its first four opponents of 1974, including Tennessee (21-0) and Miami (3-0). A 24-15 setback at Florida knocked the Tigers out of the Top 5, and in a No. 7 vs. No. 2 matchup, Alabama again came out on top, 17-13. Even though Auburn fumbled seven times in the Gator Bowl, it still dominated Darrell Royal's Texas team, 27-3. At 10-2, the Tigers were No. 8.

"Coach 'Shug' Jordan was a true gentleman, but he had a mean, cold streak to do what he had to do," defensive end Liston Eddins said.

Doug Barfield was promoted from offensive coordinator in 1976 and won 29 games in five seasons. His best showing was in 1979, with an 8-3 record resulting in a No. 16 ranking.

Auburn targeted Dooley after Barfield resigned, but without success. Instead, it interviewed Pat Dye, who might have secured the job when he answered the question, "How long will it take you to beat Alabama?" by saying, "Sixty minutes." On December 23, 1980, Dye resigned from Wyoming without knowing if he would get the job, but he was finally named the new head coach on January 2, 1981.

"We might not be the most talented team in the country, but there is no reason why we can't be the best prepared, the most disciplined, and the best conditioned team in the country," Dye said upon his hiring, and during his first spring told players practice would be like going through a briar patch during a storm.

"At Auburn, practice is hell. But when you line up across from the big, fast, smart, angry boys from Florida, and Georgia, and Alabama, where there is no quality of mercy on the ground and no place to hide, you'll know why practice is hell at Auburn."

The Dye era began with a 24-16 victory against Texas Christian, but two weeks later Auburn fumbled on fourth down at the Tennessee 1, with the Volunteers pulling out a 10-7 home victory. Following a 17-3 loss to Nebraska, Dye earned his first SEC victory with a 19-7 win against LSU.

Dye's first shot at Alabama came on November 28, when Bryant was going after milestone victory No. 315. The Tide had won eight straight against the Tigers, and all the attention was on Dye's former mentor. He was surprised during the pregame warm-ups when Dye told him, "We're coming after your butt." Bryant smiled and said, "What are you trying to do, boy, scare me?"

"I'm not trying to scare you, coach," Dye replied. "I just want you to know that we aren't scared of you anymore."

Alabama came back in the fourth quarter for a 28-17 victory, but the following year, with Auburn fresh off a 19-14 loss to No. 1 Georgia, it was a different story. The Tide had a lead heading into the fourth quarter, only to see the Tigers drive 66 yards, capped by running back Bo Jackson's 1-yard plunge—now affectionately known to Auburn fans as "Bo Over the Top." It gave the Tigers a 23-22 victory, snapped a nine-game losing streak in the series, and served as a precursor of things to come.

"Set your goals high and don't stop until you get there," Jackson once said. He was also credited with: "If my mother put on a helmet and shoulder pads and a uniform that wasn't the same as the one I was wearing, I'd run over her if she was in my way. And I love my mother."

Auburn went to the first of nine bowl games under Dye and faced future Heisman Trophy winner Doug Flutie at the Tangerine Bowl. Lionel James gained 101 rushing yards on 18 carries, and Jackson punched in two touchdowns for a 33-26 victory. At 9-3, the Tigers were No. 14.

Ranked fourth in the 1983 preseason poll, Auburn lost an early showdown with No. 3 Texas, but pounded Tennessee (37-14) and beat No. 5 Florida (28-21). Against No. 7 Maryland, Auburn went for a crucial fourth down deep in its own territory just to keep quarterback Boomer Esiason from getting the ball back. The Tigers converted and went on to a 35-23 victory.

A 13-7 victory against No. 4 Georgia provided Auburn's first SEC championship in 26 years, and against Alabama, fans ignored a tornado warning to watch Jackson accumulate 258 yards in a 23-20 victory. During the Tigers' second Sugar Bowl appearance, Al Del Greco's 19-yard field goal with 23 seconds remaining provided a 9-7 victory against Michigan. Auburn (11-1) finished No. 3, but the *New York Times* computer poll ranked the Tigers first due to their brutal schedule.

Although Auburn was ranked No. 1 in the preseason poll, 1984 began with a thud due to losses against Miami (20-18) and at Texas (35-27). A wild 42-41 victory against Florida State aided a six-game winning streak, but the Tigers lost 24-3 at Florida and 17-15 to Alabama. Jackson closed his injury-plagued season with 88 yards on 18 carries and two touchdowns for a 21-15 victory against Arkansas in the Liberty Bowl.

With Jackson entering his senior season in 1985, expectations were again high. Auburn was the preseason No. 2 team and quickly moved up to No. 1, only it didn't last. In Week 3, Tennessee proved too difficult to defeat at Neyland Stadium, 38-20. Auburn came back to upset No. 4 Florida State 59-27, but lost to No. 2 Florida, 14-10. After defeating No. 12 Georgia 24-10, the Tigers were back in the Top 10, only to wind up on the losing end of the wildest Iron Bowl ever— settled by a 52-yard field goal into the wind. Jackson won the Heisman Trophy and in his final game had 129 rushing yards on 31 carries, 73 receiving yards, and two touchdowns. But Texas A&M twice stopped Auburn on fourth down in the fourth quarter and handily won the Cotton Bowl, 36-16.

"When people tell me I could be the best athlete there is, I just let it go in one ear and out the other," Jackson said. "There is always somebody out there who is better than you are. Go ask Mike Tyson."

Even without Jackson, any potential drop-off was nearly negligible. In 1986, Lawyer Tillman's reverse helped lead Auburn to a 21-17 victory against Alabama, resulting in an invitation to the Orange Bowl. However, Dye had already given his word that the Tigers would play in the Citrus Bowl, where linebacker Aundray Bruce recorded three sacks and caused a fumble as No. 6 Auburn (10-2) defeated Southern California 16-7 to record all-time victory No. 500.

"I don't believe in miracles. I believe in character," Dye said.

In 1987, Auburn defeated Texas (31-3), Florida (29-6), Georgia (27-11), and Alabama (10-0), and tied Tennessee (20-20) to become SEC champions. The only loss was 34-6 to No. 4 Florida State, and with Win Lyle's 30-yard field goal against Syracuse the Sugar Bowl saw its first tie, 16-16, resulting in a 9-1-2 record for the No. 7 Tigers.

With defensive tackle Tracy Rocker leading the No. 1 defense in the country, the 1988 Tigers blew out Tennessee 38-6 and got their first win at Florida in 16 years, 16-0. It was just one of three shutouts, and Dooley's last game coaching Georgia was a 20-10 loss to his alma mater. Auburn clinched the SEC championship with a 15-10 victory against Alabama, and Rocker won both the Outland Trophy and Lombardi Award. But at the Sugar Bowl, Auburn's comeback bid fell short due to an interception with only 5 seconds remaining, and Florida State held on for a 13-7 victory.

Although Auburn lost an early 1989 showdown with Tennessee (21-14), and missed a chance at redemption with Florida State (22-14), it pulled out a 10-6 victory against LSU. On the last play against Florida, quarterback Reggie Slack connected with Shayne Wasden for a 10-7 win. A 20-3 victory against Georgia helped set the stage for something Tigers fans had never seen—the first-ever meeting with Alabama on the Auburn campus. After years of playing at Legion Field in Birmingham, which was perceived to be an advantage for the Crimson Tide, the game at Auburn was considered by many to be a huge turning point in the program's history.

No. 2 Alabama sported a 10-0 record, but Auburn, which was still stinging from losing nine straight Iron Bowls from 1973 to 1981, would not be denied. The Tigers pulled out an impressive 30-20 victory.

Athletic director David Housel called it the "most emotional day in Auburn history" and said there were so many people greeting the players on the way to the stadium that "It was as if the Children of Israel had been freed from Pharaoh. Or the Berlin Wall had come down." It also gave Dye his third straight SEC championship, fourth overall.

Riding an emotional high, Auburn defeated Ohio State 31-14 in the Hall of Fame Bowl for a 10-2 record and at No. 6 had its fourth straight Top 10 finish. Slack completed 16 of 22 passes for 141 yards and three touchdowns, and he ran in a fourth.

Dye's final bowl game was the 1990 Peach Bowl, with quarterback Stan White scoring on a 1-yard bootleg on fourth down for a 27-23 victory against Indiana. When Dye retired at the end of the 1992 season, his leaving closed arguably the most successful era in Auburn football. His 99 wins tied Donahue for second-most in school history, and every player who played four years for Dye won at least one SEC championship.

Auburn was on NCAA probation again in 1993 when Terry Bowden took over the program. Despite having no games on television and not being bowl eligible, the Tigers ran the table—including wins against No. 4 Florida (38-35) and defending national champion Alabama (22-14)—to finish 11-0. Perhaps the most pivotal point of that season came, not surprisingly, against the Tide. Facing fourth-and-15 at the Alabama 35-yard line, and down 14-5 midway through the third quarter, sophomore quarterback Patrick Nix had to enter the game without even having a chance to warm up. Bowden called "278Z Takeoff," and Nix threw a deep pass to receiver Frank Sanders for a touchdown.

Bowden, who was known for saying "Today, not tomorrow," set an NCAA record by winning his first 20 games—a streak that ended with a 23-23 tie against Georgia and a 21-14 loss to No. 4 Alabama. But against LSU, Auburn was down 23-9 to start the fourth quarter when safety Ken Alvis made the first of five interceptions and returned it 42 yards for a touchdown. Two fellow defenders, Fred Smith and Brian Robinson, followed suit with scores of their own, resulting in a 30-26 victory.

Coming off a 9-1-1 season, Auburn was bowl eligible again in 1995 and flirted with a top ranking, only to sustain losses at LSU (12-6), Florida (49-38), and Arkansas (30-28). Against Penn State in the Outback Bowl, the Tigers gave up 266 rushing yards and lost 43-14.

Another four-loss season in 1996 found Auburn playing surprise Army in the Independence Bowl. Quarterback Dameyune Craig passed for 370 yards and ran for 75 more, but the Tigers weren't able to secure the 32-29 victory until a 27-yard last-minute field-goal attempt by the Cadets sailed wide right.

In 1997 Auburn began the season 6-0—thanks, in part, to a 31-28 victory at No. 10 LSU. Despite stumbling 24-10 to No. 7 Florida and 20-0 to Mississippi State, an 18-17 victory against Alabama had the Tigers in their first SEC Championship Game. But after the narrow 30-29 loss to Tennessee, Auburn was paired against Clemson in the Peach Bowl. While the defense held Clemson to just four first downs, 60 rushing yards, and 86 passing, special teams struggled with two blocked punts. Craig threw for 259 yards and scored on a 22-yard scramble to lead a 21-17 victory.

Bowden stepped down during the 1998 season with Bill Oliver taking over on an interim basis, and Tommy Tuberville was hired away from Ole Miss to become Auburn's twenty-fifth coach. In 2000, he won the first of three straight SEC Western Division titles—only to lose 28-6 to Florida in the SEC Championship Game and 31-28 to Michigan in the Florida Citrus Bowl, where quarterback Ben Leard passed for 394 yards and three touchdowns.

Despite being co-division champions, Auburn didn't play for either the 2001 or 2002 SEC championship. It lost to North Carolina 16-10 in the 2001 Peach Bowl, but came back to defeat No. 10 Penn State 13-9 in the Capital One Bowl, thanks to running back Ronnie Brown outgaining counterpart Larry Johnson with 184 yards and two touchdowns. In 2003, with six sacks and quarterback Jason Campbell keying two fourth-quarter touchdown drives, the Tigers scored a 28-14 victory against Wisconsin in the Music City Bowl.

But possibly no team exemplifies Auburn better than the 2004 squad, which had four players—Williams, Brown, Campbell, and cornerback Carlos Rogers—selected in the first round of the subsequent NFL Draft. Ranked just seventeenth in the preseason, the Tigers defeated No. 5 LSU (10-9), No. 10 Tennessee (34-10), and No. 8 Georgia (24-6) to win the division title. During the rematch against Tennessee in the SEC Championship Game, Campbell passed for 374 yards and three touchdowns to lead a 38-28 victory.

While either Williams or Brown surpassed 100 rushing yards in nine of 13 games, the defense led the nation by allowing just 11.3 points per game. Auburn outscored opponents 129-19 in the first quarter and 224-39 in the first half. But despite finishing the regular season undefeated, the Tigers still couldn't crack the top two spots in the polls, with Southern California and Oklahoma 1-2 in the Bowl Championship Series and paired to play for the national title. After Auburn bested No. 9 Virginia Tech 16-13 in the Sugar Bowl to finish No. 2, USC destroyed Oklahoma 55-19, fueling debate on whether Division I-A football should have a playoff system.

"Nothing has been done to solve the problem," Tuberville said. "We have used a Band-Aid. You can have all the voting polls you want. Popular vote is not the way you have a national champion. You need to play it on the field. I think we're smart enough to be able to figure out a way to keep our bowl system, to have a true national champion. We got left out last year and rightly so. The way it was picked we were No. 3. We weren't No. 1 or 2. There's really no way to complain about it. It is the system we have, it's the only one we have, but we can do a lot better."

The perfect season was even more remarkable considering that just before the 2003 game against Alabama, Auburn school officials flew to Kentucky to offer Tuberville's job to Louisville coach Bob Petrino. Needless to say, Tuberville earned a substantial raise after the 13-0 season.

He came back in 2005 to beat Alabama for the fourth straight year, 28-18, and the Tigers finished tied with LSU atop the division standings.

"It was a beautiful sight," Tuberville said after celebrating with fans on Pat Dye Field at Jordan-Hare Stadium, which had been renamed during a halftime ceremony.

THREE THINGS THAT STAND OUT ABOUT AUBURN FOOTBALL

1. *"War Eagle":* The battle cry stems from a legend that dates back to 1864 and the Civil War's Battle of the Wilderness in Virginia. An Auburn student fighting for the Confederacy was one of many left for dead on the battlefield, and when he regained consciousness the only living thing he saw was a baby eagle. He took the wounded bird with him and nursed it back to health. Later, he went on to teach at Auburn, and during the first football game against Georgia in 1892, the eagle took off after Auburn scored and soared over the field, prompting fans to yell "War Eagle." Auburn won 10-0, but the eagle collapsed and died.

2. *Toomer's Corner:* The corner where College Street intersects Magnolia Avenue has a drugstore, Toomer's, where John Heisman supposedly would go for lemonade. Nowadays it's where Auburn fans celebrate football wins and big victories in other sports. The trees on the corner are "rolled" with toilet paper, on first glance making the center of town appear as if it had been hit by a snowstorm. FYI, they actually sell Auburn rolls of toilet paper at games.

3. *The campus:* Though game-day traffic can be a nightmare, of the 12 schools in

the SEC, the Auburn campus and surrounding community may be the most scenic. "The loveliest village on the plains" got its name from the poem "The Deserted Village," by Oliver Goldsmith (FYI, the poem's line, "where crouching tigers wait their hapless prey," is also the source of the team nickname). But on game day, the town takes on a life of its own. Thousands of fans will line up along Donahue Drive two hours before kickoff and applaud players on their way to the stadium (aka The Tiger Walk). More fans show up if the game is against Alabama.

· 14 ·

LSU

THE SCHOOL

Location: Baton Rouge, Louisiana
Founded: 1860
Enrollment: 31,234
Nickname: Tigers
Colors: Purple and gold
Mascot: Mike the Tiger
Stadium: Tiger Stadium (91,600)
2005 officials: Sean O'Keefe, chancellor; Ken Carpenter, faculty representative; Stanley "Skip" Bertman, athletics director

THE PROGRAM

National Championships (2): 1958, 2003
SEC Championships (9): 1935, 1936, 1958, 1961, 1970, 1986, 1988, 2001, 2003
Bowl appearances: 37 (18-18-1)
First season: 1893
College Football Hall of Fame (9): Dana Bible, 1916, coach, inducted 1951; Tommy Casanova, 1969–71, cornerback, 1995; Michael Donahue, 1923–27, coach, 1951; Doc Fenton, 1907–09, end/quarterback, 1971; Lawrence Jones, 1932–34, coach, 1954; Ken Kavanaugh, 1937–39, end, 1963; Charlie McClendon, 1962–79, coach, 1986; Abe Mickal, 1933–35, halfback, 1967; Bernie Moore, 1925–47, coach, 1954; Gaynell Tinsley, 1934–36, end, 1956
Heisman Winner (1): Billy Cannon, halfback, 1959
National Honors: Josh Reed, 2001 Fred Biletnikoff Award (outstanding wide receiver); Ben Wilkerson, 2004 Rimington Award (best center); Rudy Niswanger, 2005 Draddy Award (academic Heisman) and Wuerffel Award (exemplary community service with outstanding academic and athletic achievement)
First-Team All-Americans: Gaynell (Gus) Tinsley, E, 1935–36; Marvin (Moose) Stewart, C, 1935–36; Ken Kavanaugh, E, 1939; George Tarasovic, C, 1951; Sid Fournet, T, 1954; Jimmy Taylor, FB, 1957; Max Fugler, C, 1958; Bill Cannon,

HB, 1958–59; Roy (Moonie) Winston, G, 1961; Jerry Stovall, HB, 1962; Fred Miller, T, 1962; Billy Traux, E, 1963; Remi Prudhomme, T, 1964; George Rice, T, 1963; Doug Moreau, E, 1963; John Garlington, E, 1967; George Bevan, LB, 1969; Tommy Casanova, DB, 1969–71; Mike Anderson, LB, 1970; Ronnie Estay, T, 1971; Bert Jones, QB, 1972; Warren Capone, LB, 1972–73; Tyler Lafauci, G, 1973; Mike Williams, DB, 1974; Charles Alexander, RB, 1977–78; Robert Dugas, T, 1978; James Britt, DB, 1982; Al Richardson, LB, 1982; Eric Martin, SE, 1983; Lance Smith, T, 1984; Michael Brooks, LB, 1985; Wendell Davis, WR, 1986–87; Nacho Albergamo, C, 1987; Greg Jackson, DB, 1988; Kevin Faulk, RB, 1996; David LaFleur, TE, 1996; Alan Faneca, G, 1997; Chad Kessler, P, 1997; Anthony McFarland, DT, 1998; Todd McClure, C, 1998; Josh Reed, WR, 2001; Bradie James, LB, 2002; Skyler Green, RS, 2003, 2005; Chad Lavalais, DT, 2003; Stephen Peterman, OL, 2003; Corey Webster, CB, 2003; Kyle Williams, DT, 2005; Claude Wroten, DT, 2005

First-Team Academic All-Americans (CoSIDA): Mickey Mangham, E, 1959; Charles Strange, C, 1960; Billy Booth, T, 1961; Jay Michaelson, KS, 1971; Tyler Lafauci, G, 1973; Joe Winkler, DB, 1973; Brad Davis, RB, 1974; Robert Dugas, T, 1977; Juan Carlos Betanzos, K, 1984; Michael Blanchard, OL, 1994; Brad Kessler, P, 1997; Rodney Reed, OL, 2002–03; Rudy Niswanger, C, 2004–05

First-round NFL draftees: 25

Retired jersey: 20 Billy Cannon

All-Centennial Team (selected by fans): Offence—Tyler Lafauci, G, 1971–73; Eric Andolsek, G, 1984–87; Charles "Bo" Strange, T, 1958–60; Lance Smith, T, 1981–84; Nacho Albergamo, C, 1984–87; Eric Martin, WR, 1981–84; Wendell Davis, WR, 1984–87; Bert Jones, QB, 1970–72; Jimmy Taylor, RB, 1956–57; Billy Cannon, RB, 1957–59; Charles Alexander, RB, 1975–78; Dalton Hilliard, RB, 1982–85; David Browndyke, K, 1988–89 **Defense**—Fred Miller, DT, 1960–62; Ronnie Estay, DT, 1969–71; A. J. Duhe, DT, 1973–76; Henry Thomas, DT, 1983–86; Roy "Moonie" Winston, LB, 1959–61; Mike Anderson, LB, 1968–70; Warren Capone, LB, 1971–73; Liffort Hobley, LB, 1980–84; Michael Brooks, LB, 1983–86; Johnny Robinson, DB, 1957–59; Jerry Stovall, DB, 1960–62; Tommy Casanova, DB, 1969–71; Tommy Davis, P, 1953–58

Early-Day Team (selected by a panel): W. Jeff Barrett, E, 1933–35; Gaynell Tinsley, E, 1934–36; Thomas Dutton, L, 1912–13; Jess Tinsley, L, 1926–28; Jack Torrance, L, 1931–33; Justin Rukas, L, 1933–35; Martin "Moose" Stewart, L, 1934–46; G. E. "Doc" Fenton, QB, 1907–09; Jesse Fatherree, B, 1933–35; Abe Mickal, B, 1933–35; Charles "Pinky" Rohm, B, 1935–37

THE COACHES

Dr. Charles E. Coates, 1893, 0-1; Albert Simmons, 1894–95, 5-1; Allen W. Jeardeau, 1896–97, 7-1; Edmond A. Chavanne, 1898, 1900, 3-2; John P. Gregg,

1899, 3-2; W. S. Boreland, 1901–03, 15-7; D. A. Killian, 1904–06, 8-6-2; Edgar R. Wingard, 1908–09, 17-3; Joe G. Pritchard, 1909, 4-1; John W. Mayhew, 1910, 3-6; James K. (Pat) Dwyer, 1911–13, 16-7-2; E. T. McDonald, 1914–16, 14-7-1; Dana X. Bible, 1916, 1-0-2; Wayne Sutton, 1917, 3-5; Irving R. Pray, 1916, 1919, 1922, 11-9; Branch Bocock, 1920–21, 11-4-2; Mike Donahue, 1923–27, 23-19-2; Russ Cohen, 1928–31, 23-13-1; Biff Jones, 1933–34, 20-5-6; Bernie H. Moore, 1935–47, 83-39-6; Gaynell (Gus) Tinsley, 1948–54, 35-34-6; Paul F. Dietzel, 1955–61, 46-23-3; Charlie McClendon, 1962–79, 137-59-7; Bo Rein, 1979–80, 0-0; Jerry Stovall, 1980–83, 22-21-2; Bill Arnsparger, 1984–86, 26-8-2; Mike Archer, 1987–90, 27-18-1; Curley Hallman, 1991–94, 16-28-0; Gerry DiNardo, 1995–99, 32-24-1; Hal Hunter, 1999, 1-0; Nick Saban, 2000–04, 48-16; Les Miles, 2005, 11-2

National Coach of the Year: Paul Dietzel 1958, Charles McClendon 1970, Jerry Stovall 1982, Nick Saban 2003

SEC Coach of the Year, AP: Gaynell Tinsley 1949; Paul Dietzel 1958; Charlie McClendon 1969; Jerry Stovall 1982; Bill Arnsparger 1986; Nick Saban 2003 **Coaches:** Gaynell Tinsley 1949; Paul Dietzel 1959; Charlie McClendon 1969, 1970; Bill Arnsparger 1984, 1986

SEC Championships: Bernie Moore 2, Paul Dietzel 2, Nick Saban 2, Charlie McClendon 1, Bill Arnsparger 1, Mike Archer 1

National Championships: Paul Dietzel 1, Nick Saban 1

RECORDS

Rushing yards, game: 250, Alley Broussard vs. Ole Miss, Nov. 20, 2004 (26 carries)

Rushing yards, season: 1,686, Charles Alexander, 1977 (311 carries)

Rushing yards, career: 4,557, Kevin Faulk, 1995–98 (856 carries)

Passing yards, game: 528, Rohan Davey vs. Alabama, Nov. 3, 2001 (35 of 44)

Passing yards, season: 3,347, Rohan Davey, 2001 (217 of 367)

Passing yards, career: 9,115, Tommy Hodson, 1986–89 (674 of 1,163)

Receiving yards, game: 293, Josh Reed vs. Alabama, Nov. 3, 2001 (19 receptions)

Receiving yards, season: 1,740, Josh Reed, 2001 (94 receptions)

Receiving yards, career: 3,001, Josh Reed, 1999–2001 (167 receptions)

Points, game: 30, Kevin Faulk vs. Kentucky, Nov. 1, 1997 (five touchdowns); Carlos Carson vs. Rice, Sept. 24, 1977 (five touchdowns)

Points, season: 114, LaBrandon Toefield, 2001 (19 touchdowns)

Points, career: 318, Kevin Faulk, 1995–98 (53 touchdowns)

The history of Louisiana State University football is about as rich and colorful as the purple and gold uniforms the team wears, with home games played in an atmosphere so electric that it's one of college sports' most unique venues to visit.

While the school can brag of Pete Maravich, Dale Brown, and Shaquille O'Neal in men's basketball, and its baseball program is the envy of the entire nation, there's nothing quite like Saturday nights in Death Valley (aka Tiger Stadium). Not only do the Tigers draw more than 90,000 for every game, but they fill the stands with some of the most energetic and lively fans you'll ever come across.

In the words of LSU publicity director and athletic director Jim Corbett (1945–67): "In Baton Rouge, the focal point of everything is Tiger football."

But the real compliments have come from opponents like Georgia Tech's Bobby Dodd: "I'd rather face the lions in the Coliseum than the Tigers in Baton Rouge."

LSU was founded in 1860 as the Louisiana State Seminary of Learning and Military Academy, with the first superintendent Civil War commander William Tecumseh Sherman, who led the North's advance on Atlanta. After the school was moved to Baton Rouge following the war, LSU was commonly referred to as "Ole War Skule," along with "Old Lou." But it wasn't until 1893 that the first football game was played, under the direction of Dr. Charles Coates, resulting in a 34-0 loss to Tulane. Like some other Southeastern Conference pioneers of the sport, Coates had attended Johns Hopkins University.

However, under the direction of coach A. P. Simmons, the 1895 team recorded the first of six perfect seasons; LSU compiled a 3-0 record, with wins against Tulane (8-4), Centenary (16-6), and Alabama (12-6).

It's believed that the baseball team was the first to adopt the school colors, fittingly taken from those used in the region's Mardi Gras celebrations; but the 1896 football team, which finished 6-0 under coach Allen W. Jeardeau, was the first to adopt the Tigers nickname.

After stumbling along for a few years, with an impressive 5-1 record in 1901, 6-1 in 1902 (both under W. S. Borland), and 3-0 in 1905, the Tigers got a little more serious in 1907 under the guidance of coach Edgar R. Wingard. Not only did LSU play its first 10-game season (finishing 7-3), but it also became the first American college football team to play on foreign soil. The University of Havana was undefeated against service teams comprised of U.S. soldiers stationed in Cuba, and eager to test itself against a collegiate program. On Christmas Day at Almendares Park, LSU won 56-0 before 10,000 fans.

Led by G. Ellwood "Doc" Fenton, who was nicknamed the "Kandy Kid," the 1908 team posted LSU's first consequential undefeated season when the Tigers finished 10-0. The squad was dubbed the "Point a Minute Team" for scoring 442 points in 450 minutes of play, of which Fenton had 125, and the Tigers were named Southern Intercollegiate Association champions. Although LSU had already recorded four unbeaten seasons, and wouldn't do so again for another 50 years, the 1908 Tigers were considered the first great team in school history.

After the 1918 season was cancelled due to World War I, Mike Donahue, who won three Southern Intercollegiate Athletic Association championships at Auburn, brought stability to the program. He guided the Tigers from 1923 to 1927 and had only one losing season.

In 1928, athletic director T. P. "Skipper" Heard, who was also credited for making night football a LSU staple, heard that school president James Smith had proposed to use $250,000 to build new dormitories on campus. Instead, Heard convinced him to raise the stands on the east and west sides of the stadium and extend them to the end zones, with the dorm rooms underneath. It bumped the stadium capacity by 10,000.

The tradition of playing under the lights began on October 3, 1931, when LSU crushed Spring Hill 35-0. In addition to avoiding the heat and humidity, it was a way to give fans a better opportunity to see the Tigers play, as evidenced by an attendance spike. From 1960 to 2004, LSU was 187-62-4 (.747) in night home games and 16-21-3 (.438) during the day.

Coming off a 7-2-2 season under coach Lawrence M. "Biff" Jones, Bernie Moore, who would later become the second commissioner of the SEC, gave LSU fans their first significant taste of success, though the 1935 season didn't get off to a good start with a 10-7 home loss to Rice. But led by freshman end Gaynell "Gus" Tinsley and quarterback "Miracle" Abe Mickal—who had connected on a last-ditch 65-yard touchdown pass to tie Southern Methodist the year before, setting the Southern record for longest scoring pass ever—LSU rebounded by scoring two touchdowns in the fourth quarter to defeat Texas 18-6. A 7-2 victory in its SEC opener against Vanderbilt was followed by a 6-0 win against Auburn, and after defeating Mississippi State 28-13 the Tigers shut out their last three opponents to finish the regular season 9-1. Consequently, LSU received its first bowl invitation, to face Texas Christian and Sammy Baugh in the Sugar Bowl.

The game was played in a downpour, but the Tigers were able to score a safety when Tinsley forced an incompletion in the end zone (back then, it was an automatic two points), but Baugh drove the Horned Frogs for a game-winning field goal and 3-2 victory.

LSU got off to a better start in 1936 by defeating Rice (20-7) and tying Texas (6-6). A 47-7 victory against Georgia served notice of LSU's offensive prowess, and the Tigers wound up leading the nation with 281 points while compiling a 9-0-1 record. Voted No. 2 in the national poll behind Minnesota, LSU returned to the Sugar Bowl; but Santa Clara, under the direction of coach Buck Shaw, jumped out to a 14-0 lead en route to a 21-14 upset.

The two teams rematched a year later, with LSU posting similar offensive numbers despite a 7-6 loss to Vanderbilt. Again, the Broncos scored early and held on, holding the Tigers scoreless for the first time in 50 games for a 6-0 result.

Moore wouldn't return to the postseason until 1944, when during World War II the Tigers went to the Orange Bowl despite a 5-3 record. Steve Van Buren threw for two touchdowns and had a 62-yard rushing touchdown to lead a 19-14 victory against Texas A&M. Van Buren's sixteenth touchdown of the season stood as a school record until Charles Alexander scored 17 in 1977.

Led by quarterback Y. A. Tittle, only a 26-7 loss to Georgia Tech kept LSU from tying for the SEC title in 1946; but the Tigers still managed to land in the Cotton Bowl to face Arkansas and All-American Clyde Scott. In that game, played in frigid conditions (fans lit fires in stands so they could stay and watch) and nicknamed the "Ice Bowl," LSU had an advantage of 271 to 54 in total yards and 15-1 in first downs. But neither team could reach an end zone, resulting in a lackluster 0-0 tie.

Tinsley took over the program in 1948 and went 3-7 his inaugural season, but he brought about numerous changes the following year. Among them was a new numbering system, devised by the coach and Corbett, that used the first letter of the position followed by a single digit. For example, a center could wear "C-4." Although the "Gobo" yearbook predicted that the system "may revolutionize the football jersey manufacturing industry," it flopped.

But the Tigers didn't follow suit on the field, and after a 19-0 opening loss to Kentucky yielded more than seven points only once. The upstart squad was 8-1 when it returned to New Orleans for the Sugar Bowl but was overmatched against Bud Wilkinson's Oklahoma Sooners, who, led by quarterback Darrell Royal, out-gained the Tigers 286 yards to 38 on the ground for a 35-0 victory.

In 1955, LSU's fortunes changed with the hiring of innovative Paul Dietzel, though at first it didn't seem that way. After seasons of 3-5-2, 3-7, and 5-5, Corbett's patience paid off handsomely in 1958.

With a lineup dominated by juniors and sophomores, Dietzel split his team into three units. (*Note:* This was before teams were allowed unlimited substitutions.) The White Team, led by Billy Cannon, played both offense and defense, and wore that color. The Go Team concentrated on offense and wore gold. The popular defensive unit was nicknamed the Chinese Bandits, borrowed from a "Terry and the Pirates" comic strip that referred to Chinese bandits as the "most vicious people in the world." *Life* magazine featured a photograph of the players all wearing Chinese masks.

When unranked LSU won at Rice, 26-6, and defeated Alabama 13-3 in Paul "Bear" Bryant's coaching debut with the Tide, LSU began to shoot upward in the polls. After destroying Miami (41-0) and Kentucky (32-7), the Tigers were No. 3 to set up a homecoming showdown with Florida. In renovated Tigers Stadium (67,500), LSU held on for a 10-7 victory and backed it up with a 14-0 win against No. 6 Ole Miss.

After the Tigers survived a 7-6 scare against Mississippi State, only bayou rival Tulane stood in the way of a national championship. LSU built up a 6-0 half-time lead, but inspired by Green Wave tailback Claude "Boo" Mason's statement that "We'll beat LSU because they'll choke," the Tigers scored 56 points in the final two quarters for an overwhelming 62-0 win—the most lopsided score in the series (since equaled in 1961 and 1965).

With a 10-0 record and national title in tow, LSU accepted an invitation to play Clemson in the twenty-fifth annual Sugar Bowl. Although quarterback War-ren Rabb fractured his hand in the first quarter, Chinese Bandit tackle Duane Leopard recovered a fumbled punt at the 11 to set up Cannon's 9-yard touchdown pass to Mickey Mangham on a halfback option for the game's only score and 7-0 victory.

LSU was riding an 18-game winning streak in 1959 when its most famous play happened on Halloween night against Ole Miss. Ahead 3-0 in the fourth quarter, the Rebels decided to punt on third-and-17 (which wasn't uncommon then) at their own 42. Cannon fielded All-American Jake Gibbs' punt on the bounce at the 11 and headed up the sideline, avoiding numerous would-be tacklers en route to the end zone for a dramatic 7-3 victory. Many consider it not only the play that secured Cannon the Heisman Trophy, but perhaps the greatest play in college football history, and J. C. Politz's radio call is still frequently overheard in Baton Rouge.

"I got a hand on him, but he just shook me off like a puppy," said Gibbs, the last of seven defenders who were unable to bring Cannon down.

"Outside the Louisiana Purchase in 1803, many Cajuns consider Bill Cannon's run the greatest event in state history," Ole Miss coach John Vaught later said.

What most fans don't remember from that game is that Cannon and Rabb stopped Ole Miss' Doug Elmore at the 1 to save a touchdown. However, LSU subsequently lost at Tennessee, 14-13, after Dietzel went for a victory instead of settling for a tie, ending both the winning streak and hopes of defending the title.

"We came to win, not to tie," Dietzel said. "If I had it to do over a hundred times, I would do the same thing."

Ole Miss got even in the Sugar Bowl. Gibbs' 43-yard touchdown pass to Cowboy Woodruff provided an insurmountable lead—while the Tigers never crossed the Rebels' 38-yard line—for a 21-0 final. Undefeated Syracuse won the national title, but voters had Ole Miss second and LSU third. During his career, Cannon rushed for 1,867 yards on 359 carries and 21 touchdowns and led LSU to a 24-7 record, including a 19-game winning streak.

Incidentally, the 1959 season began another LSU tradition, the wearing of white jerseys at home. After the NCAA passed a rule in 1982 making all home teams wear dark jerseys, coach Gerry DiNardo personally lobbied each member of the rules committee to have it changed. When Nick Saban took over in 2000, he altered the tradition so LSU would wear purple for non-SEC home games except the home opener.

Dietzel's last hurrah was the 1961 season, which started with a 16-3 setback to Rice. However, over the last nine games the Tigers allowed only 30 points, 14 of them to Kentucky in a 24-14 victory. After finishing 6-0 in SEC play, which made the Tigers co-conference champions with Alabama, LSU was paired against Colorado in the Orange Bowl. Except for a 59-yard interception return for a touchdown, LSU dominated. Charley White Cranford (6-yard run), Jimmy Field (9-yard run), and Gene Sykes (recovered blocked punt) scored touchdowns for a 25-7 victory and a 10-1 record.

"There are no office hours for champions," Dietzel was credited with saying, along with, "The athletic field is very democratic. Each person is judged by personal merit rather than personal wealth or prestige."

Bowl games became a regular feature of the program under coach Charlie McClendon—"Cholly Mac," who had been a player and assistant for Bryant at Kentucky—beginning with the Cotton Bowl after an 8-1-1 season in 1962. Led by All-Americans Fred Miller and Jerry Stovall, the defensively potent Tigers, who gave up only 34 points all season, recorded a shutout against Texas. Field scored a 22-yard touchdown, and Lynn Amedee made field goals of 23 and 37 yards for a 13-0 victory.

Injuries took their toll on the 1963 team, and following losses to both Ole Miss (37-3) and Mississippi State (7-6), the Tigers limped into the Bluebonnet Bowl with a 7-3 record. With quarterback Don Trull completing 26 of 37 passes in frigid conditions, Baylor amassed 430 yards of total offense and scored two touchdowns in the fourth quarter for a 14-7 victory.

LSU met Ole Miss on Halloween again in 1964, when Billy Ezell connected with Doug Moreau on a two-point conversion late in the fourth quarter for an 11-10 victory. But a 17-9 loss to Alabama knocked the Tigers out of contention for the SEC championship, followed by a 20-6 regular season-ending loss to Florida. Against Syracuse in the Sugar Bowl, George Rice caught Floyd Little in the end zone for an early safety, Ezell threw a 57-yard touchdown to Moreau, and Moreau completed the scoring with a 28-yard field goal for a 13-10 victory.

The Tigers matched the eight-win season in 1965 when they were invited to play heavily favored No. 2 Arkansas, which was riding a 22-game winning streak. On their second possession, the Razorbacks drove 87 yards to take the lead, but running back Joe Labruzzo countered by scoring two touchdowns in the second quarter. Sealed by Jerry Joseph's late interception, LSU held on for a 14-7 win. With No. 1 Michigan State losing to UCLA 14-12 in the Rose Bowl, the loss cost Arkansas a chance at the national championship, which No. 4 Alabama secured with a 39-28 victory against No. 3 Nebraska in the Orange Bowl.

"Baton Rouge happens to be the worst place in the world to be a visiting team," Alabama's Bryant once said. "It's a dugout arena, and you get all of that noise. It's like being inside a drum."

After missing the postseason in 1966 due to a 5-4-1 record, LSU returned to the Sugar Bowl the following year, where it was paired against unbeaten Wyoming. Nelson Stokley threw two touchdown passes to Tommy Morel, and sophomore Glenn Smith came off the bench to be named game MVP in the 20-13 victory. The 1968 season was also rather erratic, culminating with a 31-27 victory against Florida State in the Peach Bowl. Although Bill Cappleman attempted 41 passes and scored three touchdowns (two to Ron Sellers), Morel's late reception set up Maurice LeBlanc's game-winning 2-yard touchdown run.

When Archie Manning and Ole Miss left LSU three points shy of a perfect season in 1969, and missed a chance to play Texas for the national championship in the Cotton Bowl, 9-1 LSU turned down its bowl invitation. A shot at immediate redemption was quickly dismissed when the Tigers opened the 1970 season with a 20-18 home loss to Texas A&M.

But LSU rallied to win seven straight—including 17-9 against future Heisman Trophy winner Pat Sullivan and No. 6 Auburn, and 14-9 against Alabama—before suffering a 3-0 setback against Ara Parseghian's Notre Dame team, led by quarterback Joe Theismann. Still, the Tigers got Manning, who was sporting a cast due to a broken arm, and Ole Miss at Death Valley with the SEC championship on the line. Tommy Casanova and Craig Burns combined to return three punts for touchdowns, and Ronnie Estay caught Manning for a safety in the 61-17 victory.

LSU (8-3) was rewarded by playing in the game to determine the national champion, but on the wrong end. Buddy Lee's 31-yard touchdown pass to Al Coffee gave the Tigers a two-point lead after three quarters in the Orange Bowl, but No. 3 Nebraska drove 67 yards with Jerry Tagge leaping over the top for the winning touchdown and subsequent title.

"Be as positive as you can to everyone you meet and they'll always think you're a winner," McClendon said. Two other popular McClendon-isms: "There is no single 'best' way to do something in football," and "The worst mistake any coach can make is not being himself."

In 1971, LSU got a chance to get even with Notre Dame and didn't squander the opportunity. With three goal-line stands, the first of which saw Louis Cascio and Ronnie Estay stonewall Andy Huff, the Tigers won 28-8. The victory helped project LSU into the Sun Bowl, where quarterback Bert Jones completed 12 of 18 passes for 227 yards and three touchdowns, including one to his cousin Andy Hamilton, and ran in another touchdown for a 33-15 victory against Iowa State. The Tigers finished 9-3.

Some fans refer to November 4, 1972, as the day when time stood still—literally. Supposedly, there were four seconds on the clock when Jones dropped back, pump-faked, and then threw a pass for an incompletion against Ole Miss. After all that, one second still showed on the clock; then Jones connected with running back Brad Davis in the corner of the end zone, and Rusty Jackson made the extra-point attempt for a 17-16 victory. It prompted a Rebels fan to post a sign at the state border: "You are now entering Louisiana. Set your clocks back four seconds."

LSU (9-1-1) went on to face Tennessee, which it did not play during the regular season, in an all-SEC Bluebonnet Bowl. Volunteers quarterback Condredge Holloway ran in two scores and threw for another to help give the Volunteers a 24-3 halftime lead. With Jones and Brad Davis scoring touchdowns, the Tigers came back to make it close—only to have their last-ditch effort fall short when Jones' final pass was deflected at the Tennessee 10 with less than two minutes to play. Tennessee won 24-17.

McClendon's last good opportunity to win the SEC championship came in 1973; instead, he would see an undefeated season derailed by Alabama (21-7), followed by a disappointing regular season-ending 14-0 loss at Tulane. Despite scoring on the first series of the game and limiting Heisman Trophy winner John Cappelletti to just 50 yards, LSU wasn't emotionally able to recover in time for the Orange Bowl, which Penn State won, 16-9.

During McClendon's last three seasons from 1977 to 1979, the Tigers played in the Sun, Liberty, and Tangerine bowls, losing the first two (24-14 to Stanford and 20-15 to Missouri, despite 133 rushing yards on 24 carries from All-American tailback Alexander), but crushing Wake Forest 34-10 in the final sendoff. LSU's all-time winningest coach, with 137 victories, was fired because he couldn't beat Bryant, who won six national championships at Alabama, prompting Auburn coach Shug Jordan to say: "You go by that and they'll have to fire us all."

"In football, and in life, you've got to keep proving yourself," McClendon said. "If you're looking back, you're in trouble."

After a lengthy coaching search, 34-year-old Bo Rein, who had just finished

7-4 at North Carolina State, was hired, but died before he could coach a single game for the Tigers. While on a recruiting trip to Shreveport, controllers lost contact with his small plane and sent military fighters to try to intercept it over North Carolina, approximately a thousand miles off course. Similar to when professional golfer Payne Stewart and five others died 20 years later, it was speculated that depressurization caused the deaths of Rein and his pilot, long before their plane ran out of fuel and crashed into the Atlantic Ocean; their bodies were never recovered.

The following day, Stovall took the reins. He needed three seasons to return the Tigers to the postseason, earning national coach of the year honors in the process. Coming off a 3-7-1 season, LSU opened the 1982 season with a 45-7 victory against Oregon State, but eventually saw a 24-24 tie to Tennessee and 27-24 upset at Mississippi State knock it out of contention for the SEC championship (won by Georgia). Against No. 3 Nebraska in the Orange Bowl, two Dalton Hilliard touchdown runs had LSU leading 17-7 late in the third quarter and thinking upset. But the Cornhuskers countered with two late touchdowns of their own to pull off a 21-20 heartbreaker.

Bill Arnsparger had Tigers fans quickly thinking titles again when he was hired in 1984. In his first year, he led LSU to within a whisker of the SEC championship captured by Florida (which LSU tied in the season opener, only to be foiled by Mississippi State, 16-14). At 8-2-1, the Sugar Bowl set up a rematch with heavily favored Nebraska. Hilliard, who was limited by the flu, scored a touchdown for a 10-0 lead, but the Cornhuskers scored three second-half touchdowns for a 28-10 victory.

Despite following the initial campaign with back-to-back nine-win seasons, Arnsparger wasn't able to get a bowl victory or the elusive tenth win. In 1985, Norman Jefferson's 79-yard punt return sparked Baylor—which, behind 489 yards of total offense, won 21-7. However, in 1986, even after the Tigers were shocked by the coaches' alma mater, Miami of Ohio, 21-12, in Week 2, Arnsparger was able to win the SEC championship. Led by freshman quarterback Tommy Hodson, the Tigers won at Florida (28-17) and defeated Georgia (23-14) to vault to the top of the conference standings. Ole Miss pulled off its first win at Death Valley since Archie Manning's sophomore season of 1968 (21-19), but LSU responded by winning a crucial game at Alabama, 14-10, and crushed Mississippi State 47-0 to lock up at least a share of the title.

"You can accomplish a lot if you don't worry about who gets the credit," Arnsparger said.

LSU closed the season with victories against Notre Dame and Tulane, but when Auburn upset Alabama in the Iron Bowl, it secured the Tigers' first championship since 1970. With Arnsparger having already accepted a promotion to athletic director, they faced Nebraska once again, and in similar fashion were rebuffed by the No. 6 Cornhuskers in the Sugar Bowl, 30-15.

Although Mike Archer's team finished 10-1-1 in 1987, a 22-10 loss to Alabama left the Tigers second behind Auburn in the SEC chase. Against future conference opponent South Carolina in the Gator Bowl, Wendall Davis caught nine passes from Hodson for 132 yards and three touchdowns to lead a 30-13 victory.

The 1988 season got off an unusual start against Texas A&M, when the stadium lights suddenly went out in the middle of an Aggie drive. After power was restored, the possession was eventually stopped at the LSU 2, with the 27-0 victory inspiring the nickname: "The Lights Out Defense."

LSU recorded its first victory in Knoxville with a 34-9 rout before losing a close game at Ohio State (36-33) and another game at Florida (19-6). The conference title would come down to a showdown against No. 4 Auburn, and when tailback Eddie Fuller caught a late touchdown pass in the back of the end zone from Hodson for a 7-6 victory, LSU went on to win its second SEC title in three years. The Tigers split their final two regular-season games, losing 44-3 to Miami and defeating Tulane 44-14, before playing Syracuse in the Hall of Fame Bowl. While Hodson had three passes intercepted, halfback Robert Drummond accumulated 123 rushing yards on 23 carries to lead a 23-10 victory.

Little did LSU fans know at the time, but the program was about to experience a dip. From 1989 to 1994, the Tigers never won more than three conference games; LSU compiled six straight losing seasons until hiring DiNardo away from Vanderbilt in 1995.

DiNardo's first season (7-4-1) was capped by a 45-26 victory against Michigan State in the Independence Bowl. Both teams had a kickoff return for a touchdown, the Tigers' by Eddie Kennison, and running back Kevin Faulk's 51-yard touchdown run pulled LSU to within 24-21 at the half. Keyed by end Gabe Northern's 37-yard fumble return for a touchdown, the Tigers scored 24 unanswered points and in the process set 11 bowl records.

LSU was able to tie Alabama atop the Western Division standings in 1996, but due to a 26-0 loss in Baton Rouge, the No. 10 Crimson Tide advanced to the SEC Championship Game (and lost to No. 1 Florida, LSU's other regular-season defeat). Against Clemson in the Peach Bowl, Faulk capped an 80-play drive with a 3-yard touchdown, and Aaron Adams blocked a potentially game-tying 52-yard field goal attempt, for a 10-7 victory, 10-2 record, and No. 12 finish.

The 1997 season brought another LSU milestone as Raion Hill's interception sealed a 28-21 upset of Florida, marking the first time the Tigers beat a team ranked No. 1. However, after being bumped up to No. 8, LSU lost the following Saturday, 36-21 to Ole Miss, which proved to be costly. Having already lost to No. 12 Auburn earlier in the season, Auburn only had to tie LSU in the standings to advance to the SEC Championship Game (where it lost 30-29 to Tennessee).

The Independence Bowl would be DiNardo's swan song, but against a prize program, Notre Dame. Rondell Mealey's 222 rushing yards and two touchdowns avenged a 24-6 loss during the regular season, and gave LSU both a 27-9 victory and a 9-3 record.

When Saban was hired away from Michigan State in 2000, it had been more than a decade since LSU's last SEC championship, and the team was coming off a lackluster 3-8 season. Upon announcing that the new coach would be hired with a salary of $1.2 million—nearly 17 times the average salary of a full LSU professor— LSU chancellor Mark Emmert said: "Simply put, success in LSU football is essential for the success of Louisiana State University."

The Tigers finished Saban's first year at 8-4, capped by a 28-14 win in the Peach Bowl after quarterback Rohan Davey came off the bench to pass for 174 yards and three touchdowns to lead a come-from-behind victory.

Saban's second season didn't get off to a favorable start when the SEC opener against Auburn had to be postponed in the wake of the September 11 terrorist attacks. Instead, the Tigers played their first conference game at Tennessee and lost 26-18. That was followed by a 44-15 defeat to Florida in the home opener and a 35-24 loss to Ole Miss.

However, with Davey passing for 528 yards and Josh Reed making 19 receptions for 293 yards, LSU won at Alabama, 35-21. With a 41-38 home victory against Arkansas, the Western Division title came down to the rescheduled game against Auburn. LSU won handily, 27-14, for a rematch with Tennessee in Atlanta. Even though Davey and running back LaBrandon Toefield both sustained injuries, backup quarterback Matt Mauck and the defense pulled off a shocking 31-20 upset, costing the Volunteers a chance to play Miami for the national championship in the Rose Bowl.

"I'd like to be there when the BCS [Bowl Championship Series] tries to sort this one out," Reed said.

Back in the Sugar Bowl for the first time since 1986, LSU celebrated its first win there since 1968 with a 47-34 victory against No. 7 Illinois. Davey passed for 444 yards to be named the game MVP, Reed caught 14 passes for 239 yards, and running back Domanick Davis accumulated 122 rushing yards and four touchdowns.

LSU had to regroup a bit in 2002, but still enjoyed the dramatic "Bluegrass Miracle." Down 30-27 at Kentucky on November 9, 2002, the Tigers had the ball at their own 13 with just 11 seconds remaining. As hundreds of fans prepared to storm the field, LSU completed a 12-yard pass. Already the Wildcats had doused their coach with Gatorade, and when quarterback Marcus Randall uncorked a Hail Mary pass downfield, fireworks shot out of the scoreboard while fans attacked the goalpost in the east end zone.

Meanwhile, the pass deflected off three Kentucky players before wide receiver Devery Henderson caught it inside the 20, avoided a tackle, and ran into the end zone for the stunning victory. One student already standing on the crossbar asked another, "Did we just lose this game?"

After winning six straight, LSU lost three of its final five regular-season games and was bested by Texas 35-20 in the Cotton Bowl for an 8-5 finish. Despite LSU's advantage of 187 yards of offense to zero at the end of the first quarter, and a second quarter lead of 17-7 after Davis scored a 10-yard touchdown, the Longhorns closed the half with two touchdowns and took a lead that wouldn't be relinquished.

"The brook trout look—we've got it and we've got to get rid of it," Saban said of a losing performance.

Fans weren't sure what to expect in 2003, and neither were those voting in the national polls with the Tigers the preseason No. 14 team. But when they built up a 38-0 halftime lead at Arizona and finished with 481 total yards, expectations began to rise. It set up an early test for No. 11 LSU against No. 7 Georgia, and despite a 93-yard touchdown pass from David Greene to Tyson Browning on a screen, Skyler Green's late touchdown provided a 17-10 victory, the Tigers' first against the Bulldogs in 13 years.

A 19-7 loss at Florida proved to be only a minor setback, for the following week running backs Justin Vincent, Alley Broussard, and Barrington Edwards combined for 263 rushing yards while the defense limited South Carolina to a net total of zero, for a 33-7 victory. From there, the Tigers rolled. Against Auburn, LSU scored three touchdowns in the first quarter and went on to a 31-7 win. It easily won at Alabama, 27-3, to set up a showdown with Ole Miss for the division title, and edged the Rebels, led by Eli Manning, 17-14. With only Arkansas in the way of the SEC Championship Game, LSU pounded out a 55-24 victory.

Heading into its rematch with Georgia, LSU was third in the Bowl Championship Series (BCS) standings behind Southern California and Oklahoma, and looking at possibly being on the outside of the national championship game. However, when the Tigers blasted the Bulldogs 34-13, with Vincent recording 201 rushing yards and scoring on an 87-yard run, and Oklahoma lost to Kansas 35-7 in the Big XII title game, all three teams were left with one loss. The controversial Sugar Bowl pairing for the title was LSU vs. Oklahoma, featuring the nation's best defense against the top offense.

Despite Mauck fumbling away the first possession at the Sooners' 1-yard line, LSU dictated the tempo from the start. The Tigers sacked Heisman Trophy quarterback Jason White five times and limited the Sooners to just 154 yards. End Marcus Spears returned an interception 20 yards for a touchdown, and cornerback Corey Webster set up a touchdown with his interception. Vincent, who had a 64-yard gain on the first snap of the game, finished with 117 rushing yards and one touchdown, and the Tigers never trailed. Oklahoma's last chance ended with linebacker Lionel Turner's 10-yard sack, to secure the 21-14 victory.

The coaches' poll would vote Southern California No. 1. But under the BCS system, LSU was automatically presented with the national championship trophy, and Saban was later named Coach of the Year. USC and LSU would finally meet, but not on the playing field. Instead, it was in the East Room of the White House, as part of a Champions Day event with President George W. Bush.

"What's the toughest thing about being great? It's overcoming being good," Saban said.

The 2004 Tigers weren't quite able to equal the championship season, finishing 9-3 after winding up on the losing end in one of the most dramatic bowl games ever played. After LSU erased a 12-point deficit over the final eight minutes of the Capital One Bowl, No. 11 Iowa pulled off a surprising come-from-behind victory—thanks to Drew Tate's last-second 56-yard touchdown pass to Warren Holloway, with the receiver knifing his way through the secondary en route to the end zone and 30-25 victory.

It turned out to be Saban's last game at LSU. After just four years, and a 48-16 record, he accepted the head coaching job with the Miami Dolphins. But Saban left a roster full of talent for Les Miles, who was hired away from Oklahoma State, and despite massive destruction to the region from Hurricane Katrina in 2005, the Tigers still managed to reach the SEC Championship Game.

THREE THINGS THAT STAND OUT ABOUT LSU FOOTBALL

1. *Mike the Tiger:* Yes, Mike is a real Bengal tiger who actually lives in a swank pad on campus. Before games, his cage is placed on the field near the visiting locker room, and the announcer proclaims, "It's Saturday Night in Death Valley and here come your Fighting Tigers of LSU," referring to the stadium with a capacity of 91,600. The Tigers nickname goes back to the Civil War and a battalion of confederate soldiers comprised of New Orleans Zouaves and Donaldsonville Cannoneers who distinguished themselves at the Battle of Shenandoah. Among their fellow troops, they were known as the Louisiana Tigers.
2. *The real "raging" Cajuns:* Call them raucous, unruly, or just plain crazy, but LSU fans are as devoted as any you'll find, and they're seldom quiet about it (especially after having all day to "prepare" for games). Fans arrive on campus as early as Thursday and put on a tailgating spread to be envied, often including jambalaya, crawfish, boiled shrimp, and even *cochon de lait* (pig roast). For games, they also frequently dress "up," either in costume or in clothing lavishly featuring the team colors.
3. *Under the lights:* Most LSU home games are played at night, which helps turn them into all-day celebrations. The practice began in 1931, and the crowd gets so loud that after a touchdown against Auburn in 1988, the seismograph at the university's geology department actually moved. Consequently, October 8, 1988, has been dubbed the "Night the Tigers Moved the Earth."

· 15 ·

Ole Miss

Location: Oxford, Mississippi
Founded: 1848
Enrollment: 16,498
Nickname: Rebels
Colors: Cardinal red and navy blue
Mascot: Colonel Rebel
Stadium: Vaught-Hemingway Stadium/Hollingsworth Field
2005 officials: Dr. Robert Khayat, chancellor; Dr. Robert Weems, faculty representative; Pete Boone, athletics director

THE PROGRAM

National Championship (1): 1960
SEC Championships (6): 1947, 1954, 1955, 1960, 1962, 1963
Bowl appearances: 31 (19-12)
First season: 1893
College Football Hall of Fame (8): Charlie Conerly, 1942, 1946–47, halfback, inducted 1966; Charlie Flowers, 1957–59, fullback, 1997; Jake Gibbs, 1958–60, quarterback, 1995; Parker Hall, 1936–38, halfback, 1991; Bruiser Kinard, 1935–37, tackle, 1951; Archie Manning, 1968–70, quarterback, 1989; Barney Poole, 1942, 1947–48, end, 1974; Johnny Vaught, 1947–73, coach, 1979
Heisman Winners: None
National Honors: Eli Manning, 2003 Maxwell Award (outstanding player) and Johnny Unitas Golden Arm Award (best senior quarterback); Jonathan Nichols, 2003 Lou Groza Award (top kicker)
First-Team All-Americans: Frank (Bruiser) Kinard, T, 1936–37; Parker Hill, HB, 1938; Charlie Conerly, TB, 1947; Barney Poole, E, 1947–48; John (Kayo) Dottley, fullback, 1949; Kline Gilbert, T, 1952; Jimmy Lear, QB, 1952; Crawford Mims, G, 1953; Rex Boggan, T, 1954; Paige Cothren, FB, 1956; Jackie Simpson, G, 1957; Charles Flowers, FB, 1959; Marvin Terrell, G, 1959; Jake

Gibbs, QB, 1960; Johnny Brewer, E, 1960; Billy Ray Adams, FB, 1961; Jim Dunaway, T, 1961–62; Treva Bolin, G, 1961; Doug Elmore, QB, 1961; Glynn Griffing, QB, 1962; Kenny Dill, C, 1963; Whaley Hall, T, 1963; Allen Brown, E, 1964; Stan Hindman, G, 1964; Billy Clay, DB, 1964; Jim Urbanek, T, 1967; Archie Manning, QB, 1969–70; Glenn Cannon, S, 1969; Harry Harrison, DB, 1973; Ben Williams, DL, 1975; Jim Miller, P, 1979; Freddie Joe Nunn, DE, 1984; Bill Smith, P, 1985–86; Wesley Walls, TE, 1988; Everett Lindsay, T, 1991–92; Kris Mangum, TE, 1996; Rufus French, TE, 1998; Ken Lucas, DB, 2000; Terrence Metcalf, T, 2001; Eli Manning, QB, 2003; Jonathan Nichols, K, 2003; Patrick Willis, LB, 2005

First-Team Academic All-Americans (CoSIDA): Robert Khayat, T, 1959; Charlie Flowers, B, 1959; Doug Elmore, B, 1961; Stan Hindman, G, 1965; Mack Haik, SE, 1966; Steve Hindman, HB, 1968; Julius Fagan, K, 1969; Greg Markow, DE, 1974; Robert Fabris, OE, 1977; George Plasketes, DE, 1977; Ken Toler, WR, 1980; Danny Hoskins, G, 1986–87; Wesley Walls, TE, 1988; Todd Sandroni, DB, 1989; Rob Robertson, LB, 2004; Cody Ridgeway, P, 2004

First-round NFL draftees: 15

Retired jerseys: 18 Archie Manning

All-Centennial Team: Offense—E Floyd Franks, 1968–70; E Barney Poole, 1942, 1947–48; OL Jim Dunaway, 1960–62; OL Gene Hickerson, 1955–57; OL Stan Hindman, 1963–65; OL Everett Lindsay, 1989–92; OL Marvin Terrell, 1957–59; C Dawson Pruett, 1987–90; QB Archie Manning, 1968–70; RB Charlie Conerly, 1942, 1946–47; RB John (Kayo) Dottley, 1947–50; RB Charlie Flowers, 1957–59; K Robert Khayat, 1957–59 **Defense**—DL Bruiser Kinard, 1935–37; DL Kelvin Pritchett, 1988–90; DL Ben Williams, 1972–75; LB Tony Bennett, 1986–89; LB Larry Grantham, 1957–59; LB Jeff Herrod, 1984–87; LB Freddie Joe Nunn, 1981–84; DB Billy Brewer, 1957–59; DB Glenn Cannon, 1967–69; DB Chris Mitchell, 1987–90; DB Jimmy Patton, 1952–54; DB Todd Sandroni, 1987–90; P Jim Miller, 1976–79 **Coach:** John Vaught, 1947–70, 1973

Chucky Mullins Courage Award winners (in order, from 1990 to 2005): Chris Mitchell, Jeff Carter, Trea Southerland, Johnny Dixon, Alundis Brice, Michael Lowery, Derek Jones, Nate Wayne, Gary Thigpen, Ronnie Heard, Anthony Magree, Kevin Thomas, Lanier Goethie, Jamil Northcutt, Eric Oliver, Kelvin Robinson

THE COACHES

Dr. A. L. Bondurant, 1893, 4-1; C. D. Clark, 1894, 6-1; H. L. Fairbanks, 1895, 2-1; J. W. Hollister, 1896, 1-2; T. G. Scarbrough, 1898, 1-1; W. H. Lyon, 1899, 3-4; Z. N. Estes Jr., 1900, 0-3; Daniel Martin/William Sibley, 1901, 2-4; Daniel Martin, 1902, 4-3; Mike Harvey, 1903–04, 6-4-1; T. S. Hammond, 1906, 4-2; Frank Mason, 1907, 0-6; Frank Kyle, 1908, 3-5; Dr. N. P. Stauffer, 1909–11, 17-7-2; Leo DeTray, 1912, 5-3; William Driver, 1913–14, 11-7-2;

Fred Robbins, 1915–16, 5-12; C. R. (Dudy) Noble, 1917–18, 2-7-1; R. L. Sullivan, 1919–21, 11-13; R. A. Cowell, 1922–23, 8-11-1; Chester Barnard, 1924, 4-5; Homer Hazel, 1925–29, 21-22-3; Ed L. Walker, 1930–37, 38-38-8; Harry J. Mehre, 1938–45, 39-26-1; Harold (Red) Drew, 1946, 2-7; John Vaught, 1947–70, 1973, 190-60-12; Billy Kinard, 1971–73, 16-9; Ken Cooper, 1974–77, 21-23; Steve Sloan, 1978–82, 20-34-1; Billy Brewer, 1983–93, 68-54-3; Joe Lee Dunn, 1994, 4-7; Tommy Tuberville, 1995–98, 25-20; David Cutcliffe, 1998–2004, 44-29; Ed Orgeron, 2005, 3-8

National Coach of the Year: None

SEC Coach of the Year, AP: John Vaught 1947, 1948, 1954, 1955, 1960; Ken Cooper 1975; Billy Brewer 1983; Tommy Tuberville 1997; David Cutcliffe 2003 **Coaches:** John Vaught 1947, 1962; Ken Cooper 1975; Billy Brewer 1990; David Cutcliffe 2003

SEC Championships: John Vaught 6

National Championships: John Vaught 1

RECORDS

Rushing yards, game: 242, Dou Innocent vs. Mississippi State, Nov. 25, 1995 (39 carries)

Rushing yards, season: 1,312, John Dottley, 1949 (208 carries)

Rushing yards, career: 3,060, Duece McAlister, 1997–2000 (616 carries)

Passing yards, game: 436, Archie Manning vs. Alabama, Oct. 4, 1969 (33 of 52)

Passing yards, season: 3,600, Eli Manning, 2003 (275 of 441)

Passing yards, career: 10,119, Eli Manning, 2000–03 (829 of 1,363)

Receiving yards, game: 210, Eddie Small vs. Vanderbilt, Sept. 18, 1993 (six receptions)

Receiving yards, season: 949, Chris Collins, 2003 (77 receptions)

Receiving yards, career: 2,621, Chris Collins, 2000–03 (198 receptions)

Points, game: 42, Showboat Boykin vs. Mississippi State, Dec. 1, 1995 (seven touchdowns)

Points, season: 124, Jonathan Nichols, 2003 (25 field goals, 49 PATs)

Points, career: 265, Jonathan Nichols, 2001–04 (43 field goals, 136 PATs)

When it comes to the University of Mississippi, its football team reflects both the small-town charm and big-time sophistication that the Oxford campus is known for.

No home to big-time college football is quite as quaint, gracious, charming, or Southern, and not in a geographical way. It features Rowan Oak, once the home of William Faulkner, Oxford Square, and The Grove, described by *The Sporting News* as the "Holy Grail of tailgating experiences." Just don't forget the words to the "Hotty Toddy" cheer (but if you do, they'll be more than happy to help you out).

This school that is so entrenched in its roots doesn't even use its own name.

"Ole Miss" was selected during a contest to name the yearbook in 1896, and over the years became synonymous with the university. Somehow, it's just more fitting.

"There is a valid distinction between the university and Ole Miss even though the separate threads are closely interwoven," alumnus Frank Everett Jr. wrote. "The university is buildings, trees and people. Ole Miss is mood, emotion and personality. One is physical, and the other is spiritual. One is tangible, and the other intangible. The university is respected, but Ole Miss is loved. The university gives a diploma and regretfully terminates tenure, but one never graduates from Ole Miss."

At Ole Miss, the men don't boast about having once dated the homecoming queen; they brag about having escorted a Miss America. And they take honor in remembering their sports icons, even if Casey Stengel did coach the baseball team only briefly in 1914. He's considered part of their heritage and family, as are all the football players and coaches.

Georgia coach Vince Dooley once said: "When you hear forty-six thousand Rebels screaming for your blood, and meaning it, it can be eerie." Now Vaught-Hemingway Stadium at Hollingsworth Field, the state's largest facility, has a capacity of 60,580.

Ole Miss football dates back to 1890, when Dr. A. L. Bondurant was instrumental in forming the school's athletic association. With the future dean of the graduate school serving as manager/coach, the first game was played in 1893 against Southwest Baptist University of Jackson, Tennessee, a 56-0 victory that helped lead to a 4-1 season.

Almost immediately, the sport was popular. Among one of the more telling quotes in early school history was from James "Bobo" Champion in 1893: "The athletic fever has now taken full possession of the university . . . and the time is already here when, in order to rank high in college or society, one must join the running crowd and play on the football team."

It's believed that C. D. Clark was the first paid football coach in 1894, when Ole Miss first faced a few of its future SEC rivals. It squeaked out a 6-0 victory against Alabama and beat LSU 26-6, but lost 40-0 to Vanderbilt to finish 6-1.

Like most of its collegiate counterparts, Ole Miss in the early years saw numerous coaching changes. Prior to 1925, the team had 22 different head coaches, the most noteworthy being a 7-1 finish under Dr. Nathan P. Stauffer in 1910. Over three seasons, he had a 17-7-2 record.

Homer Hazel was the first coach to provide some stability, when from 1925 to 1929 Ole Miss tallied a 21-22-3 mark. Ed Walker had a comparable record during his eight years at the helm, and led the Rebels to their first bowl appearance in 1935. A 9-2 season brought a bid from the Orange Bowl, but during the 14-6 regular season finale against Mississippi State, fullback Clarence (Big Un) Hapes sustained a knee injury. He would be missed against Catholic University from Washington, D.C.

A 67-yard sweep around the left side by Ned Peters put Ole Miss on the scoreboard, and sophomore halfback Ray Hapes returned from an injury to lead a second-half comeback, but despite being outgained 265 yards to 172, and in first downs 15 to seven, Catholic U. held on for a 20-19 victory.

Walker also coached Ole Miss' first All-American, Frank "Bruiser" Kinard in 1936–37, before Harry Mehre took over the following season. (*Note:* The 1937 season was also known for Ole Miss making the first en masse flight by a college team. The Rebels traveled from Memphis to Philadelphia on American Airlines flagship *Maryland.*)

In the pre–World War II years, the Rebels finished 9-2, 7-2, 9-2, and 6-2-1 before dipping in 1942 and having trustees ban the sport in 1943. The 1938 team featured Parker "Bullet" Hall, who led the nation in scoring (73 points), all-purpose rushing (1,558 yards), rushing average, kick-return average, interceptions, and touchdowns (22). Although his teams were best remembered for the dominating backfield of Junie Hovious and Merle Hapes, nicknamed the H-boys, Mehre's accomplishments included the first victory against Vanderbilt (14-7 in 1939), the first win in 11 years against LSU (20-7 in 1938), and the first victory against Tulane in 25 years (20-13 in 1941).

Mehre returned for two more seasons in 1944 and 1945, and left Ole Miss on the brink of its glory years. C. M. "Tad" Smith succeeded him as director of athletics, a post he would hold until 1971, and many believed that longtime Alabama assistant Harold "Red" Drew, who was hired as coach, would be the one to bring greatness to the program. He was, sort of. After a 2-7 season, Drew returned to Tuscaloosa to succeed legendary coach Frank Thomas at Alabama. When assistant John Vaught decided to stay at Ole Miss and replace Drew rather than follow him back to Tuscaloosa, it turned out to be the best thing that ever happened to the Rebels.

"I'll do anything for Ole Miss," Vaught said.

In his first season alone, the former All-American at Texas Christian guided Ole Miss to a 9-2 record and captured its first SEC title. Charlie Conerly, a combat Marine in the South Pacific during World War II, led the nation in pass completions with 133 and was the school's first Heisman candidate, finishing fourth. Prior to the start of the season, Vaught promised to play his alma mater at the Delta Bowl in nearby Memphis if possible. Even after receiving an invitation for the Sugar Bowl, the coach kept his word, though the stubborn Horned Frogs almost made him regret it.

Bobby Berry's 28-yard interception return for a touchdown and a blocked punt gave TCU a 9-0 lead heading into the fourth quarter, when Conerly connected on touchdown passes to Joe Johnson and Dixie Howell to lead the 13-9 comeback.

From there, things only got better for Ole Miss and Vaught, who brought the split-T to the South, but really made his mark on defense. During his 24 years the Rebels had just one losing season, 4-5-1 in 1949. During the 1950s, when Ole Miss won three SEC titles, only Oklahoma had a better overall record than Ole Miss' 80-21-5.

The Rebels did go to the Sugar Bowl after finishing the 1952 regular season undefeated at 8-0-2, thanks to a 21-14 victory over No. 1 Maryland, but they ran into a talented Georgia Tech team and some bad breaks. Wissy Dillard opened the scoring with a 14-yard touchdown, but when he was stopped short of the goal line on two different drives, one on a controversial call, the Rebels lost their momentum for good. Though the Ole Miss media guide called it the "game of the big grumble," with even Governor Hugh White voicing his displeasure, the Engineers won 24-7.

Ole Miss didn't have better fortune in the 1955 Sugar Bowl against Navy. Coming in, the SEC champions had outscored the opposition 283-47, but the "Team of Desire" won out that day. Navy outgained Ole Miss 442 yards to 121 and won 21-0.

The Rebels' first major bowl victory came in the 1956 Cotton Bowl. Led by Jim Swink, who scored the first two touchdowns of the game, TCU was favored against the SEC champions; but Ole Miss had Herman "Eagle" Day, who would earn the nickname "The Mississippi Gambler" that day.

With Paige Cothren setting up his own 3-yard touchdown with a 21-yard fullback draw, the Rebels drove 66 yards in four plays to close within 13-7 at half-time. Day's 25-yard run in the fourth quarter set up Billy Lott's 5-yard touchdown for the 14-13 final.

The 1958 Sugar Bowl was even more impressive. After outscoring opponents 232-52 in the regular season and posting shutouts in four of the first five games, Ole Miss was 8-1-1 heading into its showdown with Texas. Led by Ray Brown, who threw a 3-yard touchdown pass to Don Williams and ran in two more, including a 92-yarder when in punt formation he tucked the ball and ran, Ole Miss won in a rout, 39-7. Brown finished with 157 rushing yards and had three interceptions on defense to be named the game's outstanding player.

An 8-2 record, with losses to LSU and Tennessee, had Ole Miss in the 1958 Gator Bowl against Florida. With a light rain falling, the Rebels elected to take the opening kickoff and drove 70 yards for the game's only touchdown. On the way, fullback Charlie Flowers suffered an eye injury that sidelined him, but replacement Jim Anderson and Kent Lovelace kept the possession going along with quarterback Bobby Franklin.

Florida's best chance to score came early in the fourth quarter after Bobby Joe Green's surprise kick quick went 76 yards and hit an Ole Miss player, resulting in a fumble recovered at the Rebels' 10-yard line. But two stops by Jimmy Hall and one by Larry Grantham set up fourth down, when Richard Price burst through the line and dropped quarterback Jimmy Dunn.

(*Note:* The J. Richard Price Courage and Compassion Award is now presented annually to the rising senior lineman who, in the opinion of his coaches, has demonstrated extraordinary courage and unusual compassion in his dedication to the team and Ole Miss.)

Leaving the game, Grantham started chanting, "All the way in '59, national champs," and Ole Miss answered by attempting to make the leap from SEC dominance to national prominence. The Rebels gave up just three touchdowns all season, en route to a 10-1 record. The defense was so dominating—allowing just 2.1 points per game, thanks to eight shutouts—that the Rebels would often punt on first or second down.

The one gaffe that season took place on October 31 at LSU, when Billy Cannon, who went on to win the Heisman Trophy, broke an 89-yard punt return in what's still considered one of the greatest plays in college football history. Defending national champion LSU held on, 7-3. Later, Cannon said, "I realized that I could have been tackled any number of times and that if we didn't score soon the game was going to be over."

When Ole Miss rebounded by blowing out Chattanooga, Tennessee, and Mississippi State by a combined score of 137-7, it earned a rematch with LSU in the Sugar Bowl. This time, the game wasn't close. Led by Franklin and Grantham, the Rebels easily won 21-0. The Tigers mustered only six first downs, 74 yards of total offense, and minus-15 yards rushing.

Although the '59 Rebels weren't a consensus national champion (instead, the title went to Syracuse), weeks later they were named SEC Team of the Decade by an Associated Press poll.

Ole Miss did get its national championship in 1960, though once again LSU got in the way. After a 6-0 start, the Rebels could only tie the Tigers in Oxford, 6-6, which opened the door for Minnesota to finish No. 1 in both Associated Press and United Press International polls. Against Rice in the Sugar Bowl, All-American Jake Gibbs scored two touchdowns to lead the SEC champions to a 14-6 victory. The Football Writers Association of America rewarded the effort in post-bowl balloting, with Ole Miss the first SEC school to receive the Grantland Rice Trophy.

Incidentally, Gibbs went on to play for ten years as a catcher with the New York Yankees (1962–71). In six of those years, 1965–70, he returned to campus after the baseball season to serve as an assistant football coach. After his professional playing career ended, Gibbs was Ole Miss' baseball coach for 19 years.

Another setback against LSU, 10-7, cost a title run in 1961, and All-American fullback Billy Ray Adams was injured in a car accident just two days after a 37-7 victory against Mississippi State. The Rebels, who outscored opponents 326-40, were heavily favored against Texas in the Cotton Bowl, but the Longhorns got out to an early lead and were able to hold on.

"I never could get my cleats anchored to throw," All-American quarterback Glynn Griffing said of the hard surface after the 12-7 loss.

Arguably the best run the Rebels made for the consensus national title was in 1962, when they finally got the best of LSU 15-7 and went on to finish the regular season 9-0. Against Arkansas in the Sugar Bowl, Griffing completed 14 of 23 passes for 242 yards and a touchdown and ran in another. His 257 yards in total offense broke Davey O'Brien's bowl record, which had stood for 24 years.

For the first time, Ole Miss finished the season with a perfect record. The only problem was something it couldn't control—Southern California, which also ran the table in impressive fashion to be voted the consensus national champion. Ole Miss had to settle for No. 2.

Despite an opening 0-0 tie at Memphis State, the Rebels took another shot at it in 1963, and optimism prevailed following a dominating 37-3 victory at LSU. But if a 10-10 tie at Mississippi State didn't foreshadow what was to come, then four-plus inches of snow the day before the Sugar Bowl against Alabama certainly did. Ole Miss fumbled 11 times, losing six, while the Crimson Tide had six fumbles, losing three.

If one play typified the game, it was when Perry Lee Dunn completed an 11-yard pass to end Joe Pettey to the Alabama 9-yard-line, which could have set up a potential game-winning touchdown in the fourth quarter. But along the sideline, Pettey fumbled. The ball rolled out of bounds against a snowbank and then rolled back in, to be recovered by Alabama's Eddie Versprille. Tim Davis made field goals of 46, 31, 34, and 48 yards as the Tide won 12-7.

Although Ole Miss was unable to challenge for another national championship, it started a 15-year string of bowl appearances. With seconds remaining in the 1965 Liberty Bowl, Jim Urbanek, Jimmy Keyes, Marvin McQueen, and Jerry Richardson broke through and sacked Auburn quarterback Alex Bowden on fourth down at the Ole Miss 9 to preserve a 13-7 victory.

After allowing just 46 points, with five shutouts, for an 8-2 record in 1966, the defense yielded on three long drives by Texas, which won the Bluebonnet Bowl 19-0.

The 1967 season ended in similar fashion. Despite the efforts of Mac McClure, whose 47-yard interception return set up a touchdown, and tackle Dan Smith, Texas-Paso won the Sun Bowl 14-7. But there would be brighter times in the years to follow, when the Rebels were led by the most beloved player in their history.

Quarterback Archie Manning never won an SEC or national championship, or the Heisman Trophy. But his No. 18 is the only retired jersey in school history, and the road leading to the new indoor practice facility (costing, of course, $18 million) was named Manning Way.

What Ole Miss might have lacked in hardware, it made up for in excitement, even when the Rebels didn't want any.

For example, 37 seconds into the 1968 Liberty Bowl, Ole Miss was waiting for Virginia Tech to huddle when Hokies quarterback Al Kincaid scooped up the ball and pitched it to tailback Ken Edwards, who went 58 yards for a touchdown. Manning fumbled on his first possession two minutes into the game; and by the end of the first quarter, Tech had a 17-0 lead.

Starting with a 24-yard touchdown pass to Hank Shows, Ole Miss dominated thereafter. Though upset about a fourth-down play in which officials ruled that Manning was across the goal line, but the ball was not, the quarterback threw another touchdown pass, tailback Steve Hindman had 122 rushing yards on 15 carries, and middle linebacker Robert Bailey scored on a 70-yard interception return for a 34-17 final.

One of the most famous games in college football history occurred on October 4, 1969. No. 15 Alabama hosted No. 20 Ole Miss at Legion Field in Birmingham, in the first regular-season college football game televised in prime time.

In the second half, the quarterbacks—Manning and Scott Hunter of the Crimson Tide—seemed to turn the game into a version of "Anything you can do, I can do better." In the final few minutes, Alabama coach Paul "Bear" Bryant simply told his quarterback to "Run the best thing you've got." Hunter did, and the

Tide scored for a 33-32 victory. Manning completed 33 of 52 passes for 436 yards, ran for 104 yards, and had five touchdowns. Hunter completed 22 of 29 passes for 300 yards, with the game-winning touchdown pass to George Ranager.

ABC announcer Chris Schenkel described it as the "Greatest duel two quarterbacks ever had. You had to be there to believe it."

After the game, the coaches shook hands at midfield and Bryant said to his friend, "Wasn't that the worst college football game you've ever seen?"

While Alabama lost its next two games, Ole Miss went on to manhandle No. 3 Tennessee 38-0 after Volunteers linebacker Steve Kiner made the mistake of saying, "Archie who?" Next up was Arkansas, which at 9-1 was coming off a No. 1 vs. No. 2 showdown against Texas, in the Sugar Bowl.

Although the Razorbacks led the nation in scoring defense, allowing just 7.6 points per game, the Rebels dominated the first half. Fullback Bo Bowen opened the scoring with a 69-yard run. Manning had two touchdowns, the first on an 18-yard carry set up by his 57-yard pass to Vernon Studdard, followed by a 30-yard scoring strike to Studdard for a 24-12 halftime lead.

Arkansas came back, but All-American safety Glenn Cannon intercepted a tailback pass in the end zone. The following Arkansas possession stalled when he broke up three consecutive passes by quarterback Bill Montgomery, and later, with 1:15 remaining, forced and recovered a fumble to preserve the 27-22 victory.

Manning finished fourth in Heisman voting that year; he placed third in 1970, when health issues forced Vaught to resign as head coach. Their last game was a loss, but one that tugged at the hearts of Rebels fans.

No. 10 Auburn, led by 1971 Heisman Trophy winner Pat Sullivan, and Ole Miss combined for 1,063 yards of offense in the Gator Bowl. But with Manning wearing a plastic sleeve to protect a broken arm, the Rebels couldn't keep up. Before being replaced by Shug Chumbler, who threw a 23-yard pass to Jim Poole, Manning had 95 rushing yards and 180 passing in the 35-28 defeat.

"All that scrambling got me," said Manning, whose career concluded with 4,753 passing yards and 823 rushing yards, often from his legendary improvisations. "My wind left me, and those weeks out of action showed up. That old hospital bed never got off my back. As a matter of fact, I felt like it rode down the field with me a couple of times."

Manning went on to play 14 years in the National Football League, during which he was also recognized for work with the Boy Scouts, Special Olympics, Fellowship of Christian Athletes, 4-H, American Heart Association, American Cancer Society, United Negro College Fund, Easter Seals, United Way, Cystic Fibrosis, Tuberculosis, and others. He was voted Mississippian of the Year in 1981, and was the youngest person ever inducted into the Ole Miss Hall of Fame.

University of Mississippi Chancellor Porter L. Fortune Jr. said on John Vaught Day in 1971, "John Vaught trained the boys to become men while imparting to them some of his own extraordinary skills as an athlete."

Billy Kinard became the first former Ole Miss player to coach the team when he was hired by his brother "Bruiser" Kinard, the former player and offensive line coach under Vaught who was named athletic director. After early losses to No. 7

Alabama (40-6) and No. 10 Georgia (38-7), the Rebels turned things around with a 48-0 win at Mississippi State and took a 9-2 record into the Peach Bowl. Although Georgia Tech was favored, Ole Miss dominated, racking up five touchdowns and a field goal before the Engineers scored their first points in the second quarter.

The Rebels converted five turnovers, including interceptions by Mickey Fratesi and Henry Walsh, into points in the 41-18 rout. Jim Porter ran in two touchdowns, and quarterback Norris Weese scored two himself—one running, one passing. Weese was named the game's most valuable offensive player with linebacker Crowell Armstrong his defensive counterpart. The Rebels were ranked fifteenth.

It would be 12 years until Ole Miss returned to the postseason, but the program's struggles briefly brought the return of Vaught after both Kinards were fired three games into the 1973 season. Despite a 1-2 start the Rebels finished a respectable 6-5, with Vaught retiring from coaching for good while staying on as director of athletics. Vaught's impressive record of 190-61-12 made him the fourth-winningest coach in SEC history, behind only Bryant (323), Lou Holtz, and Vince Dooley.

"The worst thing a coach can do is stand pat and think the things that worked yesterday will win tomorrow," Vaught said. "Intelligent changes must be made."

From 1972 to 1985, the Rebels won more than six games in a season only once, with one bowl appearance. Both happened during former player Billy Brewer's first season as coach in 1983 (though the seventh win came from a forfeit by Tulane). A goal-line stand, with a key stop by defensive tackle Andre Townsend, kept Ole Miss in the game during the rain-soaked Independence Bowl; but Air Force prevailed, 9-3.

The biggest victory during this time period came in 1977, during coach Ken Cooper's final season. The Rebels were rotten hosts to Joe Montana and No. 3 Notre Dame, with fullback James Storey's touchdown reception leading a 20-13 victory. The Irish didn't lose again that season, beating Texas in the Cotton Bowl to edge Alabama for the national championship, while Ole Miss finished 5-6.

However, the controversy of race continued to cast a shadow over the program well into the 1980s. In 1962, enrollment of the school's first black student, James Meredith, led to riots in protest. It wasn't until 1972 that Ole Miss added its first two black players, Ben Williams and James Reed.

"If it hadn't been for football, they would have probably closed Ole Miss," Vaught later recalled.

In the '80s, heated debate questioned whether Confederate flags should continue to be waved during games; the controversy also affected recruiting. However, Brewer was able to lead the Rebels to four more bowl games, the first of which was a 20-17 victory against Texas Tech in the 1986 Independence Bowl. Mark Young threw for 343 passing yards, breaking five of Manning's bowl records, but a 48-yard field goal by Bryan Owens provided the winning points thanks to a last-minute interception by safety Jeff Nobin. Brewer was named SEC Coach of the Year.

Ole Miss picked a good time to win for the first time against the No. 12 Crimson Tide in the state of Alabama—it was 1988, and the Rebels pulled off a 22-12 victory that spoiled not only Alabama's homecoming, but the dedication of the Paul W. Bryant Museum in Tuscaloosa. The Rebels went on to finish 5-6.

Inspired by a visit from Chucky Mullins—a player who'd been paralyzed during a game earlier in the season and was making his first trip out of the hospital—Ole Miss jumped out to a huge lead in the 1989 Liberty Bowl en route to a 42-29 victory against Air Force. Quarterback John Darnell and running back Randy Baldwin combined for nearly 300 yards of offense in the first half alone, and Pat Coleman returned a punt 58 yards for a touchdown. Jeff Carter—a walk-on who wound up starting due to teammates' injuries—had eight tackles, an interception, and one pass breakup to be named the game's most outstanding defensive player.

A last-second 21-17 victory against Arkansas sparked Ole Miss to a seven-game winning streak in 1990, but a 9-2 season was overshadowed by a 35-3 loss to Michigan in the Gator Bowl. Defensive back Tyrone Ashley had a 60-yard interception, four kickoff returns for 113 yards, and made four tackles; but led by quarterback Elvis Grbac, running back Jon Vaughn, and future Heisman Trophy winner Desmond Howard, the Wolverines scored 21 points in the third quarter to secure the win.

For the third time in 10 years, Ole Miss was paired against Air Force in the postseason, though the 1992 Liberty Bowl was more of a defensive showdown than its predecessors had been. Coordinator Joe Lee Dunn's defense, ranked sixth in the nation, proved worthy of its reputation, yielding an average of just 2.9 yards per play, and earned the Rebels a shutout, 13-0. Cornerback Danny Boyd made an interception in the end zone; but linebacker Cassius Ware, who had 10 tackles, two sacks, and a fumble recovery, was named the game's defensive MVP. Ole Miss wouldn't return to the postseason until 1997, when under coach Tommy Tuberville the Rebels pulled out both a 36-21 victory at No. 8 LSU and a last-second 15-14 win against Mississippi State.

With Marshall led by quarterback Chad Pennington and wide receiver Randy Moss, the teams combined for more than 1,000 yards and swapped the lead six teams during the Motor City Bowl. Quarterback Stewart Patridge matched Pennington with 332 yards and three touchdowns. Running back Deuce McAllister had 39 of his 71 rushing yards on the game-winning drive, and both he and John Avery, who had 110 rushing yards, scored touchdowns in the 34-31 victory.

In 1998, Ole Miss scored 22 points in the final 10 minutes to pull off a stunning comeback against Southern Methodist, which had a 41-19 lead. The Rebels won in overtime 48-41, a win that proved crucial for postseason aspirations after they lost the last three games of the regular season to finish 6-5.

"They'll have to carry me out of here in a pine box," Tuberville said when asked about rumors he was up for the Auburn job—which he accepted November 29, a week before Ole Miss was invited to play Texas Tech in the Independence Bowl. David Cutcliffe, the offensive coordinator of national champion Tennessee, was hired and had less than a month to learn his players and the playbook. Making matters worse, while the Rebels were in the middle of final exams, Cutcliffe was hospitalized with pancreatitis. After hearing an "against-all-odds" pregame speech, they still came through with an inspired 35-18 victory. Quarterback Romaro Miller, who came back from an injury sustained on the final play against Georgia, passed for 216 yards with three touchdowns, and safety Anthony Magee had two interceptions.

Cutcliffe led the Rebels to four bowl appearances in his first five years at Ole Miss, beginning with an impressive 27-25 victory against Oklahoma in the 1999 Independence Bowl. McAllister had 239 all-purpose yards with two touchdowns, including a career-best 80-yard carry, Miller was 18 of 28 for 202 yards and two touchdowns, and senior cornerback Tim Strickland had both an interception in the end zone and a forced fumble. Shortly after quarterback Josh Heupel, who finished 39 of 53 for 390 yards, gave the Sooners a one-point lead with just over two minutes remaining, kicker Les Binkley made a 39-yard game-winning field goal in the final seconds.

In 2000, Cutcliffe was able to tap into a piece of Ole Miss history when Archie Manning's son Eli took over at quarterback.

Like father, like son—Manning wasn't able to lead Ole Miss to a championship, and he would finish third in Heisman voting in 2003. But once again, the Rebels were far from boring.

The changeover happened during the 2000 Music City Bowl, after Miller scored on a 7-yard touchdown run and, with Ole Miss down 49-16 to West Virginia, gave way to the redshirt freshman. Manning completed 12 of 20 passes for 267 yards with three touchdowns to pull the Rebels to within 49-38.

The 2001 team set a school record for points scored with 391, but it translated into only seven wins. One of the most dramatic defeats in Ole Miss lore came against Arkansas, in a game that took seven overtimes to decide. Eventually, the Razorbacks stopped a two-point conversion for a 58-56 final.

The biggest upset in school history came against No. 6 Florida in 2002. Manning completed 18 of 33 passes for 254 yards to lead a comeback after being down 14-2 at halftime and win his showdown with Heisman candidate Rex Grossman, 17-14.

"I knew to leave my helmet on," Eli Manning said. "Everyone was smacking me on the head. I wanted to see the goal post come down, but it was too crazy."

Not learning their lesson, the Gators lost again the following year at The Swamp, 20-17.

Ole Miss concluded the 2002 season at the Independence Bowl against Nebraska, which had won three national championships and 108 games in the 1990s but entered the game with a 7-6 record. Manning passed for 313 yards, and the defense dominated the second half, yielding just 59 rushing yards and 38 passing yards. Defensive backs Eric Oliver and Travis Blanchard and linebacker Eddie Strong all reached double digits in tackles, while defensive tackle Jesse Mitchell had nine.

After a lackluster 2-2 start in 2003, Manning keyed the turnaround as Ole Miss finished 10-3 and tied LSU, which won the national championship, for first in the SEC Western Division. Playing on New Year's Day, Manning completed 23 of 31 passes for 259 yards and scored three touchdowns to guide Ole Miss to a 31-28 victory against Oklahoma State. While Josh Cooper led the defense, Tremaine Turner scored two touchdowns to help lead the Rebels' first victory in the Cotton Bowl since 1962.

Four months later, Manning entered the NFL Draft a year early and was selected first overall, one spot higher than his father.

THREE THINGS THAT STAND OUT ABOUT OLE MISS FOOTBALL

1. *The Grove:* The 10-acre plot in the heart of campus, shaded by oak trees, is where fans gather hours before kickoff to tailgate. They dress up, enjoy a cocktail or two, and indulge in elaborate food spreads. In 1983, coach Billy Brewer began the tradition of the team walking through The Grove en route to the stadium two hours before kickoff, which evolved into fans forming a narrow gauntlet extending from the Walk of Champions arch, erected on the east end in 1998 and donated by the 10-0 1962 team. "If you ain't ready to play after walking through the Grove, you're probably dead," Brewer said.
2. *The Rebels:* The name, which would later become controversial, was suggested by Judge Ben Guider of Vicksburg and voted on by a panel of sportswriters in 1936. Two years later, the "Colonel Rebel" first appeared in the university yearbook. According to University of Mississippi historian David Sansing, a black man named Blind Jim Ivy was the original model for the emblem, but others believe Gen. Robert E. Lee was the inspiration. Ivy was a mainstay at athletic events and is remembered for frequently saying, "I've never seen Ole Miss lose." Prior to 1936, Ole Miss' nickname was "The Flood."
3. *Chucky Mullins:* The defensive back was paralyzed during the 1989 homecoming game, but considered a national hero for his spirit and determination. "I may give out, but I'll never give up," was one of the many inspirational things he said. Shortly after returning to school, Mullins died in 1991. Each year the team's most outstanding defensive player receives both the Chucky Mullins Award and the honor of wearing his No. 38. "There are a lot of awards, the Heisman, the Doak Walker, and then you have the Chucky Mullins Award," 1996 winner Derek Jones said. "Not too many people can win this award. It belongs to us, and we should cherish it."

Mississippi State

THE SCHOOL

Location: Starkville, Mississippi
Founded: 1878
Enrollment: 15,934
Nickname: Bulldogs
Colors: Maroon and white
Mascot: Bully
Stadium: Davis Wade Stadium at Scott Field (55,082)
2005 officials: Dr. J. Charles Lee, president; Dr. Steve Turner, faculty representative; Larry Templeton, athletics director

THE PROGRAM

National Championships: None
SEC Championship (1): 1941
Bowl appearances: 12 (6-6)
First season: 1895
College Football Hall of Fame (5): Bernie Bierman, 1925–26, coach, inducted 1955; D. D. Lewis, 1965–67, linebacker, 2001; Allyn McKeen, 1939–48, coach, 1991; Jackie Parker, 1952–53, quarterback, 1976; Darrell Royal, 1954–55, coach, 1983
Heisman Winners: None
National Honors: None
First-Team All-Americans: Erwin (Buddy) Elrod, E, 1940; Joe Fortunato, FB, 1951; Jackie Parker, QB, 1953; Hal Easterwood, C, 1954; Scott Suber, G, 1955; Art Davis, HB, 1955; Tom Goode, C, 1960; Pat Watson, C, 1963; D. D. Lewis, LB, 1967; Frank Dowsing, DB, 1972; Jimmy Webb, DE, 1974; Stan Black, S, 1976; Mardye McDole, WR, 1980; Johnie Cooks, LB, 1981; Glenn Collins, DT, 1981; Billy Jackson, DE, 1981; Wayne Harris, G, 1982; Walt Harris, DB, 1995; Barrin Simpson, LB, 1999; Fred Smoot, DB, 2000; Pork Chop Womack, T, 2000

First-Team Academic All-Americans (CoSIDA): Jackie Parker, B, 1953; Hal
Easterwood, C, 1954; Ron Bennett, E, 1956; Frank Dowsing, DB, 1972; Ken
Phares, QB, 1972; Jimmy Webb, DE, 1973; Will Coltharp, DE, 1976; Bo Russell, DB, 1989; Scott Westerfield, K, 2000
First-round NFL draftees: Nine
Retired jerseys: None

THE COACHES

W. M. Matthews, 1895, 0-2; J. B. Hildebrand, 1896, 0-4; L. B. Harvey, 1901, 2-2-1; L. Gwinn, 1902, 1-4-1; Dan Martin, 1903–06, 10-11-3; Fred Furman, 1907–08, 9-7; W. D. Chadwick, 1909–13, 29-12-2; E. C. Hayes, 1914–16, 15-8-2; Sid Robinson, 1917–19, 15-5; Fred Holtkamp, 1920–21, 9-7-1; C. R. (Dudy) Noble, 1922, 3-4-2; Earl Able, 1923–24, 10-6-2; Bernie Bierman, 1925–26, 8-8-1; J. W. Hancock, 1927–29, 8-12-4; Chris Cagle, 1930, 2-7; Ray Dauber, 1931–32, 5-11; Ross McKechnie, 1933–34, 7-12-1; Ralph Sasse, 1935–37, 20-10-2; Emerson (Spike) Nelson, 1938, 4-6; Allyn McKeen, 1939–48, 65-19-3; Arthur (Slick) Morton, 1949–51, 8-18-1; Murray Warmath, 1952–53, 10-6-3; Darrell Royal, 1954–55, 12-8; Wade Walker, 1956–61, 23-32-2; Paul Davis, 1962–66, 20-28-2; Charley Shira, 1967–72, 16-45-2; Bob Tyler, 1973–78, 21-44-2; Emory Bellard, 1979–85, 37-42; Rockey Felker, 1986–90, 21-34; Jackie Sherrill, 1991–2003, 75-75-2; Sylvester Croom, 2004–05, 6-16
National Coach of the Year: None
SEC Coach of the Year, AP: Paul Davis 1963; Charlie Shira 1970 **Coaches:** Allyn
McKeen 1940; Wade Walker 1957
SEC Championships: Allyn McKeen 1
National Championships: None

RECORDS

Rushing yards, game: 257 Jerious Norwood vs. Houston, Oct. 22, 2005 (24 carries)
Rushing yards, season: 1,383, James Johnson, 1998 (236 carries)
Rushing yards, career: 3,222, Jerious Norwood, 2002–05 (573 carries)
Passing yards, game: 466, Derrick Taite vs. Tulane, Oct. 22, 1994 (21 of 30)
Passing yards, season: 2,422, Dave Marler, 1978 (163 of 287)
Passing yards, career: 6,336, Wayne Madkin, 1998–2001 (462 of 887)
Receiving yards, game: 215, David Smith vs. Texas Tech, Oct. 17, 1970 (12 receptions)
Receiving yards, season: 1,035, Mardye McDole, 1978 (48 receptions)
Receiving yards, career: 2,214, Mardye McDole, 1977–80 (116 receptions)

Points, game: 42, Harry McArthur vs. Cumberland, Oct. 10, 1914 (seven touch-downs)

Points, season: 120, Jackie Parker, 1952 (16 touchdowns, 24 PATs)

Points, career: 218, Brian Hazelwood, 1995–98 (43 field goals, 90 PATs)

It's never been known as a football powerhouse, but don't tell that to fans of Mississippi State, who have proven to be as resilient as, well, an undeterred Bulldog.

No program in the Southeastern Conference has had such a roller-coaster history, and while the baseball team has enjoyed enormous success—providing the likes of Will Clark, Rafael Palmeiro, and Buck Showalter—the football program has been continually searching for an identity and reinventing itself. Still, Mississippi State is seemingly always tough and has never been a team to take lightly.

"Football doesn't build character," coach Darrell Royal (1954–55) said. "It eliminates weak ones."

The first football game at Mississippi A&M College (later to become Mississippi State University) took place between the faculty and students on Thanksgiving Day 1892. The teachers won 4-0.

The first intercollegiate game was played on November 16, 1895, a 21-0 loss to Southwestern Baptist (now Union University). Beforehand, coach/captain W. M. Mathews chose maroon and white as the team's colors, which for the most part are the same ones used today. Seventeen players made up the roster, and a second game was played, against the Memphis Athletic Club, a 16-0 loss.

After the student body raised roughly $300 to hire J. B. Hildebrand as coach, Mississippi A&M scheduled both its first home game and its first meeting with nearby Alabama (just 90 miles away), losing both. Due to an epidemic of yellow fever followed by the Spanish-American Civil War, football didn't return to the school until 1901. Its resurgence was thanks, in part, to the lobbying of Irwin Dancy Sessums, a military science instructor who gained the approval of college president John Crumton Hardy.

Finally, two days after playing Christian Brothers College in Memphis to a scoreless tie, the program under the direction of L.B. Harvey recorded its first victory on October 28, 1901. Fittingly, it came in Starkville, in the inaugural meeting against long-standing rival Ole Miss, 17-0. Harvey was also credited with recording the first points in Mississippi A&M history.

The 1901 team finished 2-2-1, and with Sessions appointed chairman of the faculty athletic committee, football's place on campus was firmly established. Two years later, under the direction of Dan Martin, the "Boss Team" finished 3-0-2 and outscored opponents 71-6.

In 1905, the school's first football facility opened and was named in honor of Hardy, with its inaugural game a 44-0 victory against Howard. The season also saw the program's first forward pass, from Ham McGeorge to Spike Gully against Alabama, one year before the play was officially legalized.

Fred Furman was hired as the school's first full-time coach and athletic director in 1907 and enjoyed a 6-3 season that featured back-to-back wins against

Union and Mercer, outscoring them by a combined 155-0. But the biggest high-light was a 15-0 victory against Ole Miss, and A&M won the following meeting as well, 44-6.

W. D. Chadwick became one of the few Northerners to coach the Aggies in 1909, and in five seasons never had a losing record (29-12-2 overall) while collecting 27 shutouts. The 1910 team gave up only six points through its first eight games, including a 48-0 drubbing of Tennessee and 82-0 against Howard, before losing to Ole Miss 30-0 to finish 7-2.

Led by Morley Jennings, the 1911 team again won seven games, tying Alabama (6-6) and losing close games to Auburn (11-5) and Tulane (5-4) before defeating Ole Miss 6-0. On January 1, 1912, A&M had the distinction of playing outside of the United States when it defeated Club Atletico de Cuba in Havana, 12-0.

Chadwick's last season—before he started concentrating on his duties as athletic director—was 1913, when the Aggies finished 6-1-1. Assistant E. C. Hayes replaced him and had similar success during his three seasons, posting a 15-8-2 record that included a 65-0 victory against Ole Miss in Tupelo in 1915. Led by C. R. "Dudy" Noble, the Aggies yielded more than 19 points only once under Hayes, a 25-0 loss to Auburn in 1915.

Again a medical epidemic and war affected football, but this time A&M didn't suspend play. Under the direction of Sid Robinson, the Aggies posted an impressive 6-1 record in 1917, with the lone loss 13-6 against Auburn in Birmingham, Alabama. Again, they defeated rival Ole Miss, by a convincing 41-14 score.

After the armistice in 1918, Robinson came back from serving in naval aviation to guide two more wins against Ole Miss, 34-0 and 14-0, during the only season the rivals would play twice. It was the same result in 1919—33-0, improving A&M to 6-0 by outscoring opponents 152-13. But after losing 7-0 to Auburn and 14-6 to Alabama, both in Birmingham, Robinson left for Mississippi College with a .750 winning percentage, still the second best in A&M history.

New Athletic Field opened in 1914 and in 1920 was renamed Scott Field, in honor of Magruder Scott, an Olympic sprinter and one of the school's first football standouts. Additions and renovations in 1928, 1936, and 1948 brought capacity up to 35,000. Thanks to alumni and booster Floyd Davis Wade Sr., the latest renovation, costing $30 million, increased seating to 55,082 in 2000. The name was then changed to Davis Wade Stadium at Scott Field, and it's the second oldest on-campus stadium in Division I football.

Ohio State's Fred J. Holtkamp was the first of five coaches to head the program in the 1920s, and when A&M finished 3-4-2 under Noble again in 1922, it marked the first losing season since 1908. The most notable coach of the decade was future Hall of Famer Bernie Bierman, who brought his "Minnesota Shift" offense to the SEC for two seasons. His last game in 1926 was truly memorable, but not because of the coach. When Ole Miss snapped its 13-game losing streak to rival A&M (7-6) in Starkville, visiting fans rushed the field and went for the home goalposts. But they were rebuffed by A&M fans, and a melee resulted.

Before the teams met again, the student bodies decided that in an effort to avoid a repeat incident, the rivals would play for a trophy. Thus, the "Golden Egg" football-shaped trophy was created, with the annual regular season-ending game later simply called the Egg Bowl.

Other changes were at hand. When the school's name changed from Mississippi A&M to Mississippi State College in 1932, the nickname switched to the Maroons—a reference to the team's uniform color. It wasn't until the school obtained university status in 1961 that the official nickname was changed to Bulldogs. However, the maroon uniforms remained a constant—except in 1938, when coach Spike Nelson put his players in gold, which went over so well that neither he nor the uniforms returned in 1939.

When Mississippi State became one of the 13 charter members of the SEC, the football program was struggling, both on and off the field. Limited finances and facilities put the team at a disadvantage; and between 1928 and 1933, including their first year in the new SEC, the Maroons didn't win more than three games in any season. They lost their first four conference games by a combined score of 78-7 before finally defeating Sewanee 26-13—the most points they tallied in any game during that time.

Enter college president George Duke Humphrey, who was hired in 1934 and made football a priority. In addition to expanding Scott Field to accompany 26,000 fans, one of his first moves was to hire Major Ralph I. Sasse, a former cavalry officer, as head coach. It didn't take long to see the difference on the field.

Two weeks into the 1935 season, visiting Mississippi State played Vanderbilt tough, but lost 14-9. Two weeks after that, the Maroons won in Tuscaloosa, beating Alabama 20-7. Mississippi State was 5-1 when it traveled to West Point to face Army, where Sasse had both served and previously coached. MSU hung around against the heavily-favored home team and in the final minute trailed only 7-6. Quarterback Pee Wee Armstrong threw a 65-yard touchdown pass to Fred Walters, and the 13-7 outcome is still considered one of the program's biggest victories.

Despite playing eight games on the road, the Maroons finished 8-3, with a 14-6 loss at Ole Miss serving as a minor disappointment. The momentum carried over into the 1936 season, when Mississippi State posted seven shutouts and sustained only two narrow losses—7-0 at Alabama and 12-0 at LSU—but received its first bowl invitation, to play Duquesne in the Orange Bowl.

Ike Pickle, who later set a bowl record with an 82-yard punt, opened the scoring with a 10-yard touchdown run, and Armstrong connected with Waters for a 40-yard score. But in the final moments of the game, the Dukes' Boyd Brumbaugh threw a desperation pass that end Ernie Hefferlie caught to score a 72-yard touchdown and pull off a 13-12 victory. According to a local newspaper, the 9,210 people in attendance "went wild."

The 1937 season wasn't as kind to the Maroons or to Sasse, who was still serving military assignments. Shortly after falling in a stairway, the coach—to everyone's surprise—resigned with three games remaining. The staff stayed on to finish the 5-4-1 season, but Sasse's brief tenure had left its mark; as the yearbook proclaimed, "If ever a man gave his all for State, Sasse was that man."

On the advice of Tennessee's legendary coach Robert Neyland, Mississippi State hired Allyn McKeen in 1939. Like Sasse, McKeen had an impact on the field that was immediately noticeable. Although picked to finish eleventh in the conference, the Maroons opened the season with three shutouts before losing 7-0 to both Auburn and Alabama. Undeterred, Mississippi State won at Ole Miss, 18-6, and at 8-2 was on the doorstep of its first national ranking.

Despite a difficult schedule that featured five ranked opponents, Ole Miss earned its national ranking the following season when four opponents failed to score and just two reached double digits. With an early season tie against Auburn serving as the lone blemish, Mississippi State closed the schedule with wins against Ole Miss (19-0) and at No. 17 Alabama (13-0) and returned to the Orange Bowl to play No. 13 Georgetown. This time, there would be no last-minute heartache.

Led by Buddy Elrod and Hunter Corhern, line play ruled the day for the "Maroon Machine." Tackle John Tripson recovered a blocked punt in the end zone for an early lead, and when the offenses were only able to trade touchdowns, Mississippi State held on for a 14-7 victory. In addition to an undefeated season (10-0-1), but no SEC championship thanks to 10-0 Tennessee, the Maroons finished ranked ninth. Elrod was the school's first consensus All-American, and McKeen was named SEC Coach of the Year.

McKeen's machine continued to make history over the next two years. Although a 21-game unbeaten streak came to an end in 1941, the Maroons finally secured their first and only conference title by finishing the season 8-1-1 overall and 4-0-1 in conference play, including shutouts against Florida (6-0), Alabama (14-0), LSU (0-0), and No. 14 Ole Miss. A 38-yard end-around by quarterback Jennings Moates sealed both the title and a 6-0 victory against the Rebels. Mississippi State was No. 16 after winning at San Francisco, 26-13, on December 6; but with the bombing of Pearl Harbor the following day, the team was temporarily stranded on the West Coast and didn't play in a bowl game.

Despite the advent of World War II, Mississippi State played the 1942 season and posted an impressive 8-2 record, with only early-season losses at No. 4 Alabama (21-6) and LSU (16-6). After winning seven straight, including 34-13 against Ole Miss, for a No. 18 finish, the program—like many others in the SEC—shut down for a year.

When play resumed in 1944, the Maroons picked up where they left off, winning their first six games before stumbling at Alabama (19-0) and at Ole Miss (13-8). For the first time, Mississippi State had a Heisman Trophy candidate in freshman back Tom "Shorty" McWilliams, who finished tenth in voting, but the departure of assistant coaches Bowden Wyatt and Murray Warmath began to be felt.

The Maroons didn't live up to expectations in 1945. They finished 6-3 with a season-ending 55-13 loss at No. 3 Alabama, which at 9-0 went on to beat Southern California in the Rose Bowl. Likewise, a loss for No. 19 Mississippi State at Alabama at the end of the 1946 season left a bad taste, despite an 8-2 record and a 20-0 victory against Ole Miss. Fans started to wonder if McKeen was stuck in the past while other teams had converted to the modern wing-T offensive scheme.

Though Mississippi State started the 1947 season 6-1, it lost 21-6 at LSU and then 33-14 at home to No. 15 Ole Miss for a 7-3 record. When he lost to No. 16 Ole Miss again in 1948, 34-7, McKeen was fired. His winning percentage of .764 (65-19-3) has yet to be equaled at the school, and no one has come close to challenging his three-year record of 26-3-2 from 1939 to 1941.

"Some of the school's greatest wins came during the 1939 season, but I have to go with the 1940 team as my best," McKeen said.

Years later, when McKeen was voted into the College Football Hall of Fame, his widow, Susan, was seriously ill when notified of the honor. "The news was given her January 25, 1991, and made her very happy," reported the family. "She died the next day."

Without McKeen in 1949, the Maroons finished 0-8-1 and were outscored 224-38. Despite the poor showing, back Harper Davis became the first player in Mississippi State history to be selected in the first round of the NFL Draft, by the Chicago Bears.

The program would have only six winning seasons and one bowl bid between 1949 and 1972, but at the same time was home to some of college football's most interesting characters.

For example, Arthur "Slick" Morton lasted only three seasons, but in 1950 engineered a 7-0 victory against No. 1 Tennessee and coached All-American fullback Joe Fortunato in 1950. He's also the founder of the annual Mississippi High School All-Star Game.

In 1952 Warmath, who went on to win the 1960 national championship at Minnesota, was re-hired as head coach and immediately led the Maroons to 5-4 and 5-2-3 seasons. Although he never beat Ole Miss (going 0-1-1), quarterback Jackie Parker set the SEC single-season scoring record with 120 points, thanks in part to an amazing performance against Auburn. In the first three quarters Mississippi State accumulated 49 points, and Parker had a hand in 42. He had touchdown runs of 34, 11, and 6 yards, passes of 27 and 11 yards, and six extra points—all before watching the fourth quarter from the sideline. A year later in 1953, he was named an All-American.

Assistant coach Royal left the Maroons to coach in Canada, but when Warmath moved on, athletic director Noble called Royal back. With All-Americans Hal Easterwood and Scott Suber blocking for Art Davis, Mississippi State went 6-4 in both 1954 and 1955 but failed to score a point against Ole Miss (losing 14-0 and 26-0).

Royal was also known for being a human quote machine, and he spewed forth some of football's finest philosophy:

"Luck is what happens when preparation meets opportunity."

"You can't be aggressive and confused at the same time."

"Treat turnovers like a copperhead in the bedclothes; avoid them at all costs."

"When good things have happened over a period of years, and you expect good things to happen again, that's tradition."

"Never try to fool a player. You can't kid a kid."

"You've got to be in position for luck to happen. Luck doesn't go around looking for a stumblebum."

"On game day, I'm as nervous as a pig in a packing plant."

Like his predecessor, Royal left after two seasons; he went on to win a national championship at Texas.

Assistant Wade Walker was promoted to head coach in 1956 and again to athletic director in 1961 despite having only one winning season, 6-2-1 in 1957. But it was a pretty memorable season; MSU posted wins at Alabama (25-13) and at LSU (14-6) before tying Ole Miss (7-7) to finish No. 14.

Mississippi State University wouldn't have another winning season until 1963, under coach Paul Davis. Behind All-American Pat Watson and fellow linemate Tommy Neville, the Bulldogs pulled out a tie at Florida (9-9) and won at Tennessee (7-0) before losing back-to-back games at Memphis State (17-10) and at No. 7 Alabama (20-19). Unlike previous teams, they rebounded to win close games against Auburn (13-10) and LSU (7-6) and tied Ole Miss 10-10 to earn the school's third bowl invitation.

In eight-degree weather and 17-mph winds in Philadelphia, MSU took a page from its brief postseason history to pull out a 16-12 victory against North Carolina State in the Liberty Bowl. End Bill McGuire blocked a punt and lineman Tommy Inman returned it 11 yards for a touchdown, and quarterback Sonny Fisher scored a 3-yard touchdown to provide a lead that would hold up. Despite 11 penalties for 122 yards, the Bulldogs had an advantage of 275-176 in rushing yards. When Davis emerged from a Plexiglas canopy, which along with heaters was used to protect the players and coaches, MSU was No. 11 in the country.

"The defense did a good job all day, especially considering the conditions," Davis said. "We had a stronger line."

In 1966, university president William Giles made what many fans considered to be a colossal mistake when he fired both athletic director Walker and coach Davis on December 10, football signing day for recruits. Charley Shira was hired to pick up the pieces, but it would take years for the program to recover. Even with end Sammy Milner, linebacker D. D. Lewis, and Tommy Pharr setting school passing records, the Bulldogs finished 1-9 in 1967, 0-8-2 in 1968 (though one of the ties was 17-17 at Ole Miss), and 3-7 in 1969. Despite the record, Alabama coach Paul "Bear" Bryant said about Lewis, "No doubt about it, the best linebacker in the country."

"Football is a lot like engineering," Shira said. "If you work long and hard enough you can come up with the answer to the problem."

In 1970, flanker David Smith set an MSU record with 215 receiving yards on 12 passes from Joe Reed to lead a 20-16 victory against Texas Tech. Also notable during the 6-5 season, which included a 19-14 upset of Ole Miss, was MSU's first black player, defensive back Frank Dowsing, who was named an All-American in 1972. That was the same year Shira handed over the coaching duties to assistant Bob Tyler, whose controversial coaching reign could be called anything but boring.

Although Tyler had never played football and had graduated from rival Ole Miss, he did improve the program. Despite quarterback Rockey Felker having an injury-plagued 1973 season, and the Bulldogs losing their last four games, the 4-

5-2 campaign included wins against No. 16 Florida (33-12), Florida State (37-12), and Louisville (18-7).

With Felker and halfback Walter Packer leading the veer offense, and All-American tackle Jimmy Webb keying the defense, Mississippi State finished the 1974 regular season with eight wins, its best showing since 1946. Against Memphis State, the Bulldogs drove 98 yards in the last two minutes to pull out a 29-28 victory, and they concluded the schedule with a 7-6 victory against LSU and a 31-13 pounding of Ole Miss.

No. 18 Mississippi State was invited to only its fourth bowl game, against North Carolina—coached by MSU graduate Bill Dooley—in foggy conditions at the ironically named Sun Bowl. Terry Vitrano scored a 55-yard touchdown on the first snap of the game and went on to accumulate 164 rushing yards on 20 carries, including a game-winning 2-yard touchdown run in the fourth quarter. Packer added 183 rushing yards on 24 attempts and scored two touchdowns, but again the victory came as the result of a late drive, with the final score 26-24.

"This team was a lot better than we expected in a lot of ways," Tyler said. "I think we're a year ahead. We established unity in our program that usually takes two seasons to establish. I've never been more confident or enthusiastic about the future than I am right now."

Despite six Bulldogs being named to various All-SEC teams, the following 1975 season didn't meet expectations. After early losses to Georgia and Florida, Mississippi State won four straight games only to have the season derailed by No. 6 Alabama (21-10), Auburn (21-21), and Ole Miss (13-7).

Or so fans thought. Actually, the Bulldogs' situation would soon be much worse than the 6-4-1 record. In 1976, the National Collegiate Athletic Association issued penalties and probation for rules violations. The school fought the ruling in court, but eventually lost. As a result, all but two of the program's 20 victories between 1975 and 1977 were forfeited.

Particularly painful to fans was learning that the 1976 season would be turned from a 9-2 finish to 0-11. Safety Stan Black was named an All-American that year, and linebacker Ray Costict (who had a school-record 29 tackles in a 14-7 victory against Kentucky) and nose guard Harvey Hull had helped lead the Bulldogs to a No. 20 finish.

By 1977, the strain showed on the field. The team accumulated only five wins in 1977 (all forfeited) and six the subsequent year, with victories against No. 15 Florida State (55-27) and No. 17 LSU (16-14) before a 27-7 loss to Ole Miss. When Tyler refused to give up his athletic director duties to concentrate on coaching, school president James McComas fired him.

LSU's Carl Maddox was brought in as athletic director, and former Texas A&M coach Emory Bellard, who had invented the wishbone offense, was hired to turn the program around. After a 3-8 season in 1979, things started to click for the Bulldogs, who found themselves 6-2 and hosting defending national champion Alabama, which was No. 1 and riding a 28-game winning streak.

Led by linebackers Johnie Cooks and Glen Collins, MSU didn't buckle and had a 6-3 lead in the final minute when Alabama drove deep into Bulldog territory.

With freshman defensive end Billy Jackson recovering a fumble at the 3 with 6 seconds remaining, the goal-line stand held for Mississippi State's first victory against the Crimson Tide since 1957. In many ways, the win surpassed the 1935 Army game in terms of prominent victories, and it's still proudly celebrated in Starkville.

While Georgia went on to win the national championship, Mississippi State received an invitation to represent the conference against Nebraska at the Sun Bowl. Although option quarterback John Bond and the offense had set numerous school records that season, Tom Osborne's defense limited him to minus-8 yards rushing en route to a convincing 31-17 victory for the Cornhuskers. The Bulldogs finished No. 19.

"I'm proud of our team and the season we had," Bellard said. "We just flat out gave Nebraska too many opportunities. Our defense played well enough to win. Looking at what we have, we will be back next year."

Bellard's prediction was close. Led by linemen Kent Hull and Jacobs Trophy winner Wayne Harris, Mississippi State got off to a 6-1 start despite a schedule that featured five ranked teams, including No. 13 Miami (a 14-10 victory), during the 1981 season. After a 21-17 victory at Auburn, MSU held its highest ranking ever at No. 7, but in the following two weeks stumbled at No. 8 Alabama (13-10) and No. 19 Southern Miss (7-6) before losing 21-17 to Ole Miss. Nevertheless, the Bulldogs still received a bowl invitation, marking the first time in school history they would play in back-to-back postseason games.

On a day dominated by the defenses, and All-American Cooks, the only touchdown against Kansas in the Hall of Fame Bowl fittingly came off a turnover. Defensive back Rob Fesmire recovered a fumble on the opening kickoff, and Bond ran in a 17-yard touchdown on the following play.

"The whole defensive unit played extremely well," Bellard said after the 10-0 victory. "We didn't ring the bell quite enough on offense, but we did move the ball down the field a good bit."

Cooks was named SEC Defensive Player of the Year. In 45 games during his collegiate career, he made 392 tackles. The following spring, he was the second-overall pick in the National Football League draft by the Baltimore Colts and went on to play 10 more years. Collins went twenty-sixth overall to the Cincinnati Bengals. In 1983 running back Michael Haddix was the eighth pick by the Philadelphia Eagles.

However, it was another high point for the roller-coaster program that would soon take another downward turn. From 1982 to 1990 the Bulldogs had just one winning season, 6-5 in 1986, and didn't qualify for any bowl games. When Bellard couldn't match his postseason success, he was fired after the 1985 season and replaced by former player Felker, who at the time was the youngest head coach in the country. After winning his first game, 24-17 at Syracuse, he pulled off a memorable 27-3 upset at defending SEC champion Tennessee en route to winning six of his first seven games and a No. 13 ranking. But with 42,700 fans packed into Scott Field, Mississippi State lost to both No. 7 Auburn (35-6) and No. 8 Alabama (38-3) and plunged into a winless final month.

Felker finished 4-7 in 1987 and 1-10 in 1988, but after some solid recruiting posted 5-6 seasons in 1989 and 1990. Three straight losses to Ole Miss proved to be his downfall, much to the dismay of the MSU faithful, who didn't support the firing.

President Donald Zacharias and athletic director Larry Templeton looked to former Alabama player Jackie Sherrill, who, following a two-year layoff after coaching at Pittsburgh and Texas A&M, was ready to get back into football. Once again, the Bulldogs were led by a controversial coach who was anything but boring.

"Is coaching at Mississippi State tougher than coaching at Florida? Yes," Sherrill once said. "Tougher than Tennessee? Yes. Tougher than Alabama? Yes. But nobody made me take the job at Mississippi State and nobody is making me stay there. I've made the decision that this is my last rodeo and it is."

That confidence, combined with a strong group of assistant coaches, put MSU back on track. In only Sherrill's second game, the Bulldogs upset No. 13 Texas, 13-6. After solid wins against LSU (28-19) and Ole Miss (24-9) in the first Egg Bowl played on campus since 1972, Mississippi State was paired against Air Force in the Liberty Bowl. But it was unable to stop the potent running attack, which amassed 318 yards on 69 carries, compared to just two passes attempted; the result was a 38-15 victory for the Falcons.

Prior to the 1992 season opener against the Texas Longhorns, Sherrill captured the attention of his players, and the nation, when he showed his team on the practice field how a bull is castrated.

"The whole story came up when I asked our players what a steer was and none of them knew what a steer was," Sherrill said "People say (the Texas mascot) is a longhorn steer. Is that a bull, or is he a steer?"

Despite the uproar regarding Wild Willie, MSU upset Texas again, 28-10, after which Sherrill issued a formal apology.

The '92 squad had the potential to be one of the best teams Mississippi State ever had and spent most of the season ranked in the Top 25. When quarterback Sleepy Robinson was injured in a 30-6 victory against No. 13 Florida—which was played before the largest home-opening crowd (38,886) in Scott Field history and on national television—along with other key injuries, it may have been a death blow that didn't take hold until mid-November. The Bulldogs lost 30-21 to eventual national champion Alabama, 17-10 at Ole Miss, and squandered a two-touchdown lead before losing 21-17 to North Carolina in the Peach Bowl. MSU finished 7-5, ranked No. 23.

After retooling in 1993, Mississippi State returned to the Peach Bowl in 1994. With Derrick Taite passing for a school-record 466 yards against Tulane, a 66-22 victory, the No. 16 Bulldogs were 8-3, and two of their losses were against No. 6 Alabama (29-25) and No. 9 Auburn (42-18). Despite Tim Rogers' five field goals and safety Andrew Bennett's blocked punt in the end zone for a safety, the Bulldogs were rebuffed by North Carolina State, 28-24. No. 24 MSU finished 8-4.

MSU's "100 Years of Football" was celebrated in 1995, but it was rebuilding time again as the Bulldogs finished just 3-8. The following year saw two more victories, including wins against No. 8 Alabama (17-16) and Ole Miss (17-0) in a rainstorm. However, the NCAA came calling again; and due to recruiting violations, the program was issued scholarship penalties effective in 1997.

After upsetting No. 11 Auburn 20-0 and Alabama 32-20, Mississippi State found itself atop the Western Division standings and ranked fifteenth. But after losing to Arkansas, 17-7, the Bulldogs' 1997 season came down to one game; the winner of the Egg Bowl would head to a bowl game, while the losing team stayed home. The Bulldogs had a 14-7 lead in the final minutes, when Ole Miss drove the field, scored a touchdown, and converted a two-point conversion for the victory. Despite the 7-4 season finish, that year's Egg Bowl is considered one of the most disappointing losses in MSU history.

While still recovering from the NCAA reprimand, the Bulldogs went on a late-season run in 1998 with victories against Alabama (26-14), No. 9 Arkansas (22-21), and Ole Miss (28-6) to earn its first SEC Western Division title. Against the Tide, senior J. J. Johnson set school records for rushing (237) and all-purpose yards (312), and he went on to become the first MSU player ever to rush for 1,000 or more yards in two straight years.

Against Tennessee in the SEC Championship Game, MSU led 14-10 in the fourth quarter—before the Volunteers, who went on to win the national championship, pulled out a 24-14 victory. Mississippi State received its first invitation in 60 years to play in a major New Year's Day bowl against Texas in the Cotton Bowl, but led by Heisman Trophy winner Ricky Williams, the Longhorns treated MSU like the Bulldogs did Wild Willie. The running back had 203 rushing yards and scored two touchdowns, while quarterback Major Applewhite passed for 225 yards and three touchdowns as Texas snapped a seven-game losing streak against Sherrill, 38-11.

MSU wasn't able to defend its division title in 1999, but did pull off the school's second 10-win season. Led by its stingy defense, the Bulldogs got off to an 8-0 start, climbing to No. 8, lost back-to-back games against No. 11 Alabama (19-7) and Arkansas (14-9), but redeemed themselves with a 23-20 win against Ole Miss.

Despite giving up a season-high 391 yards, of which 301 came on the arm of quarterback Brandon Streeter, Mississippi State defeated Clemson 17-7 in the Peach Bowl. Robert Bean blocked his seventh kick, Pig Prather's 45-yard kickoff return set up a field goal, and quarterback Wayne Madkin ran in one score and threw for another. Voters placed the 10-2 Bulldogs thirteenth.

Mississippi State made an unprecedented third straight postseason appearance in 2000, thanks in part to back-to-back wins against No. 3 Florida (47-35) and No. 15 Auburn (17-10). But it lost two overtime games (45-38 at LSU and 17-10 vs. Arkansas—which snapped a 16-game home winning streak) and to Ole Miss 45-30. The Bulldogs faced Texas A&M at the Independence Bowl in a game that was as wild as the driving snowstorm blanketing Shreveport, Louisiana.

Even though Dontae Walker had 143 rushing yards and three touchdowns, and Willie Blade made 16 tackles, they were countered by 193 rushing yards by Aggies fullback Ja'Mar Toombs, and the game had to be settled in overtime. Blade blocked his second point-after attempt, Julius Griffith returned it for a two-point conversion, and Madkin ran in a 6-yard touchdown for a 43-41 victory in "Snow Bowl 2000."

For No. 24 MSU (8-4), Dicenzo Miller became the Bulldogs' fifth career 1,000-yard rusher, Madkin their all-time leading passer (6,336 yards), and Sherrill the school's all-time winningest coach. But Sherrill's legacy, like Tyler's, was to leave the program with a cloud hanging over it; the Bulldogs finished 3-8, 3-9, and 2-10 from 2001 to 2003, and more NCAA penalties loomed on the horizon.

On December 1, 2003, Mississippi State reinvented both itself and the conference when former Alabama All-American center Sylvester Croom became the SEC's first black head football coach. Although his first campaign resulted in a 3-8 record, a 38-31 victory against No. 20 Florida gave him an immediate signature win; and the Gators subsequently fired coach Ron Zook.

"I'm the first African-American coach in the SEC," said Croom, "but there ain't but one color that matters here, and that color is maroon."

THREE THINGS THAT STAND OUT ABOUT MISSISSIPPI STATE FOOTBALL

1. *The cowbells:* Even though the SEC banned all artificial noisemakers in 1974, Bulldog fans have been ringing them since the 1940s and still do openly (though "officially" only during non-conference and bowl games . . . and in this case, *officially* means nonstop for every opponent). According to legend, the tradition started when a cow wandered onto the field during a game won by Mississippi State. Bulldogs fans also see it as defying Ole Miss' smugness.
2. *The Bulldog:* Though the nickname wasn't officially changed until 1961, references go back to 1905. Coach Ralph Sasse, on "orders" from his team, went to Memphis in 1935 to select a bulldog to be the official game mascot; MSU then promptly defeated Alabama 20-7. A littermate became the first mascot named "Bully," and when a campus bus ended his "eligibility," he was buried under the bench at the 50-yard line of Scott Field.
3. *Giant killers:* Since 1980, when Mississippi State defeated both No. 18 Miami and No. 1 Alabama, the Bulldogs have recorded 17 victories against teams ranked in the Top 25 poll. Nearly all were considered upsets.

Part IV

THE SEC CHAMPIONSHIP

· 17 ·

The Champions

It began with a novel idea that would transform college football. According to National Collegiate Athletic Association rules, Division I-A football teams could play in only one postseason game per season, unless it was a playoff to determine a conference champion. In 1992, with the addition of Arkansas and South Carolina, the Southeastern Conference split into two divisions; the winners of each would meet to decide the championship.

Though it was the first Division I-A conference to take advantage of the loophole, the trend quickly caught on. Among those following suit would be the Atlantic Coast Conference, Big 12, Conference USA, and Mid-American Conference.

Previously, the conference title went to the team with the best record. Considering that for years the SEC didn't have a balanced schedule, or even have teams playing the same number of conference games every season, there were some discrepancies.

Year	Champion	SEC	Overall	Coach
1933	Alabama	5-0-1	7-1-1	Frank Thomas
1934	Tulane	8-0	10-1	Ted Cox
	Alabama	7-0	10-0	Frank Thomas
1935	LSU	5-0	9-2	Bernie Moore
1936	LSU	6-0	9-1-1	Bernie Moore
1937	Alabama	6-0	9-1	Frank Thomas
1938	Tennessee	7-0	11-0	Bob Neyland
1939	Tennessee	6-0	10-1	Bob Neyland
	Georgia Tech	6-0	8-2	Bill Alexander
	Tulane	5-0	8-1-1	"Red" Dawson
1940	Tennessee	5-0	10-1	Bob Neyland
1941	Mississippi State	4-0-1	8-1-1	Allyn McKeen
1942	Georgia	6-1	11-1	Wally Butts
1943	Georgia Tech	3-0	7-4	Bill Alexander
1944	Georgia Tech	4-0	9-2	Bill Alexander
1945	Alabama	6-0	10-0	Frank Thomas
1946	Georgia	5-0	11-0	Wally Butts
	Tennessee	5-0	9-2	Bob Neyland

1947	Ole Miss	6-1	9-2	John Vaught
1948	Georgia	6-0	9-2	Wally Butts
1949	Tulane	5-1	7-2-1	Henry Frnka
1950	Kentucky	5-1	11-1	Paul Bryant
1951	Georgia Tech	7-0	11-0-1	Bobby Dodd
	Tennessee	5-0	10-1	Bob Neyland
1952	Georgia Tech	6-0	12-0	Bobby Dodd
1953	Alabama	4-0-3	6-3-3	Red Drew
1954	Ole Miss	5-1	9-2	John Vaught
1955	Ole Miss	5-1	10-1	John Vaught
1956	Tennessee	6-0	10-1	Bowden Wyatt
1957	Auburn	7-0	10-0	Ralph Jordan
1958	LSU	6-0	11-0	Paul Dietzel
1959	Georgia	7-0	10-1	Wally Butts
1960	Ole Miss	5-0-1	10-0-1	John Vaught
1961	Alabama	7-0	11-0	Paul Bryant
	LSU	6-0	10-1	Paul Dietzel
1962	Ole Miss	6-0	10-0	John Vaught
1963	Ole Miss	5-0-1	7-1-2	John Vaught
1964	Alabama	8-0	10-1	Paul Bryant
1965	Alabama	6-1-1	9-1-1	Paul Bryant
1966	Alabama	6-0	11-0	Paul Bryant
	Georgia	6-0	10-1	Vince Dooley
1967	Tennessee	6-0	9-2	Doug Dickey
1968	Georgia	5-0-1	8-1-2	Vince Dooley
1969	Tennessee	5-1	9-2	Doug Dickey
1970	LSU	5-0	9-3	Charlie McClendon
1971	Alabama	7-0	11-1	Paul Bryant
1972	Alabama	7-1	10-2	Paul Bryant
1973	Alabama	8-0	11-1	Paul Bryant
1974	Alabama	6-0	11-1	Paul Bryant
1975	Alabama	6-0	11-1	Paul Bryant
1976	Georgia	5-1	10-2	Vince Dooley
	Kentucky	5-1	9-3	Fran Curci
1977	Alabama	7-0	11-1	Paul Bryant
1978	Alabama	6-0	11-1	Paul Bryant
1979	Alabama	6-0	12-0	Paul Bryant
1980	Georgia	6-0	12-0	Vince Dooley
1981	Georgia	6-0	10-2	Vince Dooley
	Alabama	6-0	9-2-1	Paul Bryant
1982	Georgia	6-0	11-1	Vince Dooley
1983	Auburn	6-0	11-1	Pat Dye
1984	Vacated			
1985	Tennessee	5-1	9-1-2	Johnny Majors
1986	LSU	5-1	9-3	Bill Arnsparger

1987	Auburn	5-0-1	9-1-2	Pat Dye
1988	Auburn	6-1	10-2	Pat Dye
	LSU	6-1	8-4	Mike Archer
1989	Alabama	6-1	10-2	Bill Curry
	Tennessee	6-1	11-1	Johnny Majors
	Auburn	6-1	10-2	Pat Dye
1990	Tennessee	5-1-1	9-2-2	Johnny Majors
1991	Florida	7-0	10-2	Steve Spurrier
1992	Alabama	8-0	13-0	Gene Stallings
1993	Florida	7-1	11-2	Steve Spurrier
1994	Florida	7-1	10-2-1	Steve Spurrier
1995	Florida	8-0	12-1	Steve Spurrier
1996	Florida	8-0	12-1	Steve Spurrier
1997	Tennessee	7-1	11-2	Phillip Fulmer
1998	Tennessee	8-0	13-0	Phillip Fulmer
1999	Alabama	7-1	10-3	Mike DuBose
2000	Florida	7-1	10-3	Steve Spurrier
2001	LSU	5-3	10-3	Nick Saban
2002	Georgia	7-1	13-1	Mark Richt
2003	LSU	7-1	13-1	Nick Saban
2004	Auburn	8-0	13-0	Tommy Tuberville
2005	Georgia	6-2	10-2	Mark Richt

Source: SEC.

· 18 ·

The Championship Game

With ABC set to televise the first SEC championship game nationally (with CBS later securing the broadcast rights) and earn an impressive 9.8 rating, conference officials knew they had a hit from the start. Additionally, 83,091 fans packed Legion Field in Birmingham on December 5, 1992, to see Alabama pull off another victory on its way to winning another national title.

1992

Alabama 28, Florida 21
MVP: Antonio Langham, Alabama

The matchup of Florida's high-powered offense against Alabama's top-ranked defense got off to a surprising start when Gators quarterback Shane Matthews opened the game by completing his first seven passes, including a 5-yard touchdown to running back Errict Rhett.

Alabama countered by pounding the ball, with 55 of the 72 yards on the ground during its first touchdown drive, capped by a 3-yard carry by Derrick Lassic. The Tide made it 14-7 on Jay Barker's 30-yard touchdown pass to Curtis Brown. It was only Barker's seventh touchdown pass of the season. A 39-yard reception by David Palmer sparked an Alabama four-play drive in the third quarter, and Lassic's 15-yard run into the corner of the end zone provided a 21-7 lead.

Florida came back, and when Alabama had punts of 16, 18, and 26 yards, the Gators took advantage to tie the game 21-21 on Rhett's 1-yard plunge.

With 3:16 remaining, Florida had first-and-10 at its own 21, when Alabama cornerback Antonio Langham jumped in front of a receiver and returned the interception 27 yards for the game-winning score. Just one week previous, it was Langham's interception returned 61 yards for a touchdown that broke open the Iron Bowl.

"When we hit [Matthews] and got pressure on him, he threw interceptions," defensive end Jeremy Nunley said. "Antonio Langham just made an awesome play. He's a great guy and I love him to death."

Barker threw for 154 yards and one touchdown, Lassic had 117 yards on 21 carries, and Palmer accumulated 122 all-purpose yards, 101 of which were receiving.

1993

Florida 28, Alabama 13
MVP: Terry Dean, Florida

Though Florida coach Steve Spurrier had won the 1991 SEC championship in the final year without a playoff, his team lost the inaugural title game. However, in the rematch at Legion Field, quarterback Terry Dean passed for 256 yards and two touchdowns to lead the Gators.

Willie Jackson was his favorite target, catching nine passes for 114 yards, but it was Jack Jackson who made the key reception of the game.

Up by one point and facing fourth-and-8, Florida kept possession thanks to punter Shayne Edge's 20-yard run for a first down. On the next play, Dean's 43-yard touchdown pass to Jack Jackson provided an insurmountable 21-13 lead. With Larry Kennedy making 11 tackles, the defense didn't yield, while Florida tagged on another touchdown with a 3-yard carry by Rhett, who finished with 88 yards and 22 carries.

Florida went on to record its first victory in the Sugar Bowl—41-7 against West Virginia, for a school-record 11 wins—and finished the season ranked fifth.

1994

Florida 24, Alabama 23
MVP: Ellis Johnson, Florida

While the location was different, with the championship moving to the Georgia Dome, the teams were the same. Despite having young players in key positions, Florida had been No. 1 in seven of the first nine polls and came in at No. 6.

Alabama opened the scoring with a 70-yard touchdown pass from Barker to Rick Brown, but it was Florida's passing game that eventually got the upper hand. Danny Wuerffel completed 23 of 41 passes for 227 yards and two touchdowns, including a 26-yard score to freshman wide receiver Reidel Anthony.

After trailing 17-10 at halftime, Alabama took the lead with two third-quarter field goals and linebacker Dwayne Rudd's 23-yard interception return for a touchdown. Florida answered with a 10-play, 80-yard drive, which concluded with a 2-yard touchdown reception by Chris Doering. Judd Davis' extra point proved to be the winning margin.

For the first time, a defensive player was the game MVP, with Ellis Johnson making two sacks and five tackles as well as breaking up one pass. ABC's broadcast earned a 10.5 rating, making it the network's most-watched college football game since the 1991 season.

1995

Florida 34, Arkansas 3
MVP: Danny Wuerffel, Florida

While the game was moved to a prime-time kickoff, Florida continued its domination of the championship with its most-impressive showing yet.

Wuerffel completed 20 of 28 passes for 276 yards and two touchdowns, and ran in another as the Gators gained 396 offensive yards and took advantage of four Arkansas turnovers—including nicklebacker Ben Hanks' 95-yard fumble return for a touchdown.

The Razorbacks scored first, on Todd Latourette's 36-yard field goal midway through the first quarter; but sophomore running back Madre Hill, who finished third in conference rushing, sustained a knee injury that sidelined him for the rest of the game.

After the subsequent kickoff, Florida drove 80 yards in seven plays, with Doering's 22-yard touchdown reception providing the only lead the Gators would need. Ike Hilliard, who finished with 125 yards on seven receptions, caught Wuerffel's other touchdown pass of 29 yards.

Florida went on to play Nebraska for the national championship in the Fiesta Bowl, but lost 62-24. Still, the No. 2 finish was its best to date.

1996

Florida 45, Alabama 30
MVP: Danny Wuerffel, Florida

With Alabama hoping to give coach Gene Stallings win No. 70 as a retirement gift, the game again featured Florida's top-ranked offense against Alabama's conference-leading defense—only someone forgot to tell Wuerffel, who turned it into a shootout and passed for an SEC Championship Game record 401 yards and six touchdowns. Anthony led all receivers with 171 yards on 11 catches and three touchdowns.

Although the Tide scored first on a 36-yard touchdown pass from Freddie Kitchens to Dennis Riddle, and Michael Vaughn's 94-yard touchdown reception was the longest ever in Alabama history, at one point Florida rattled off 24 straight points.

Following Vaughn's touchdown in the third quarter, the Gators needed just 57 seconds to counter with an 85-yard score by Jacquez Green.

While the Tide did get the coveted win for Stallings at the Outback Bowl, the Gators went on to defeat Florida State 52-20 in the Sugar Bowl to claim their first national title, with Wuerffel becoming the only player over a 20-year span to win the national championship and Hesiman Trophy in the same season.

"You know, I didn't think of it as pressure," Wuerffel told the *Times-Picayune* in 2004. "I think pressure is something that you perceive. The whole season was a lot of pressure, and playing for the national championship is a lot of pressure and the stakes are high. It was a very exciting time with very high stakes."

1997

Tennessee 30, Auburn 29
MVP: Peyton Manning, Tennessee

For the first time a team other than Florida emerged from the Eastern Division, and Auburn was making its SEC Championship Game debut as well.

Although Tennessee scored first, on a 40-yard touchdown pass from Peyton Manning to Peerless Price, Auburn led for most of the first half. A 24-yard fumble return by Brad Ware, a 51-yard touchdown pass from Dameyune Craig to Tyrone Goodson, and two field goals by Jaret Holmes helped the Tigers build a 20-7 lead.

Manning and Craig both had touchdown passes in the third quarter before the Volunteers started to take control. A 46-yard touchdown reception by Price nearly pulled Tennessee to within a field goal, but Auburn's Quinton Reese returned the blocked extra-point attempt for a two-point conversion and 29-23 score.

Instead, a 73-yard touchdown pass to Marcus Nash tied the game, with Jeff Hall's extra point the difference.

Manning completed 25 of 43 passes for 373 yards, four touchdowns, and two interceptions; Craig had 262 yards passing (14 of 34). Price had 161 yards on eight catches and Nash 126 on nine receptions, while running back Jamal Lewis pounded out 127 yards on 31 carries.

Ranked No. 3, Tennessee went on to lose 42-17 to Nebraska in the Orange Bowl.

1998

Tennessee 24, Mississippi State 14
MVP: Peerless Price, Tennessee

With undefeated Tennessee ranked No. 1, the game appeared to be a mismatch, but No. 25 Mississippi State hung tough. Thanks to a 70-yard interception return for a touchdown by Robert Bean and an 83-yard punt return by Kevin Prentiss, the Bulldogs had a 14-10 lead midway through the fourth quarter.

With its national title aspirations on the line, Tennessee rallied for two late touchdowns. Quarterback Tee Martin connected with Price for a 41-yard score with 6:15 remaining to take the lead, and after a Mississippi State fumble the Volunteers needed one play to reach the end zone again, a 26-yard pass to Cedric Wilson.

Martin completed 15 of 32 passes for 208 yards, with two touchdowns and one interception. Price had six catches for 97 yards and a touchdown, to go with two kickoff returns for 55 yards. Travis Henry was the leading rusher, with 120 yards on 26 carries.

With the win finally in hand, coupled with losses by No. 2 Kansas State and No. 3 UCLA, Tennessee was the clear choice to play for the national championship in the Fiesta Bowl, where it defeated Florida State, 23-16.

1999

Alabama 34, Florida 7
MVP: Freddie Milons, Alabama

Alabama was up only 15-7 when it scored 19 points in the fourth quarter to win going away.

Two plays in particular did in the Gators. With 11:54 left in the game, Freddie Milons scored on a 77-yard run, and 18 seconds later defensive tackle Reggie Grimes scored on a 38-yard interception return. Running back Shaun Alexander, who had 97 rushing yards on 30 carries, finished off Florida with a final 7-yard touchdown run.

Running back Earnest Graham was responsible for Florida's only touchdown, on a 3-yard pass to Erron Kinney in the first quarter. Otherwise, Alabama's defense dominated, allowing just 59 offensive yards and after the touchdown no third-down conversions while making four interceptions. It was Florida's lowest output in total offense, passing yards, pass completions, and first downs under Spurrier.

Behind quarterbacks Andrew Zow, who had a 27-yard touchdown pass to Jason McAddley, and Tyler Watts, Alabama accumulated 426 offensive yards; Milons finished with 116 rushing yards after lining up at wide receiver and quarterback, in addition to returning kicks.

2000

Florida 28, Auburn 6
MVP: Rex Grossman, Florida

After the Gators had played the nation's toughest schedule, Spurrier's sixth SEC championship proved to be his last at Florida.

The Gators never trailed as quarterback Rex Grossman completed 17 of 26 passes for 238 yards and four touchdowns, and Graham set an SEC Championship Game record with 169 rushing yards on 19 carries.

Wide receiver Jabar Gaffney, the SEC Freshman of the Year, had five catches for 84 yards and a touchdown, and Reche Caldwell added three catches for 91 yards and touchdown receptions of 10 and 66 yards. Grossman's final touchdown, 12 yards, was to Brian Haugabrook.

"Rex Grossman can make plays out there," Spurrier said. "In big ball games somebody has to make the plays and some of the passes he got off today were sensational. He hung in there and got the ball where it was supposed to be."

Auburn quarterback Ben Leard completed 17 of 30 passes for 158 yards before leaving the game with an injury. Running back Rudi Johnson, SEC Player of the Year, was limited to just 47 rushing yards on 17 carries.

2001

LSU 31, Tennessee 20
MVP: Matt Mauck, LSU

Concerns that having a championship game might cost an SEC team the opportunity to play for a national title became reality in 2001, thanks to a backup quarterback.

After Rohan Davey took a pair of vicious shots to the ribs, Matt Mauck came in and ran for two touchdowns, costing the No. 2 Volunteers a Rose Bowl trip.

"Everyone dreams about doing it," said Mauck, a 22-year-old freshman who had spent three years as a catcher in the Chicago Cubs organization. "For it to actually happen is something that is very special to me."

Mauck completed just 5 of 15 passes for 67 yards, but had 43 rushing yards on 12 carries as LSU overcame an early 17-7 deficit. Running back Domanick Davis, who was in for injured starter LaBrandon Toefield, finished off the Vols by diving over the top on fourth-and-goal from the 1 with 2:26 remaining.

Tennessee quarterback Casey Clausen had two touchdown passes in the first half, when Kelley Washington had 103 of his 140 receiving yards. But second-half miscues, including fumbles by Travis Stephens and Donte Stallworth, doomed the Vols.

LSU's Josh Reed had four catches for 60 yards, giving him 3,001 for his career and breaking the SEC mark of 2,964 set by Vanderbilt's Boo Williams (1985–88).

2002

Georgia 30, Arkansas 3
MVP: Musa Smith, Georgia

Georgia scored on its first five possessions to win its first SEC championship in 20 years. Running back Musa Smith gained 106 rushing yards and scored two touchdowns, quarterback David Greene passed for 237 yards and a touchdown, and receiver Terrence Edwards had seven catches for 92 yards—and in the process became the SEC's career leader in receiving yards (3,093).

Just as impressive was the Bulldogs' defense, which was led by senior linebackers Boss Bailey and Tony Gilbert along with sophomore defensive end David Pollack, the SEC Player of the Year. It set the tone on the first series by moving Arkansas back 2 yards before Decory Bryant blocked a subsequent punt. On the following play, Smith scored a 2-yard touchdown.

"I felt like they were playing with 12 men," Arkansas coach Houston Nutt said. "They have few weaknesses."

It was the ninth kick blocked by Georgia that season. Razorbacks running back Fred Talley was limited to 51 rushing yards on 17 carries, and quarterback Matt Jones had 12 yards on nine carries with 60 yards passing.

Earlier in the day, Miami defeated Virginia Tech 56-45 to clinch a spot in the national championship game against Ohio State in the Fiesta Bowl, knocking Georgia out of contention. If anything, it only fired up the Bulldogs even more, resulting in a game-record five personal foul penalties called. Georgia went on to defeat Florida State 26-13 in the Sugar Bowl to finish No. 3.

2003

LSU 34, Georgia 13
MVP: Justin Vincent, LSU

By dominating No. 5 Georgia, No. 3 LSU moved up just enough in the polls to play for the national championship in the Sugar Bowl.

Unlike their previous meeting earlier in the season, won by LSU 17-10 at Baton Rouge on Mauck's 34-yard touchdown pass to Skyler Green with 1:22 remaining, the Tigers finished with 293 rushing yards and outgained the Bulldogs 444-249. Freshman running back Justin Vincent opened the scoring with an 87-yard touchdown and went on to set the SEC Championship Game rushing record with 201 yards.

Mauck also had a 43-yard touchdown pass to Michael Clayton, and midway through the second quarter LSU led 17-0 on the scoreboard, and posted 196 to Georgia's minus-8 in yards. Linebacker Lionel Turner tipped a pass to himself and returned the interception 18 yards for the Tigers' sixth defensive touchdown of the season. While Georgia had only 50 rushing yards, Greene had three passes intercepted, was sacked five times, and completed just 17 of 41 passes for 199 yards.

"I'm very proud of the accomplishments of this team," LSU coach Nick Saban said. "Georgia is a very good team. Coming into this game there were a lot of questions about whether you could beat the same team twice in a season and our team was out to prove that you could do that."

With No. 1 Oklahoma demolished by Kansas State 35-7 in the Big 12 Championship Game, and No. 2 Southern Cal easily defeating Oregon State 52-28, the top three teams all had one loss. Although the Associated Press had USC ranked first, the Bowl Championship Series paired LSU against Oklahoma. LSU won 21-14.

2004

Auburn 38, Tennessee 28
MVP: Jason Campbell, Auburn

The situation was similar to the year before; an SEC team needed a dominating performance and a little good fortune to play for the national championship. Undefeated No. 3 Auburn got the win it needed, but not the help.

Senior quarterback Jason Campbell had the first 300-yard passing game of his career by completing 27 of 35 passes for 374 yards, and with 57 rushing yards set an SEC Championship Game record with 431 yards of total offense.

Auburn dominated early and was up 14-0 before Tennessee made a first down, and at halftime the Tigers had leads of 303-39 in total yards, 17-2 in first downs, and more than 12 minutes in time of possession.

But after giving up just one rushing touchdown during the regular season, the Tigers yielded three. An 80-yard touchdown run by Gerald Riggs Jr. pulled Tennessee even at 21-21 in the third quarter, and he went on to finish with 182 yards on 11 carries. But miscues cost the Volunteers, with penalties wiping out both Cedric Houston's 70-yard touchdown run and third-string quarterback Rick Clausen's 44-yard pass to wide receiver Robert Meachem.

Campbell connected with wide receiver Devin Aromashodu for a 53-yard touchdown to regain the lead and capped the victory with a 43-yard touchdown pass to wide receiver Ben Obomanu.

"We definitely deserve a chance to play for the national championship," Campbell said. "We've done all we can do. We've done what people asked. But one thing they can't take away is our SEC championship."

The national championship game didn't happen for Auburn. No. 1 Southern California also finished 12-0 by holding off UCLA 29-24, and No. 2 Oklahoma crushed Colorado, 42-3, to secure spots in the Orange Bowl.

"It's been 15 long years since Auburn won an SEC championship, and we've never won 12 games in a season," coach Tommy Tuberville said. "This is a special team."

2005

Georgia 34, LSU 14
MVP: D. J. Shockley, Georgia

No. 3 LSU's remote chances of playing in the national championship quickly evaporated when Georgia quarterback D. J. Shockley threw early touchdown passes of 45 and 29 yards to junior flanker Sean Bailey to provide a lead the Tigers would never challenge.

"It was shocking that they got those two big plays on us at the start," LSU senior defensive tackle Kyle Williams said. "It just slipped away from us at that point and got out of hand."

An interception by senior cornerback DeMario Minter set up the second touchdown, and senior cornerback Tim Jennings returned an interception 15 yards into the end zone. Overall, LSU was limited to 74 rushing yards, 219 fewer than it accumulated against Georgia in the 2003 SEC Championship Game.

LSU's first touchdown capped a 14-play, 80-yard drive, with sophomore quarterback JaMarcus Russell scoring on a 1-yard run. But any momentum shift disappeared when LSU lost 6 yards on its next possession, and senior Bryan McClendon blocked junior Chris Jackson's punt. Three plays later, the score was 21-7 on Shockley's 7-yard scramble into the end zone.

"What can I say, other than I'm excited as I can be," said Georgia coach Mark Richt, who secured his fourth straight 10-win season.

· Appendix A ·

The SEC

SEC COMMISSIONERS

Martin S. Conner	1940–46
Bernie H. Moore	1948–66
A. M. (Tonto) Coleman	1966–72
Dr. H. Boyd McWhorter	1972–86
Dr. Harvey W. Schiller	1986–89
Roy F. Kramer	1990–2002
Michael L. Slive	2002–06

2005 EXECUTIVE COMMITTEE

Dr. Michael Adams, Georgia, president
Dr. Andrew Sorensen, South Carolina, vice president
Dr. Robert Weems, Ole Miss, secretary
Dr. John White, Arkansas
Marcia Boosinger, Auburn
Judy Southard, LSU
Larry Templeton, Mississippi State

2005 SEC FOOTBALL

Michael L. Slive, Commissioner
Mark Womack, Executive Associate Commissioner
Brad Davis, Associate Commissioner
Mark Whitworth, Associate Commissioner
Charles Bloom, Associate Commissioner
Debbie Corum, Associate Commissioner
Greg Sankey, Associate Commissioner
Kathryn Poe-Switzer, Executive Associate to the Commissioner
Craig Mattox, Assistant Commissioner
Gil Grimes, Assistant Commissioner
Laronica Conway, Assistant Commissioner
Peggy Blake, Director of Business Operations
Sylvia Hagan, Association Director of Sports Administration
Tammy Wilson, Associate Media Relations Director
DeWayne Peevy, Associate Media Relations Director
Chuck Dunlap, Assistant Media Relations Director
Megan Patterson, Assistant Director of Football Administration
Charlie Hussey, Assistant Director of Championships/Marketing
David Knight, Assistant Director of Championship Ticket Operations
Dauna Koonce, Administrative Assistant
Torie Johnson, Director of National Letter of Intent
Brenda Gray, Receptionist
Bobby Gaston, Supervisor of Football Officials

Eric SanInocencio, Media Relations Intern
Edgar Gantt, Compliance Intern

SEC NATIONAL CHAMPIONS
(Through 2004–05 Academic Year)

Men (92)

Baseball (6): 1990 Georgia (52-19); 1991 LSU (55-18); 1993 LSU (53-17-1); 1996 LSU (52-15); 1997 LSU (57-13); 2000 LSU (52-17)

Basketball (8): 1948 Kentucky (36-3); 1949 Kentucky (32-2); 1951 Kentucky (32-2); 1958 Kentucky (23-6); 1978 Kentucky (30-2); 1994 Arkansas (31-3); 1996 Kentucky (34-2); 1998 Kentucky (35-4)

Boxing (1): 1949 LSU (20)

Cross Country (8): 1972 Tennessee (134); 1991 Arkansas (52); 1992 Arkansas (46); 1993 Arkansas (31); 1995 Arkansas (100); 1998 Arkansas (97); 1999 Arkansas (58); 2000 Arkansas (83)

Football (15): 1951 Tennessee (10-1); 1957 Auburn (10-0); 1958 LSU (11-0); 1960 Ole Miss (10-0-1); 1961 Alabama (11-0); 1964 Alabama (10-1); 1965 Alabama (9-1-1); 1973 Alabama (11-1); 1978 Alabama (11-1); 1979 Alabama (12-0); 1980 Georgia (12-0); 1992 Alabama (13-0); 1996 Florida (12-1); 1998 Tennessee (13-0); 2003 LSU (13-1)

Golf (10): 1940 LSU (601-tie); 1942 LSU (590-tie); 1947 LSU (606); 1955 LSU (574); 1968 Florida (1154); 1973 Florida (1149); 1993 Florida (1145); 1999 Georgia (1180); 2001 Florida (1126); 2005 Georgia (1135)

Swimming and Diving (7): 1978 Tennessee (307); 1983 Florida (238); 1984 Florida (287.5); 1997 Auburn (496.5); 1999 Auburn (467.5); 2003 Auburn (609.5); 2004 Auburn (634); 2005 Auburn (491)

Tennis (5): 1959 Tulane (tie); 1985 Georgia (36-1); 1987 Georgia (24-3); 1999 Georgia (26-5); 2001 Georgia (28-1)

Indoor Track and Field (13): 1992 Arkansas (53); 1993 Arkansas (66); 1994 Arkansas (94); 1995 Arkansas (59); 1997 Arkansas (59); 1998 Arkansas (56); 1999 Arkansas (65); 2000 Arkansas (69.5); 2001 LSU (34); 2002 Tennessee (52); 2003 Arkansas (54); 2004 LSU (44.5); 2005 Arkansas (56)

Outdoor Track and Field (18): 1933 LSU (58); 1974 Tennessee (60); 1989 LSU (53); 1990 LSU (44); 1991 Tennessee (51); 1992 Arkansas (60); 1993 Arkansas (69); 1994 Arkansas (83); 1995 Arkansas (61.5); 1996 Arkansas (55); 1997 Arkansas (55); 1998 Arkansas (58.5); 1999 Arkansas (59); 2001 Tennessee (50); 2002 LSU (64); 2003 Arkansas (59); 2004 Arkansas (65.5); 2005 Arkansas (60)

Women (61)

Basketball (6): 1987 Tennessee (28-6); 1989 Tennessee (35-2); 1991 Tennessee (30-5); 1996 Tennessee (32-4); 1997 Tennessee (29-10); 1998 Tennessee (39-0)

Cross Country (1): 1988 Kentucky (75)

Golf (3): 1985 Florida (1218); 1986 Florida (1180); 2001 Georgia (1176)

Gymnastics (10): 1987 Georgia (187.90); 1988 Alabama (190.05); 1989 Georgia (192.65); 1991 Alabama (195.125); 1993 Georgia (198.000); 1996 Alabama (198.025); 1998 Georgia (197.725); 1999 Georgia (196.850); 2002 Alabama (197.575); 2005 Georgia (197.825)

Soccer (1): 1998 Florida (26-1)

Swimming and Diving (8): 1982 Florida (505); 1999 Georgia (504.5); 2000 Georgia (490.5); 2001 Georgia (389); 2002 Auburn (474); 2003 Auburn (536); 2004 Auburn (569); 2005 Georgia (609.5)

Tennis (6): 1992 Florida (30-0); 1994 Georgia (27-2); 1996 Florida (31-0); 1998 Florida (27-0); 2000 Georgia (27-2); 2003 Florida (31-2)

Indoor Track and Field (13): 1987 LSU (49); 1989 LSU (61); 1991 LSU (48); 1992 Florida (50);

1993 LSU (49); 1994 LSU (48); 1995 LSU (40); 1996 LSU (52); 1997 LSU (49); 2002 LSU (57); 2003 LSU (62); 2004 LSU (52); 2005 Tennessee (46)

Outdoor Track and Field (14): 1987 LSU (62); 1988 LSU (61); 1989 LSU (86); 1990 LSU (53); 1991 LSU (78); 1992 LSU (87); 1993 LSU (93); 1994 LSU (86); 1995 LSU (69); 1996 LSU (81); 1997 LSU (63); 2000 LSU (58); 2002 South Carolina (82); 2003 LSU (64)

· Appendix B ·

Standings

1933

	Conference W-L-T	Pts.	Opp.	Overall W-L-T	Pts.	Opp.
Alabama	5-0-1	69	15	7-1-1	130	17
LSU	3-0-2	73	20	7-0-3	176	27
Georgia	3-1-0	53	33	8-2-0	148	86
Tennessee	5-2-0	134	37	7-3-0	176	47
Tulane	4-2-1	127	55	6-3-1	160	68
Auburn	2-2-0	40	43	5-5-0	133	104
Mississippi	2-2-1	78	66	6-3-2	167	79
Vanderbilt	2-2-2	56	74	4-3-3	126	107
Florida	2-3-0	58	53	5-3-1	114	53
Kentucky	2-3-0	14	87	5-5-0	91	116
Georgia Tech	2-5-0	62	55	5-5-0	117	63
Mississippi State	1-5-1	39	143	3-6-1	69	149
Sewanee	0-6-0	36	158	3-6-0	75	165

1934

	Conference W-L-T	Pts.	Opp.	Overall W-L-T	Pts.	Opp.
Tulane	8-0-0	148	49	9-1-0	195	69
Alabama	7-0-0	223	32	9-0-0	287	32
Tennessee	5-1-0	98	32	8-2-0	175	58
LSU	4-2-0	133	41	7-2-2	172	77
Georgia	3-2-0	51	33	7-3-0	141	56
Vanderbilt	4-3-0	66	94	6-3-0	105	100
Florida	2-2-1	52	74	6-3-1	113	110
Mississippi	2-3-1	39	78	4-5-1	114	98
Kentucky	1-3-0	30	73	5-5-0	123	86
Auburn	1-6-0	37	87	2-8-0	58	107
Sewanee	0-4-0	12	105	2-7-0	40	147
Mississippi State	0-5-0	6	94	4-6-0	79	126
Georgia Tech	0-6-0	42	125	1-9-0	56	187

Bowls: Rose (Alabama 29, Stanford 13); Sugar (Tulane 20, Temple 14)

1935

	Conference W-L-T	Pts.	Opp.	Overall W-L-T	Pts.	Opp.
LSU	5-0-0	95	15	9-1-0	221	38
Vanderbilt	5-1-0	103	42	7-3-0	179	68

	Conference W-L-T	Pts.	Opp.	Overall W-L-T	Pts.	Opp.
Mississippi	3-1-0	87	26	9-2-0	292	66
Auburn	5-2-0	118	39	8-2-0	201	46
Alabama	4-2-0	106	48	6-2-1	185	55
Tulane	3-3-0	85	97	6-4-0	156	123
Kentucky	3-3-0	80	68	5-4-0	167	94
Georgia Tech	3-4-0	123	123	5-5-0	162	142
Mississippi State	2-3-0	73	63	8-3-0	190	76
Tennessee	2-3-0	34	84	4-5-0	98	155
Georgia	2-4-0	54	81	6-4-0	169	88
Florida	1-6-0	51	134	3-7-0	113	154
Sewanee	0-6-0	0	189	2-7-0	15	228

Bowls: Orange (Catholic 20, Ole Miss 19); Sugar (Texas Christian 3, LSU 2)

1936

	Conference W-L-T	Pts.	Opp.	Overall W-L-T	Pts.	Opp.
LSU	6-0-0	143	13	9-0-1	281	33
Alabama	5-0-1	89	29	8-0-1	168	35
Auburn	4-1-1	58	44	7-2-2	160	63
Tennessee	3-1-2	79	25	6-2-2	147	52
Mississippi State	3-2-0	101	25	7-2-1	220	25
Georgia	3-3-0	74	133	5-4-1	115	159
Georgia Tech	3-3-1	164	63	5-5-1	251	103
Tulane	2-3-1	73	91	6-3-1	163	117
Vanderbilt	1-3-1	33	59	3-5-1	115	87
Kentucky	1-3-0	13	55	6-4-0	179	84
Florida	1-5-0	40	98	4-6-0	99	125
Mississippi	0-3-1	12	46	5-5-2	150	98
Sewanee	0-5-0	13	211	0-6-1	20	230

Bowls: Bacardi (Auburn 7, Villanova 7); Orange (Duquesne 13, Mississippi State 12); Sugar (Santa Clara 21, LSU 14)

1937

	Conference W-L-T	Pts.	Opp.	Overall W-L-T	Pts.	Opp.
Alabama	6-0-0	145	20	9-0-0	225	20
LSU	5-1-0	108	21	9-1-0	234	27
Auburn	4-1-2	95	23	5-2-3	121	36
Vanderbilt	4-2-0	80	36	7-2-0	121	42
Mississippi State	3-2-0	42	94	5-4-1	119	117
Georgia Tech	3-2-1	64	34	6-3-1	177	54
Tennessee	4-3-0	130	47	6-3-1	189	47
Florida	3-4-0	46	59	4-7-0	86	89
Tulane	2-3-1	66	50	5-4-1	164	69
Georgia	1-2-2	13	50	6-3-2	151	64
Mississippi	0-4-0	14	68	4-5-1	127	106
Kentucky	0-5-0	0	104	4-6-0	93	130
Sewanee	0-6-0	7	204	2-7-0	78	213

Bowls: Orange (Auburn 6, Michigan State 0); Rose (California 13, Alabama 0); Sugar (Santa Clara 6, LSU 0)

1938

	Conference W-L-T	Pts.	Opp.	Overall W-L-T	Pts.	Opp.
Tennessee	7-0-0	167	9	10-0-0	276	16
Alabama	4-1-1	82	33	7-1-1	149	40

Tulane	4-1-1	107	9	7-2-1	211	53
Mississippi	3-2-0	85	73	9-2-0	232	120
Georgia Tech	2-1-3	47	51	3-4-3	72	84
Vanderbilt	4-3-0	54	49	6-3-0	86	49
Florida	2-2-1	25	54	4-6-1	112	149
Auburn	3-3-1	84	49	4-5-1	110	88
Georgia	1-2-1	39	57	5-4-1	145	143
LSU	2-4-0	58	83	6-4-0	160	89
Mississippi State	1-4-0	41	98	4-6-0	123	131
Kentucky	0-4-0	31	105	2-7-0	150	160
Sewanee	0-6-0	9	159	1-8-0	59	213

Bowl: Orange (Tennessee 17, Oklahoma 0)

1939

	Conference W-L-T	Pts.	Opp.	Overall W-L-T	Pts.	Opp.
Tennessee	6-0-0	120	0	10-0-0	212	0
Georgia Tech	6-0-0	74	25	7-2-0	129	49
Tulane	5-0-0	128	26	8-0-1	181	46
Mississippi State	3-2-0	47	32	8-2-0	216	32
Mississippi	2-2-0	40	50	7-2-0	230	64
Kentucky	2-2-1	47	58	6-2-1	161	64
Auburn	3-3-1	48	40	5-5-1	71	69
Alabama	2-3-1	53	47	5-3-1	101	53
Georgia	1-3-0	12	35	5-6-0	113	98
LSU	1-5-0	58	109	4-5-0	111	116
Vanderbilt	1-6-0	57	120	2-7-1	96	165
Florida	0-3-1	16	48	5-5-1	78	66
Sewanee	0-3-0	7	117	3-5-0	43	150

Bowls: Orange (Georgia Tech 21, Missouri 7); Rose (Southern California 14, Tennessee 0); Sugar (Texas A&M 14, Tulane 13)

1940

	Conference W-L-T	Pts.	Opp.	Overall W-L-T	Pts.	Opp.
Tennessee	5-0-0	122	12	10-0-0	319	26
Mississippi State	4-0-1	88	21	9-0-1	233	51
Mississippi	3-1-0	60	46	9-2-0	251	100
Alabama	4-2-0	89	80	7-2-0	166	80
Auburn	3-2-1	89	70	6-4-1	170	153
LSU	3-3-0	55	82	6-4-0	139	112
Georgia	2-3-1	82	106	5-4-1	209	134
Florida	2-3-0	48	81	5-5-0	136	141
Kentucky	1-2-2	40	79	5-3-2	190	107
Tulane	1-3-0	41	60	5-5-0	144	126
Vanderbilt	1-5-1	55	91	3-6-1	101	98
Georgia Tech	1-5-0	72	93	3-7-0	139	160
Sewanee	0-1-0	0	20	3-5-0	132	125

Bowls: Orange (Mississippi State 14, Georgetown 7); Sugar (Boston College 19, Tennessee 13)

1941

	Conference W-L-T	Pts.	Opp.	Overall W-L-T	Pts.	Opp.
Mississippi State	4-0-1	40	7	8-1-1	191	55
Tennessee	3-1-0	61	29	8-2-0	182	73

Alabama	5-2-0	105	51	8-2-0	234	64
Georgia	3-1-1	75	44	8-1-1	279	59
Mississippi	2-1-1	47	45	6-2-1	131	67
Vanderbilt	3-2-0	81	82	8-2-0	260	89
LSU	2-2-2	54	40	4-4-2	119	93
Tulane	2-3-0	93	72	5-4-0	220	95
Georgia Tech	2-4-0	62	96	3-6-0	82	130
Florida	1-3-0	24	42	4-6-0	149	97
Auburn	0-4-1	28	88	4-5-1	123	115
Kentucky	0-4-0	35	109	5-4-0	151	154

Bowls: Cotton (Alabama 29, Texas A&M 21); Orange (Georgia 40, Texas Christian 26)

1942

	Conference W-L-T	Pts.	Opp.	Overall W-L-T	Pts.	Opp.
Georgia	6-1-0	238	56	10-1-0	367	76
Georgia Tech	4-1-0	89	48	9-1-0	212	73
Tennessee	4-1-0	85	15	8-1-1	245	54
Mississippi State	5-2-0	188	62	8-2-0	200	77
Alabama	4-2-0	80	41	7-3-0	209	76
LSU	3-2-0	62	70	7-3-0	192	117
Auburn	3-3-0	79	60	6-4-1	174	133
Vanderbilt	2-4-0	61	113	6-4-0	232	113
Florida	1-3-0	25	121	3-7-0	106	185
Tulane	1-4-0	47	113	4-5-0	121	154
Kentucky	0-5-0	19	101	3-6-1	155	154
Mississippi	0-5-0	33	136	2-7-0	132	163

Bowls: Cotton (Texas 14, Georgia Tech 7); Orange (Alabama 37, Boston College 21); Rose (Georgia 9, UCLA 0); Sugar (Tennessee 14, Tulsa 7)

1943

	Conference W-L-T	Pts.	Opp.	Overall W-L-T	Pts.	Opp.
Georgia Tech	3-0-0	123	7	7-3-0	280	124
Tulane	1-1-0	27	33	3-3-0	92	94
LSU	2-2-0	68	102	5-3-0	143	144
Georgia	0-3-0	33	109	6-4-0	264	153
Vanderbilt	0-0-0	0	0	5-0-0	145	33

Bowls: Orange (LSU 19, Texas A&M 14); Sugar (Georgia Tech 20, Tulsa 18)

1944

	Conference W-L-T	Pts.	Opp.	Overall W-L-T	Pts.	Opp.
Georgia Tech	4-0-0	119	13	8-2-0	241	75
Tennessee	5-0-1	120	27	7-0-1	173	48
Georgia	4-2-0	121	103	7-3-0	269	130
Alabama	3-1-2	128	47	5-1-2	246	54
Mississippi State	3-2-0	73	59	6-2-0	219	79
LSU	2-3-1	79	80	2-5-1	92	101
Mississippi	2-3-0	59	95	2-6-0	77	178
Tulane	1-2-0	29	72	4-3-0	113	125
Kentucky	1-5-0	59	134	3-6-0	125	147

Florida	0-3-0	18	104	4-3-0	106	136
Auburn	0-4-0	47	118	4-4-0	181	137
Vanderbilt	0-0-0	0	0	3-0-1	67	23

Bowls: Orange (Tulsa 26, Georgia Tech 12); Rose (Southern California 25, Tennessee 0); Sugar (Duke 29, Alabama 26)

1945

	Conference			Overall		
	W-L-T	Pts.	Opp.	W-L-T	Pts.	Opp.
Alabama	6-0-0	265	60	9-0-0	396	66
Tennessee	3-1-0	100	25	8-1-0	238	52
LSU	5-2-0	172	80	7-2-0	245	92
Georgia	4-2-0	164	66	8-2-0	294	94
Mississippi	3-3-0	68	112	4-5-0	100	183
Georgia Tech	2-2-0	68	56	4-6-0	157	165
Mississippi State	2-3-0	79	96	6-3-0	221	108
Auburn	2-3-0	46	89	5-5-0	172	129
Vanderbilt	2-4-0	40	175	3-6-0	71	215
Florida	1-3-1	32	79	4-5-1	155	100
Tulane	1-3-1	41	113	2-6-1	93	212
Kentucky	0-5-0	38	162	2-8-0	96	217

Bowls: Oil (Georgia 20, Tulsa 6); Rose (Alabama 34, Southern California 14)

1946

	Conference			Overall		
	W-L-T	Pts.	Opp.	W-L-T	Pts.	Opp.
Georgia	5-0-0	151	34	10-0-0	372	100
Tennessee	5-0-0	57	29	9-1-0	175	89
LSU	5-1-0	140	101	9-1-0	240	123
Georgia Tech	4-2-0	128	75	8-2-0	243	108
Mississippi State	3-2-0	80	44	8-2-0	271	71
Alabama	4-3-0	85	84	7-4-0	186	110
Vanderbilt	3-4-0	66	43	5-4-0	108	43
Kentucky	2-3-0	50	69	7-3-0	233	97
Tulane	2-4-0	106	110	3-7-0	179	209
Auburn	1-5-0	53	164	4-6-0	132	210
Mississippi	1-6-0	61	130	2-7-0	76	144
Florida	0-5-0	46	140	0-9-0	104	264

Bowls: Cotton (LSU 0, Arkansas 0); Oil (Georgia Tech 41, St. Mary's 19); Orange (Rice 8, Tennessee 0); Sugar (Georgia 20, North Carolina 10)

1947

	Conference			Overall		
	W-L-T	Pts.	Opp.	W-L-T	Pts.	Opp.
Mississippi	6-1-0	157	82	8-2-0	256	101
Georgia Tech	4-1-0	88	21	9-1-0	220	35
Alabama	5-2-0	122	61	8-2-0	203	74
Mississippi State	2-2-0	54	54	7-3-0	169	89
Georgia	3-3-0	104	81	7-4-0	192	115
Vanderbilt	3-3-0	72	58	6-4-0	182	85
Tulane	2-3-2	88	100	2-5-2	94	192
LSU	2-3-1	95	121	5-3-1	149	161
Kentucky	2-3-0	53	40	7-3-0	151	59
Tennessee	2-3-0	38	93	5-5-0	164	152

Auburn	1-5-0	33	151	2-7-0	78	204
Florida	0-3-1	33	75	4-5-1	125	156

Bowls: Delta (Mississippi 13, Texas Christian 9); Gator (Georgia 20, Maryland 20); Great Lakes (Kentucky 24, Villanova 14); Orange (Georgia Tech 20, Kansas 14); Sugar (Texas 29, Alabama 7)

1948

	Conference			Overall		
	W-L-T	Pts.	Opp.	W-L-T	Pts.	Opp.
Georgia	6-0-0	175	51	9-1-0	278	100
Mississippi	6-1-0	160	73	8-1-0	226	93
Tulane	5-1-0	124	40	9-1-0	207	60
Vanderbilt	4-2-1	170	67	8-2-1	328	73
Georgia Tech	4-3-0	126	62	7-3-0	226	69
Alabama	4-4-1	153	164	6-4-1	228	170
Mississippi State	3-3-0	62	59	4-4-1	103	87
Tennessee	2-3-1	59	77	4-4-2	140	98
Kentucky	1-3-1	60	96	5-3-2	199	128
Florida	1-5-0	78	153	5-5-0	213	206
LSU	1-5-0	52	178	3-7-0	99	271
Auburn	0-7-0	29	228	1-8-1	68	262

Bowl: Orange (Texas 41, Georgia 28)

1949

	Conference			Overall		
	W-L-T	Pts.	Opp.	W-L-T	Pts.	Opp.
Tulane	5-1-0	155	61	7-2-1	251	142
Kentucky	4-1-0	126	6	9-2-0	304	53
Tennessee	4-1-1	97	64	7-2-1	214	104
Georgia Tech	5-2-0	134	99	7-3-0	197	129
LSU	4-2-0	122	53	8-2-0	231	74
Alabama	4-3-1	145	96	6-3-1	227	130
Vanderbilt	4-4-0	144	170	5-5-0	177	183
Auburn	2-4-2	114	168	2-4-3	134	188
Mississippi	2-4-0	107	151	4-5-1	246	243
Florida	1-4-1	86	156	4-5-1	180	218
Georgia	1-4-1	47	94	4-6-1	177	134
Mississippi State	0-6-0	25	184	0-8-1	38	224

Bowls: Orange (Santa Clara 21, Kentucky 13); Sugar (Oklahoma 35, LSU 0)

1950

	Conference			Overall		
	W-L-T	Pts.	Opp.	W-L-T	Pts.	Opp.
Kentucky	5-1-0	157	48	10-1-0	380	62
Tennessee	4-1-0	99	16	10-1-0	315	57
Alabama	6-2-0	214	101	9-2-0	328	107
Tulane	3-1-1	118	66	6-2-1	260	97
Georgia Tech	4-2-0	89	95	5-6-0	182	193
Georgia	3-2-1	65	44	6-2-3	158	65
Mississippi State	3-4-0	95	123	4-5-0	169	137
LSU	2-3-2	107	88	4-5-2	165	151
Vanderbilt	3-4-0	128	178	7-4-0	252	216
Florida	2-4-0	90	137	5-5-0	157	181
Mississippi	1-5-0	75	169	5-5-0	207	183
Auburn	0-7-0	17	189	0-10-0	31	255

Bowls: Cotton (Tennessee 20, Texas 14); Presidential Cup (Texas A&M 40, Georgia 20); Sugar (Kentucky 13, Oklahoma 7)

1951

	Conference W-L-T	Pts.	Opp.	Overall W-L-T	Pts.	Opp.
Georgia Tech	7-0-0	175	41	10-0-1	278	76
Tennessee	5-0-0	150	61	10-0-0	373	88
LSU	4-2-1	63	71	7-3-1	128	111
Mississippi	4-2-1	181	130	6-3-1	254	157
Kentucky	3-3-0	102	68	7-4-0	294	114
Auburn	3-4-0	101	164	5-5-0	180	212
Vanderbilt	3-5-0	147	167	6-5-0	201	195
Alabama	3-5-0	116	140	5-6-0	263	188
Georgia	2-4-0	73	97	5-5-0	176	184
Florida	2-4-0	88	96	5-5-0	174	131
Mississippi State	2-5-0	23	107	4-5-0	82	127
Tulane	1-5-0	40	117	4-6-0	143	172

Bowls: Cotton (Kentucky 20, Texas Christian 7); Orange (Georgia Tech 17, Baylor 14); Sugar (Maryland 28, Tennessee 13)

1952

	Conference W-L-T	Pts.	Opp.	Overall W-L-T	Pts.	Opp.
Georgia Tech	6-0-0	124	26	11-0-0	301	52
Tennessee	5-0-1	142	36	8-1-1	259	63
Mississippi	4-0-2	122	69	8-0-2	237	96
Alabama	4-2-0	121	85	9-2-0	264	133
Georgia	4-3-0	108	131	7-4-0	226	208
Florida	3-3-0	127	84	7-3-0	290	109
Mississippi State	3-4-0	170	172	5-4-0	225	186
Tulane	3-5-0	107	132	5-5-0	188	146
Kentucky	1-3-2	75	121	5-4-2	161	173
LSU	2-5-0	101	138	3-7-0	148	214
Vanderbilt	1-4-1	55	145	3-5-2	151	199
Auburn	0-7-0	75	188	2-8-0	139	208

Bowls: Cotton (Texas 16, Tennessee 0); Gator (Florida 14, Tulsa 13); Orange (Alabama 61, Syracuse 6); Sugar (Georgia Tech 24, Mississippi 7)

1953

	Conference W-L-T	Pts.	Opp.	Overall W-L-T	Pts.	Opp.
Alabama	4-0-3	91	51	6-2-3	172	124
Georgia Tech	4-1-1	140	44	8-2-1	246	92
Mississippi	4-1-1	129	62	7-2-1	236	113
Kentucky	4-1-1	137	89	7-2-1	201	116
Auburn	4-2-1	136	99	7-2-1	257	138
Mississippi State	3-1-3	121	80	5-2-3	196	219
Tennessee	3-2-1	95	80	6-4-1	240	153
LSU	2-3-3	123	138	5-3-3	194	159
Florida	1-3-2	69	79	3-5-2	200	113
Vanderbilt	1-5-0	59	172	3-7-0	131	258
Georgia	1-5-0	71	149	3-8-1	155	250
Tulane	0-7-0	68	196	1-8-1	129	228

Bowls: Cotton (Rice 28, Alabama 6); Gator (Texas Tech 35, Auburn 13); Sugar (Georgia Tech 42, West Virginia 19)

1954

	Conference W-L-T	Pts.	Opp.	Overall W-L-T	Pts.	Opp.
Mississippi	5-1-0	119	29	9-1-0	283	47
Georgia Tech	6-2-0	145	63	7-3-0	175	91
Florida	5-2-0	94	66	5-5-0	115	128
Kentucky	5-2-0	90	95	7-3-0	151	125
Georgia	3-2-1	40	69	6-3-1	89	89
Auburn	3-3-0	124	54	7-3-0	243	73
Mississippi State	3-3-0	58	47	6-4-0	192	120
Alabama	3-3-2	74	74	4-5-2	123	104
LSU	2-5-0	66	115	5-6-0	125	173
Tulane	1-6-1	26	124	1-6-3	46	144
Vanderbilt	1-5-0	68	91	2-7-0	134	169
Tennessee	1-5-0	39	116	4-6-0	105	164

Bowls: Cotton (Georgia Tech 14, Arkansas 6); Gator (Auburn 33, Baylor 13); Sugar (Navy 21, Mississippi 0)

1955

	Conference W-L-T	Pts.	Opp.	Overall W-L-T	Pts.	Opp.
Mississippi	5-1-0	135	73	9-1-0	251	97
Auburn	5-1-1	123	92	8-1-1	211	98
Georgia Tech	4-1-1	87	33	8-1-1	182	46
Tennessee	3-2-1	74	57	6-3-1	188	92
Vanderbilt	4-3-0	123	66	7-3-0	215	73
Mississippi State	4-4-0	120	135	6-4-0	173	142
Kentucky	3-3-1	89	108	6-3-1	178	131
Tulane	3-3-1	101	94	5-4-1	163	136
LSU	2-3-1	106	81	3-5-2	139	149
Florida	3-5-0	77	119	4-6-0	111	126
Georgia	2-5-0	91	123	4-6-0	173	170
Alabama	0-7-0	36	181	0-10-0	48	256

Bowls: Cotton (Mississippi 14, Texas Christian 13); Gator (Vanderbilt 25, Auburn 13); Sugar (Georgia Tech 7, Pittsburgh 0)

1956

	Conference W-L-T	Pts.	Opp.	Overall W-L-T	Pts.	Opp.
Tennessee	6-0-0	139	28	10-0-0	268	75
Georgia Tech	7-1-0	211	26	9-1-0	227	33
Florida	5-2-0	124	58	6-3-1	158	98
Mississippi	4-2-0	122	68	7-3-0	207	82
Auburn	4-3-0	108	110	7-3-0	174	117
Kentucky	4-4-0	72	105	6-4-0	119	105
Tulane	3-3-0	56	83	6-4-0	124	123
Vanderbilt	2-5-0	72	91	5-5-0	147	113
Alabama	2-5-0	53	152	2-7-1	85	208
Mississippi State	2-5-0	104	119	4-6-0	148	152
LSU	1-5-0	50	158	3-7-0	104	197
Georgia	1-6-0	30	143	3-6-1	66	162

Bowls: Gator (Georgia Tech 21, Pittsburgh 14); Sugar (Baylor 13, Tennessee 7)

1957

| | Conference | | | Overall | | |
	W-L-T	Pts.	Opp.	W-L-T	Pts.	Opp.
Auburn	7-0-0	90	7	10-0-0	207	28
Mississippi	5-0-1	128	26	8-1-1	232	52
Mississippi State	4-2-1	118	81	6-2-1	175	100
Florida	4-2-1	92	70	6-2-1	133	70
Tennessee	4-3-0	82	62	7-3-0	161	75
Vanderbilt	3-3-1	47	81	5-3-2	113	108
LSU	4-4-0	126	76	5-5-0	159	110
Georgia Tech	3-4-1	62	71	4-4-2	75	71
Georgia	3-4-0	72	71	3-7-0	93	150
Tulane	1-5-0	41	135	2-8-0	94	195
Alabama	1-6-1	40	143	2-7-1	69	173
Kentucky	1-7-0	48	120	3-7-0	128	127

Bowls: Gator (Tennessee 3, Texas A&M 0); Sugar (Mississippi 39, Texas 7)

1958

| | Conference | | | Overall | | |
	W-L-T	Pts.	Opp.	W-L-T	Pts.	Opp.
LSU	6-0-0	138	23	10-0-0	275	53
Auburn	6-0-1	102	40	9-0-1	173	62
Mississippi	4-2-0	83	46	8-2-0	215	65
Vanderbilt	2-1-3	45	30	5-2-3	131	71
Tennessee	4-3-0	64	77	4-6-0	77	122
Alabama	3-4-1	63	69	5-4-1	106	75
Kentucky	3-4-1	65	109	5-4-1	136	115
Florida	2-3-1	66	56	6-3-1	171	93
Georgia Tech	2-3-1	53	60	5-4-1	98	91
Georgia	2-4-0	70	64	4-6-0	196	114
Tulane	1-5-0	35	148	3-7-0	195	189
Mississippi State	1-6-0	61	123	3-6-0	127	129

Bowls: Gator (Mississippi 7, Florida 3); Sugar (LSU 7, Clemson 0)

1959

| | Conference | | | Overall | | |
	W-L-T	Pts.	Opp.	W-L-T	Pts.	Opp.
Georgia	7-0-0	123	53	9-1-0	214	89
LSU	5-1-0	79	23	9-1-0	164	29
Mississippi	5-1-0	184	21	9-1-0	329	21
Alabama	4-1-2	65	45	7-1-2	95	52
Auburn	4-3-0	90	33	7-3-0	174	58
Vanderbilt	3-2-2	57	79	5-3-2	138	106
Georgia Tech	3-3-0	76	69	6-4-0	129	107
Tennessee	3-4-1	60	111	5-4-1	112	118
Florida	2-4-0	60	62	5-4-1	169	107
Kentucky	1-6-0	45	97	4-6-0	140	107
Tulane	0-5-1	39	143	3-6-1	94	176
Mississippi State	0-7-0	19	161	2-7-0	96	198

Bowls: Gator (Arkansas 14, Georgia Tech 7); Liberty (Penn State 7, Alabama 0); Orange (Georgia 14, Missouri 0); Sugar (Mississippi 21, LSU 0)

1960

	Conference			Overall		
	W-L-T	Pts.	Opp.	W-L-T	Pts.	Opp.
Mississippi	5-0-1	138	37	9-0-1	266	64
Florida	5-1-0	93	57	8-2-0	144	74
Alabama	5-1-1	81	47	8-1-1	180	53
Auburn	5-2-0	68	52	8-2-0	155	80
Tennessee	3-2-2	85	58	6-2-2	209	79
Georgia	4-3-0	88	95	6-4-0	174	118
Georgia Tech	4-4-0	102	78	5-5-0	118	97
LSU	2-3-1	42	37	5-4-1	105	50
Kentucky	2-4-1	79	81	5-4-1	206	81
Tulane	1-4-1	57	84	3-6-1	132	139
Mississippi State	0-5-1	41	96	2-6-1	101	119
Vanderbilt	0-7-0	7	159	3-7-0	74	193

Bowls: Bluebonnet (Alabama 3, Texas 3); Gator (Florida 13, Baylor 12); Sugar (Mississippi 14, Rice 6)

1961

	Conference			Overall		
	W-L-T	Pts.	Opp.	W-L-T	Pts.	Opp.
Alabama	7-0-0	178	15	10-0-0	287	22
LSU	6-0-0	143	27	9-1-0	234	50
Mississippi	5-1-0	176	33	9-1-0	326	40
Tennessee	4-3-0	128	114	6-4-0	221	149
Georgia Tech	4-3-0	90	43	7-3-0	162	50
Florida	3-3-0	57	92	4-5-1	97	146
Auburn	3-4-0	94	109	6-4-0	174	137
Kentucky	2-4-0	81	101	5-5-0	138	123
Georgia	2-5-0	60	128	3-7-0	84	177
Mississippi State	1-5-0	34	112	5-5-0	111	135
Tulane	1-5-0	20	175	2-8-0	60	225
Vanderbilt	1-6-0	51	163	2-8-0	95	220

Bowls: Cotton (Texas 12, Mississippi 7); Gator (Penn State 30, Georgia Tech 15); Orange (LSU 25, Colorado 7); Sugar (Alabama 10, Arkansas 3)

1962

	Conference			Overall		
	W-L-T	Pts.	Opp.	W-L-T	Pts.	Opp.
Mississippi	6-0-0	117	19	9-0-0	230	40
Alabama	6-1-0	187	27	9-1-0	272	39
LSU	5-1-0	113	25	8-1-1	162	34
Georgia Tech	5-2-0	141	51	7-2-1	201	83
Florida	4-2-0	106	74	6-4-0	204	132
Auburn	4-3-0	88	134	6-3-1	173	168
Georgia	2-3-1	68	123	3-4-3	109	174
Kentucky	2-3-1	32	54	3-5-2	85	101
Mississippi State	2-5-0	60	101	3-6-0	76	132
Tennessee	2-6-0	108	120	4-6-0	179	134
Vanderbilt	1-6-0	34	141	1-9-0	62	215
Tulane	0-7-0	43	228	0-10-0	76	293

Bowls: Bluebonnet (Missouri 14, Georgia Tech 10); Cotton (LSU 13, Texas 0); Gator (Florida 17, Penn State 7); Orange (Alabama 17, Oklahoma 0); Sugar (Mississippi 17, Arkansas 13)

1963

	Conference W-L-T	Pts.	Opp.	Overall W-L-T	Pts.	Opp.
Mississippi	5-0-1	146	27	7-0-2	207	33
Auburn	6-1-0	119	74	9-1-0	189	103
Alabama	6-2-0	177	63	8-2-0	215	88
Mississippi State	4-1-2	96	65	6-2-2	169	82
LSU	4-2-0	78	57	7-3-0	135	98
Georgia Tech	4-3-0	101	76	7-3-0	173	89
Florida	3-3-1	61	71	6-3-1	130	120
Tennessee	3-5-0	85	108	5-5-0	168	121
Georgia	2-4-0	61	95	4-5-1	133	151
Vanderbilt	0-5-2	23	113	1-7-2	73	146
Kentucky	0-5-1	41	109	3-6-1	142	168
Tulane	0-6-1	23	153	1-8-1	43	191

Bowls: Bluebonnet (Baylor 14, LSU 7); Liberty (Mississippi State 16, North Carolina State 12); Orange (Nebraska 13, Auburn 7); Sugar (Alabama 12, Mississippi 7)

1964

	Conference W-L-T	Pts.	Opp.	Overall W-L-T	Pts.	Opp.
Alabama	8-0-0	188	60	10-0-0	233	67
Georgia	4-2-0	52	59	6-3-1	123	98
Florida	4-2-0	101	64	7-3-0	181	98
Kentucky	4-2-0	95	97	5-5-0	150	194
LSU	4-2-1	83	70	7-2-1	115	79
Auburn	3-3-0	43	65	6-4-0	123	91
Mississippi	2-4-1	113	104	5-4-1	210	113
Mississippi State	2-5-0	82	102	4-6-0	155	143
Vanderbilt	1-4-1	37	67	3-6-1	79	122
Tennessee	1-5-1	32	87	4-5-1	80	121
Tulane	1-5-0	31	82	3-7-0	79	147

Bowls: Bluebonnet (Tulsa 14, Mississippi 7); Orange (Texas 21, Alabama 17); Sugar (LSU 13, Syracuse 10); Sun (Georgia 7, Texas Tech 0)

1965

	Conference W-L-T	Pts.	Opp.	Overall W-L-T	Pts.	Opp.
Alabama	6-1-1	161	65	8-1-1	217	79
Auburn	4-1-1	113	115	5-4-1	165	162
Florida	4-2-0	126	76	7-3-0	221	129
Tennessee	3-1-2	73	40	7-1-2	193	92
Mississippi	5-3-0	129	77	6-4-0	166	108
LSU	3-3-0	144	109	7-3-0	251	157
Kentucky	3-3-0	120	90	6-4-0	202	160
Georgia	3-3-0	81	90	6-4-0	186	158
Vanderbilt	1-5-0	40	125	2-7-1	85	180
Tulane	1-5-0	37	192	2-8-0	71	268
Mississippi State	1-5-0	78	123	4-6-0	202	172

Bowls: Bluebonnet (Tennessee 27, Tulsa 6); Cotton (LSU 14, Arkansas 7); Liberty (Mississippi 13, Auburn 7); Orange (Alabama 39, Nebraska 28); Sugar (Missouri 20, Florida 18)

1966

	Conference			Overall		
	W-L-T	Pts.	Opp.	W-L-T	Pts.	Opp.
Alabama	6-0-0	149	37	10-0-0	267	37
Georgia	6-0-0	104	58	9-1-0	211	89
Florida	5-1-0	109	68	8-2-0	238	135
Mississippi	5-2-0	116	33	8-2-0	170	46
Tennessee	4-2-0	101	44	7-3-0	222	87
LSU	3-3-0	54	73	5-4-1	135	124
Kentucky	2-4-0	65	119	3-6-1	107	196
Auburn	1-5-0	60	127	4-6-0	104	162
Mississippi State	0-6-0	45	129	2-8-0	75	176
Vanderbilt	0-6-0	16	131	1-9-0	72	237

Bowls: Bluebonnet (Texas 19, Mississippi 0); Cotton (Georgia 24, Southern Methodist 9); Gator (Tennessee 18, Syracuse 12); Orange (Florida 27, Georgia Tech 12); Sugar (Alabama 34, Nebraska 7)

1967

	Conference			Overall		
	W-L-T	Pts.	Opp.	W-L-T	Pts.	Opp.
Tennessee	6-0-0	146	68	9-1-0	259	115
Alabama	5-1-0	96	61	8-1-1	188	111
Florida	4-2-0	123	120	6-4-0	201	161
Georgia	4-2-0	114	53	7-3-0	250	105
Mississippi	4-2-1	120	97	6-3-1	174	151
LSU	3-2-1	155	50	6-3-1	248	114
Auburn	3-3-0	126	79	6-4-0	237	123
Kentucky	1-6-0	65	187	2-8-0	111	230
Vanderbilt	0-6-0	71	143	2-7-1	165	241
Mississippi State	0-6-0	10	168	1-9-0	49	259

Bowls: Cotton (Texas A&M 20, Alabama 16); Liberty (North Carolina State 14, Georgia 7); Orange (Oklahoma 26, Tennessee 24); Sugar (LSU 20, Wyoming 13); Sun (UTEP 14, Mississippi 7)

1968

	Conference			Overall		
	W-L-T	Pts.	Opp.	W-L-T	Pts.	Opp.
Georgia	5-0-1	173	47	8-0-2	282	98
Tennessee	4-1-1	106	68	8-1-1	248	110
Alabama	4-2-0	108	63	8-2-0	174	104
LSU	4-2-0	64	62	7-3-0	190	144
Auburn	4-2-0	123	75	6-4-0	223	149
Florida	3-2-1	74	117	6-3-1	151	179
Mississippi	3-2-1	91	115	6-3-1	178	180
Vanderbilt	2-3-1	40	87	5-4-1	163	147
Mississippi State	0-4-2	60	114	0-8-2	146	260
Kentucky	0-7-0	59	150	3-7-0	141	206

Bowls: Cotton (Texas 36, Tennessee 13); Gator (Missouri 35, Alabama 10); Liberty (Mississippi 34, Virginia Tech 17); Peach (LSU 31, Florida State 27); Sugar (Arkansas 16, Georgia 2); Sun (Auburn 34, Arizona 10)

1969

	Conference			Overall		
	W-L-T	Pts.	Opp.	W-L-T	Pts.	Opp.
Tennessee	5-1-0	174	127	9-1-0	315	165
LSU	4-1-0	162	77	9-1-0	349	91

Auburn	5-2-0	238	123	8-2-0	363	137
Florida	3-1-1	144	112	8-1-1	329	187
Mississippi	4-2-0	178	105	7-3-0	307	140
Georgia	2-3-1	106	79	5-4-1	212	101
Vanderbilt	2-3-0	111	137	4-6-0	242	264
Alabama	2-4-0	121	175	6-4-0	281	221
Kentucky	1-6-0	61	224	2-8-0	104	295
Mississippi State	0-5-0	95	231	3-7-0	193	385

Bowls: Astro-Bluebonnet (Houston 36, Auburn 7); Gator (Florida 14, Tennessee 13); Liberty (Colorado 47, Alabama 33); Sugar (Mississippi 27, Arkansas 22); Sun (Nebraska 45, Georgia 6)

1970

	Conference W-L-T	Pts.	Opp.	Overall W-L-T	Pts.	Opp.
LSU	5-0-0	144	49	9-2-0	277	96
Tennessee	4-1-0	154	49	10-1-0	336	103
Auburn	5-2-0	247	128	8-2-0	355	149
Mississippi	4-2-0	156	157	7-3-0	285	220
Florida	3-3-0	118	190	7-4-0	224	256
Georgia	3-3-0	131	85	5-5-0	242	153
Alabama	3-4-0	176	151	6-5-0	310	240
Mississippi State	3-4-0	72	189	6-5-0	171	264
Vanderbilt	1-5-0	60	159	4-7-0	201	213
Kentucky	0-7-0	72	173	2-9-0	131	233

Bowls: Astro-Bluebonnet (Alabama 24, Oklahoma 24); Gator (Auburn 35, Mississippi 28); Orange (Nebraska 17, LSU 12); Sugar (Tennessee 34, Air Force 13)

1971

	Conference W-L-T	Pts.	Opp.	Overall W-L-T	Pts.	Opp.
Alabama	7-0-0	238	45	11-0-0	362	84
Auburn	5-1-0	160	94	9-1-0	313	142
Georgia	5-1-0	200	56	10-1-0	353	112
Mississippi	4-2-0	147	127	9-2-0	322	204
Tennessee	4-2-0	94	76	9-2-0	256	108
LSU	3-2-0	122	61	8-3-0	320	138
Vanderbilt	1-5-0	70	146	4-6-1	136	208
Florida	1-6-0	79	232	4-7-0	174	298
Kentucky	1-6-0	84	186	3-8-0	144	284
Mississippi State	1-7-0	80	251	2-9-0	120	311

Bowls: Gator (Georgia 7, North Carolina 3); Liberty (Tennessee 14, Arkansas 13); Orange (Nebraska 38, Alabama 6); Peach (Mississippi 41, Georgia Tech 18); Sugar (Oklahoma 40, Auburn 22); Sun (LSU 33, Iowa State 15)

1972

	Conference W-L-T	Pts.	Opp.	Overall W-L-T	Pts.	Opp.
Alabama	7-1-0	258	97	10-1-0	393	133
Auburn	6-1-0	120	103	9-1-0	185	138
LSU	4-1-1	114	75	9-1-1	235	121
Tennessee	4-2-0	94	44	9-2-0	273	83
Georgia	4-3-0	82	96	7-4-0	174	163
Florida	3-3-1	121	76	5-5-1	218	144
Mississippi	2-5-0	124	104	5-5-0	192	142

Kentucky	2-5-0	45	141	3-8-0	131	232
Mississippi State	1-6-0	81	202	4-7-0	197	254
Vanderbilt	0-6-0	60	161	3-8-0	129	243

Bowls: Astro-Bluebonnet (Tennessee 24, LSU 17); Cotton (Texas 17, Alabama 13); Gator (Auburn 24, Colorado 3)

1973

| | Conference | | | Overall | | |
	W-L-T	Pts.	Opp.	W-L-T	Pts.	Opp.
Alabama	8-0-0	268	70	11-0-0	454	89
LSU	5-1-0	156	72	9-2-0	258	153
Mississippi	4-3-0	124	137	6-5-0	202	177
Tennessee	3-3-0	127	136	8-3-0	272	219
Florida	3-4-0	82	141	7-4-0	180	171
Kentucky	3-4-0	148	130	5-6-0	226	196
Georgia	3-4-0	128	114	6-4-1	207	150
Auburn	2-5-0	73	140	6-5-0	153	159
Mississippi State	2-5-0	133	205	4-5-2	219	255
Vanderbilt	1-5-0	87	181	5-6-0	181	262

Bowls: Gator (Texas Tech 28, Tennessee 19); Orange (Penn State 16, LSU 9); Peach (Georgia 17, Maryland 16); Sugar (Notre Dame 24, Alabama 23); Sun (Missouri 34, Auburn 17); Tangerine (Miami-Ohio 16, Florida 7)

1974

| | Conference | | | Overall | | |
	W-L-T	Pts.	Opp.	W-L-T	Pts.	Opp.
Alabama	6-0-0	168	50	11-0-0	318	83
Auburn	4-2-0	120	88	9-2-0	260	126
Georgia	4-2-0	155	122	6-5-0	317	264
Kentucky	3-3-0	139	128	6-5-0	248	194
Florida	3-3-0	128	123	8-3-0	251	184
Mississippi State	3-3-0	109	121	8-3-0	301	200
Vanderbilt	2-3-1	122	144	7-3-1	307	193
Tennessee	2-3-1	90	144	6-3-2	204	178
LSU	2-4-0	77	91	5-5-1	202	168
Mississippi	0-6-0	65	192	3-8-0	135	241

Bowls: Gator (Auburn 27, Texas 3); Liberty (Tennessee 7, Maryland 3); Orange (Notre Dame 13, Alabama 11); Peach (Vanderbilt 6, Texas Tech 6); Sugar (Nebraska 13, Florida 10); Sun (Mississippi State 26, North Carolina 24); Tangerine (Miami-Ohio 21, Georgia 10)

1975

| | Conference | | | Overall | | |
	W-L-T	Pts.	Opp.	W-L-T	Pts.	Opp.
Alabama	6-0-0	174	40	10-1-0	361	66
Mississippi	5-1-0	104	78	6-5-0	170	162
Georgia	5-1-0	147	70	9-2-0	289	166
Florida	5-1-0	182	47	9-2-0	302	104
Tennessee	3-3-0	89	110	7-5-0	253	193
Vanderbilt	2-4-0	47	156	7-4-0	119	200
f-LSU	2-4-0	62	128	5-6-0	159	202
f-Auburn	2-4-0	80	138	4-6-1	174	243
Kentucky	0-6-0	59	131	2-8-1	132	188
f-Mississippi State	0-6-0	70	116	2-9-0	165	166

f-Includes forfeit imposed on Mississippi State by NCAA and SEC.

Bowls: Cotton (Arkansas 31, Georgia 10); Gator (Maryland 13, Florida 0); Sugar (Alabama 13, Penn State 6)

1976

	Conference			Overall		
	W-L-T	Pts.	Opp.	W-L-T	Pts.	Opp.
Georgia	5-1-0	183	55	10-1-0	324	118
f-Kentucky	5-1-0	84	61	8-3-0	188	151
Alabama	5-2-0	169	99	8-3-0	291	134
Florida	4-2-0	142	159	8-3-0	314	255
f-Mississippi	4-3-0	68	142	6-5-0	153	180
f-LSU	3-3-0	138	118	7-3-1	255	149
f-Auburn	3-3-0	93	146	4-7-0	194	267
Tennessee	2-4-0	104	101	6-5-0	237	162
Vanderbilt	0-6-0	47	167	2-9-0	131	282
f-Mississippi State	0-6-0	138	118	0-11-0	269	178

f-Includes forfeit imposed on Mississippi State by NCAA and SEC.
Bowls: Liberty (Alabama 36, UCLA 6); Peach (Kentucky 21, North Carolina 0); Sugar (Pittsburgh 27, Georgia 3); Sun (Texas A&M 37, Florida 14)

1977

	Conference			Overall		
	W-L-T	Pts.	Opp.	W-L-T	Pts.	Opp.
Alabama	7-0-0	209	76	10-1-0	345	133
Kentucky	6-0-0	152	50	10-1-0	252	111
f-Auburn	5-1-0	131	130	6-5-0	204	243
LSU	4-2-0	135	131	8-3-0	375	196
Florida	3-3-0	108	135	6-4-1	251	235
f-Mississippi	3-4-0	145	143	6-5-0	208	196
Georgia	2-4-0	79	132	5-6-0	157	191
Tennessee	1-5-0	112	136	4-7-0	229	229
Vanderbilt	0-6-0	67	172	2-9-0	141	276
f-Mississippi State	0-6-0	105	138	0-11-0	193	227

f-Includes forfeit imposed on Mississippi State by NCAA and SEC.
Bowls: Sugar (Alabama 35, Ohio State 6); Sun (Stanford 24, LSU 14)

1978

	Conference			Overall		
	W-L-T	Pts.	Opp.	W-L-T	Pts.	Opp.
Alabama	6-0-0	204	97	10-1-0	331	161
Georgia	5-0-1	160	90	9-1-1	268	162
Auburn	3-2-1	129	104	6-4-1	238	191
LSU	3-3-0	126	100	8-3-0	264	173
Tennessee	3-3-0	159	139	5-5-1	251	209
Florida	3-3-0	138	104	4-7-0	249	223
Kentucky	2-4-0	123	104	4-6-1	193	189
Mississippi	2-4-0	107	154	5-6-0	181	240
Mississippi State	2-4-0	71	137	6-5-0	232	205
Vanderbilt	0-6-0	72	260	2-9-0	164	418

Bowls: Bluebonnet (Stanford 25, Georgia 22); Liberty (Missouri 20, LSU 15); Sugar (Alabama 14, Penn State 7)

1979

	Conference			Overall		
	W-L-T	Pts.	Opp.	W-L-T	Pts.	Opp.
Alabama	6-0-0	185	45	11-0-0	359	58
Georgia	5-1-0	142	94	6-5-0	206	189

Team	W-L-T	Pts.	Opp.	W-L-T	Pts.	Opp.
Auburn	4-2-0	153	124	8-3-0	330	238
LSU	4-2-0	106	73	6-5-0	241	141
Tennessee	3-3-0	132	143	7-4-0	289	208
Kentucky	3-3-0	116	79	5-6-0	180	143
Mississippi	3-3-0	169	123	4-7-0	251	298
Mississippi State	2-4-0	74	92	3-8-0	162	179
Vanderbilt	0-6-0	96	262	1-10-0	179	418
Florida	0-6-0	39	167	0-10-1	106	265

Bowls: Bluebonnet (Purdue 27, Tennessee 22); Sugar (Alabama 24, Arkansas 9); Tangerine (LSU 34, Wake Forest 10)

1980

	Conference			Overall		
	W-L-T	Pts.	Opp.	W-L-T	Pts.	Opp.
Georgia	6-0-0	169	78	11-0-0	316	127
Mississippi State	5-1-0	143	104	9-2-0	284	216
y-Alabama	5-1-0	178	31	9-2-0	322	96
LSU	4-2-0	138	133	7-4-0	213	193
Florida	4-2-0	102	93	7-4-0	221	166
Tennessee	3-3-0	162	90	5-6-0	256	189
y-Mississippi	2-4-0	101	123	3-8-0	263	266
Kentucky	1-5-0	70	161	3-8-0	167	280
Auburn	0-6-0	87	173	5-6-0	235	238
Vanderbilt	0-6-0	51	215	2-9-0	140	352

y-Alabama vs. Ole Miss did not count toward standings.

Bowls: Cotton (Alabama 30, Baylor 2); Sugar (Georgia 17, Notre Dame 10); Sun (Nebraska 31, Mississippi State 17); Tangerine (Florida 35, Maryland 20)

1981

	Conference			Overall		
	W-L-T	Pts.	Opp.	W-L-T	Pts.	Opp.
Georgia	6-0-0	205	62	10-1-0	352	98
y-Alabama	6-0-0	150	70	9-1-1	284	137
Mississippi State	4-2-0	122	76	7-4-0	278	137
Florida	3-3-0	145	93	7-4-0	278	140
Tennessee	3-3-0	105	164	7-4-0	216	244
Auburn	2-4-0	87	102	5-6-0	186	166
Kentucky	2-4-0	70	117	3-8-0	186	244
y-Ole Miss	1-4-1	101	185	4-6-1	167	284
LSU	1-4-1	84	121	3-7-1	167	281
Vanderbilt	1-5-0	108	188	4-7-0	211	281

y-Alabama vs. Ole Miss did not count toward standings.

Bowls: Cotton (Texas 14, Alabama 12); Garden State (Tennessee 28, Wisconsin 21); Hall of Fame (Mississippi State 10, Kansas 0); Peach (West Virginia 26, Florida 6); Sugar (Pittsburgh 24, Georgia 20)

1982

	Conference			Overall		
	W-L-T	Pts.	Opp.	W-L-T	Pts.	Opp.
Georgia	6-0-0	179	73	11-0-0	315	133
LSU	4-1-1	171	92	8-2-1	365	170
Auburn	4-2-0	131	94	8-3-0	241	171
Vanderbilt	4-2-0	135	121	8-3-0	265	206
Tennessee	3-2-1	152	128	6-4-1	259	211

Florida	3-3-0	127	146	8-3-0	272	200
Alabama	3-3-0	146	125	7-4-0	317	201
Mississippi State	2-4-0	122	145	5-6-0	352	244
Ole Miss	0-6-0	69	196	4-7-0	208	262
Kentucky	0-6-0	57	169	0-10-1	96	287

Bowls: Bluebonnet (Arkansas 28, Florida 24); Hall of Fame (Air Force 36, Vanderbilt 28); Liberty (Alabama 21, Illinois 15); Orange (Nebraska 21, LSU 20); Peach (Iowa 28, Tennessee 22); Sugar (Penn State 27, Georgia 23); Tangerine (Auburn 33, Boston College 26)

1983

| | Conference | | | Overall | | |
	W-L-T	Pts.	Opp.	W-L-T	Pts.	Opp.
Auburn	6-0-0	178	96	10-1-0	302	179
Georgia	5-1-0	140	74	9-1-1	264	149
Florida	4-2-0	149	84	8-2-1	290	150
Tennessee	4-2-0	129	114	8-3-0	252	142
Alabama	4-2-0	205	132	7-4-0	338	222
f-Ole Miss	4-2-0	96	147	7-4-0	176	255
Kentucky	2-4-0	87	151	6-4-1	212	217
Mississippi State	1-5-0	118	168	3-8-0	196	279
LSU	0-6-0	112	176	4-7-0	251	253
Vanderbilt	0-6-0	93	165	2-9-0	183	274

f-includes forfeits imposed on Tulane by NCAA.

Bowls: Cotton (Georgia 10, Texas 9); Florida Citrus (Tennessee 30, Maryland 23); Gator (Florida 14, Iowa 6); Hall of Fame (West Virginia 20, Kentucky 16); Independence (Air Force 9, Mississippi 3); Sugar (Auburn 9, Michigan 7); Sun (Alabama 28, Southern Methodist 7)

1984

| | Conference | | | Overall | | |
	W-L-T	Pts.	Opp.	W-L-T	Pts.	Opp.
v-Florida	5-0-1	167	83	9-1-1	341	170
LSU	4-1-1	153	117	8-2-1	305	198
Auburn	4-2-0	109	97	8-4-0	338	239
Georgia	4-2-0	153	116	7-4-0	246	213
Kentucky	3-3-0	95	141	8-3-0	273	202
Tennessee	3-3-0	150	146	7-3-1	300	248
Vanderbilt	2-4-0	160	193	5-6-0	276	277
Alabama	2-4-0	117	134	5-6-0	226	208
Ole Miss	1-5-0	115	148	4-6-1	194	203
Mississippi State	1-5-0	85	130	4-7-0	198	230

v-championship vacated.

Bowls: Florida Citrus (Georgia 17, Florida State 17); Hall of Fame (Kentucky 20, Wisconsin 19); Liberty (Auburn 21, Arkansas 15); Sugar (Nebraska 28, LSU 20); Sun (Maryland 28, Tennessee 27)

1985

| | Conference | | | Overall | | |
	W-L-T	Pts.	Opp.	W-L-T	Pts.	Opp.
Tennessee	5-1-0	170	65	8-1-2	290	133
n-Florida	5-1-0	105	79	9-1-1	286	162
LSU	4-1-1	104	56	9-1-1	220	113
Alabama	4-1-1	157	117	8-2-1	294	178
Georgia	3-2-1	138	87	7-3-1	284	158
Auburn	3-3-0	139	96	8-3-0	328	172
Ole Miss	2-4-0	115	172	4-6-1	210	276

	W-L-T	Pts.	Opp.	W-L-T	Pts.	Opp.
Vanderbilt	1-4-1	78	191	3-7-1	166	308
Kentucky	1-5-0	76	143	5-6-0	194	211
Mississippi State	0-6-0	120	196	5-6-0	257	288

n-Not eligible for championship.

Bowls: Aloha (Alabama 24, Southern California 3); Cotton (Texas A&M 36, Auburn 16); Liberty (Baylor 21, LSU 7); Sugar (Tennessee 35, Miami 7); Sun (Georgia 13, Arizona 13)

1986

	Conference			Overall		
	W-L-T	Pts.	Opp.	W-L-T	Pts.	Opp.
LSU	5-1-0	156	78	9-2-0	291	155
Auburn	4-2-0	154	78	9-2-0	379	115
Alabama	4-2-0	184	83	9-3-0	323	157
Georgia	4-2-0	136	105	8-3-0	285	206
Ole Miss	4-2-0	126	83	7-3-1	220	150
Tennessee	3-3-0	144	156	6-5-0	272	235
Florida	2-4-0	86	111	6-5-0	223	173
Mississippi State	2-4-0	55	177	6-5-0	195	275
Kentucky	2-4-0	91	141	5-5-1	228	207
Vanderbilt	0-6-0	89	208	1-10-0	193	347

Bowls: Florida Citrus (Auburn 16, Southern California 7); Hall of Fame (Boston College 27, Georgia 23); Independence (Mississippi 20, Texas Tech 17); Liberty (Tennessee 21, Minnesota 14); Sugar (Nebraska 30, LSU 13); Sun (Alabama 28, Washington 6)

1987

	Conference			Overall		
	W-L-T	Pts.	Opp.	W-L-T	Pts.	Opp.
Auburn	5-0-1	172	59	9-1-1	298	116
LSU	5-1-0	159	91	9-1-1	335	171
Tennessee	4-1-1	197	142	9-2-1	395	224
Georgia	4-2-0	157	115	8-3-0	291	187
Alabama	4-2-0	128	106	7-4-0	244	185
Florida	3-3-0	114	96	6-5-0	283	158
Kentucky	1-5-0	123	146	5-6-0	258	185
Vanderbilt	1-5-0	150	239	4-7-0	286	355
Mississippi State	1-5-0	82	189	4-7-0	169	259
Ole Miss	1-5-0	108	207	3-8-0	223	309

Bowls: Aloha (UCLA 20, Florida 16); Gator (LSU 30, South Carolina 13); Hall of Fame (Michigan 28, Alabama 24); Liberty (Georgia 20, Arkansas 17); Peach (Tennessee 27, Indiana 22); Sugar (Auburn 16, Syracuse 16)

1988

	Conference			Overall		
	W-L-T	Pts.	Opp.	W-L-T	Pts.	Opp.
Auburn	6-1-0	148	43	10-1-0	331	79
LSU	6-1-0	132	87	8-3-0	239	181
Georgia	5-2-0	193	125	8-3-0	324	185
Alabama	4-3-0	196	147	8-3-0	288	160
Florida	4-3-0	99	106	6-5-0	254	175
Ole Miss	3-4-0	150	160	5-6-0	221	223
Tennessee	3-4-0	114	171	5-6-0	212	286
Kentucky	2-5-0	122	141	5-6-0	217	208
Vanderbilt	2-5-0	128	178	3-8-0	202	277
Mississippi State	0-7-0	98	222	1-10-0	172	332

Bowls: All-American (Florida 14, Illinois 10); Gator (Georgia 34, Michigan State 27); Hall of Fame (Syracuse 23, LSU 10); Sugar (Florida State 13, Auburn 7); Sun (Alabama 29, Army 28)

1989

	Conference			Overall		
	W-L-T	Pts.	Opp.	W-L-T	Pts.	Opp.
Alabama	6-1-0	219	130	10-1-0	332	184
Tennessee	6-1-0	194	155	10-1-0	315	190
Auburn	6-1-0	122	69	9-2-0	253	117
Florida	4-3-0	145	103	7-4-0	261	168
Ole Miss	4-3-0	164	189	7-4-0	267	285
Georgia	4-3-0	139	109	6-5-0	233	179
Kentucky	2-5-0	118	174	6-5-0	212	220
LSU	2-5-0	174	180	4-7-0	295	252
Mississippi State	1-6-0	89	153	5-6-0	205	207
Vanderbilt	0-7-0	85	187	1-10-0	162	265

Bowls: Cotton (Tennessee 31, Arkansas 27); Freedom (Washington 34, Florida 7); Hall of Fame (Auburn 31, Ohio State 14); Liberty (Mississippi 42, Air Force 29); Peach (Syracuse 19, Georgia 18); Sugar (Miami 33, Alabama 25)

1990

	Conference			Overall		
	W-L-T	Pts.	Opp.	W-L-T	Pts.	Opp.
n-Florida	6-1-0	221	116	9-2-0	387	171
Tennessee	5-1-1	230	106	8-2-2	442	198
Ole Miss	5-2-0	140	119	9-2-0	257	191
Alabama	5-2-0	159	78	7-4-0	253	127
Auburn	4-2-1	170	132	7-3-1	256	194
Kentucky	3-4-0	163	214	4-7-0	228	316
LSU	2-5-0	112	168	5-6-0	183	238
Georgia	2-5-0	122	187	4-7-0	185	293
Mississippi State	1-6-0	102	173	5-6-0	207	236
Vanderbilt	1-6-0	140	266	1-10-0	227	457

n-Not eligible for championship.

Bowls: Fiesta (Louisville 34, Alabama 7); Gator (Michigan 35, Mississippi 3); Peach (Auburn 27, Indiana 23); Sugar (Tennessee 23, Virginia 22)

1991

	Conference			Overall		
	W-L-T	Pts.	Opp.	W-L-T	Pts.	Opp.
Florida	7-0-0	226	74	10-1-0	361	152
Alabama	6-1-0	128	101	10-1-0	294	118
Tennessee	5-2-0	190	136	9-2-0	335	221
Georgia	4-3-0	192	163	8-3-0	312	204
Mississippi State	4-3-0	145	119	7-4-0	276	156
LSU	3-4-0	116	157	5-6-0	248	263
Vanderbilt	3-4-0	127	192	5-6-0	205	267
Auburn	2-5-0	128	170	5-6-0	233	214
Ole Miss	1-6-0	148	189	5-6-0	242	223
Kentucky	0-7-0	113	212	3-8-0	190	268

Bowls: Blockbuster (Alabama 30, Colorado 25); Fiesta (Penn State 42, Tennessee 17); Independence (Georgia 24, Arkansas 15); Liberty (Air Force 38, Mississippi State 15); Sugar (Notre Dame 39, Florida 28)

1992

Eastern Division	Conference W-L-T	Pts.	Opp.	Overall W-L-T	Pts.	Opp.
Florida	6-2-0	188	164	8-4-0	288	274
Georgia	6-2-0	231	117	9-2-0	352	141
Tennessee	5-3-0	205	149	8-3-0	309	173
South Carolina	3-5-0	104	194	5-6-0	160	240
Kentucky	2-6-0	136	224	4-7-0	207	280
Vanderbilt	2-6-0	149	193	4-7-0	224	277

Western Division	W-L-T	Pts.	Opp.	W-L-T	Pts.	Opp.
Alabama	8-0-0	237	78	12-0-0	332	109
Ole Miss	5-3-0	165	· 147	8-3-0	230	174
Mississippi State	4-4-0	131	144	7-4-0	235	176
Arkansas	3-4-1	144	153	3-7-1	172	209
Auburn	2-5-1	132	173	5-5-1	228	205
LSU	1-7-0	115	201	2-9-0	175	261

SEC Championship Game: Alabama 28, Florida 21
Bowls: Gator (Florida 27, North Carolina State 10); Florida Citrus (Georgia 21, Ohio State 14); Hall of Fame (Tennessee 38, Boston College 23); Liberty (Mississippi 13, Air Force 0); Peach (North Carolina 21, Mississippi State 17); Sugar (Alabama 34, Miami 13)

1993

Eastern Division	Conference W-L-T	Pts.	Opp.	Overall W-L-T	Pts.	Opp.
Florida	7-1-0	318	171	10-2	472	237
f-Tennessee	7-1-0	324	115	10-1	471	144
Kentucky	4-4-0	158	168	6-5	207	195
Georgia	2-6-0	179	218	5-6	328	289
f-South Carolina	3-5-0	114	192	5-6	188	214
f-Vanderbilt	2-6-0	52	264	5-6	137	290

Western Division	W-L-T	Pts.	Opp.	W-L-T	Pts.	Opp.
n-Auburn	8-0-0	228	147	11-0-0	353	192
Arkansas	4-3-1	131	185	6-4-1	165	208
LSU	3-5-0	128	257	5-6-0	190	308
f-Ole Miss	4-4-0	155	116	6-5-0	242	142
f-Mississippi State	3-4-1	155	175	4-5-2	241	245
f-Alabama	0-8-0	176	110	0-12-0	316	158

f-Includes forfeits imposed on Alabama by NCAA.
n-Not eligible for championship.
SEC Championship Game: Florida 28, Alabama 13
Bowls: Florida Citrus (Penn State 31, Tennessee 13); Gator (Alabama 24, North Carolina 10); Peach (Clemson 14, Kentucky 13); Sugar (Florida 41, West Virginia 14)

1994

Eastern Division	Conference W-L-T	Pts.	Opp.	Overall W-L-T	Pts.	Opp.
Florida	7-1-0	341	136	10-1-1	521	205
Tennessee	5-3-0	261	138	7-4-0	318	185
South Carolina	4-4-0	170	186	6-5-0	276	255
Georgia	3-4-1	211	249	6-4-1	351	283

	W-L-T	Pts.	Opp.	W-L-T	Pts.	Opp.
Vanderbilt	2-6-0	117	223	5-6-0	203	277
Kentucky	0-8-0	86	311	1-10-0	149	405

Western Division	W-L-T	Pts.	Opp.	W-L-T	Pts.	Opp.
Alabama	8-0-0	176	120	11-1-0	281	173
n-Auburn	6-1-1	239	166	9-1-1	359	199
Mississippi State	5-3-0	217	203	8-3-0	349	234
LSU	3-5-0	188	208	4-7-0	268	271
Arkansas	2-6-0	136	151	4-7-0	215	208
Ole Miss	2-6-0	133	185	4-7-0	246	205

n-Not eligible for championship.
SEC Championship Game: Florida 24, Alabama 23
Bowls: Carquest (South Carolina 24, West Virginia 21); Florida Citrus (Alabama 24, Ohio State 17); Gator (Tennessee 45, Virginia Tech 23); Peach (North Carolina State 28, Mississippi State 24); Sugar (Florida State 23, Florida 17)

1995

Eastern Division	Conference W-L-T	Pts.	Opp.	Overall W-L-T	Pts.	Opp.
Florida	8-0-0	396	136	12-0-0	534	201
Tennessee	7-1-0	311	207	10-1-0	411	214
Georgia	3-5-0	154	200	6-5-0	233	247
South Carolina	2-5-1	239	314	4-6-1	401	387
Kentucky	2-6-0	163	186	4-7-0	223	269
Vanderbilt	1-7-0	90	218	2-9-0	122	281

Western Division	W-L-T	Pts.	Opp.	W-L-T	Pts.	Opp.
Arkansas	6-2-0	209	213	8-4-0	274	263
Auburn	5-3-0	276	203	8-3-0	424	240
n-Alabama	5-3-0	171	138	8-3-0	260	188
LSU	4-3-1	143	113	6-4-1	279	160
n-Ole Miss	3-5-0	99	178	6-5-0	209	208
Mississippi State	1-7-0	171	284	3-8-0	261	357

n-Not eligible for championship.
SEC Championship Game: Florida 34, Arkansas 3
Bowls: Carquest (North Carolina 20, Arkansas 10); Fiesta (Nebraska 62, Florida 24); Florida Citrus (Tennessee 20, Ohio State 14); Independence (LSU 45, Michigan State 26), Outback (Penn State 43, Auburn 14); Peach (Virginia 34, Georgia 27)

1996

Eastern Division	Conference W-L-T	Pts.	Opp.	Overall W-L-T	Pts.	Opp.
Florida	8-0	376	112	11-1	559	201
Tennessee	7-1	275	113	9-2	389	157
South Carolina	4-4	171	170	6-5	245	238
Georgia	3-5	189	224	5-6	230	257
Kentucky	3-5	118	260	4-7	138	322
Vanderbilt	0-8	65	198	2-9	122	234

Western Division	W-L-T	Pts.	Opp.	W-L-T	Pts.	Opp.
Alabama	6-2	204	100	9-3	299	181
LSU	6-2	192	145	9-2	325	203

Auburn	4-4	247	224	7-4	366	248
Mississippi State	3-5	136	181	5-6	249	229
Arkansas	2-6	88	202	4-7	174	267
n-Ole Miss	2-6	96	228	5-6	203	270

n-Not eligible for championship.
SEC Championship Game: Florida 45, Alabama 30
Bowls: Florida Citrus (Tennessee 45, Northwestern 28); Independence (Auburn 32, Army 29); Outback (Alabama 17, Michigan 14); Peach (LSU 10, Clemson 7); Sugar (Florida 52, Florida State 20)

1997

Eastern Division	Conference W-L-T	Pts.	Opp.	Overall W-L-T	Pts.	Opp.
Tennessee	7-1	255	154	11-1	411	244
Georgia	6-2	240	155	9-2	347	189
Florida	6-2	274	158	9-2	419	199
South Carolina	3-5	178	201	5-6	258	279
Kentucky	2-6	212	317	5-6	348	362
Vanderbilt	0-8	52	169	3-8	138	204

Western Division	W-L-T	Pts.	Opp.	W-L-T	Pts.	Opp.
Auburn	6-2	172	159	9-3	319	233
LSU	6-2	229	152	8-3	346	179
Ole Miss	4-4	145	147	7-4	233	209
Mississippi State	4-4	154	167	7-4	226	215
Arkansas	2-6	127	224	4-7	181	284
Alabama	2-6	157	192	4-7	246	248

SEC Championship Game: Tennessee 30, Auburn 29
Bowls: Florida Citrus (Florida 21, Penn State 6); Independence (LSU 27, Notre Dame 9); Motor City (Mississippi 34, Marshall 31); Orange (Nebraska 42, Tennessee 17); Outback (Georgia 33, Wisconsin 6); Peach (Auburn 21, Clemson 17)

1998

Eastern Division	Conference W-L-T	Pts.	Opp.	Overall W-L-T	Pts.	Opp.
Tennessee	8-0	271	106	12-0	408	173
Florida	7-1	246	112	9-2	349	155
Georgia	6-2	166	156	8-3	257	189
Kentucky	4-4	266	281	6-5	417	349
Vanderbilt	1-7	66	290	2-9	142	369
South Carolina	0-8	129	258	1-10	207	330

Western Division	W-L-T	Pts.	Opp.	W-L-T	Pts.	Opp.
Mississippi State	6-2	235	140	8-4	349	218
Arkansas	6-2	254	139	9-2	359	182
Alabama	4-4	153	176	7-4	244	252
Ole Miss	3-5	137	188	6-5	245	256
LSU	2-6	206	214	4-7	337	279
Auburn	1-7	124	193	3-8	166	235

SEC Championship Game: Tennessee 24, Mississippi State 14
Bowls: Cotton (Texas 38, Mississippi State 11); Fiesta (Tennessee 23, Florida State 16); Florida Citrus (Michigan 45, Arkansas 31); Independence (Mississippi 35, Texas Tech 18); Music City

(Virginia Tech 35, Alabama 7); Orange (Florida 31, Syracuse 10); Outback (Penn State 26, Kentucky 14); Peach (Georgia 35, Virginia 33)

1999

Eastern Division	Conference W-L-T	Pts.	Opp.	Overall W-L-T	Pts.	Opp.
Florida	7-1	226	118	9-3	369	235
Tennessee	6-2	251	116	9-2	348	163
Georgia	5-3	198	204	7-4	311	282
Kentucky	4-4	198	218	6-5	315	323
Vanderbilt	2-6	129	211	5-6	252	256
South Carolina	0-8	63	216	0-11	87	278

Western Division	W-L-T	Pts.	Opp.	W-L-T	Pts.	Opp.
Alabama	7-1	210	170	10-2	344	230
Mississippi State	6-2	156	121	9-2	238	149
Ole Miss	4-4	235	176	7-4	296	203
Arkansas	4-4	198	196	7-4	326	208
Auburn	2-6	153	188	5-6	233	236
LSU	1-7	135	218	3-8	223	259

SEC Championship Game: Alabama 34, Florida 7
Bowls: Cotton (Arkansas 27, Texas 6); Fiesta (Nebraska 31, Tennessee 21); Florida Citrus (Michigan State 37, Florida 34); Independence (Mississippi 27, Oklahoma 25); Music City (Syracuse 20, Kentucky 13); Orange (Michigan 35, Alabama 34 OT); Outback (Georgia 28, Purdue 25 OT); Peach (Mississippi State 17, Clemson 7)

2000

Eastern Division	Conference W-L-T	Pts.	Opp.	Overall W-L-T	Pts.	Opp.
Florida	7-1	318	181	10-2	448	236
Georgia	5-3	213	164	7-4	294	198
South Carolina	5-3	173	152	7-4	259	174
Tennessee	5-3	251	176	8-3	359	212
Vanderbilt	1-7	120	223	3-8	193	273
Kentucky	0-8	152	300	2-9	254	383

Western Division	W-L-T	Pts.	Opp.	W-L-T	Pts.	Opp.
Auburn	6-2	178	144	9-3	288	235
LSU	5-3	196	195	7-4	292	221
Ole Miss	4-4	187	210	7-4	314	280
Mississippi State	4-4	225	199	7-4	347	265
Arkansas	3-5	136	221	6-5	264	258
Alabama	3-5	166	150	3-8	228	246

SEC Championship Game: Florida 28, Auburn 6
Bowls: Cotton (Kansas State 35, Tennessee 21); Florida Citrus (Michigan 31, Auburn 28); Independence (Mississippi State 43, Texas A&M 41 OT); Las Vegas (UNLV 31, Arkansas 14); Music City (West Virginia 49, Ole Miss 38); Oahu (Georgia 37, Virginia 14); Outback (South Carolina 24, Ohio State 7); Peach (LSU 28, Georgia Tech 14); Sugar (Miami 37, Florida 20)

2001

Eastern Division	Conference W-L-T	Pts.	Opp.	Overall W-L-T	Pts.	Opp.
Tennessee	7-1	225	148	10-2	355	234
Florida	6-2	341	122	9-2	482	155

	W-L-T	Pts.	Opp.	W-L-T	Pts.	Opp.
South Carolina	5-3	189	160	8-3	279	202
Georgia	5-3	204	167	8-3	315	208
Kentucky	1-7	206	285	2-9	259	367
Vanderbilt	0-8	128	315	2-9	226	402
Western Division	**W-L-T**	**Pts.**	**Opp.**	**W-L-T**	**Pts.**	**Opp.**
LSU	5-3	231	203	9-3	371	268
Auburn	5-3	152	193	7-4	244	265
Alabama	4-4	203	177	6-5	304	219
Arkansas	4-4	208	220	7-4	291	269
Ole Miss	4-4	262	262	7-4	391	310
Mississippi State	2-6	119	216	3-8	196	288

SEC Championship Game: LSU 31, Tennessee 20

Bowls: Cotton (Oklahoma 10, Arkansas 3); Florida Citrus (Tennessee 45, Michigan 17); Independence (Alabama 14, Iowa State 13); Music City (Boston College 20, Georgia 16); Orange (Florida 56, Maryland 23); Outback (South Carolina 31, Ohio State 28); Peach (North Carolina 16, Auburn 10); Sugar (LSU 47, Illinois 34)

2002

	Conference			Overall		
Eastern Division	**W-L-T**	**Pts.**	**Opp.**	**W-L-T**	**Pts.**	**Opp.**
Georgia	7-1	226	144	12-1	424	199
Florida	6-2	191	160	8-4	306	241
Tennessee	5-3	182	147	8-4	293	197
South Carolina	3-5	108	156	5-7	225	262
n-Kentucky	3-5	215	228	7-5	385	301
Vanderbilt	0-8	121	260	2-10	221	368
Western Division	**W-L-T**	**Pts.**	**Opp.**	**W-L-T**	**Pts.**	**Opp.**
n-Alabama	6-2	227	99	10-3	377	200
Arkansas	5-3	223	184	9-4	356	248
Auburn	5-3	213	150	8-4	375	222
LSU	5-3	179	160	8-4	303	203
Ole Miss	3-5	175	230	6-6	324	308
Mississippi State	0-8	123	265	3-9	227	339

n-Not eligible for championship.

SEC Championship Game: Georgia 30, Arkansas 3

Bowls: Capital One (Auburn 13, Penn State 9); Cotton (Texas 35, LSU 20); Independence (Ole Miss 27, Nebraska 23); Music City (Minnesota 29, Arkansas 14); Outback (Michigan 38, Florida 30); Peach (Maryland 30, Tennessee 3); Sugar (Georgia 26, Florida State 13)

2003

	Conference			Overall		
Eastern Division	**W-L-T**	**Pts.**	**Opp.**	**W-L-T**	**Pts.**	**Opp.**
Georgia	6-2	215	102	10-3	337	176
Tennessee	6-2	260	170	10-2	351	212
Florida	6-2	178	152	8-4	373	234
South Carolina	2-6	164	227	5-7	268	314
Vanderbilt	1-7	126	261	2-10	235	358
Kentucky	1-7	198	244	4-8	328	321

Western Division	W-L-T	Pts.	Opp.	W-L-T	Pts.	Opp.
LSU	7-1	228	90	12-1	454	140
Ole Miss	7-1	218	150	9-3	411	257
Auburn	5-3	190	148	7-5	314	198
Arkansas	4-4	247	223	8-4	409	291
n-Alabama	2-6	216	237	4-9	331	333
Mississippi State	1-7	93	329	2-10	225	471

n-Not eligible for championship.

SEC Championship Game: LSU 34, Georgia 13

Bowls: Capital One (Georgia 34, Purdue 27 OT); Cotton (Ole Miss 31, Oklahoma State 28); Independence (Arkansas 27, Missouri 14); Music City (Auburn 28, Wisconsin 14); Outback (Iowa 37, Florida 17); Peach (Clemson 27, Tennessee 14); Sugar (LSU 21, Oklahoma 14)

2004

Eastern Division	Conference			Overall		
	W-L-T	Pts.	Opp.	W-L-T	Pts.	Opp.
Tennessee	7-1	215	199	9-3	340	288
Georgia	6-2	231	133	9-2	311	177
Florida	4-4	251	187	7-4	372	226
South Carolina	4-4	185	190	6-5	243	229
Kentucky	1-7	106	253	2-9	173	341
Vanderbilt	1-7	133	213	2-9	212	286

Western Division	W-L-T	Pts.	Opp.	W-L-T	Pts.	Opp.
Auburn	8-0	247	96	12-0	401	134
LSU	6-2	220	131	9-2	319	175
Arkansas	3-5	196	215	5-6	328	270
Alabama	3-5	152	149	6-5	279	169
Ole Miss	3-5	142	200	4-7	215	278
n-Mississippi State	2-6	125	237	3-8	173	280

n-Not eligible for championship.

SEC Championship Game: Auburn 38, Tennessee 28

Bowls: Capital One (Iowa 30, LSU 25); Cotton (Tennessee 38, Texas A&M 7); Music City (Minnesota 20, Alabama 16); Outback (Georgia 24, Wisconsin 21); Peach (Miami 27, Florida 10); Sugar (Auburn 16, Virginia Tech 13)

2005

Eastern Division	Conference			Overall		
	W-L-T	Pts.	Opp.	W-L-T	Pts.	Opp.
Georgia	6-2	209	134	10-3	384	213
South Carolina	5-3	175	193	7-5	284	279
Florida	5-3	205	178	9-3	343	226
Vanderbilt	3-5	223	271	5-6	299	321
Tennessee	2-5	147	130	5-6	205	205
Kentucky	2-6	160	277	3-7	239	375

Western Division	W-L-T	Pts.	Opp.	W-L-T	Pts.	Opp.
LSU	7-1	214	114	11-2	383	185
Auburn	7-1	262	122	9-3	386	186
Alabama	6-2	159	87	10-2	263	128
Arkansas	2-6	173	169	4-7	283	271

Mississippi State	1-7	78	211	3-8	153	259
Ole Miss	1-7	97	208	4-7	148	245

SEC Championship Game: Georgia 34, LSU 14

Bowls: Capital One (Wisconsin 24, Auburn 10); Cotton (Alabama 13, Texas Tech 10); Independence (Missouri 38, South Carolina 31); Outback (Florida 31, Iowa 24); Peach (LSU 40, Miami 3); Sugar (West Virginia 38, Georgia 35)

Appointed Conference Games

While the SEC rule requiring six football games with member schools was in effect, 16 games with outside schools were appointed to serve as conference games to avoid a violation for the members. The won-loss records, but not the point totals, are included in the conference standings.

1954: Arkansas 6, Ole Miss 0

1958: Ole Miss 56, Houston 7

1964: Miami 21, Tulane 0

1965: Georgia 23, Clemson 9; Tennessee 24, South Carolina 3

1966: Florida 31, Tulane 10; Georgia 28, North Carolina 3; LSU 21, Tulane 7; Tennessee 29, South Carolina 17; Vanderbilt 21, Tulane 3

1967: Georgia 24, Clemson 17; Tulane 27, Vanderbilt 14

1968: Florida 24, Tulane 3; LSU 10, Texas Christian 7; LSU 34, Tulane 10; Mississippi State 28, Texas Tech 28; Vanderbilt 21, Tulane 7

· Appendix C ·

Bowls

ALL-TIME BOWL APPEARANCES (Through 2005 Season)

1.	**Alabama**	**53 (30-20-3)**
2.	**Tennessee**	**45 (24-21)**
	Texas	45 (22-21-2)
4.	Southern California	44 (28-16)
5.	Nebraska	43 (22-21)
6.	**Georgia**	**41 (22-16-3)**
7.	Oklahoma	39 (24-14-1)
8.	Penn State	38 (24-12-2)
9.	**LSU**	**37 (18-18-1)**
	Ohio State	37 (18-19)
	Michigan	37 (18-19)
12.	**Arkansas**	**34 (11-20-3)**
	Georgia Tech	34 (22-12)
	Florida State	34 (19-13-2)
15.	**Florida**	**33 (15-18)**
16.	**Auburn**	**32 (17-13-2)**
17.	**Ole Miss**	**31 (19-12)**
18.	Miami	30 (17-13)
19.	Washington	29 (14-14-1)
	Texas Tech	29 (8-20-1)
21.	Texas A&M	28 (13-15)
	Clemson	28 (15-13)
23.	Colorado	27 (12-15)
	UCLA	27 (13-13-1)
25.	Notre Dame	26 (13-13)

ALL-TIME BOWL VICTORIES
(Through 2005 Season)

1.	**Alabama**	**30-20-3**
2.	Southern California	28-16
3.	Penn State	24-11-2
	Oklahoma	24-14-1
	Tennessee	**24-21**
6.	**Georgia**	**22-16-3**
	Texas	22-21-2
	Georgia Tech	22-12
	Nebraska	22-21
10.	Florida State	19-13-2
	Ole Miss	**19-12**

12.	**LSU**	**18-18-1**
	Michigan	18-19
	Ohio State	18-19
15.	**Auburn**	**17-13-2**
	Miami	17-13
17.	**Florida**	**15-18**
	Clemson	15-13
19.	Washington	14-14-1
20.	UCLA	13-13-1
	Notre Dame	13-13
	Texas A&M	13-15
23.	Syracuse	12-8-1
	Colorado	12-15
25.	**Arkansas**	**11-20-3**
	North Carolina	11-14

BOWL GAMES

Alabama (30-20-3)

1926	Rose	Alabama 20, Washington 19
1927	Rose	Alabama 7, Stanford 7
1931	Rose	Alabama 24, Washington State 0
1935	Rose	Alabama 29, Stanford 13
1938	Rose	California 13, Alabama 0
1942	Cotton	Alabama 29, Texas A&M 21
1943	Orange	Alabama 37, Boston College 21
1945	Sugar	Duke 29, Alabama 26
1946	Rose	Alabama 34, Southern Cal 14
1948	Sugar	Texas 27, Alabama 7
1953	Orange	Alabama 61, Syracuse 6
1954	Cotton	Rice 28, Alabama 6
1959	Liberty	Penn State 7, Alabama 0
1960	Bluebonnet	Alabama 3, Texas 3
1962	Sugar	Alabama 10, Arkansas 3
1963	Orange	Alabama 17, Oklahoma 0
1964	Sugar	Alabama 12, Mississippi 7
1965	Orange	Texas 21, Alabama 17
1966	Orange	Alabama 39, Nebraska 28
1967	Sugar	Alabama 34, Nebraska 7
1968	Cotton	Texas A&M 20, Alabama 16
1968	Gator	Missouri 35, Alabama 10
1969	Liberty	Colorado 47, Alabama 33
1970	Bluebonnet	Alabama 24, Oklahoma 24
1972	Orange	Nebraska 38, Alabama 6
1973	Cotton	Texas 17, Alabama 13
1973	Sugar	Notre Dame 24, Alabama 23
1975	Orange	Notre Dame 13, Alabama 11
1975	Sugar	Alabama 13, Penn State 6
1976	Liberty	Alabama 33, UCLA 6
1978	Sugar	Alabama 35, Ohio State 6
1979	Sugar	Alabama 14, Penn State 7
1980	Sugar	Alabama 24, Arkansas 9
1981	Cotton	Alabama 30, Baylor 2
1982	Cotton	Texas 14, Alabama 12
1982	Liberty	Alabama 21, Illinois 15
1983	Sun	Alabama 28, Southern Methodist 7

1985	Aloha	Alabama 24, Southern Cal 3
1986	Sun	Alabama 28, Washington 6
1988	Hall of Fame	Michigan 28, Alabama 24
1988	Sun	Alabama 29, Army 28
1990	Sugar	Miami 33, Alabama 25
1991	Fiesta	Louisville 34, Alabama 7
1991	Blockbuster	Alabama 30, Colorado 25
1993	Sugar	Alabama 34, Miami 13
1993	Gator	Alabama 24, North Carolina 10
1995	Florida Citrus	Alabama 24, Ohio State 17
1997	Outback	Alabama 17, Michigan 14
1998	Music City	Virginia Tech 38, Alabama 7
2000	Orange	Michigan 35, Alabama 34 (OT)
2001	Independence	Alabama 14, Iowa State 13
2004	Music City	Minnesota 20, Alabama 16
2006	Cotton Bowl	Alabama 13, Texas Tech 10

Arkansas (11-20-3)

1934	Dixie Classic	Arkansas 7, Centenary 7
1947	Cotton	Arkansas 0, LSU 0
1948	Dixie	Arkansas 21, William & Mary 19
1955	Cotton	Georgia Tech 14, Arkansas 6
1960	Gator	Arkansas 14, Georgia Tech 7
1961	Cotton	Duke 7, Arkansas 6
1962	Sugar	Alabama 10, Arkansas 3
1963	Sugar	Ole Miss 17, Arkansas 13
1965	Cotton	Arkansas 10, Nebraska 7
1966	Cotton	LSU 14, Arkansas 7
1969	Sugar	Arkansas 16, Georgia 2
1970	Sugar	Ole Miss 27, Arkansas 22
1971	Liberty	Tennessee 14, Arkansas 13
1976	Cotton	Arkansas 31, Georgia 10
1978	Orange	Arkansas 31, Oklahoma 6
1978	Fiesta	Arkansas 10, UCLA 10
1980	Sugar	Alabama 24, Arkansas 9
1980	Hall of Fame	Arkansas 34, Tulane 15
1981	Gator	North Carolina 31, Arkansas 27
1982	Bluebonnet	Arkansas 28, Florida 24
1984	Liberty	Auburn 21, Arkansas 15
1985	Holiday	Arkansas 18, Arizona State 17
1987	Orange	Oklahoma 42, Arkansas 8
1987	Liberty	Georgia 20, Arkansas 17
1989	Cotton	UCLA 17, Arkansas 3
1990	Cotton	Tennessee 31, Arkansas 27
1991	Independence	Georgia 24, Arkansas 15
1995	Carquest	North Carolina 20, Arkansas 10
1999	Florida Citrus	Michigan 45, Arkansas 31
2000	Cotton	Arkansas 27, Texas 6
2000	Las Vegas	UNLV 31, Arkansas 14
2002	Cotton	Oklahoma 10, Arkansas 3
2002	Music City	Minnesota 29, Arkansas 14
2003	Independence	Arkansas 27, Missouri 14

Auburn (17-13-2)

| 1937 | Bacardi | Auburn 7, Villanova 7 |
| 1938 | Orange | Auburn 6, Michigan State 0 |

1954	Gator	Texas Tech 35, Auburn 13
1954	Gator	Auburn 33, Baylor 13
1955	Gator	Vanderbilt 25, Auburn 13
1964	Orange	Nebraska 13, Auburn 7
1965	Liberty	Ole Miss 13, Auburn 7
1968	Sun	Auburn 34, Arizona 10
1969	Bluebonnet	Houston 36, Auburn 7
1971	Gator	Auburn 35, Ole Miss 28
1972	Sugar	Oklahoma 40, Auburn 22
1972	Gator	Auburn 24, Colorado 3
1973	Sun	Missouri 34, Auburn 17
1974	Gator	Auburn 27, Texas 3
1982	Tangerine	Auburn 33, Boston College 26
1984	Sugar	Auburn 9, Michigan 7
1984	Liberty	Auburn 21, Arkansas 15
1986	Cotton	Texas A&M 36, Auburn 16
1987	Florida Citrus	Auburn 16, Southern Cal 7
1988	Sugar	Auburn 16, Syracuse 16
1989	Sugar	Florida State 13, Auburn 7
1990	Hall of Fame	Auburn 31, Ohio State 14
1990	Peach	Auburn 27, Indiana 23
1996	Outback	Penn State 43, Auburn 14
1996	Independence	Auburn 32, Army 29
1998	Peach	Auburn 21, Clemson 17
2001	Florida Citrus	Michigan 31, Auburn 28
2001	Peach	North Carolina 16, Auburn 10
2003	Capital One	Auburn 13, Penn State 9
2003	Music City	Auburn 28, Wisconsin 14
2005	Sugar	Auburn 16, Virginia Tech 13
2006	Capital One	Wisconsin 24, Auburn 10

Florida (15-18)

1953	Gator	Florida 14, Tulsa 13
1958	Gator	Ole Miss 7, Florida 3
1960	Gator	Florida 13, Baylor 12
1962	Gator	Florida 17, Penn State 7
1966	Sugar	Missouri 20, Florida 18
1967	Orange	Florida, 27, Georgia Tech 12
1969	Gator	Florida 14, Tennessee 13
1973	Tangerine	Miami (Ohio) 16, Florida 7
1974	Sugar	Nebraska 13, Florida 10
1975	Gator	Maryland 13, Florida 0
1977	Sun	Texas A&M 37, Florida 14
1980	Tangerine	Florida 35, Maryland 20
1981	Peach	West Virginia 26, Florida 6
1982	Bluebonnet	Arkansas 28, Florida 24
1983	Gator	Florida 14, Iowa 6
1987	Aloha	UCLA 20, Florida 16
1988	All-American	Florida 14, Illinois 10
1989	Freedom	Washington 34, Florida 7
1992	Sugar	Notre Dame 39, Florida 28
1992	Gator	Florida 27, North Carolina State 10
1994	Sugar	Florida 41, West Virginia 7
1995	Sugar	Florida State 23, Florida 17
1996	Fiesta	Nebraska 62, Florida 24

1997	Sugar	Florida 52, Florida State 20
1998	Florida Citrus	Florida 21, Penn State 6
1999	Orange	Florida 31, Syracuse 10
2000	Florida Citrus	Michigan State 37, Florida 34
2001	Sugar	Miami 37, Florida 20
2002	Orange	Florida 56, Maryland 23
2003	Outback	Michigan 38, Florida 30
2003	Outback	Iowa 37, Florida 17
2004	Peach	Miami 27, Florida 10
2006	Outback	Florida 31, Iowa 24

Georgia (22-16-3)

1942	Orange	Georgia 40, Texas Christian 26
1943	Rose	Georgia 9, UCLA 0
1946	Oil	Georgia 20, Tulsa 6
1947	Sugar	Georgia 20, North Carolina 10
1948	Gator	Georgia 20, Maryland 20
1949	Orange	Texas 41, Georgia 28
1950	Presidential	Texas A&M 40, Georgia 20
1960	Orange	Georgia 14, Missouri 0
1964	Sun	Georgia 7, Texas Tech 0
1966	Cotton	Georgia 24, Southern Methodist 9
1967	Liberty	North Carolina State 14, Georgia 7
1969	Sugar	Arkansas 16, Georgia 2
1969	Sun	Nebraska 45, Georgia 6
1971	Gator	Georgia 7, North Carolina 3
1973	Peach	Georgia 17, Maryland 16
1974	Tangerine	Miami (Ohio) 21, Georgia 10
1976	Cotton	Arkansas 31, Georgia 10
1977	Sugar	Pittsburgh 27, Georgia 3
1978	Bluebonnet	Stanford 25, Georgia 22
1981	Sugar	Georgia 17, Notre Dame 10
1982	Sugar	Pittsburgh 24, Georgia 20
1983	Sugar	Penn State 27, Georgia 23
1984	Cotton	Georgia 10, Texas 9
1984	Florida Citrus	Georgia 17, Florida State 17
1985	Sun	Georgia 13, Arizona 13
1986	Hall of Fame	Boston College 27, Georgia 24
1987	Liberty	Georgia 20, Arkansas 17
1989	Gator	Georgia 34, Michigan State 27
1989	Peach	Syracuse 19, Georgia 18
1991	Independence	Georgia 24, Arkansas 15
1993	Florida Citrus	Georgia 21, Ohio State 14
1995	Peach	Virginia 34, Georgia 27
1998	Outback	Georgia 33, Wisconsin 6
1998	Peach	Georgia 35, Virginia 33
2000	Outback	Georgia 28, Purdue 25 (OT)
2000	Oahu	Georgia 37, Virginia 14
2001	Music City	Boston College 20, Georgia 16
2003	Sugar	Georgia 26, Florida State 13
2004	Capital One	Georgia 34, Purdue 27 (OT)
2005	Outback	Georgia 24, Wisconsin 21
2006	Sugar	West Virginia 38, Georgia 35

Kentucky (5-5)

| 1947 | Great Lakes | Kentucky 24, Villanova 14 |
| 1950 | Orange | Santa Clara 21, Kentucky 13 |

1951	Sugar	Kentucky 13, Oklahoma 7
1952	Cotton	Kentucky 20, Texas Christian 7
1976	Peach	Kentucky 21, North Carolina 0
1983	Hall of Fame	West Virginia 20, Kentucky 16
1984	Hall of Fame	Kentucky 20, Wisconsin 19
1993	Peach	Clemson 14, Kentucky 13
1999	Outback	Penn State 26, Kentucky 14
1999	Music City	Syracuse 20, Kentucky 13

LSU (18-18-1)

1936	Sugar	Texas Christian 3, LSU 2
1937	Sugar	Santa Clara 21, LSU 14
1938	Sugar	Santa Clara 6, LSU 0
1944	Orange	LSU 19, Texas A&M 14
1947	Cotton	LSU 0, Arkansas 0
1950	Sugar	Oklahoma 35, LSU 0
1959	Sugar	LSU 7, Clemson 0
1960	Sugar	Ole Miss 21, LSU 0
1962	Orange	LSU 25, Colorado 7
1963	Cotton	LSU 13, Texas 0
1963	Bluebonnet	Baylor 14, LSU 7
1965	Sugar	LSU 13, Syracuse 10
1966	Cotton	LSU 15, Arkansas 7
1968	Sugar	LSU 20, Wyoming 13
1968	Peach	LSU 31, Florida State 27
1971	Orange	Nebraska 17, LSU 12
1971	Sun	LSU 33, Iowa State 15
1972	Bluebonnet	Tennessee 24, LSU 17
1974	Orange	Penn State 16, LSU 9
1977	Sun	Stanford 24, LSU 14
1978	Liberty	Missouri 20, LSU 15
1979	Tangerine	LSU 34, Wake Forest 10
1983	Orange	Nebraska 21, LSU 20
1985	Sugar	Nebraska 28, LSU 10
1985	Liberty	Baylor 21, LSU 7
1987	Sugar	Nebraska 30, LSU 15
1987	Gator	LSU 30, South Carolina 13
1989	Hall of Fame	Syracuse 23, LSU 10
1995	Independence	LSU 45, Michigan State 26
1996	Peach	LSU 10, Clemson 7
1997	Independence	LSU 27, Notre Dame 9
2000	Peach	LSU 28, Georgia Tech 14
2002	Sugar	LSU 47, Illinois 34
2003	Cotton	Texas 35, LSU 20
2004	Sugar	LSU 21, Oklahoma 14
2005	Capital One	Iowa 30, LSU 25
2005	Peach	LSU 40, Miami 3

Ole Miss (19-12)

1936	Orange	Catholic U 20, Ole Miss 19
1949	Delta	Ole Miss 13, Texas Christian 9
1953	Sugar	Georgia Tech 24, Ole Miss 7
1955	Sugar	Navy 21, Ole Miss 0
1956	Cotton	Ole Miss 14, Texas Christian 13
1958	Sugar	Ole Miss 39, Texas 7

1958	Gator	Ole Miss 7, Florida 3
1960	Sugar	Ole Miss 21, LSU 0
1961	Sugar	Ole Miss 14, Rice 6
1962	Cotton	Texas 12, Ole Miss 7
1963	Sugar	Ole Miss 17, Arkansas 13
1964	Sugar	Alabama 12, Ole Miss 7
1964	Bluebonnet	Tulsa 14, Ole Miss 7
1965	Liberty	Ole Miss 13, Auburn 7
1966	Bluebonnet	Texas 19, Ole Miss 0
1967	Sun	Texas El Paso 14, Ole Miss 7
1968	Liberty	Ole Miss 34, Virginia Tech 17
1970	Sugar	Ole Miss 27, Arkansas 22
1971	Gator	Auburn 35, Ole Miss 28
1971	Peach	Ole Miss 41, Georgia Tech 18
1983	Independence	Air Force 9, Ole Miss 3
1986	Independence	Ole Miss 20, Texas Tech 17
1989	Liberty	Ole Miss 42, Air Force 29
1991	Gator	Michigan 35, Ole Miss 3
1992	Liberty	Ole Miss 13, Air Force 0
1997	Motor City	Ole Miss 34, Marshall 31
1998	Independence	Ole Miss 35, Texas Tech 18
1999	Independence	Ole Miss 27, Oklahoma 25
2000	Music City	West Virginia 49, Ole Miss 38
2002	Independence	Ole Miss 27, Nebraska 23
2004	Cotton Bowl	Ole Miss 31, Oklahoma State 28

Mississippi State (6-6)

1937	Orange	Duquesne 13, Mississippi State 12
1941	Orange	Mississippi State 14, Georgetown 7
1963	Liberty	Mississippi State 16, North Carolina State 12
1974	Sun	Mississippi State 26, North Carolina 24
1980	Sun	Nebraska 31, Mississippi State 17
1981	Hall of Fame	Mississippi State 10, Kansas 0
1991	Liberty	Air Force 38, Mississippi State 15
1993	Peach	North Carolina 21, Mississippi State 17
1995	Peach	North Carolina State 28, Mississippi State 24
1999	Cotton	Texas 38, Mississippi State 11
1999	Peach	Mississippi State 17, Clemson 7
2000	Independence	Mississippi State 43, Texas A&M 41 (OT)

South Carolina (3-9)

1946	Gator	Wake Forest 26, South Carolina 14
1969	Peach	West Virginia 14, South Carolina 3
1975	Tangerine	Miami (Ohio) 20, South Carolina 7
1979	Hall of Fame	Missouri 24, South Carolina 14
1980	Gator	Pittsburgh 37, South Carolina 9
1984	Gator	Oklahoma State 21, South Carolina 14
1987	Gator	LSU 30, South Carolina 13
1988	Liberty	Indiana 34, South Carolina 10
1994	Carquest	South Carolina 24, West Virginia 21
2001	Outback	South Carolina 24, Ohio State 7
2002	Outback	South Carolina 31, Ohio State 28
2005	Independence	Missouri 38, South Carolina 31

Tennessee (24-21)

1931	New York-x	Tennessee 13, NYU 0
1939	Orange	Tennessee 17, Oklahoma 0
1940	Rose	Southern California 14, Tennessee 0
1941	Sugar	Boston College 19, Tennessee 13
1943	Sugar	Tennessee 14, Tulsa 7
1945	Rose	Southern California 25, Tennessee 0
1947	Orange	Rice 8, Tennessee 0
1951	Cotton	Tennessee 20, Texas 14
1952	Sugar	Maryland 28, Tennessee 13
1953	Cotton	Texas 16, Tennessee 0
1957	Sugar	Baylor 13, Tennessee 7
1957	Gator	Tennessee 3, Texas A&M 0
1965	Bluebonnet	Tennessee 27, Tulsa 6
1966	Gator	Tennessee 18, Syracuse 12
1968	Orange	Oklahoma 26, Tennessee 24
1969	Cotton	Texas 36, Tennessee 13
1969	Gator	Florida 14, Tennessee 13
1971	Sugar	Tennessee 34, Air Force 13
1971	Liberty	Tennessee 14, Arkansas 13
1972	Bluebonnet	Tennessee 24, LSU 17
1973	Gator	Texas Tech 28, Tennessee 19
1974	Liberty	Tennessee 7, Maryland 3
1979	Bluebonnet	Purdue 27, Tennessee 22
1981	Garden State	Tennessee 28, Wisconsin 21
1982	Peach	Iowa 28, Tennessee 22
1983	Florida Citrus	Tennessee 30, Maryland 23
1984	Sun	Maryland 28, Tennessee 27
1986	Sugar	Tennessee 35, Miami 7
1986	Liberty	Tennessee 21, Minnesota 14
1988	Peach	Tennessee 27, Indiana 22
1990	Cotton	Tennessee 31, Arkansas 27
1991	Sugar	Tennessee 23, Virginia 22
1992	Fiesta	Penn State 42, Tennessee 17
1993	Hall of Fame	Tennessee 38, Boston College 23
1994	Florida Citrus	Penn State 31, Tennessee 13
1994	Gator	Tennessee 45, Virginia Tech 23
1996	Florida Citrus	Tennessee 20, Ohio State 14
1997	Florida Citrus	Tennessee 48, Northwestern 28
1998	Orange	Nebraska 42, Tennessee 17
1999	Fiesta	Tennessee 23, Florida State 16
2000	Fiesta	Nebraska 31, Tennessee 21
2001	Cotton	Kansas State 35, Tennessee 21
2002	Florida Citrus	Tennessee 45, Michigan 17
2002	Peach	Maryland 30, Tennessee 3
2004	Peach	Clemson 27, Tennessee 14
2005	Cotton	Tennessee 38, Texas A&M

x-not recognized by the NCAA

Vanderbilt (1-1-1)

1955	Gator	Vanderbilt 25, Auburn 13
1974	Peach	Vanderbilt 6, Texas Tech 6
1982	Hall of Fame	Air Force 36, Vanderbilt 28

FORMER SEC SCHOOLS

Georgia Tech (11-5)

1929	Rose	Georgia Tech 8, California 7
1940	Orange	Georgia Tech 21, Missouri 7
1943	Cotton	Texas 14, Georgia Tech 7
1944	Sugar	Georgia Tech 20, Tulsa 18
1945	Orange	Tulsa 26, Georgia Tech 12
1947	Oil	Georgia Tech 41, St. Mary's 19
1948	Orange	Georgia Tech 20, Kansas 14
1952	Orange	Georgia Tech 17, Baylor 14
1953	Sugar	Georgia Tech 24, Ole Miss 7
1954	Sugar	Georgia Tech 42, West Virginia 19
1955	Cotton	Georgia Tech 14, Arkansas 6
1956	Sugar	Georgia Tech 7, Pittsburgh 0
1956	Gator	Georgia Tech 21, Pittsburgh 14
1960	Gator	Arkansas 14, Georgia Tech 7
1961	Gator	Penn State 30, Georgia Tech 15
1962	Bluebonnet	Missouri 14, Georgia Tech 10

(*Note:* Georgia Tech became independent in 1964 and is currently in the ACC.)

Tulane (1-2)

1932	Rose	Southern California 21, Tulane 12
1935	Sugar	Tulane 20, Temple 14
1940	Sugar	Texas A&M 14, Tulane 13

(*Note:* Tulane became independent in 1966 and is currently in Conference USA.)

· Appendix D ·

Polls

ALL-TIME FINAL ASSOCIATED PRESS POLL

Former SEC assistant director of media relations Charles Woodroof came up with the idea of creating a compiled ranking for the Associated Press Poll, which began in 1936. From 1936 to 1961, the wire service ranked 20 teams. From 1962 to 1967, only 10 teams were recognized. From 1968 to 1988, it went back to 20 teams before expanding to 25 in 1989. Points are awarded based on a team's finish in the final AP of each year. Points were awarded on a 20-19-18 . . . 3-2-1 basis from 1936 to 1988, and a 25-24-23 . . . 3-2-1 basis from 1989 through 2005.

Rank	Team	Points	Top 20	Top 10	Top 5	1st	2nd
1.	Michigan	715	51	36	15	2	2
2.	Notre Dame	701.5	47	35	22	8	5
3.	Oklahoma	689.5	44	32	27	6	4
4.	**Alabama**	**637**	**44**	**32**	**18**	**6**	**2**
5.	Ohio State	630	44	26	17	4	6
6.	Nebraska	617	41	30	13	4	2
7.	Texas	544.5	37	23	8	3	1
8.	**Tennessee**	**533**	**39**	**23**	**13**	**2**	**4**
9.	Southern Cal	530	39	22	15	5	5
10.	Penn State	484	37	22	14	2	3
11.	Miami	439	27	15	10	5	4
12.	Florida State	413	23	15	15	2	2
13.	**Georgia**	**373**	**27**	**17**	**8**	**1**	**1**
14.	**Auburn**	**368**	**30**	**15**	**7**	**1**	**1**
15.	**LSU**	**364**	**29**	**17**	**6**	**1**	**2**
16.	UCLA	352	30	16	9	0	1
17.	**Florida**	**333**	**22**	**13**	**8**	**1**	**1**
18.	**Arkansas**	**282**	**25**	**13**	**3**	**0**	**1**
19.	Michigan State	266	20	13	7	1	4
20.	Texas A&M	264	22	11	2	1	0
21.	Washington	260	20	10	5	0	2
22.	Georgia Tech	227.5	20	10	5	0	2
23.	**Ole Miss**	**223.5**	**18**	**10**	**4**	**0**	**2**
24.	Colorado	218	18	8	5	1	0
25.	Iowa	217	18	11	3	0	1
26.	Pittsburgh	207	17	10	6	2	1
27.	Clemson	198	20	6	1	1	0
28.	Wisconsin	184	14	9	3	0	1
29.	Minnesota	175	14	9	5	4	0
30.	Army	174	14	8	6	2	2
31.	Maryland	164.5	17	5	3	1	0

32.	Arizona State	157.5	14	7	3	0	1
33.	Syracuse	150.5	12	5	2	1	0
34.	North Carolina	144	15	7	1	0	0
35.	Navy	143.5	11	8	7	0	1
36.	Kansas State	143	8	6	0	0	0
37.	California	141	11	6	4	0	1
38.	Virginia Tech	137	9	5	2	0	1
39.	Purdue	135.5	15	5	1	0	0
40.	Illinois	131	10	6	3	0	0
41.	Duke	130	16	5	2	0	1
42.	Missouri	120.5	12	6	1	0	0
43.	Stanford	116	12	5	1	0	1
44.	Southern Methodist	113	11	6	3	0	1
45.	Texas Christian	111	9	4	1	1	0
46.	Houston	106.5	12	5	2	0	0
47.	Brigham Young	106	9	3	2	1	0
48.	West Virginia	100	11	4	2	0	0
49.	Boston College	98	8	3	2	0	0
	Oregon	98	6	3	1	0	1
	Washington State	98	9	4	0	0	0
52.	Northwestern	96	8	5	0	0	0
53.	Oregon State	75	5	3	1	0	0
54.	North Carolina State	69	10	0	0	0	0
55.	Baylor	68.5	10	1	0	0	0
56.	Rice	66	8	4	1	0	0
57.	Oklahoma State	61	6	2	1	0	0
	Texas Tech	61	7	0	0	0	0
59.	Pennsylvania	60	7	3	0	0	0
60.	Fordham	58	6	2	1	0	0
61.	Kansas	57	5	2	0	0	0
62.	**Kentucky**	**56**	**8**	**2**	**0**	**0**	**0**
	Virginia	56	6	0	0	0	0
64.	Santa Clara	55	6	2	0	0	0
	Air Force	55	5	2	0	0	0
66.	Mississippi State	53.5	8	1	0	0	0
	Utah	53	4	2	1	0	0
68.	Arizona	51	6	2	1	0	0
69.	Tulane	50.5	7	2	1	0	0
70.	Louisville	48	4	1	0	0	0
	Miami (Ohio)	48	5	2	0	0	0
72.	Tulsa	47	6	1	1	0	0
73.	Cornell	43	5	1	1	0	0
74.	**South Carolina**	**42**	**5**	**0**	**0**	**0**	**0**
75.	Indiana	38	5	2	2	0	0
76.	Dartmouth	35	5	1	0	0	0
	Princeton	35	4	2	0	0	0
	Boise State	35	3	0	0	0	0
79.	Yale	34	4	0	0	0	0
	Iowa Pre-Flight	34	2	2	1	0	1
81.	Wyoming	33	3	1	0	0	0
82.	Duquesne	31	3	2	0	0	0
	Colorado Springs	31	3	0	0	0	0
84.	Holy Cross	26.5	5	1	0	0	0
85.	Villanova	26	3	1	0	0	0
86.	March Field	22	3	1	0	0	0
87.	Southern Miss	19	2	0	0	0	0

	Great Lakes	19	2	1	0	0	0
	Brainbridge NTS	20	2	1	1	0	0
90.	Marshall	18	1	1	0	0	0
	William & Mary	18	1	1	1	0	0
	East Carolina	19	2	1	0	0	0
	Toledo	18	2	0	0	0	0
	Randolph Field	18	1	1	1	0	0
95.	Carnegie Tech	15	1	1	0	0	0
96.	St. Mary's	14	1	1	0	0	0
97.	Pacific	13	2	1	0	0	0
	Del Monte P-F	13	1	1	0	0	0
99.	Rutgers	11	3	0	0	0	0
	Utah State	11	1	1	0	0	0
101.	**Vanderbilt**	**9**	**1**	**0**	**0**	**0**	**0**
102.	Georgetown	8	1	0	0	0	0
103.	Norman P-F	7.5	1	0	0	0	0
104.	San Francisco	7	1	0	0	0	0
105.	Hawaii	6	1	0	0	0	0
	Fresno State	6	0	0	0	0	0
107.	Boston University	5	1	0	0	0	0
	San Diego State	5	1	0	0	0	0
	El Toro Maines	5	1	0	0	0	0
110.	Wake Forest	4	2	0	0	0	0
	George Washington	4	1	0	0	0	0
	New Mexico State	4	1	0	0	0	0
	Temple	4	1	0	0	0	0
	Hardin-Simmons	4	1	0	0	0	0
115.	Colorado College	3	1	0	0	0	0
	Iowa State	3	1	0	0	0	0
	Bowling Green	3	0	0	0	0	0
	Washington & Lee	3	1	0	0	0	0
	Fort Pierce	3	1	0	0	0	0
120.	Columbia	2	2	0	0	0	0
	Delaware	2	1	0	0	0	0
	Lafayette	2	1	0	0	0	0
	St. Mary's P-F	2	1	0	0	0	0
124.	Marquette	1	1	0	0	0	0
	Ohio University	1	1	0	0	0	0
	Virginia Military	1	1	0	0	0	0
	Second Air Force	1	1	0	0	0	0

Source: SEC

Associated Press Final Rankings
[*Author's note:* For simplicity, only the AP rankings are used in this book unless otherwise noted. The UPI poll was conducted from 1950 to 1995. The USA Today/ESPN poll, commonly called the coaches' poll, began in 1982.]

1936:   2. LSU; 4. Alabama; 17. Tennessee.
1937:   4. Alabama; 8. LSU.
1938:   2. Tennessee; 13. Alabama.
1939:   2. Tennessee; 5. Tulane; 16. Georgia Tech.
1940:   4. Tennessee; 9. Mississippi State.
1941:   14. Georgia; 16. Mississippi State; 17. Ole Miss; 18. Tennessee; 20. Alabama.
1942:   2. Georgia; 5. Georgia Tech; 7. Tennessee; 10. Alabama; 16. Auburn; 18. Mississippi State.
1943:   13. Georgia Tech.
1944:   12. Tennessee; 13. Georgia Tech.

1945:   3. Alabama; 14. Tennessee; 15. LSU; 18. Georgia.
1946:   3. Georgia; 7. Tennessee; 8. LSU.
1947:   6. Alabama; 10. Georgia Tech; 13. Ole Miss.
1948:   8. Georgia; 12. Vanderbilt; 13. Tulane; 15. Ole Miss.
1949:   9. LSU; 11. Kentucky; 17. Tennessee.
1950:   4. Tennessee; 7. Kentucky; 16. Alabama; 20. Tulane.
1951:   1. Tennessee; 5. Georgia Tech; 15. Kentucky.
1952:   2. Georgia Tech; 7. Ole Miss; 8. Tennessee; 9. Alabama; 15. Florida; 20. Kentucky.
1953:   8. Georgia Tech; 13. Alabama; 16. Kentucky; 17. Auburn.
1954:   6. Ole Miss; 13. Auburn.
1955:   7. Georgia Tech; 8. Auburn; 10. Ole Miss.
1956:   2. Tennessee; 4. Georgia Tech.
1957:   1. Auburn; 7. Ole Miss; 13. Tennessee; 14. Mississippi State; 17. Florida.
1958:   1. LSU; 4. Auburn; 11. Ole Miss; 14. Florida.
1959:   2. Ole Miss; 3. LSU; 5. Georgia; 10. Alabama; 19. Florida.
1960:   2. Ole Miss; 9. Alabama; 13. Auburn; 18. Florida.
1961:   1. Alabama; 4. LSU; 5. Ole Miss; 13. Georgia Tech.
1962:   3. Ole Miss; 5. Alabama; 7. LSU.
1963:   5. Auburn; 7. Ole Miss; 8. Alabama.
1964:   1. Alabama; 7. LSU.
1965:   1. Alabama; 7. Tennessee; 8. LSU
1966:   3. Alabama; 4. Georgia.
1967:   2. Tennessee; 8. Alabama.
1968:   8. Georgia; 13. Tennessee; 16. Auburn; 17. Alabama; 19. LSU.
1969:   8. Ole Miss; 10. LSU; 14. Florida; 15. Tennessee; 20. Auburn.
1970:   4. Tennessee; 7. LSU; 10. Auburn; 20. Ole Miss.
1971:   4. Alabama; 7. Georgia; 9. Tennessee; 11. LSU; 12. Auburn; 15. Ole Miss.
1972:   5. Auburn; 7. Alabama; 8. Tennessee; 11. LSU.
1973:   4. Alabama; 13. LSU; 19. Tennessee.
1974:   5. Alabama; 8. Auburn; 15. Florida; 17. Mississippi State; 20. Tennessee.
1975:   3. Alabama; 19. Georgia.
1976:   10. Georgia; 11. Alabama; 18. Kentucky; 20. Mississippi State.
1977:   2. Alabama; 6. Kentucky.
1978:   1. Alabama; 16. Georgia.
1979:   1. Alabama; 16. Auburn.
1980:   1. Georgia; 6. Alabama; 19. Mississippi State.
1981:   6. Georgia; 7. Alabama.
1982:   4. Georgia; 11. LSU; 14. Auburn.
1983:   3. Auburn; 4. Georgia; 6. Florida; 15. Alabama.
1984:   3. Florida; 14. Auburn; 15. LSU; 19. Kentucky.
1985:   4. Tennessee; 5. Florida; 13. Alabama; 20. LSU.
1986:   6. Auburn; 9. Alabama; 10. LSU.
1987:   5. LSU; 7. Auburn; 13. Georgia; 14. Tennessee.
1988:   8. Auburn; 15. Georgia; 17. Alabama; 19. LSU.
1989:   5. Tennessee; 6. Auburn; 9. Alabama.
1990:   8. Tennessee; 13. Florida; 19. Auburn; 21. Ole Miss.
1991:   5. Alabama; 7. Florida; 14. Tennessee; 17. Georgia.
1992:   1. Alabama; 8. Georgia; 10. Florida; 12. Tennessee; 16. Ole Miss; 23. Mississippi State.
1993:   4. Auburn; 5. Florida; 12. Tennessee; 14. Alabama.
1994:   5. Alabama; 7. Florida; 9. Auburn; 22. Tennessee; 24. Mississippi State.
1995:   2. Florida; 3. Tennessee; 21. Alabama; 22. Auburn.
1996:   1. Florida; 9. Tennessee; 11. Alabama; 12. LSU; 24. Auburn.
1997:   4. Florida; 7. Tennessee; 10. Georgia; 11. Auburn; 13. LSU; 22. Ole Miss.
1998:   1. Tennessee; 5. Florida; 14. Georgia; 16. Arkansas.
1999:   8. Alabama; 9. Tennessee; 12. Florida; 13. Mississippi State; 16. Georgia; 17. Arkansas; 22. Ole Miss.

2000: 10. Florida; 18. Auburn; 19. South Carolina; 20. Georgia; 22. LSU; 24. Mississippi State.
2001: 3. Florida; 4. Tennessee; 7. LSU; 13. South Carolina; 22. Georgia.
2002: 3. Georgia; 11. Alabama; 14. Auburn.
2003: 2. LSU; 7. Georgia; 13. Ole Miss; 15. Tennessee; 24. Florida.
2004: 2. Auburn; 7. Georgia; 13. Tennessee; 16. LSU.
2005: 6. LSU; 8. Alabama; 10. Georgia; 12. Florida; 14. Auburn.

SEC Teams Ranked No. 1 (week by week; italicized teams won national championship)
1939: Tennessee (Oct. 24, 31, Nov. 7, 14).
1942: Georgia (Nov. 3, 10, 17).
1951: *Tennessee (preseason, Oct. 23, 30, Nov. 6, 20, 27, Dec. 4).*
1956: Tennessee (Nov. 13).
1957: *Auburn (Nov. 26, Dec. 3).*
1958: Auburn (Oct. 7); *LSU (Oct. 28, Nov. 4, 11, 18, 25, Dec. 2).*
1959: LSU (Sept. 22, 29, Oct. 6, 13, 20, 27, Nov. 3).
1960: Ole Miss (Sept. 20, 27, Oct. 11).
1961: Ole Miss (Oct. 10); *Alabama (Nov. 21, 28, Dec. 5).*
1962: Alabama (Sept. 25, Oct. 9, Nov. 13).
1964: Ole Miss (preseason); *Alabama (Dec. 1).*
1965: *Alabama (Dec. 4).*
1966: Alabama (preseason).
1973: Alabama (Nov. 27, Dec. 4).
1978: *Alabama (preseason, Sept. 12, 19, Dec. 4, Jan. 3).*
1979: *Alabama (Oct. 16, 23, 30, Nov. 6, 13, 20, 27, Dec. 3, Jan. 3).*
1980: Alabama (Sept. 16, 23, 30, Oct. 7, 14, 21, 28); *Georgia (Nov. 11, 18, 25, Dec. 2, 9, Jan. 3).*
1982: Georgia (Nov. 9, 16, 23, 30, Dec. 7).
1984: Auburn (preseason).
1985: Auburn (Sept. 10, 17, 24); Florida (Nov. 5).
1992: *Alabama (Jan. 2).*
1994: Florida (preseason, Aug. 30, Sept. 11, 18, 26, Oct. 3, 10).
1996: *Florida (Sept. 23, 30, Oct. 6, 13, 20, 27, Nov. 4, 11, 18, 25, Jan. 3).*
1997: Florida (Sept. 21, 28, Oct. 5).
1998: *Tennessee (Nov. 8, 15, 22, 29. Dec. 6, Jan. 5).*
2001: Florida (preseason, Aug. 26, Oct. 7).

(*Note:* Arkansas was No. 1 in the AP poll on Oct. 19, 1965, but was not in the SEC yet.)

· Appendix E ·

Records

Individuals

Total offense

Plays, game: 78, Whit Taylor, Vanderbilt vs. Georgia (20 rushes, 58 passes) 1982
Plays, season: 635, Jared Lorenzen, Kentucky (76 rushes, 559 passes) 2000
Plays, career: 1,793, Jared Lorenzen, Kentucky (279 rushes, 1,574 passes) 2000–03
Yards gained, game: 540, Archie Manning, Ole Miss vs. Alabama (104 rushing, 436 passing) 1969
Yards gained, season: 4,151, Tim Couch, Kentucky (–124 rushing, 4,275 passing) 1998
Yards gained, career: 11,270, David Greene, Georgia (–258 rushing, 11,528 passing) 2001–04
Yards per game, season: 377.4, Tim Couch, Kentucky (–124 rush, 4,275 pass, 11 games) 1998
Yards per game, career: 281.4, Tim Couch, Kentucky (8,160 yards in 29 games) 1996–98
Yards per play (minimum 10 plays): 21.4, Eagle Day, Ole Miss vs. Villanova (10 for 214) 1954
Yards per play, game (minimum 20 plays): 14.18, Derrick Taite, Mississippi State vs. Tulane (33 for 468) 1994
Yards per play, game (minimum 40 plays): 11.9, Tim Couch, Kentucky vs. Louisville (42 for 498) 1998
Yards per play, game (minimum 50 plays): 10.04, Steve Taneyhill, South Carolina vs. Miss. State (51 for 512) 1995
Yards per play, season (minimum 300 plays): 9.10, Rex Grossman, Florida (429 for 3,904) 2001
Yards per play, career (minimum 900 plays): 7.75, Danny Wuerffel, Florida (1,355 for 10,500) 1993–96
Touchdowns, game: 7 (tie), Tim Couch, Kentucky vs. Louisville (all passing) 1998; Danny Wuerffel, Florida vs. Tennessee (1 rushing, 6 passing) 1995; Tim Couch, Kentucky vs. Indiana (all passing) 1997; Showboat Boykin, Ole Miss vs. Miss. State (all rushing) 1951; Terry Dean, Florida vs. New Mexico State (all passing) 1994; Tim Couch, Kentucky vs. Northeast Louisiana (1 rushing, 6 passing) 1997; Doug Johnson, Florida vs. Central Michigan (all passing) 1997
Touchdowns, season: 41, Danny Wuerffel, Florida (2 rushing, 39 passing) 1996
Touchdowns, career: 122, Danny Wuerffel, Florida (8 rushing, 114 passing) 1993–96

Rushing

Most rushes, game: 47, Herschel Walker, Georgia vs. Florida (192 yards) 1981
Most rushes, season: 385, Herschel Walker, Georgia (1,891 yards) 1981
Most rushes, career: 994, Herschel Walker, Georgia (5,259 yards) 1980–82 (NCAA record for three years)
Rushes per game, season: 35.0, Herschel Walker, Georgia (385 in 11 games) 1981
Rushes per game, career: 30.1, Herschel Walker, Georgia (994 in 33 games) 1980–82
Yards gained, game: 321, Frank Mordica, Vanderbilt vs. Air Force (22 rushes) 1978
Yards gained, season: 1,891, Herschel Walker, Georgia (385 rushes) 1981

Yards gained, career: 5,259, Herschel Walker, Georgia (33 games) 1980–82 (NCAA record for three years)

Yards per game, season: 171.9, Herschel Walker, Georgia (1,891 in 11 games) 1981

Yards per game, career: 159.4, Herschel Walker, Georgia (5,259 in 33 games) 1980–82

Yards per rush, game (minimum 40): 7.5, Moe Williams, Kentucky vs. South Carolina (299 on 40) 1995

Yards per rush, game (minimum 30): 10.2, Emmitt Smith, Florida vs. New Mexico (316 on 31) 1989

Yards per rush, game (minimum 20): 14.58, Frank Mordica, Vanderbilt vs. Air Force (321 on 22) 1978

Yards per rush, game (minimum 10): 19.6, Harvey Williams, LSU vs. Rice (196 on 10) 1987

Yards per rush, season (minimum 200): 6.8, Garrison Hearst, Georgia (1,547 on 228) 1992

Yards per rush, season (minimum 100): 8.3, Brent Fullwood, Auburn (1,391 on 167) 1986

Yards per rush, career (minimum 400): 6.6, Bo Jackson, Auburn (4,303 on 650) 1982–85

Touchdown rushing, season: 19 (tie), Garrison Hearst, Georgia 1992; Shaun Alexander, Alabama 1999; LaBrandon Toefield, LSU 2001

Touchdown rushing, career: 49, Herschel Walker, Georgia 1980–82

Longest touchdown rushing: 99, Kelsey Finch, Tennessee vs. Florida 1977

All-purpose yards

Game: 429, Moe Williams, Kentucky vs. South Carolina (299 rush, 57 rec., 73 KR) 1995

Season: 2,120, Domanick Davis, LSU (931 rush, 130 rec., 499 PR, 560 KR) 2002

Season average: 191.7, Kevin Faulk, LSU (1,279 rush, 287 rec., 265 PR, 278 KR in 11 games) 1998

Career: 6,833, Kevin Faulk, LSU (4,557 rush, 600 rec., 832 PR, 844 KR) 1995–98

Career yards per game average: 174.2, Herschel Walker, Georgia (5,749 yards in 33 games) 1980–82

Passing

Attempts, game: 67, Tim Couch, Kentucky vs. Arkansas (47 comp., 499 yards) 1998

Attempts, season: 559, Jared Lorenzen, Kentucky (321 comp., 3,687 yards) 2000

Attempts, career: 1,514, Jared Lorenzen, Kentucky (862 comp., 10,354 yards) 2000–03

Completions, game: 47, Tim Couch, Kentucky vs. Arkansas (67 atts., 499 yards) 1998

Completions, season: 400, Tim Couch, Kentucky (553 atts., 4,275 yards) 1998

Completions, career: 863, Peyton Manning, Tennessee (1,402 atts., 11,201 yards) 1994–97

Consecutive completions: 24, Tee Martin, Tennessee (1 vs. Alabama, 23 vs. South Carolina) 1998

Completions percentage, game (minimum 10): 100.0, Rohan Davey, LSU vs. Western Carolina (11 of 11) 2000

Completions percentage, game (minimum 20): 95.8, Tee Martin, Tennessee vs. South Carolina (23 of 24) 1998

Completions percentage, game (minimum 30): 86.4, Steve Taneyhill, South Carolina vs. Miss. State (38 of 44) 1995

Completions percentage, season (minimum 100): 70.7, Wayne Peace, Florida (174 of 246) 1982

Completions percentage, season (minimum 200): 72.3, Tim Couch, Kentucky (400 of 553) 1998

Completions percentage, career (minimum 300): 67.1, Tim Couch, Kentucky (795 of 1,184) 1996–98

Yards gained, game: 544, Eric Zeier, Georgia vs. Southern Miss. (30 of 47) 1993

Yards gained, season: 4,275, Tim Couch, Kentucky (400 of 553) 1998

Yards gained, career: 11,528, David Greene, Georgia (849 of 1,440) 2001–04

Touchdown passes, game: 7 (tie), Terry Dean, Florida vs. New Mexico State 1994 (NCAA record for touchdowns in a half); Tim Couch, Kentucky vs. Indiana 1997; Tim Couch, Kentucky vs. Louisville 1998; Doug Johnson, Florida vs. Central Michigan 1997

Touchdown passes, season: 39, Danny Wuerffel, Florida 1996

Touchdown passes, career: 114, Danny Wuerffel, Florida 1993–96

Interceptions, game: 9, John Reaves, Florida vs. Auburn (66 atts.) 1969

Interceptions, season: 29, Zeke Bratkowski, Georgia (248 atts.) 1951; Kurt Page, Vanderbilt (493 atts.)

Interceptions, career: 68, Zeke Bratkowski, Georgia (734 atts.) 1951–53
Consecutive attempts without an interception: 214, David Greene, Georgia 2004
Ratio of attempts/interceptions, season (minimum 100 attempts): 1:157.0, Ben Leard, Auburn (1 in 157) 1999
Ratio of attempts/interceptions, season (minimum 200 attempts): 1:74.8, David Greene, Georgia (4 in 299) 2004
Ratio of attempts/interceptions, season (minimum 300 attempts): 1:95.0, Peyton Manning, Tennessee (4 in 380) 1995
Ratio of attempts/interceptions, career (minimum 200 attempts): 1:60.0, Randy Campbell, Auburn (5 in 300) 1982–83
Ratio of attempts/interceptions, career (minimum 400 attempts): 1:46.4, Stewart Patridge, Ole Miss (11 in 510) 1994–97
Ratio of attempts/interceptions, career (minimum 600 attempts): 1:45.0, David Greene, Georgia (32 in 1,440) 2001–04
Longest touchdown passes: 99 (tie), Cris Collinsworth to Derrick Gaffney, Florida vs. Rice 1977; Dondrial Pinkins to Troy Williamson, South Carolina vs. Virginia 2003

Receiving

Catches, game: 19, Josh Reed, LSU vs. Alabama (293 yards) 2001
Catches, season: 97, Keith Edwards, Vanderbilt (909 yards) 1983
Catches, career: 208, Craig Yeast, Kentucky (2,899 yards) 1995–98
Yards gained, game: 293, Josh Reed, LSU vs. Alabama (19 catches) 2001
Yards gained, season: 1,740, Josh Reed, LSU (94 catches) 2001
Yards gained, career: 3,093, Terrence Edwards, Georgia (204 catches) 1999–2002
Yards per game, season: 145.0, Josh Reed, LSU (1,740 in 12 games) 2001
Yards per game, career: 103.3, Jabar Gaffney, Florida (2,375 in 23 games) 2000–01
Yards per catch, game (minimum five): 52.6, Alexander Wright, Auburn vs. Pacific (5 for 263) 1989
Yards per catch, game (minimum 10): 23.3, Kelley Washington, Tennessee vs. LSU (11 for 256) 2001
Yards per catch, game (minimum 15): 16.8, Craig Yeast, Kentucky vs. Vanderbilt (16 for 269) 1998
Yards per catch, season (minimum 25): 29.3, Bucky Curtis, Vanderbilt (27 for 791) 1950
Yards per catch, season (minimum 50): 20.5, Eric Martin, LSU (52 for 1,064) 1983
Yards per catch, season (minimum 75): 18.5, Josh Reed, LSU (94 for 1,740) 2001
Yards per catch, career (minimum 50): 24.5, Bucky Curtis, Vanderbilt (61 for 1,496) 1947–50
Yards per catch, career (minimum 100): 21.0, Anthony Lucas, Arkansas (137 for 2,879) 1995–99
Touchdown catches, game: 5, Carlos Carson, LSU vs. Rice 1977
Touchdown catches, season: 18, Reidel Anthony, Florida (12 games) 1996
Touchdown catches, career: 31, Chris Doering, Florida (40 games) 1992–95

Scoring

Most points, game: 42, Showboat Boykin, Ole Miss vs. Miss. State (7 TDs) 1951
Most points, season: 144, Shaun Alexander, Alabama (24 TDs) 1999
Most points, career: 409, Billy Bennett, Georgia (148 PAT, 87 FGs, 50 games) 2000–03
Most touchdowns, game: 7, Showboat Boykin, Ole Miss vs. Miss. State 1951 (NCAA record)
Most touchdowns, season: 24, Shaun Alexander, Alabama 1999
Most touchdowns, career: 53, Kevin Faulk, LSU (41 games) 1995–98

Field goals

Attempts, game: 7 (tie), Al Del Greco, Auburn vs. Kentucky (made 6) 1982; Doug Pelfrey, Kentucky vs. Miss. State (made 5) 1992
Attempts, season: 38, Billy Bennett, Georgia (made 31) 2003
Attempts, career: 110, Billy Bennett, Georgia (made 87) 2000–03
Made, game: 6 (tie), Al Del Greco, Auburn vs. Kentucky (7 atts.) 1982; Bobby Raymond, Florida vs. Florida State (6 atts.) 1983; Bobby Raymond, Florida vs. Kentucky (6 atts.) 1984; Philip Doyle,

Alabama vs. SW Louisiana (6 atts.) 1990; Billy Bennett, Georgia vs. Georgia Tech (6 atts.) 2001; Jonathan Nichols, Ole Miss vs. Texas Tech (6 atts.) 2003

Attempts, season: 31, Billy Bennett, Georgia (38 atts.) 2003

Attempts, career: 87, Billy Bennett, Georgia (110 atts.) 2000–03

Longest field goal: 60 (tie), Fuad Reveiz, Tennessee vs. Georgia Tech 1982; Kevin Butler, Georgia vs. Clemson 1984; Chris Perkins, Florida vs. Tulane 1984

Consecutive field goals: 18, Fuad Reveiz, Tennessee 1984

Field goal percentage, season (minimum 10): 100.0, David Browndyke, LSU (14 of 14) 1989

Field goal percentage, career (minimum 20): 88.4, Bobby Raymond, Florida (23 of 26) 1984

Field goal percentage, career (minimum 25): 87.8, Bobby Raymond, Florida (43 of 49) 1982–84 (NCAA record)

PAT kicks attempted, game: 13, Red Lutz, Alabama vs. Delta State (made 11) 1951

PAT kicks attempted, season: 71, Bart Edmiston, Florida (made 71) 1995

PAT kicks attempts, career: 194, Jeff Hall, Tennessee (made 188) 1995–98

PAT kicks made, game: 11 (tie), Reed Morton, South Carolina vs. Kent (11 atts.) 1995; Bill Davis, Alabama vs. Virginia Tech (11 atts.) 1973; Red Lutz, Alabama vs. Delta State (13 atts.) 1951

PAT kicks, season: 71, Bart Edmiston, Florida (71 atts.) 1995

PAT kicks, career: 188, Jeff Hall, Tennessee (194 atts.) 1995–98

PAT kicks, percentage, game (minimum 10): 100 (tie), Bill Davis, Alabama vs. Virginia Tech (11 of 11) 1973; Reed Morton, South Carolina (11 of 11) 1995; Bob Gain, Kentucky vs. North Dakota (10 of 10) 1950; Bobby Moreau, LSU vs. Rice (10 of 10) 1977; Judd Davis, Florida vs. Kentucky (10 of 10) 1994; Judd Davis, Florida vs. New Mexico State (10 of 10) 1994; Alex Walls, Tennessee vs. Louisiana–Monroe (10 of 10) 2000

PAT kicks, percentage, season (minimum 40): 100 (tie), Bart Edmiston, Florida (71 of 71) 1995; Judd Davis, Florida (65 of 65) 1994; John Becksvoort, Tennessee (59 of 59) 1993; Billy Bennett, Georgia (52 of 52) 2002; Greg Burke, Tennessee (50 of 50) 1990; Chris Knapp, Auburn (49 of 49) 1986; Jonathan Nichols, Ole Miss (49 of 49) 2003; Jeff Hall, Tennessee (47 of 47) 1998; Scott Etheridge, Auburn (45 of 45) 1993; Arden Czyzewski, Florida (44 of 44) 1991; David Browndyke, LSU (41 of 41) 1987; Todd Latourette, Arkansas (41 of 41) 1998; Matt Leach, Florida (41 of 41) 2003; James Wilhoit, Tennessee (41 of 41) 2003; Van Tiffin, Alabama (40 of 40) 1983; Jonathan Nichols, Ole Miss (40 of 40) 2002; Damon Duval, Auburn (40 of 40) 2002; Taylor Begley, Kentucky (40 of 40) 2003

PAT kicks, percentage, career (minimum 100): 100 (tie), John Becksvoort, Tennessee (161 of 161) 1991–94; Van Tiffin, Alabama (135 of 135) 1983–86; Damon Duval, Auburn (125 of 125) 1999–2002; David Browndyke, LSU (109 of 109) 1986–89; Brian Clark, Florida (62 of 62) 1979–81 (ties NCAA record)

Consecutive PAT kicks made: 161, John Becksvoort, Tennessee 1991–94

Total points scored by kicking, game: 23, Bobby Raymond, Florida vs. Florida State (6 FGs, 5 PATs) 1983

Total points scored by kicking, season: 131, Billy Bennett, Georgia (31 FGs, 38 PATs) 2003

Total points scored by kicking, career: 409, Billy Bennett, Georgia (87 FGs, 148 PATs) 2000–03

Punting

Most punts, game: 30, Bert Johnson, Kentucky vs. Washington & Lee 1934

Most punts, season: 101, Ralph Kercheval, Kentucky (4,413 yards for 43.5 avg.) 1933

Most punts, career: 277, Jim Arnold, Vanderbilt (12,171 yards for 43.9 avg.) 1979–82

Most punts, 50 yards or more: 86, Bill Smith, Ole Miss 1983–86 (NCAA record)

Most consecutive games one punt of 50 yards or more: 32, Bill Smith, Ole Miss 1983–86 (NCAA record)

Most games averaging 40 yards or more (minimum four): 36, Bill Smith, Ole Miss 1983–86 (NCAA record)

Longest punt: 92, Bill Smith, Ole Miss vs. Southern Miss 1984

Yards punted, game: 1,155, Bert Johnson, Kentucky vs. Washington & Lee (30 for 38.5 avg.) 1934

Yards punted, season: 4,413, Ralph Kercheval, Kentucky (101 for 43.5 avg.) 1933

Yards punted, career: 12,171, Jim Arnold, Vanderbilt (277 for 43.9 avg.) 1979–82

Punting average, game (minimum two): 84.5, Bill Smith, Ole Miss vs. Southern Miss (2 for 169) 1984

Punting average, game (minimum 7): 53.1, Jim Arnold, Vanderbilt vs. North Carolina (8 for 425) 1982

Punting average, game (minimum 10): 52.0, Ralph Kercheval, Kentucky vs. Cincinnati (10 for 520) 1933

Punting average, game (minimum 20): 43.0, Hawk Cavette, Georgia Tech vs. Florida (21 for 904) 1938

Punting average, season (minimum 30): 50.3, Chad Kessler, LSU (39 for 1,961) 1997

Punting average, season (minimum 50): 48.2, Ricky Anderson, Vanderbilt (58 for 2,793) 1984

Punting average, season (minimum 75): 46.6, Bill Marinangel, Vanderbilt (77 for 3,586) 1996

Punting average, season (minimum 100): 43.5, Ralph Kercheval, Kentucky (101 for 4,394) 1933

Punting average, career (minimum 100): 45.6, Ricky Anderson, Vanderbilt (111 for 5,067) 1983–84

Punting average, career (minimum 250): 44.3, Bill Smith, Ole Miss (254 for 11,260) 1983–86 (NCAA record)

Punt returns

Most returns, game: 17, A. B. Stubbs, Miss. State vs. TCU (122 yards) 1936

Most returns, season: 45, Willie Shelby, Alabama (396 yards) 1975

Most returns, career: 125, Greg Richardson, Alabama (1,011 yards) 1983–86

Yards returned, game: 203, Lee Nalley, Vanderbilt vs. Kentucky (6 returns) 1948

Yards returned, season: 791, Lee Nalley, Vanderbilt (43 returns) 1948 (NCAA record)

Yards returned, career: 1,695, Lee Nalley, Vanderbilt (109 returns) 1947–49 (NCAA record)

Gain per return, game (minimum 3): 57.6, Mike Fuller, Auburn vs. Chattanooga (3 for 173) 1974

Gain per return, season (minimum 10): 26.7, Hal Griffin, Florida (10 for 267) 1947

Gain per return, season (minimum 12): 25.9, Bill Blackstock, Tennessee (12 for 311) 1951 (NCAA record)

Gain per return, season (minimum 20): 19.1, Mike Fuller, Auburn (20 for 381) 1973

Gain per return, season (minimum 40): 18.4, Lee Nalley, Vanderbilt (43 for 791) 1948

Gain per return, career (minimum 50): 17.7, Mike Fuller, Auburn (50 for 883) 1973–74

Gain per return, career (minimum 100): 15.6, Lee Nalley, Vanderbilt (109 for 1,695) 1947–49

Punt return touchdowns, game: 2 (tie), Tommy Casanova, LSU vs. Ole Miss 1970; Buzy Rosenberg, Georgia vs. Oregon State 1971; David Langner, Auburn vs. Alabama 1972; Mike Fuller, Auburn vs. Chattanooga 1974; Jacquez Green, Florida vs. Kentucky 1996; Derek Abney, Kentucky vs. Miss. State 2002 (NCAA record)

Punt return touchdowns, season: 4, Derek Abney, Kentucky 2002

Punt return touchdowns, career: 6, Derek Abney, Kentucky 2000–03

Long punt returns, game: 100 (tie), Bert Rechichar, Tennessee vs. Washington & Lee 1950; Jim Campagna, Georgia vs. Vanderbilt 1952; Eddie Kennison, LSU vs. Miss. State 1994 (NCAA record)

Kickoff returns

Most returns, game: 7 (tie), Doug Matthews, Vanderbilt vs. Florida (168 yards) 1969; Jeff Peeples, Vanderbilt vs. Ole Miss (138 yards) 1970; Willie Gault, Tennessee vs. USC (123 yards) 1981; Kio Sanford, Kentucky vs. Tennessee (133 yards) 1994; Fred Talley, Arkansas vs. Boise State (135 yards) 2000; Ronald Hatcher, Vanderbilt vs. Florida (122 yards) 2001; Fred Reid, Miss. State vs. Kentucky (176 yards) 2002; Nick Turner, Miss. State vs. Tennessee (163 yards) 2003

Most returns, season: 34, Kendrick Shanklin, Kentucky (730 yards) 2000

Most returns, career: 107, Mark Johnson, Vanderbilt (2,263 yards) 1986–88, 1990

Yards returned, game: 243, Kwane Doster, Vanderbilt vs. Ole Miss (8 returns) 2002

Yards returned, season: 820, Kio Sanford, Kentucky (33 returns) 1994

Yards returned, career: 2,315, Derek Abney, Kentucky (95 returns) 2000–03

Yards per return, season (minimum 20): 27.9, Dan Bland, Miss. State (20 for 558) 1964

Yards per return, season (minimum 30): 26.8, Derek Abney, Kentucky (30 for 804) 2002

Yards per return, career (minimum 30): 27.6, Bo Carroll, Florida (36 for 992) 1997

Yards per return, career (minimum 50): 25.4, Robert Dow, LSU (70 for 1,780) 1973–76

Kickoff return touchdowns, season: 3, Willie Gault, Tennessee 1980

Kickoff return touchdowns, career: 4, Willie Gault, Tennessee 1979–82

Long kickoff returns, game: 100, Pat Reen, Florida vs. Miami 1940; Jim Burkett, Alabama vs. Duquesne 1949; Bobby Duke, Alabama vs. Auburn 1953; Jimmy Burson, Auburn vs. Tennessee–Chattanooga 1960; Gary Martin, Alabama vs. Miami 1963; Ray Ogden, Alabama vs. Auburn 1964; Sammy Grezaffi, LSU vs. Tennessee 1967; George Ranager, Alabama vs. Auburn 1969; Vernon Studdard, Ole Miss vs. Alabama 1970; Willie Shelby, Alabama vs. Kentucky 1973; Preston Brown, Vanderbilt vs. Ole Miss 1977; Sam DeJarnette, Auburn vs. Miss. State 1980; Willie Gault, Tennessee vs. Pittsburgh 1980; Glen Young, Miss. State vs. LSU 1980; Eric Martin, LSU vs. Kentucky 1981; Pierre Goode, Alabama vs. Ole Miss 1988; Kurt Johnson, Kentucky vs. Georgia 1989; Jack Jackson, Florida vs. Miss. State 1993; Madre Hill, Arkansas vs. LSU 1994; John Avery, Ole Miss vs. LSU 1996; Boo Williams, South Carolina vs. Vanderbilt 1997; John Avery, Ole Miss vs. Alabama 1997; Craig Yeast, Kentucky vs. Florida 1998; Peerless Price, Tennessee vs. Alabama 1998; Leonard Scott, Tennessee vs. Georgia 1999; Bo Carroll, Florida vs. LSU 1999; Deuce McAllister, Ole Miss vs. Arkansas 1999; Tim Carter, Auburn vs. LSU 2000; Derek Abney, Kentucky vs. Florida 2002; Fred Reid, Miss. State vs. Memphis 2003

Total kick returns, most returns, season: 66 (tie), Thomas Bailey, Auburn (42 PR, 24 KR) 1991; Derek Abney, Kentucky (36 PR, 30 KR) 2002

Total kick returns, most returns, career: 199, Tony James, Miss. State (121 PR, 78 KR) 1989–92; 199, Thomas Bailey, Auburn (125 PR, 74 KR) 1991–94 (NCAA record)

Most return yards, game: 266, Nick Turner, Miss. State vs. Tennessee (4/103 PR, 7/163 KR) 2003

Most return yards, season: 1,348, Derek Abney, Kentucky (36/544 PR, 30/804 KR) 2002

Most return yards, career: 3,357, Derek Abney, Kentucky (88/1,042 PR, 95/2,315 KR) 2000–03

Yards per return, game: 52.7, Deuce McAllister, Ole Miss vs. Arkansas (158 yds., 3 rets.) 1999

Yards per return, season (minimum 20): 24.8, Calvin Bird, Kentucky (10/169 PR, 14/426 KR) 1959

Yards per return, career (minimum 100): 19.1, Robert Dow, LSU (37/360 PR, 70/1,780 KR) 1973–76

Kick return touchdowns, season: 6, Derek Abney, Kentucky (4 PR, 2 KR) 2002 (NCAA record)

Kick return touchdowns, career: 8, Derek Abney, Kentucky (6 PR, 2 KR) 2002

Interceptions

Game: 4, Jack Nix, Mississippi State vs. Arkansas 1939; Junior Rosegreen, Auburn vs. Tennessee 2004

Season: 12, Terry Hoage, Georgia (51 yards) 1982

Career: 20, Bobby Wilson, Ole Miss (379 yards) 1946–49; Chris Williams, LSU (91 yards) 1977–80

Yards returned, game: 162, Joe Brodsky, Florida vs. Miss. State (3 int.) 1956

Yards returned, season: 244, Joe Brodsky, Florida (5 int.) 1956

Yards returned, career: 379, Bobby Wilson, Ole Miss (20 int.) 1946–49

Yards per interception, game (minimum 3): 54.0, Joe Brodsky, Florida vs. Miss. State (3/162) 1956

Yards per interception, season (minimum 5): 48.8, Joe Brodsky, Florida (5/244) 1956

Yards per interception, season (minimum 10): 17.7, Bobby Majors, Tennessee (10/177) 1970

Yards per interception, career (minimum 10): 28.2, Wilbur Jamerson, Kentucky (11 for 310) 1947–50

Yards per interception, career (minimum 15): 19.7, Jake Scott, Georgia (16/315) 1967–68

Touchdowns, game: 2 (tie), Joe Brodsky, Florida vs. Miss. State 1956; Jake Scott, Georgia vs. Kentucky 1968 (NCAA record)

Touchdowns, career: 5, Jackie Walker, Tennessee (32 games) 1969–71 (NCAA record)

Long interception returns, game: 100 (tie), Ray Hapes, Ole Miss vs. Ouachita 1937; Bob Davis, Kentucky vs. Washington & Lee 1937; Ray Martin, Tennessee vs. Louisville 1953; Jackie Simpson, Florida vs. Miss. State 1955; Joe Brodsky, Florida vs. Miss. State 1956; Charlie Britt, Georgia vs. Florida 1959; Louis Guy, Ole Miss vs. Tennessee 1962; White Graves, LSU vs. Kentucky 1964; Dave Hunter, Kentucky vs. West Virginia 1968; Greg Jackson, LSU vs. Mississippi State 1988

TEAM RECORDS

Rushing

Most rushes, game: 89, Georgia vs. Kentucky 1967
Most rushes, season: 763, Alabama (3,792 yards in 11 games) 1979
Most rushes, yards gained, game: 748, Alabama vs. Virginia Tech (73 rushes) 1973
Most rushes, season: 4,027, Alabama (664 rushes in 11 games) 1973
Yards per game, season: 366.1, Alabama (4,927 in 11 games) 1973
Yards per rush, game: 10.7, Tennessee vs. Tennessee Tech (44 for 469) 1951
Yards per rush, season: 6.8, LSU (360 for 2,632) 1945

Passing

Most attempts, game: 69, LSU vs. Auburn (33 comp.) 1999
Most attempts, season: 574, Kentucky (414 comp.) 1998
Completions, game: 47, Kentucky vs. Vanderbilt (58 attempts) 1998; Kentucky vs. Arkansas (67 attempts) 1998
Completions, season: 414, Kentucky (574 attempts) 1998
Completion percentage, game (minimum 20): 96.0, Tennessee vs. South Carolina (24 of 25) 1998
Completion percentage, game (minimum 30): 82.4, Georgia vs. Vanderbilt (28 of 34) 2002
Completion percentage, game (minimum 40): 86.9, South Carolina vs. Miss. State (40 of 46) 1995
Completion percentage, season (minimum 100): 68.8, Florida (203 of 295) 1982
Completion percentage, season (minimum 300): 72.1, Kentucky (414 of 574) 1998
Yards gained, game: 585, Kentucky vs. Vanderbilt (47 of 58) 1998
Yards gained, season: 4,534, Kentucky (414 of 574) 1998
Yards per game: 412.2, Kentucky (4,534 in 11 games) 1998
Yards per attempt, season: 13.4, Alabama (94 for 1,261) 1973 (NCAA record)
Passing touchdowns, game: 9, Florida vs. Central Michigan 1997
Passing touchdowns, season: 48, Florida (12 games) 1995
Interceptions, game: 9, Florida vs. Auburn 1969
Interceptions, season: 33, Kentucky (227 atts., 110 comp.) 1967
Fewest interceptions, season (minimum 100 attempts): 1:104.0, Alabama (1 in 104) 1980
Fewest interceptions, season (minimum 150 attempts): 1:87.5, Auburn (2 in 175) 1982
Fewest interceptions, season (minimum 200 attempts): 1:74.8, Alabama (4 in 299) 1997
Fewest interceptions, season (minimum 300 attempts): 1:97.8, Tennessee (4 in 391) 1995 (NCAA record)
Fewest interceptions, season (minimum 400 attempts): 1:61.7, Georgia (7 in 432) 1993

Total offense

Most plays, game: 106, Arkansas vs. Ole Miss 2001
Most plays, season: 1,023, Georgia (5,324 yards) 2003
Yards gained, game: 833, Alabama vs. Virginia Tech (748 rushing, 85 passing) 1973
Yards gained, season: 6,413, Florida (2,083 rush, 4,330 pass, 12 games) 1995
Yards gained, two teams: 1,329, Tennessee (695) vs. Kentucky (634) 1997
Yards per game: 534.4, Florida (6,413 in 12 games) 1995
Yards per play, game: 11.9, Alabama vs. Virginia Tech (70 for 833) 1973
Yards per play, season: 7.40, Florida (6,413 in 867) 1995
First downs, most rushing, game: 28, Auburn vs. Ole Miss 1985
First downs, most rushing, season: 213, Alabama 1979
First downs, most passing, game: 25, South Carolina vs. Miss. State 1995
First downs, most passing, season: 196, Kentucky 1998
First downs, total, game: 40, Vanderbilt vs. Davidson 1969
First downs, total, season: 327, Florida 1995

Punting

Most punts, game: 36, Kentucky vs. Washington & Lee 1934
Most punts, season: 139, Tennessee 1937 (NCAA record)

Yards, game: 1,386, Kentucky vs. Washington & Lee (36 punts) 1934
Yards, season: 5,620, Tennessee (139 punts) 1937
Average (minimum 10): 52.0, Kentucky vs. Cincinnati (10 for 520) 1944
Average (minimum 20): 43.0, Georgia Tech vs. Florida 1938
Average, season: 47.6, Vanderbilt (59 for 2,810) 1984

Punt returns

Most returns, game: 20, Mississippi State vs. TCU (128 yards) 1936
Most returns, season: 71, Alabama (783 yards) 1946
Yards returned, game: 272, Florida vs. Kentucky (11 returns) 1996
Yards returned, season: 974, Tennessee (68 returns) 1940
Yards per return, game (minimum 3): 45.0, Ole Miss vs. Arkansas (3 for 135) 2000
Yards per return, season: 20.8, Mississippi State (25 for 521) 1971

Kick returns

Most returns, game: 11 (tie), Ole Miss vs. Alabama 1989; Kentucky vs. Florida 1994
Most returns, season: 62, Kentucky 2000
Yards returned, game: 259, Alabama vs. Auburn (8 returns) 1969
Yards returned, season: 1,263, Kentucky (54 returns) 1994
Yards per return, game (minimum 3): 66.7, Kentucky vs. Vanderbilt (3 for 200) 1945
Yards per return, season: 28.8, Mississippi State (19 for 547) 1940

Scoring

Most points, game: 93, LSU vs. Southwestern Louisiana 1936
Most points, season: 559, Florida (12 games) 1996
Most points, two teams (overtime games only): 134, Arkansas (71) vs. Kentucky (63) [7 OT] 2003
Most points, two teams (non-overtime games): 104, South Carolina (65) vs. Mississippi State (39) 1995
Points per game: 46.6, Florida (559 in 12) 1996
Most touchdowns, game: 14 (tie), Ole Miss vs. West Tennessee Teachers 1935; LSU vs. Southwestern Louisiana 1936
Most touchdowns, season: 76, Florida (12 games) 1996
Most points in a tie game: 37-37, Alabama vs. Florida State 1967

Field goals

Game: 6 (tie), Florida vs. Kentucky 1984; Florida vs. Florida State 1983; Auburn vs. Kentucky 1982; Georgia vs. Georgia Tech 2001
Season: 31, Georgia 2003
PAT kicks, game: 11 (tie), South Carolina vs. Kent 1995; Kentucky vs. North Dakota 1950; Alabama vs. Delta State 1951; Alabama vs. Virginia Tech 1973; LSU vs. Rice 1977; Florida vs. West Texas State 1982; Kentucky vs. Texas–El Paso 2002
PAT kicks, season: 72, Florida 1995
Consecutive PAT kicks: 199, Alabama (Peter Kim 54, Paul Trodd 4, Terry Sanders 1, Van Tiffin 135, Philip Doyle 5) 1981–87

Defense

Fewest rushes allowed, game: 13 (tie), Florida vs. Vanderbilt 1983; Alabama vs. Vanderbilt 1989
Fewest rushes allowed, season: 231, Tennessee (9 games) 1945
Fewest yards allowed, game: Minus-93, Kentucky vs. Kansas State 1970
Fewest rushing yards allowed, season: 305, Alabama (9 games) 1938
Fewest rushing yards per game: 33.9, Alabama (305 yards in 9 games) 1938
Fewest rushing yards per rush, game: Minus-3.95, Kentucky vs. Kansas State (–91 in 23 rushes) 1970
Fewest yards per rush, season: 0.95, Alabama (305 yards in 321 rushes) 1938

Fewest rushing touchdowns allowed, season: 0, Tennessee 1939 (NCAA record)

Fewest passes, game: 0 (tie), Kentucky vs. Tennessee 1952; Tennessee vs. Georgia Tech 1977 (NCAA record)

Fewest passes, season: 73, Georgia Tech (10 games) 1957

Fewest completions, game: Several teams with 0

Fewest completions, season: 31 (tie), Alabama (9 games) 1938; Georgia Tech (10 games) 1957

Lowest completion percentage, season: 27.1, Auburn (36 of 133) 1950

Fewest passing yards, game: Minus-10, Auburn vs. Alabama (1 comp.) 1952

Fewest passing yards, season: 291, Alabama (9 games) 1945

Fewest passing touchdowns: 0, Tennessee (10 games) 1939; Florida (10 games) 1954 (NCAA record)

Interceptions, game: 9 (tie), Georgia vs. Presbyterian (42 passes) 1943; Auburn vs. Florida (66 passes) 1969

Interceptions, season: 36, Tennessee 1970

Interception return yards, game: 240, Kentucky vs. Ole Miss (6 ints.) 1949 (NCAA record)

Interception return yards, season: 782, Tennessee (25 ints.) 1971 (NCAA record)

Interception return touchdowns, season: 7, Tennessee 1971 (NCAA record)

Total defense

Fewest plays, game: 24, Ole Miss vs. South Carolina 1947

Fewest plays, season: 368, Tennessee 1945

Fewest yards, game: Minus-30, Auburn vs. Tennessee 1958

Fewest yards, season: 701, Alabama (9 games) 1938

Fewest yards per game, season: 77.9, Alabama (701 yards in 9 games) 1938

First downs, fewest rushing, game: 0 (tie), South Carolina vs. Kent 1995; Auburn vs. Florida 2001

First downs, fewest rushing, season: 24, Alabama (9 games) 1938

First downs, fewest passing, game: 0, several teams

First downs, fewest passing, season: 11, Alabama (9 games) 1938

First downs, fewest total, game: 0, Auburn vs. Tennessee 1958

First downs, fewest total, season: 35, Alabama (9 games) 1938

Scoring defense

Fewest points, season: 0, Tennessee (10 games) 1939 (NCAA record)

Fewest points per game, season: 0.0, Tennessee (0 points in 10 games) 1939 (NCAA record)

Fewest points per season (since 1975): 5.3, Alabama (58 points in 11 games) 1979

· Appendix F ·

Awards

NATIONAL AWARDS

Heisman Trophy

Most outstanding football player by the Downtown Athletic Club of New York.
1942   Frank Sinkwich, HB, Georgia
1959   Billy Cannon, HB, LSU
1966   Steve Spurrier, QB, Florida
1971   Pat Sullivan, QB, Auburn
1982   Herschel Walker, RB, Georgia
1985   Bo Jackson, RB, Auburn
1996   Danny Wuerffel, QB, Florida
(*Note:* Running back George Rogers won in 1980 before South Carolina joined the SEC.)

Maxwell Award

Most outstanding football player by the Maxwell Football Club of Philadelphia.
1946   Charley Trippi, HB, Georgia
1982   Herschel Walker, RB, Georgia
1996   Danny Wuerffel, QB, Florida
1997   Peyton Manning, QB, Tennessee
2003   Eli Manning, QB, Ole Miss

Walter Camp Award

Presented by the Walter Camp Foundation to the nation's top overall player.
1971   Pat Sullivan, QB, Auburn
1982   Herschel Walker, RB, Georgia
1985   Bo Jackson, RB, Auburn
1996   Danny Wuerffel, QB, Florida

Outland Trophy

Outstanding interior lineman by the Football Writers Association of America.
1950   Bob Gain, T, Kentucky
1958   Zeke Smith, G, Auburn
1964   Steve DeLong, T, Tennessee
1968   Bill Stanfill, T, Georgia
1988   Tracy Rocker, DT, Auburn
1999   Chris Samuels, T, Alabama
2000   John Henderson, DT, Tennessee
(*Note:* Bill Brooks won in 1954 and Lloyd Phillips in 1966 before Arkansas joined the SEC.)

Jim Thorpe Award

Best defensive back by the Jim Thorpe Athletic Club.
1993   Antonio Langham, Alabama
1996   Lawrence Wright, Florida
2004   Carlos Rogers, Auburn

Fred Biletnikoff Award

Outstanding wide receiver by the Football Writers Association of America.
2001   Josh Reed, LSU

Vince Lombardi/Rotary Award

Outstanding lineman of the year, sponsored by the Rotary Club of Houston.
1986   Cornelius Bennett, LB, Alabama
1988   Tracy Rocker, DT, Auburn
2004   David Pollack, DE, Georgia

Butkus Award

Top linebacker, established by the Downtown Athletic Club of Orlando.
1988   Derrick Thomas, LB, Alabama

Lou Groza Award

Top kicker, sponsored by the Palm Beach County Sports Authority in conjunction with the Orange Bowl committee.
1993   Judd Davis, Florida
2003   Jonathan Nichols, Ole Miss

Davey O'Brien Award

Best quarterback by the Football Writers Association of America.
1995   Danny Wuerffel, Florida
1996   Danny Wuerffel, Florida
1997   Peyton Manning, Tennessee

Mike Fox/Bronco Nagurski Award

Top defensive player by the Football Writers Association of America and Charlotte, N.C. Touchdown Club.
1998   Champ Bailey, Georgia

Johnny Unitas Golden Arm Award

Top senior quarterback by the Kentucky Chapter of the National Football Foundation.
1994   Jay Barker, Alabama
1996   Danny Wuerffel, Florida
1997   Peyton Manning, Tennessee
2003   Eli Manning, Ole Miss

Chuck Bednarik Trophy

Nation's top defensive player by the Maxwell Club
2004   David Pollack, DE, Georgia

Rimington Trophy

Outstanding center
2005   Ben Wilkerson, LSU

Mosi Tatupu Award

Top special teams player by the Honolulu and Maui Quarterbacks Clubs.
2002   Glenn Pakulak, Kentucky

Doak Walker Award

Best running back among Division IA juniors or seniors, sponsored by the GTE/Southern Methodist Athletic Forum.
1992   Garrison Hearst, Georgia

Ted Hendricks Award

Top defensive end
2003   David Pollack, Georgia
2004   David Pollack, Georgia

Lott Trophy

Recognizes athletic performance and character, presented by The Pacific Club Impact Foundation of Newport Beach, Calif.
2004   David Pollack, Georgia
2005   DeMeco Ryans, Alabama

Wuerffel Award

Honors the player who best combines exemplary community service with outstanding academic and athletic achievement.
2005   Rudy Niswanger, C, LSU

Draddy Trophy

The "Academic Heisman"
1991   John B. Culpepper, Florida
1996   Danny Wuerffel, Florida
1997   Peyton Manning, Tennessee
1998   Matt Stinchcomb, Georgia
2004   Michael Munoz, Tennessee
2005   Rudy Niswanger, LSU

National Coach of the Year (named by various organizations)

1942   Bill Alexander, Georgia Tech
1956   Bowden Wyatt, Tennessee
1958   Paul Dietzel, LSU
1961   Paul W. "Bear" Bryant, Alabama
1970   Charlie McClendon, LSU
1971   Paul W. "Bear" Bryant, Alabama
1973   Paul W. "Bear" Bryant, Alabama
1980   Vince Dooley, Georgia
1982   Jerry Stovall, LSU
1992   Gene Stallings, Alabama
1993   Terry Bowden, Auburn
1998   Phillip Fulmer, Tennessee
2003   Nick Saban, LSU
2004   Tommy Tuberville, Auburn

SOUTHEASTERN CONFERENCE AWARDS

SEC MVP

1933   Beattie Feathers, HB, Tennessee
1934   Dixie Howell, TB, Alabama

1935   Willie Geny, E, Vanderbilt
1936   Walter Gilbert, C, Auburn
1937   Carl Hinkle, C, Vanderbilt
1938   George Cafego, HB, Tennessee
1939   Ken Kavanaugh, E, LSU/Bob Foxx, WB, Tennessee
1940   Erwin Elrod, E, Mississippi State
1941   Jack Jenkins, FB, Vanderbilt
1942   Frank Sinkwich, TB, Georgia
1943   No selection
1944   Tom McWilliams, HB, Mississippi State
1945   Harry Gilmer, QB, Alabama
1946   Charley Trippi, HB, Georgia
1947   Charlie Conerly, TB, Ole Miss
1948   John Rauch, QB, Georgia
1949   Travis Tidwell, QB, Auburn
1950   Babe Parilli, QB, Kentucky
1951   Bill Wade, QB, Vanderbilt
1952   Jackie Parker, QB, Mississippi State
1953   Jackie Parker, QB, Mississippi State
1954   Art Davis, HB, Mississippi State
1955   John Majors, TB, Tennessee
1956   John Majors, TB, Tennessee
1957   Lou Michaels, T, Kentucky
1958   Billy Cannon, HB, LSU
1959   Billy Cannon, HB, LSU
1960   Jake Gibbs, QB, Ole Miss
1961   Pat Trammell, QB, Alabama
1962   Jerry Stovall, HB, LSU
1963   Jimmy Sidle, QB, Auburn
1964   Tucker Frederickson, FB, Auburn
1965   Steve Sloan, QB, Alabama
1966   Steve Spurrier, QB, Florida
1967   Bob Goodridge, E, Vanderbilt
1968   Jake Scott, S, Georgia
1969   Archie Manning, QB, Ole Miss
1970   Pat Sullivan, QB, Auburn
1971   Johnny Musso, HB, Alabama
1972   Terry Davis, QB, Alabama
1973   Sonny Collins, TB, Kentucky
1974   Rockey Felker, QB, Mississippi State
1975   Jimmy DuBose, FB, Florida
1976   Ray Goff, QB, Georgia
1977   Charles Alexander, TB, LSU
1978   Willie McClendon, TB, Georgia
1979   Joe Cribbs, RB, Auburn
1980   Herschel Walker, RB, Georgia
1981   Herschel Walker, RB, Georgia
1982   Herschel Walker, RB, Georgia
1983   Reggie White, DT, Tennessee
1984   Kerwin Bell, QB, Florida
1985   Bo Jackson, RB, Auburn
1986   Cornelius Bennett, LB, Alabama
1987   Wendell Davis, WR, LSU
1988   Tracy Rocker, DT, Auburn
1989   Emmitt Smith, RB, Florida
1990   Shane Mathews, QB, Florida

1991   Shane Mathews, QB, Florida
1992   Garrison Hearst, RB, Georgia
1993   Heath Shuler, QB, Tennessee
1994   Jay Barker, QB, Alabama
1995   Danny Wuerffel, QB, Florida
1996   Danny Wuerffel, QB, Florida
1997   Peyton Manning, QB, Tennessee
1998   Tim Couch, QB, Kentucky
1999   Shaun Alexander, RB, Alabama
2000   Rudi Johnson, RB, Auburn
2001   Rex Grossman, QB, Florida
2002   David Pollack, DE, Georgia
2003   Eli Manning, QB, Ole Miss (offense)
        Chad Lavalais, DT, LSU (defense)
2004   Jason Campbell, QB, Auburn (offense)
        David Pollack, DE, Georgia (defense)
        Carnell Williams, RB, Auburn (special teams)
2005   Jay Cutler, QB, Vanderbilt (offense)
        DeMeco Ryans, LB, Alabama (defense)
        Skyler Green, WR/RS (special teams)

Jacobs Award (Outstanding SEC Blocker)

1935   Riley Smith, Alabama
1936   Billy May, LSU
1937   Leroy Monsky, Alabama
1938   Sam Bartholomew, Tennessee
1939   Sam Bartholomew, Tennessee
1940   Lloyd Cheatham, Auburn
1941   Jack Jenkins, Vanderbilt
1942   Jack Jenkins, Vanderbilt
1943   John Steber, Georgia Tech
1944   Billy Bevis, Tennessee
1945   Billy Bevis, Tennessee
1946   Hal Self, Alabama
1947   Buddy Bowen, Ole Miss
1948   Truitt Smith, Mississippi State
1949   Butch Avinger, Alabama
1950   Butch Avinger, Alabama
1951   Jimmy Hahn, Tennessee
1952   John Michels, Tennessee
1953   Crawford Mims, Ole Miss
1954   Charles Evans, Mississippi State
1955   Paige Cothren, Ole Miss
1956   Stockton Adkins, Tennessee
1957   Stockton Adkins, Tennessee
1958   J. W. Brodnax, LSU
1959   Jim Cartwright, Tennessee
1960   Jim Cartwright, Tennessee
1961   Billy Neighbors, Alabama
1962   Butch Wilson, Alabama
1963   Tucker Frederickson, Auburn
1964   Tucker Frederickson, Auburn
1965   Hal Wantland, Tennessee
1966   Cecil Dowdy, Alabama
1967   Bob Johnson, Tennessee

1968   Brad Johnson, Georgia
1969   Chip Kell, Tennessee
1970   Chip Kell, Tennessee
1971   Royce Smith, Georgia
1972   John Hannah, Alabama
1973   Buddy Brown, Alabama
1974   Sylvester Croom, Alabama
1975   Randy Johnson, Georgia
1976   Warren Bryant, Kentucky
1977   Bob Cryder, Alabama
1978   Robert Dugas, LSU
1979   Dwight Stephenson, Alabama
1980   Nat Hudson, Georgia
1981   Wayne Harris, Mississippi State
1982   Wayne Harris, Mississippi State
1983   Guy McIntyre, Georgia
1984   Lomas Brown, Florida
1985   Peter Anderson, Georgia
1986   Wes Neighbors, Alabama
1987   Harry Galbreath, Tennessee
1988   Howard Cross, Alabama
1989   Eric Still, Tennessee
1990   Antone Davis, Tennessee
1991   Cal Dixon, Florida
1992   Everett Lindsay, Ole Miss
1993   Tobie Sheils, Alabama
1994   Jason Odom, Florida
1995   Jason Odom, Florida
1996   Donnie Young, Florida
1997   Alan Faneca, LSU
1998   Matt Stinchcomb, Georgia
1999   Chris Samuels, Alabama
2000   Kenyatta Walker, Florida
2001   Kendall Simmons, Auburn
2002   Shawn Andrews, Arkansas
2003   Shawn Andrews, Arkansas
2004   Wesley Britt, Alabama
2005   Marcus McNeill, Auburn

COACHES' ALL-SEC (FIRST TEAMS)

1984

Offense: Chuck Scott, WR, Vanderbilt; Eric Martin, WR, LSU; Jim Popp, TE, Vanderbilt; Corwyn Aldredge, TE, Mississippi State; Lomas Brown, T, Florida; Lance Smith, T, LSU; Bill Mayo, G, Tennessee; Jeff Lott, G, Auburn; Phil Bromley, C, Florida; Kurt Page, QB, Vanderbilt; Dalton Hilliard, RB, LSU; Johnnie Jones, RB, Tennessee; Kevin Butler, K, Georgia.

Defense: Freddie Joe Nunn, DE, Mississippi; Alonzo Johnson, DE, Florida; Jon Hand, DT, Alabama; Ben Thomas, DT, Auburn; Tim Newton, NG, Florida; Gregg Carr, LB, Auburn; Cornelius Bennett, LB, Alabama; Knox Culpepper, LB, Georgia; Jeff Sanchez, DB, Georgia; Paul Calhoun, DB, Kentucky; Liffort Hobley, DB, LSU; Jeffrey Dale, DB, LSU; Ricky Anderson, P, Vanderbilt.

1985

Offense: Tim McGee, WR, Tennessee; Al Bell, WR, Alabama; Jim Popp, TE, Vanderbilt; Will Wolford, OL, Vanderbilt; Jeff Zimmerman, OL, Florida; Bruce Wilkerson, OL, Tennessee; Steve Wallace, OL,

Auburn; Peter Anderson, C, Georgia; Mike Shula, QB, Alabama; Bo Jackson, RB, Auburn; Dalton Hilliard, RB, LSU; Carlos Reveiz, K, Tennessee.

Defense: Jon Hand, DL, Alabama; Gerald Williams, DL, Auburn; Roland Barbay, DL, LSU; Greg Waters, DL, Georgia; Harold Hallman, NG, Auburn; Michael Brooks, LB, LSU; Alonzo Johnson, LB, Florida; Cornelius Bennett, LB, Alabama; Dale Jones, LB, Tennessee; Chris White, DB, Tennessee; Tom Powell, DB, Auburn; John Little, DB, Georgia; Norman Jefferson, DB, LSU; Freddie Robinson, DB, Alabama; Bill Smith, P, Mississippi.

1986

Offense: Wendell Davis, WR, LSU; Ricky Nattiel, WR, Florida; Brian Kinchen, TE, LSU; Eric Andolsek, OL, LSU; Bruce Wilkerson, OL, Tennessee, Jeff Zimmerman, OL, Florida; Wilbur Stozier, OL, Georgia; Wes Neighbors, C, Alabama; Ben Tamburello, C, Auburn; Don Smith, QB, Mississippi State; Tommy Hodson, QB, LSU; Brent Fullwood, RB, Auburn; Bobby Humphrey, RB, Alabama; Van Tiffin, K, Alabama.

Defense: Tracy Rocker, DL, Auburn; Henry Thomas, DL, LSU; Roland Barbay, DL, LSU; Jeff Herrod, LB, Mississippi; Toby Caston, LB, LSU; Cornelius Bennett, OLB, Alabama; Aundray Bruce, OLB, Auburn; Dale Jones, OLB, Tennessee; Stevon Moore, DB, Mississippi; Freddie Robinson, DB, Alabama; Jarvis Williams, DB, Florida; Adrian White, DB, Florida; Jeff Noblin, DB, Mississippi; Bill Smith, P, Mississippi.

1987

Offense: Wendell Davis, WR, LSU; Lawyer Tillman, WR, Auburn; Howard Cross, TE, Alabama; Walter Reeves, TE, Auburn; Kim Stephens, OL, Georgia; Stacy Searels, OL, Auburn; Harry Galbreath, OL, Tennessee; Eric Andolsek, OL, LSU; Nacho Albergamo, C, LSU; Jeff Burger, QB, Auburn; Tommy Hodson, QB, LSU; Bobby Humphrey, RB, Alabama; Emmitt Smith, RB, Florida; Win Lyle, K, Auburn.

Defense: Tracy Rocker, DL, Auburn; Jerry Reese, DL, Kentucky; Mark Hovanic, DL, Tennessee; Darrell Phillips, NG, LSU; Derrick Thomas, LB, Alabama; Aundray Bruce, LB, Auburn; Chris Gaines, LB, Vanderbilt; Kurt Crain, LB, Auburn; Terry McDaniel, DB, Tennessee; Chris Carrier, DB, LSU; Kevin Porter, DB, Auburn; Brian Shulman, P, Auburn.

1988

Offense: Boo Mitchell, WR, Vanderbilt; Tony Moss, WR, LSU; Wesley Walls, TE, Ole Miss; Ralph Norwood, OL, LSU; David Williams, OL, Florida; Larry Rose, OL, Alabama; Eric Still, OL, Tennessee; Jim Thompson, OL, Auburn; Todd Wheeler, C, Georgia; Tommy Hodson, QB, LSU; Tim Worley, RB, Georgia; Eddie Fuller, RB, LSU; Emmitt Smith, RB, Florida; David Browndyke, K, LSU.

Defense: Trace Armstrong, DT, Florida; Tracy Rocker, DT, Auburn; Bill Goldberg, DL, Georgia; Darrell Phillips, DL, LSU; Jeff Roth, DL, Florida; Keith DeLong, LB, Tennessee; Quentin Riggins, LB, Auburn; Eric Hill, OLB, LSU; Derrick Thomas, OLB, Alabama; Carlo Cheattom, DB, Auburn; Louis Oliver, DB, Florida; Todd Sandroni, DB, Mississippi; Ben Smith, DB, Georgia; Brian Shulman, P, Auburn.

1989

Offense: Tony Moss, WR, LSU; Willie Green, WR, Mississippi; Lamonde Russell, TE, Alabama; John Durden, OL, Florida; Ed King, OL, Auburn; Eric Still, OL, Tennessee; Terrill Chatman, OL, Alabama; Antone Davis, OL, Tennessee; Mike Pfeifer, OL, Kentucky; John Hudson, C, Auburn; Gary Hollingsworth, QB, Alabama; Emmitt Smith, RB, Florida; Chuck Webb, RB, Tennessee; Philip Doyle, K, Alabama.

Defense: Oliver Barnett, DT, Kentucky; Marion Hobby, DT, Tennessee; Willie Wyatt, NG, Alabama; Keith McCants, ILB, Alabama; Quentin Riggins, ILB, Auburn; Huey Richardson, OLB, Florida; Tony Bennett, OLB, Mississippi; Craig Ogletree, OLB, Auburn; Richard Fain, DB, Florida; John Mangum, DB, Alabama; Ben Smith, DB, Georgia; Efrum Thomas, DB, Alabama; Kent Elmore, P, Tennessee.

1990

Offense: Todd Kinchen, WR, LSU; Carl Pickens, WR, Tennessee; Kirk Kirkpatrick, TE, Florida; Terrill Chatman, OL, Alabama; Antone Davis, OL, Tennessee; Ed King, OL, Auburn; Charles McRae, OL, Tennessee; Rob Selby, OL, Auburn; Blake Miller, C, LSU; Roger Shultz, C, Alabama; Shane Matthews, QB, Florida; Randy Baldwin, RB, Ole Miss; Tony Thompson, RB, Tennessee; Phillip Doyle, K, Alabama.

Defense: Kelvin Pritchett, DL, Ole Miss; David Rocker, DL, Auburn; George Thornton, DL, Alabama; Randy Holleran, OLB, Kentucky; John Sullins, OLB, Alabama; Godfrey Myles, OLB, Florida; Huey Richardson, OLB, Florida; Dale Carter, DB, Tennessee; Richard Fain, DB, Florida; Efrum Thomas, DB, Alabama; Will White, DB, Florida; David Lawrence, P, Vanderbilt.

1991

Offense: Todd Kinchen, WR, LSU; Carol Pickens, WR, Tennessee; Victor Hall, TE, Auburn; Eddie Blake, OK, Auburn; Hesham Ismail, OL, Florida; Tom Myslinski, OL, Tennessee; John James, OL, Mississippi State; Kevin Mawae, OL, LSU; Cal Dixon, C, Florida; Shane Matthews, QB, Florida; Corey Harris, RB, Vanderbilt; Siran Stacy, RB, Alabama; Arden Czyzewski, K, Florida.

Defense: Brad Culpepper, FL, Florida; Robert Stewart, DL, Alabama; Nate Williams, DL, Mississippi State; Tim Paulk, ILB, Florida; Dwayne Simmons, ILB, Georgia; Ephesians Bartley, OLB, Florida; Darryl Hardy, OLB, Tennessee; Corey Barlow, DB, Auburn; Dale Carter, DB, Tennessee; Jeremy Lincoln, DB, Tennessee; Will White, DB, Florida; Shayne Edge, P, Florida.

1992

Offense: Andre Hastings, WR, Georgia; Willie Jackson, WR, Florida; Kirk Botkin, TE, Arkansas; Everett Lindsay, OL, Mississippi; Ernest Dye, OL, USC; Mike Stowell, OL, Tennessee; John James, OL, Mississippi State; Tobie Sheils, C, Alabama; Shane Matthews, QB, Florida; Garrison Hearst, RB, Georgia; James Bostic, RB, Auburn; Scott Etheridge, K, Auburn.

Defense: Eric Curry, DL, Alabama; John Copeland, DL, Alabama; Todd Kelly, DL, Tennessee; ILB Derrick Oden, Alabama; James Willis, ILB, Auburn; Mitch Davis, OLB, Georgia; Lemanski Hall, OLB, Alabama; Antonio Langham, DB, Alabama; George Teague, DB, Alabama; Will White, DB, Florida; Johnny Dixon, DB, Ole Miss; Todd Jordan, P, Mississippi State.

1993

Offense: David Palmer, WR, Alabama; Cory Fleming, WR, Tennessee; Shannon Mitchell, TE, Georgia; Wayne Grady, OL, Auburn; Bernard Williams, OL, Georgia; Jeff Smith, OL, Tennessee; Reggie Green, OL, Florida; Tobie Sheils, C, Alabama; Heath Shuler, QB, Tennessee; Errict Rhett, RB, Florida; James Bostic, RB, Auburn; Michael Proctor, K, Alabama.

Defense: Henry Ford, DL, Arkansas; William Gaines, DL, Florida; Jeremy Nunley, DL, Alabama; Dewayne Dotson, OLB, Ole Miss; Ernest Dickson, OLB, South Carolina; Lemanski Hall, OLB, Alabama; Marty Moore, ILB, Kentucky; Randall Godfrey, ILB, Georgia; Antonio Langham, DB, Alabama; Marcus Jenkins, DB, Kentucky; Orlando Watters, DB, Arkansas; Johnny Dixon, DB, Ole Miss; Terry Daniel, P, Auburn.

1994

Offense: Jack Jackson, WR, Florida; Frank Sanders, WR, Auburn; David LaFleur, TE, LSU; Jason Odom, OL, Florida; Kevin Mays, OL, Tennessee; Jesse James, OL, Mississippi State; Jon Stevenson, OL, Alabama; Willie Anderson, OL, Auburn; Shannon Roubique, C, Auburn; Jay Barker, QB, Alabama; Sherman Williams, RB, Alabama; Stephen Davis, RB, Auburn; Michael Proctor, K, Alabama.

Defense: Kevin Carter, DL, Florida; Mike Pelton, DL, Auburn; Ellis Johnson, DL, Florida; Abdul Jackson, ILB, Ole Miss; Dwayne Curry, ILB, Mississippi State; Ben Hanks, OLB, Florida; Gabe Northern, OLB, LSU; Larry Kennedy, DB, Florida; Brian Robinson, DB, Auburn; Walt Harris, DB, Mississippi State; Willie Gaston, DB, Alabama; Alundis Brice, DB, Ole Miss; Terry Daniel, P, Auburn.

1995

Offense: Andy Fuller, TE, Auburn; Jason Odom, OL, Florida; Reggie Green, OL, Florida; Willie Anderson, OL, Auburn; Jason Layman, OL, Tennessee; Jeff Smith, C, Tennessee; Chris Doering, WR, Florida; Eric Moulds, WR, Mississippi State; Peyton Manning, QB, Tennessee; Moe Williams, RB, Kentucky; Madre Hill, RB, Arkansas; Jeff Hall, K, Tennessee.

Defense: Shannon Brown, DL, Alabama; Mark Campbell, FL, Florida; Steven Conley, DL, Arkansas; Gabe Northern, OLB, LSU; Ben Hanks, OLB, Florida; Dexter Daniels, ILB, Florida; Mark Smith, ILB, Arkansas; Anthone Lott, DB, Florida; Lawrence Wright, DB, Florida; Walt Harris, DB, Mississippi State; DeRon Jenkins, DB, Tennessee; Chad Kessler, P, LSU.

1996

Offense: David LaFleur, TE, LSU; Donnie Young, OL, Florida; Adam Meadows, OL, Georgia; Brent Smith, OL, Mississippi State; Alan Faneca, OL, LSU; Jeff Mitchell, C, Florida; Joey Kent, WR, Tennessee; Ike Hilliard, WR, Florida; Reidel Anthony, WR, Florida; Danny Wuerffel, QB, Florida; Duce Staley, RB, South Carolina; Kevin Faulk, RB, LSU; Jeff Hall, K, Tennessee; Jaret Holmes, K, Auburn.

Defense: Leonard Little, DL, Tennessee; Michael Myers, DL, Alabama; Ed Chester, DL, Florida; Dwayne Rudd, OLB, Alabama; Ralph Staten, OLB, Alabama; Jamie Duncan, ILB, Vanderbilt; James Bates, ILB, Florida; Takeo Spikes, ILB, Auburn; Kevin Jackson, DB, Alabama; Lawrence Wright, DB, Florida; Fred Weary, DB, Florida; Anthone Lott, DB, Florida; Terry Fair, DB, Tennessee; Bill Marinangel, P, Vanderbilt.

1997

Offense: Rufus French, TE, Ole Miss; Alan Faneca, OL, LSU; Robert Hicks, OL, Mississippi State; Victor Riley, OL, Auburn; Matt Stinchcomb, OL, Georgia; Todd McClure, C, LSU; Jacquez Green, WR, Florida; Hines Ward, WR, Georgia; Peyton Manning, QB, Tennessee; Fred Taylor, RB, Florida; Kevin Faulk, RB, LSU; Jaret Holmes, K, Auburn.

Defense: Chuck Wiley, DL, LSU; Mike Moten, DL, Florida; Greg Favors, DL, Mississippi State; Jevon Kearse, OLB, Florida; Al Wilson, OLB, Tennessee; Jamie Duncan, ILB, Vanderbilt; Takeo Spikes, ILB, Auburn; Fred Weary, DB, Florida; Champ Bailey, DB, Georgia; Cedric Donaldson, DB, LSU; Corey Chavous, DB, Vanderbilt; Terry Fair, DB, Tennessee; Chad Kessler, P, LSU.

1998

Offense: Rufus French, TE, Ole Miss; Matt Stinchcomb, OL, Georgia; Brandon Burlsworth, OL, Arkansas; Zach Piller, OL, Florida; Chris Terry, OL, Georgia; Todd McClure, C, LSU; Craig Yeast, WR, Kentucky; Travis McGriff, WR, Florida; Tim Couch, QB, Kentucky; James Johnson, RB, Mississippi State; Kevin Faulk, RB, LSU; Jeff Hall, K, Tennessee.

Defense: Anthony McFarland, DL, LSU; Reggie McGrew, DL, Florida; Leonardo Carson, DL, Auburn; Melvin Bradley, DL, Arkansas; Jevon Kearse, OLB, Florida; Raynoch Thompson, OLB, Tennessee; Al Wilson, ILB, Tennessee; Johnny Rutledge, ILB, Florida; Zac Painter, DB, Arkansas; Champ Bailey, DB, Georgia; Teako Brown, DB, Florida, Tony George, DB, Florida; Fernando Bryant, DB, Alabama; Daniel Pope, P, Alabama.

1999

Offense: James Whalen, TE, Kentucky; Chris Samuels, OL, Alabama; Cooper Carlisle, OL, Florida; Todd Wade, OL, Ole Miss; Cosey Coleman, OL, Tennessee; Paul Hogan, C, Alabama; Freddie Milons, WR, Alabama; Darrell Jackson, WR, Florida; Tee Martin, QB, Tennessee; Shaun Alexander, RB, Alabama; Deuce McAllister, RB, Ole Miss; Jeff Chandler, K, Florida.

Defense: Alex Brown, DL, Florida; Shaun Ellis, DL, Tennessee; Darwin Walker, DL, Tennessee; Jeff Snedegar, OLB, Kentucky; Raynoch Thompson, OLB, Tennessee; Barrin Simpson, ILB, Mississippi State; Jamie Winborn, ILB, Vanderbilt; Kenoy Kennedy, DB, Arkansas; Ashley Cooper, DB, Mississippi State; Deon Grant, DB, Tennessee; Dwayne Goodrich, DB, Tennessee; Andy Smith, P, Kentucky.

2000

Offense: Derek Smith, TE, Kentucky; Robert Royal, TE, LSU; Kenyatta Walker, OL, Florida; Terrence Metcalf, OL, Ole Miss; Mike Pearson, OL, Florida; Kendall Simmons, OL, Auburn; Jonas Jennings, OL, Georgia; Pork Chop Womack, OL, Mississippi State; Paul Hogan, C, Alabama; Jabar Gaffney, WR, Florida; Josh Reed, WR, LSU; Josh Booty, QB, LSU; Rudi Johnson, RB, Auburn; Travis Henry, RB, Tennessee; Alex Walls, P, Tennessee.

Defense: Alex Brown, DL, Florida; John Henderson, DL, Tennessee; Richard Seymour, DL, Georgia; Kalimba Edwards, OLB, South Carolina; Eric Westmoreland, OLB, Tennessee; Quinton Caver, OLB, Arkansas; Jamie Winborn, ILB, Vanderbilt; Lito Sheppard, DB, Florida; Fred Smoot, DB, Mississippi State; Tim Wansley, DB, Georgia; Rodney Crayton, DB, Auburn; Ken Lucas, DB, Ole Miss; Damon Duval, P, Auburn.

2001

Offense: Randy McMichael, TE, Georgia; Terrence Metcalf, OL, Ole Miss; Fred Weary, OL, Tennessee; Mike Pearson, OL, Florida; Kendall Simmons, OL, Auburn; Zac Zedalis, C, Florida; Jabar Gaffney, WR, Florida; Josh Reed, WR, Florida; Rex Grossman, QB, Florida; Travis Stephens, RB, Tennessee; LaBrandon Toefield, RB, LSU; Damon Duval, K, Auburn.

Defense: Alex Brown, DL, Florida; John Henderson, DL, Tennessee; Will Overstreet, DL, Tennessee; Kalimba Edwards, OLB, South Carolina; Bradie James, OLB, LSU; Trev Faulk, ILB, LSU; Saleem Rasheed, ILB, Alabama; Lito Sheppard, DB, Florida; Syniker Taylor, DB, Ole Miss; Tim Wansley, DB, Georgia; Andre Lott, DB, Tennessee; Sheldon Brown, DB, South Carolina; Damon Duval, P, Auburn.

2002

Offense: Jason Witten, TE, Tennessee; Shawn Andrews, OL, Arkansas; Jon Stinchcomb, OL, Georgia; Antonio Hall, OL, Kentucky; Stephen Peterman, OL, LSU; Marico Portis, OL, Alabama; Wesley Britt, OL, Alabama; Ben Nowland, C, Auburn; Taylor Jacobs, WR, Florida; Terrence Edwards, WR, Georgia; David Greene, QB, Georgia; Artose Pinner, RB, Kentucky; Fred Talley, RB, Arkansas.

Defense: David Pollack, DL, Georgia; Kindal Moorehead, DL, Alabama; Kenny King, DL, Alabama; Boss Bailey, OLB, Georgia; Karlos Dansby, OLB, Auburn; Bradie James, ILB, LSU; Eddie Strong, OLB, Ole Miss; Hunter Hillenmeyer, OLB, Vanderbilt; Ken Hamlin, DB, Arkansas; Corey Webster, DB, LSU; Travaris Robinson, DB, Auburn; Matt Grier, DB, Ole Miss; Julian Battle, DB, Tennessee; Rashad Baker, DB, Tennessee.

Specialists: Glenn Pakulak, P, Kentucky; Billy Bennett, K, Georgia; Derek Abney, RS, Kentucky.

2003

Offense: Ben Troupe, TE, Florida; Shawn Andrews, OL, Arkansas; Max Starks, OL, Florida; Antonio Hall, OL, Kentucky; Wesley Britt, OL, Alabama; Scott Wells, C, Tennessee; Michael Clayton, WR, LSU; Chris Collins, WR, Ole Miss; Eli Manning, QB, Ole Miss; Carnell Williams, RB, Auburn; Cedric Cobbs, RB, Arkansas.

Defense: David Pollack, DL, Georgia; Chad Lavalais, DL, LSU; Antwan Odom, DL, Alabama; Karlos Dansby, OLB, Auburn; Derrick Pope, OLB, Alabama; Dontarrious Thomas, ILB, Auburn; Odell Thurman, OLB, Georgia; Kerwin Ratliff, DB, Florida; Corey Webster, DB, LSU; Ahmad Carroll, DB, Arkansas; Tony Bua, DB, Arkansas; Sean Jones, DB, Georgia.

Specialists: Dustin Colquitt, P, Tennessee; Jonathan Nichols, K, Ole Miss; Derek Abney, RS, Kentucky.

2004

Offense: Leonard Pope, TE, Georgia; Wesley Britt, OL, Alabama; Marcus McNeill, OL, Auburn; Max Jean-Giles, OL, Georgia; Mo Mitchell, OL, Florida; Andrew Whitworth, OL, LSU; Ben Wilkerson, C, LSU; Fred Gibson, WR, Georgia; Reggie Brown, WR, Georgia; Jason Campbell, QB, Auburn; Carnell Williams, RB, Auburn; Ronnie Brown, RB, Auburn.

Defense: Marcus Spears, DL, LSU; David Pollack, DL, Georgia; Jeb Huckeba, DL, Arkansas; Kevin Burnett, LB, Tennessee; Travis Williams, LB, Auburn; Cornelius Wortham, LB, Alabama; Channing Crowder, LB, Florida; Moses Osemwegie, LB, Vanderbilt; Odell Thurman, LB, Georgia; Lionel

Turner, LB, LSU; Jason Allen, DB, Tennessee; Thomas Davis, DB, Georgia; Carlos Rogers, DB, Auburn; Junior Rosegreen, DB, Auburn.

Specialists: Jared Cook, P, Mississippi State; Brian Bostick, K, Alabama; Carnell Williams, RS, Auburn.

2005

Offense: Leonard Pope, TE, Georgia; Marcus McNeill, OL, Auburn; Max Jean-Gilles, OL, Georgia; Andrew Whitworth, OL, LSU; Tre' Stallings, OL, Ole Miss; Arron Sears, OL, Tennessee; Mike Degory, C, Florida; Sidney Rice, WR, South Carolina; Earl Bennett, WR, Vanderbilt; Jay Cutler, QB, Vanderbilt; Kenny Irons, RB, Auburn; Kenneth Darby, RB, Alabama; Darren McFadden, RB, Arkansas.

Defense: Willie Evans, DL, Mississippi State; Quentin Moses, DL, Georgia; Claude Wroten, DL, LSU; DeMeco Ryans, LB, Alabama; Patrick Willis, LB, Ole Miss; Moses Osemwegie, LB, Vanderbilt; Sam Olajubutu, LB, Arkansas; Greg Blue, DB, Georgia; Roman Harper, DB, Alabama; LaRon Landry, DB, LSU; Ko Simpson, DB, South Carolina.

Specialists: Kody Bliss, P, Auburn; Brandon Coutu, K, Georgia; Skyler Green, RS, LSU.

· Appendix G ·

They Said It . . .

Famous SEC quotes not listed elsewhere . . .

ALABAMA

"I grew up pickin' cotton on my daddy's farm. To me, football is like a day off."

—Lee Roy Jordan (linebacker, 1960–62)

"I'm home now . . . we have a plan . . . we intend to see it through . . . and I plan on staying at Alabama for the rest of my coaching career."

—Dennis Franchione (coach, 2001–02) before he left for Texas A&M

"He had those eyes that walked right through you. He presented his philosophy. He told us, 'I'm not worried about whether I'm going to win or lose. I know I'm going to win. I know that. And I'm not worried about my assistant coaches. I know they're winners. And I'm not worried about whether Alabama is going to win. I know that. The only thing I don't know is how many of you in this room are winners, and how many of you will be with us.' You could've heard a pin drop. That was pretty strong stuff. None of us had ever heard anything like that before."

—Dave Sington (tackle, 1957–59) recalling Bear Bryant's first speech to his new team

ARKANSAS

"You don't think about the close games you win. It's the close ones you lose that you think about."

—Frank Broyles (coach, 1958–76)

"No, but you can see it from here."

—Lou Holtz (coach, 1977–83) when asked if Fayetteville was at the end of the world.

"Sometimes the light at the end of the tunnel is a runaway train."

—Holtz

AUBURN

"Baseball and football are very different games. In a way, both of them are easy. Football is easy if you're crazy as hell. Baseball is easy if you've got patience. They'd both be easier for me if I were a little more crazy and a little more patient."

—Bo Jackson (halfback, 1982–85)

"You can never tell when a break is coming your way. That's why you've got to go all out on every play."

> —Shug Jordan (coach, 1951–75)

"I was born and raised on a farm and when you watch those crops grow, you'd learn to be patient."

> —Pat Dye (coach, 1981–92)

FLORIDA

"In the SEC, every Saturday game is like the Super Bowl."

> —Jesse Palmer (quarterback, 1997–2000)

"But the real tragedy was that 15 hadn't been colored yet."

> —Steve Spurrier in 1991 after telling fans that a fire at Auburn's football dorm had destroyed 20 books (coach, 1990–2001)

"I enjoy football, but it has never been the most important thing in my life."

> —Danny Wuerffel (quarterback, 1993–96)

GEORGIA

"He better go to Georgia."

> —Herschel Walker (running back, 1980–82) to *Georgia Bulldog Magazine* about where his son might play college football

"It's a lonesome walk to the sidelines, especially when thousands of people are cheering your replacement."

> —Fran Tarkenton (quarterback, 1958–60)

"I don't care where a man comes from or how he spells his name. All I ask is that he be loyal to Georgia, proud of that jersey and try like the devil to win."

> —Vince Dooley (coach, 1964–88)

KENTUCKY

"Potential is a French word that means you aren't worth a damn yet."

> —Announcer and former player (defensive lineman, 1966–68) Jeff Van Note

"Both teams used basically the same offense, which is based on having the ball."

> —Fran Curci (coach, 1973–81) in a weekly newsletter

"[Quarterback] Babe Parilli was as good at deception as anyone I've ever seen. I was in a game in Atlanta against Georgia Tech, and a Tech fan was sitting beside me. He said, 'It looks like Parilli is shaking hands with everybody in the backfield before he hands the ball off.'"

> —Fan Jim Brown, who heading into the 2005 season had attended 381 consecutive home games (and many road games too)

LSU

"You can last a little longer if you know when to hit the big licks and when to avoid them."

> —Jim Taylor (fullback, 1956–57)

"It's Baton Rouge. It's not a law to love LSU, but the city fathers could probably get one passed if they needed to."

—Charles McClendon (coach, 1962–79)

"I thought we had some tough situations with our pass protection. I guess our quarterback's mother is going to sue me for child abuse. That old boy took a beating back there."

—Lafayette coach Rickey Bustle after a 48-0 loss in 2002

OLE MISS

"I miss football so much. Heck, I even miss the interceptions."

—Archie Manning (quarterback, 1968–70)

"I looked up the information on the guy who was going to be across from me. He was an All-American candidate named Joe Rushing. He outweighed me by 25 pounds, was 26 years old, married with four kids and had been to Vietnam. I said, 'Uh oh.'"

—Skip Jernigan (guard, 1968–70)

"I have no interest in the Auburn head coaching job."

—Tommy Tuberville (coach, 1995–98) before he left for Auburn

MISSISSIPPI STATE

"A little bit of perfume doesn't hurt you if you don't drink it."

—Darrell Royal (coach, 1954–55)

"Three-fourths of the world is covered by water. The rest is covered by Smoot."

—Fred Smoot (cornerback, 1999–2000)

"My first goal is to lay a solid foundation. I could do a quick fix, but the walls would come tumbling down."

—Sylvester Croom (coach, 2004–05)

SOUTH CAROLINA

"The difference between involvement and commitment can be illustrated by the story of the kamikaze pilot who flew 20 missions. He was involved, but he wasn't committed."

—Lou Holtz (coach, 1999–2004)

"I want to rush for 1,000 or 1,500 yards, whichever comes first."

—George Rogers (running back, 1977–80) with the
New Orleans Saints

"Here's a health, Carolina."

—Popular South Carolina alumni toast

TENNESSEE

"The biggest myth about Southern women is that they wear too much makeup."

—Peyton Manning (quarterback, 1994–97)

"Knock a man down, and if you can't, step aside and let me through."

> —Gene McEver (halfback, 1928–29, 1931)

"Wealth and status mean nothing on the football field. Effort and unselfishness mean everything."

> —Johnny Majors (coach, 1977–92)

VANDERBILT

"My special trouble is that I'm not head-coaching one of the teams that I'd want to play."

> —Steve Sloan (coach, 1973–74)

"You've never heard anything [until you've heard] two grown women crying."

> —Wide receiver Erik Davis on receiving the phone call that teammate Kwane Doster had been killed in 2004

"You see grown men crying and you realize how long it's been since we've won. It tells us how much it means to this program."

> —Quarterback Jay Cutler after Vanderbilt snapped a 22-year losing streak against Tennessee in 2005

Acknowledgments

My apologies to anyone I missed, but in an effort to try and keep this somewhat brief, special thanks go to:

- My family, as always, for their love and support, even when I don't necessarily deserve it. The same goes for my extended family of friends around the country.
- Rick Rinehart for approaching me about doing this project, and everyone else at Taylor Trade Publishing who worked on it, including Jehanne Schweitzer, Dulcie Wilcox, and Christianne Thillen. Three books in one year was an unbelievable challenge (that I hope to never do again).
- Everyone at the *Tuscaloosa News*, especially Tim Thompson, David Wasson, and the entire sports staff, who had to put up with my going mental while tying to make deadline during the 2005 season. Helping with the photos were Dan Lopez, Michael Palmer, and Robert Sutton.
- Charles Bloom and everyone at SEC headquarters. In addition, my deepest sympathies to the family of Brad Davis, who passed away during the writing of this book.
- Brad Green and the entire staff at the Bryant Museum.
- Anyone who ever wrote a press release or helped compile a media guide for an SEC football team.

Some specific people from various SEC schools who need to be thanked include Steven Colquitt, Todd Ellis, Claude Felton, Stephen Franz, Joe Galbraith, John Hayden, John Hines, Tom Price, Chris Rushing, Michelle Schmitt, and Tommy Suggs.

Most of all, thank you to the fans of the most amazing conference in college sports.